Erica Harrison

Radio and the Performance of Government:
Broadcasting by the Czechoslovaks in Exile in London, 1939–1945

CHARLES UNIVERSITY
KAROLINUM PRESS 2023

KAROLINUM PRESS
Karolinum Press is a publishing department of Charles University
Ovocný trh 560/5, 116 36 Prague 1, Czech Republic
www.karolinum.cz
© Erica Harrison, 2023
Set in Czech Republic by Karolinum Press
Layout by Jan Šerých
First edition

A catalogue record for this book is available from the National Library
of the Czech Republic.

ISBN 978-80-246-5521-5
ISBN 978-80-246-5522-2 (pdf)

The original manuscript was reviewed by doc. PhDr. Barbara Köpplová, CSc.,
Faculty of Social Sciences, and Mark Cornwall, Professor of Modern European
History, University of Southampton.

Contents

Acknowledgements	7
List of Abbreviations	9
Introduction	10
Czechoslovakia: "The Child of Propaganda"	20
Radio: The Ideal Medium for Exile	24
Less Trouble than the Rest: The Czechoslovak Government within the British Propaganda Structure	30
Scope and Sources	46
Chapter One:	
"Legal, loyal, and internationally recognised": Legitimacy and the Performance of Government	59
"In the name of the Czechoslovak Republic": The Authority of Legality	63
"We are the Masaryk nation": The Authority of Tradition	70
"We are close together at heart": The Authority of Charisma	85
Exercising Authority: The *odsun* and "Rabble-rousing" from London	98
Chapter Two:	
Populating the "Free Republic": Performing Nationhood over the Radio	108
Radio as a Medium for Nation-Building	113
"Faithful to the spirit of our history": Reading the War into the National Narrative	119
"Anything that is dear to their hearts": The Mobilisation of Culture	131

Chapter Three:
Idiots and Traitors? Addressing Slovakia from London   151
  "The admirable and loyal Czechoslovak nation"   161
  "Do not betray yourselves": A Policy of Negative Propaganda   171
    "There is no free Slovakia": Political Arguments   171
    "The most blatant ingratitude": The Slovak State and the USA   176
    "Your Catholic, Christian, and Slovak conscience compels you":
    Religious Arguments   179
    Russians, Not Monsters: Tackling the Bolshevik Bogey   186

Chapter Four:
"We will manage our own affairs": The Soviet Union
and Broadcasting the Future of Czechoslovakia   196
  Neither Hell nor Paradise: 1940 to June 1941   198
  "Our Brother Slavs": June 1941 to 1943   201
  When Propaganda Diverges from Policy: Mid-1943 Onwards   208
    "If it doesn't work, it will not be our fault": The Changing
    Representation of Poland and the Central European
    Confederation   208
    "Subcarpathian Ruthenia is Czechoslovak": Broadcasting
    to a Lost Territory   218

Conclusions   247

Bibliography of Sources   253
Index   264

Acknowledgements

There are many people to thank for their help in producing this book, and the doctoral thesis on which it is based. First of all, I would like to thank my PhD supervisors at the University of Bristol, Dr. Rajendra Chitnis and Dr. James Thompson, for helping me to complete (and to enjoy completing) this project. Special thanks should go to Rajendra for designing the original project and for always being on hand with constructive feedback and support. I am also very grateful to my examiners, Professor Mark Cornwall and Professor Tim Cole, for all their positive comments and useful feedback.

I would like to thank the staff at the Czech National Archive, the Czech Ministry of Foreign Affairs, the National Archives at Kew, and the BBC Written Archive Centre in Caversham for all their help. Special thanks are also due to the Český rozhlas (Czech Radio) Archive, not only for their help with this project but also for hosting me and making my time in Prague so productive and enjoyable. In particular, I would like to thank Tomáš Černý, Miloslav Turek, Eva Ješutová, Jiří Hubička, and Tomáš Bělohlávek.

I am also grateful to the AHRC and Český rozhlas for originally funding this project.

For their help in transitioning this work from PhD to book, I would like to thank the team at Karolinum Press, and the reviewers Dr. Barbara Köpplová and Professor Mark Cornwall. Thanks are also due to Dr. Carolyn Birdsall at the University of Amsterdam for her understanding and encouragement.

On a personal note, thanks to all my friends who kept me going through the original PhD, and especially to those who continued to nag me about getting this published when I was distracted by other things. Special thanks to Prague friends past and present – in particular, Lenka Kudláčková and Lani Hartikainen, to whom at least part of this work should be dedicated for being the only person who really understands my love of all things Czech.

Last, but certainly not least, my family. To my mother and brother: I can't articulate all that I'm grateful for, but I hope you know. I also want to thank my grandmother Joanna for first inspiring the interests that led me here. Particular thanks are also due to my partner Alex for having to sit through more than his fair share of complaints and crises over the years. Thanks to all of you for always having faith in me, even when I wasn't so sure.

This book is dedicated to my father, who never got to read it but would have been proud of it anyway.

List of Abbreviations

BBC	British Broadcasting Corporation
BBC WAC	BBC Written Archives Centre
BBC WBC	BBC Wartime Broadcasts Collection
CNA	Czech National Archive, Chodov, Prague
CRA	Český rozhlas (Czech Radio) Archive, Prague
FO	Foreign Office
HSĽS	Hlinkova slovenská ľudová strana (Hlinka Slovak People's Party)
LN Z	Londýn Zpravodajství (*London News*)
LTS	London Transcription Service
MNO	Ministerstvo národní obrany (Ministry of National Defence)
MOI	Ministry of Information
MSP	Ministerstvo sociální péče (Ministry of Social Welfare)
MZV	Ministerstvo zahraničních věcí (Ministry of Foreign Affairs)
PKWN	Polski Komitet Wyzwolenia Narodowego (Polish Committee of National Liberation)
PRS	Poradní rozhlasový sbor (Radio Advisory Committee)
PWE	Political Warfare Executive
SNR	Slovenská národná rada (Slovak National Council)
TNA	The National Archives, Kew, UK
ÚVOD	Ústřední vedení odboje domácího (Central Leadership of the Home Resistance)

Introduction

"At one time, [radio] really was the only weapon left to us."
Prokop Drtina, *Hlas svobodné republiky,* 4 March 1945[1]

Between March 1939 and April 1945, the Czechoslovak Republic disappeared from the maps of Europe, continuing to exist only as an imagined "free republic" of the radio waves. Following the German invasion and annexation of Bohemia and Moravia, and the declaration of independence by Slovakia on 15 March 1939, the short-lived Second Czechoslovak Republic was no more, and it would take six years of war before its successor could again be declared by government representatives on state territory. From their position in exile in wartime London, former Czechoslovak president Edvard Beneš and the government which formed around him were dependent on access to radio microphones in order to communicate with the public they strove to represent. The broadcasts made by government figures in London from 1939 to 1945, culminating in the government's own programme, were the most prominent public platform on which they could perform as a government, enabling a performance of authority to impress their hosts, allies, occupying enemies, and claimed constituents. An examination of the content of these broadcasts offers a new means by which to explore the exile government's understanding of the republic it worked to reinstate – both its past and

---

1 Prokop Drtina, *A nyní promluví Pavel Svatý...: Londýnské rozhlasové epištoly Dr. Prokopa Drtiny z let 1940–1945* (Prague: Vladimír Žikeš, 1945), 450. Unless otherwise stated, all translations in this work are the author's own.

its future. The challenge of projecting certainty at a time when even the most fundamental issues were in doubt is highlighted by contrasting the confident claims made over the radio with the heated behind-the-scenes negotiations, both within the Czechoslovak government itself and with various British authorities. Would there be a Czechoslovak state after the war? If so, where would its borders be drawn? Who would be permitted to live there and who would be excluded? Who would lead such a state, and to which allies would they pledge allegiance?

Although such questions were pivotal to Beneš and those around him, they were generally of peripheral interest to the British political and broadcasting structures who controlled access to the radio and had rather different priorities. The frequency and content of the Czechoslovak government broadcasts were determined by the particular relationship the exiles had with the BBC (British Broadcasting Corporation), with various branches of the British government and propaganda structure, and with other allies, such as the Soviet Union. The Czechoslovaks navigated the challenging landscape of wartime London with greater success than some contemporaries, alternately helped and hampered by their status in British eyes as a minor ally. While they had to fight against British indifference towards Czechoslovak issues, as well as occasional outright obstruction, they were also able to achieve greater latitude in their radio work by virtue of the fact that such issues were of lesser concern to Britain than, for example, French or Polish matters.

This book touches on multiple topics – the history of the former Czechoslovakia and the specific activities of the wartime Czechoslovak government-in-exile, the history of Britain, of the BBC, of European radio – and the period of the Second World War looms large in the core mythology of each of these. Since the end of the First Czechoslovak Republic (1918–38), following the Munich Agreement, the experience and legacy of that state has been much reflected upon, both by its erstwhile citizens and by its promoters and detractors abroad. Study of the war period – wedged in between the pre-eminent First Czechoslovak Republic and the start of the Communist era in Czechoslovakia (1948–89) – offers an opportunity to trace early assessments of the former and the roots of the latter, as the wartime exile movement featured both democratic and Communist branches (the latter largely based in Moscow). It also marks the beginning of the end of the political careers of prominent figures of the pre-Communist period, notably Edvard Beneš and Jan Masaryk, whose fate and reputations are much entangled with that of the state. The ongoing influence of the Second World War on British culture and self-perception is readily apparent in the still frequent references to the "spirit" of both Dunkirk and the Blitz, which are invoked by politicians and the media whenever the country faces a challenge (both became early clichés of the COVID-19 pandemic). However, the transnational aspect of what has been termed the "London moment" tends to be forgotten, with the Churchillian image of Britain standing alone against Germany continuing to hold sway in the British public memory, in defiance of the reality of a multicultural and multilingual wartime capital.[2] For the BBC, which celebrated its centenary in 2022, the war remains a definitive period, in which the broadcaster acquired its international reputation for impartial, accurate news reporting, and produced landmark broadcasts, such as Chamberlain's announcement of war and Richard Dimbleby's report from Bergen Belsen, which now form part of the timeline of British radio. For the medium of radio as a whole, the war period represented a coming-of-age moment, in which its ability to cross borders and defy local censorship, and to immediately "break" important news, enabled it to outstrip the written press and dominate a media landscape as yet unthreatened by television. As the many shelves of books on the topic will proclaim, wartime radio is radio in its prime, weaponised by all sides and hosting a babble of voices, all competing with each other for their own imagined audience. This wartime "moment," then, centred on London, forms a key point in the histories of both Europe and the media, which continues to offer new avenues for study.

This is the first publication to take as its subject matter all the broadcasts made by the Czechoslovak exiles in London via the BBC, the vast majority of which are preserved in script form at Český rozhlas (Czech Radio) in Prague. As will be described in further detail later in this book, the exile government co-operated closely with the BBC from the summer of 1940 within the programme *Hovory s domovem* (*Conversations with Home*), and later took on its own "free time" programme entitled *Hlas svobodné republiky* (*Voice of the Free Republic*), with government figures also appearing in broadcasts by the BBC's own Czech(oslovak)

---

[2] The project "The London Moment: Exile Governments, Academics and Activists in the Capital of Free Europe, 1940–1945," funded by the Volkswagen Foundation at Humboldt-Universität zu Berlin, examines multiple aspects of this transnational "moment" in history as representatives of many nations gathered in London. Wendy Webster has also sought to update public understandings of the diversity of wartime Britain more generally, in *Mixing It: Diversity in World War Two Britain* (Oxford: Oxford University Press, 2018).

service.[3] Approaching this corpus as a whole and contextualising the broadcasts within the political negotiations going on behind the scenes offers new insights not only into the thinking of the Czechoslovak government-in-exile, but also into the wartime working of the BBC and of the British government. Although such an examination reveals several interesting themes that will form the basis of the rest of this work, it cannot, of course, be exhaustive, and there remains much material for historians pursuing particular topics not examined in detail here.[4] A close study of the wartime broadcasts by the Czechoslovak government-in-exile therefore offers something new not only to historians of Czechoslovakia and Central-Eastern Europe, but also to those seeking to understand the war more widely, as well as historians of nationalism, of broadcasting, and of radio studies.

Before beginning analysis of the wartime performance of the Czechoslovak exiles, I should explain that my use of the term "performance" is not intended to imply insincerity or intentional deception on behalf of the performers. As I hope to show in this study, all the Allied exiles in London were forced to tread a difficult path between their wishes for their home countries and the limits of what their hosts would permit. The Czechoslovaks faced even greater challenges here than some other nationalities, as British policymakers were by no means as committed to the post-war recreation of a Czechoslovak state as they were to some other countries, and Beneš and his allies acknowledged from the start that they would not be in a position to make any binding decisions about the post-war settlement alone. With limited means by which to enact policy or deploy resources, this radio performance was one of the few means by which the London exiles could work to protect their country and try to ensure its future, and they valued it as such.

It is my contention that all government in exile is a performance of government in the absence of power, and the Czechoslovaks were one of many Allied governments that sought to establish themselves in London during the conflict, putting on a show to convince the public of their

---

[3] BBC terminology is as inconsistent as many other British sources, using the words *Czech* and *Czechoslovak* largely interchangeably. BBC sources thus refer to the "Czech Service," "Czech Section," "Czechoslovak Service," and "Czechoslovak Section." The use of *Czech* slightly predominates – although this is possibly favoured purely for length rather than any considered reasons – and so this is the term most often used within this book. However, it should by no means be interpreted as an erasure of the contribution of Slovak staff and broadcasters.

[4] See, for example, Jan Láníček, "The Czechoslovak Service of the BBC and the Jews during World War II," *Yad Vashem Studies* 38, no. 2 (2010): 123–53.

authority and legitimacy. The Czechoslovak exiles used the radio for more than this, however, as radio was the stage on which they performed not only politically but also nationally. Performance of this kind was nothing new to the Czechs as, prior to the creation of the Czechoslovak state in 1918, individuals could "perform" their Czech national identity within Austria-Hungary through small acts, such as purchasing certain newspapers and attending certain events, that demonstrated their participation in a growing Czech civil society. Historians of Czech nationalism and the Czech National Revival – a period with which the London exiles explicitly sought to link themselves – have described the performative aspects of Czech national identity on an individual scale, identifying the appropriation of this identity as a decision to openly participate in the Czech national "project."[5] In the wartime context, this performance graduated from the personal to the public, and was intended to be both demonstrative and attractive to listeners in what had been Czechoslovakia, encouraging them to follow the exile government's lead and to accept their interpretation of what Czechoslovakia was and would be after the war. The exile government's wartime broadcasting is thus best understood as an attempt to represent a nation, its state, and its government over the radio.

Isolated from its territory and unable to exercise executive or administrative authority over the population it claimed to represent, the exile government that formed around Edvard Beneš created an alternative Czechoslovak state in miniature, complete with ministries, schools, armed forces, and national celebrations. The Czechoslovak exile community in Britain during the war was one of many, and all the gathered European nations created their own clubs and organisations, seeking to continue part of the national life abroad. While Britain was not the only country to host exiles in this period (several countries also had exile movements in the USSR, with varying degrees of rivalry, as well as in the USA and elsewhere), the communities there tended to be the most structured, and many gained an "official" air as more and more governments-in-exile were established in London. These communities included a wide range of organisations, from chamber orchestras and children's choirs to air squadrons and refugee committees, all to some degree or

---

[5] Vladimír Macura has written on the performative nature of Czech national identity in this early period; see, for example, *Masarykovy boty a jiné semi(o)fejetony* (Prague: Pražská imaginace, 1993), 11–13. Chad Bryant has done likewise; see, for example, *Prague in Black: Nazi Rule and Czech Nationalism* (Cambridge, MA: Harvard University Press, 2007), 4–5, 12–16.

another representing their home country in Britain.[6] The only means by which these alternative wartime mini-states could be shared with the majority of their compatriots, however, was via the medium of radio, and the BBC's European broadcasts formed a vital connection between London and occupied Europe. For those living under occupation, the radio became more than just a source of information: reports reached London from the Nazi-controlled Protectorate of Bohemia and Moravia, describing how "in spite of threats of a death sentence, the English Radio is always listened to," with speeches by figures such as Beneš and Masaryk providing "the ELIXIR which keep [sic] us all going."[7] Listeners highly valued news they felt they could trust, with one letter from the Protectorate explaining that "the London broadcasting has another meaning for us, in that it helps us to survive the evil times in which we are living since it far surpasses everything which we are obliged to listen to and read all the time here."[8]

Although the BBC shared this commitment to accurate news, in other ways its broadcasting priorities diverged significantly from those of the Allied governments. While BBC hosts were seeking to promote a positive projection of Britain and prioritising official requirements on the British side, the various Allied governments were subject to different pressures in their on-air performances.[9] Although the show of legitimacy and leadership put on by the London exiles was partly for the benefit of Britain and the other Allied nations, who could endorse this legitimacy by formally recognising exile governments as representatives of their state, the real audience for much of this performance was the peoples of occupied Europe. Exile politics relies on belief, and politicians abroad must convince those left at home that they truly represent them, that they are

---

[6] For studies of various aspects of these communities, see Martin Conway and Jose Gotovitch, eds., *Europe in Exile: European Exile Communities in Britain, 1940–45* (New York: Berghahn Books, 2001).

[7] Surveys of European Audiences, Enemy Occupied Countries Other than France [SEA, EOCOTF], 5 July 1941, pp. 4–5, 27/41, file 1A (April–July 1941), European Intelligence Papers [EIP] series 1c, E2/192/1, BBC Written Archives Centre [WAC], Caversham. Emphasis in original.

[8] SEA, EOCOTF, 2 August 1941, pp. 3–4, 31/41, file 1B (Aug–Nov 1941), EIP series 1c, E2/192/2, BBC WAC.

[9] In his history of British broadcasting, Asa Briggs described the provision of wartime news as the BBC's most important work, and many BBC memos testify to its perceived importance, in *The History of Broadcasting in the United Kingdom*, vol. 3, *The War of Words* (Oxford: Oxford University Press, 1970), 11. The projection of Britain was also promoted as an important task for European broadcasts; see, for example, "British Broadcasting and Allied Governments," undated, E2/15, BBC WAC.

connected by a shared vision of the future as well as a shared past. The wartime broadcasts by the Czechoslovak government-in-exile were thus a performance of government, predicated on the belief that a Czechoslovak Republic would be restored, and that those in London and those at home shared certain ideas and values that would define that state.

A note on sources should be recorded here. Although this study aims to analyse the government broadcasts as broadcasts – that is, as audio transmissions intended to be heard by an audience – in most cases the only surviving record of a given broadcast is the written script. While some speeches by prominent figures such as President Beneš and Jan Masaryk were recorded, they represent only a fraction of the hours broadcast, not all of these recordings have survived, and those which have seem to be re-recordings done at a later date (rather than an actual recording of the live broadcast), and as such are not a record of the programme as broadcast.[10] The written record, by contrast, is extremely robust, as BBC wartime censorship demanded the submission of scripts in full, both in the original language and in English translation, prior to broadcast. An almost complete collection of these scripts survives at Český rozhlas in Prague, and this forms the largest primary source base for this study. Research into other BBC wartime services faces this same issue and, while there will inevitably be some audio aspects that cannot be examined without audio sources, the BBC's requirement that announcers stick closely to their submitted scripts or risk being taken off air means that the written record can be taken as a reliable record of the content of the broadcasts.[11] I aim to analyse the government's programmes not only as political texts, but also as radio broadcasts, intended to be spoken and heard rather than read. This approach, drawing on broadcasting theory alongside historical sources, demonstrates the unique characteristics of radio as a medium which can contribute to this mission of nation-building from a distance, showing it to be the ideal medium for exile politics.

---

10 A BBC memo from August 1941 explains that the Czech and Polish section of the LTS is exceeding its monthly budget because the recordings "in almost every case, had to be specially produced"; Transcription Manager to O.C.Ex, "London Transcription Service – Possible Increase in Programme Expenditure for 1942," 26 August 1941, London Transcription Service, R13/163/1, BBC WAC.
11 Vike Martina Plock faced the same issue for her recent study of the BBC German Service during the war, based largely on the scripts retained at the BBC Written Archives Centre in Caversham; see *The BBC German Service during the Second World War: Broadcasting to the Enemy* (Basingstoke: Palgrave Macmillan, 2021), 2.

The primacy of the nation and the validity of the nation-state were central to the Czechoslovak exile government's work, and this is reflected in the prominence of national themes in both its public broadcasting and its off-air discussions. In the wartime context, however, when states disappeared from the map and Nazi Germany proposed a "new order" that challenged existing understandings of the nations and states that made up Europe, the conceptual nature of nationhood was made clear.[12] Removed from the borders that previously defined them, the occupied nations instead formed a "miniature Europe" in London, represented by small groups of exiles all seeking to establish bonds that united them with a distant population and justified their respective political causes.[13] Study of these exile movements raises questions not only about how the representatives of each individual nation sought to define and represent their compatriots, but also how complex ethnic, historical, and linguistic ties between peoples can be appropriated and reinterpreted for political purposes. While this project naturally focuses on the Czechoslovak expression of these issues, both exile politics and broadcasting defy traditional borders and are by their very nature international; research into the political maelstrom of wartime London and the complex negotiations between allies still uncertain of the war's eventual outcome highlights the fact that no single nation or state resolves either its political or ideological affairs in a vacuum. The Czechoslovaks, like all their fellow exiles in London, were affected by their position in Britain and their current and historic relations with both their allies and their enemies. This study therefore seeks to examine the exile government in its international context, so as best to understand the work done by this particular group of exiles, striving to use wartime propaganda to guarantee a future for the nation they wished to represent.

---

12 Understandings of nationhood in Europe are now undergoing further changes under the influence of the political structure of the European Union and the economic interdependence of Europe as a unit. James Casteel has argued that the process of "Europeanization" has not advanced as quickly in historical studies as in other areas and the nation as a concept continues to be central to European understandings of the past; see "Historicizing the Nation: Transnational Approaches to the Recent European Past," in *Transnational Europe: Promise, Paradox, Limits*, ed. Joan DeBardeleben and Achim Hurrelmann (Basingstoke: Macmillan, 2011), 153–69, esp. 153–54.

13 "We have in London at the present time a miniature Europe," said Richard A. Butler, undersecretary of state for foreign affairs, during a House of Lords debate on the Diplomatic Privileges (Extension) Bill on 20 February 1941; see *Hansard*, HL Deb., vol. 369, col. 329, 20 February 1941, accessed 15 May 2022, https://hansard.parliament.uk.

The term *propaganda* is used repeatedly in this work and should also be defined for the sake of clarity. *Propaganda* is used here to describe any and all attempts to present information or ideas with the intention of impressing a certain aspect or interpretation upon the audience. Studies of propaganda have tended to draw similarly wide definitions to cover what has been variously termed *propaganda*, *information*, *political warfare*, and *psychological warfare* by those working within it but is, essentially, information presented with an agenda, or in accordance with a certain point of view. In public discourse, however, *propaganda* has negative connotations of disinformation and dishonesty, as a result of which it is a term which political figures tend to employ to accuse their enemies of misleading communications, rather than being a word they would use to describe their own activities. These negative connotations are nothing new and were apparently already sufficiently well established in British discourse by 1940 for writer John Hargrave to wish to argue against them in his book *Propaganda, The Mightiest Weapon of Them All: Words Win Wars*. Hargrave summarised the matter simply: "Where there is Information plus Direction, there is Propaganda." While some claimed propaganda to be the province of fascist or totalitarian governments, Hargrave maintained that the presentation of information is propaganda when it is influenced even slightly by a given point of view and that, therefore, "no government has ever been possible without it."[14] More recent studies of propaganda have also tended to favour broader and more forgiving definitions of the controversial term; in his study of the relationship between British radio and resistance in occupied Europe, Michael Stenton suggested that "every society has a need to proclaim truths, to publish useful instruction and to work up the collective capacity to change its ways. This is propaganda."[15] In a 2013 collection of essays on propaganda, the editors framed their understanding of the term widely enough to incorporate everything from Nazi anti-Semitism to modern-day commercial advertising and the work of NGOs such as Greenpeace, stressing that propaganda takes many forms and that the attempt to influence a target audience with information "need not necessarily

---

[14] John Hargrave, *Propaganda, The Mightiest Weapon of Them All: Words Win Wars* (London: Wells Gardener, Darton & Co., 1940), 29–30.
[15] Michael Stenton, *Radio London and Resistance in Occupied Europe: British Political Warfare 1939–1943* (Oxford: Oxford University Press, 2000), 114.

be misleading or biased."[16] Within this book, the use of *propaganda* to describe BBC broadcasts (both those emanating from purely British sources and those created in collaboration with representatives of exile groups) is an acknowledgement of the different perspectives that shaped their construction and is not intended to convey any further connotations, either positive or negative.

Analysis of propaganda also demands good knowledge of the context in which it was produced, both in a historical and national sense. As the list of alternative phrases above demonstrates, the term *propaganda* has elicited caution among English speakers and generated many euphemistic equivalents. In Czech sources, however, the term was rarely viewed negatively, and it was openly used by the London exiles to describe their own work. The Czechoslovak understanding of propaganda and the use of politics in the media more generally differed significantly from both contemporary and modern Anglo-American views and must be analysed accordingly. A grounding in the history of the First Czechoslovak Republic is therefore essential, not only to appreciate the context for the themes discussed in the government broadcasts, but also the manner in which the Czechoslovak exiles perceived radio and the role of state propaganda. Unlike many in Britain who viewed the whole concept of propaganda with suspicion, Czechoslovak politicians knew it to be a vital tool of statecraft.[17] Propaganda for the Czechoslovak cause among the Allies had been an integral part of the campaign carried out during the First World War by Tomáš Garrigue Masaryk (later the first Czechoslovak president) and his eventual successor, Edvard Beneš, which had resulted in the original creation of the Czechoslovak state in 1918. Masaryk himself wrote extensively about what he described as his campaign of "democratic propaganda," which aimed to promote the goal of Czech and Slovak independence from Austria-Hungary in the foreign press and to generate sympathy among the political elite of Britain, France, and America.[18] Beneš also had no qualms about describing much of his own

---

16 See editors' introduction to *Propaganda*, vol. 1, *Historical Origins, Definitions and the Changing Nature of Propaganda*, ed. Paul R. Baines and Nicholas J. O'Shaughnessy (London: SAGE, 2013), xxiv.
17 Research into the truth behind propaganda myths from the First World War led Arthur Ponsonby to conclude that "the injection of the poison of hatred into men's minds by means of falsehood is a greater evil in war-time than the actual loss of life." Public distrust of the concept of propaganda was perpetuated in books such as his *Falsehood in Wartime, Containing an Assortment of Lies Circulated throughout the Nations during the Great War* (London: Allen & Unwin, 1928).
18 Tomáš Masaryk, *Světová revoluce: za války a ve válce, 1914–1918* (Prague: Čin a Orbis, 1925), 99.

work during the war as "mainly propagandist," on the grounds that the idea of a Czechoslovak state should be spread as widely as possible; the public "had so imperfect a knowledge of us," he argued, that "this was the kind of work of which we stood most in need."[19] Historian Herbert Fisher wrote of the surprising success of Masaryk and his colleagues in establishing the novel idea of the independent and united Czechoslovak nation in the minds of the state's future citizens and allies, describing the Czechoslovak path to independence as "perhaps the most striking monument of the success of war-time propaganda," and going so far as to christen the state "the child of propaganda."[20]

Czechoslovakia: "The Child of Propaganda"

The Czechoslovak commitment to propaganda did not end with the successful foundation of the state, however, but rather remained a fundamental part of the work of its interwar governments, both internationally and within their own borders. As well as seeking to convince the world of the viability of this new Czechoslovak entity, the various governments of the First Republic also worked to promote the same idea among the state's citizens, by sponsoring the creation of a Czechoslovak national identity with which the majority of people could identify. Founder and first president T. G. Masaryk wrote that successful democracy was reliant on the political education of the public, in a spiritual rather than formal sense, and the media structure of the First Republic helped to further this education by presenting the public with a historical tradition of democracy in Czech thought.[21] The pivotal position of propaganda within the Czechoslovak political system was ensured by the creation of the Third Section within the Ministry of Foreign Affairs (Ministerstvo zahraničních věcí, MZV), tasked with managing the propaganda and promotion of the ruling government and its policies. Under foreign minister and later president Edvard Beneš, the Third Section's main task was the publishing of magazines and pamphlets on Czechoslovak topics for both domestic and foreign readers. However, it also influenced

---

19 Edvard Beneš, *My War Memoirs*, trans. Paul Selver (London: George Allen & Unwin, 1928), 103.
20 Herbert Fisher, *A History of Europe from the Beginning of the 18th Century to 1937* (London: Eyre & Spottiswoode, 1952), 1155.
21 Masaryk, *Světová revoluce*, 543.

the image of Czechoslovakia abroad, by clearing information for use by foreign journalists and sponsoring research trips for influential writers and academics from other countries.[22] The MZV also had its own publishing house, Orbis, which was heavily involved in the publication of foreign books on Czechoslovak topics and also brought out some of the most influential pro-government works of the First Republic for domestic readers, including Karel Čapek's much-feted book of interviews with Masaryk, entitled *Hovory s T. G. Masarykem (Conversations with T. G. Masaryk)*.[23]

Politics and political propaganda were an established feature of the media in the First Czechoslovak Republic and the public was used to being exposed to political topics in print and over the wireless. Before the advent of radio the print media had boomed in Czechoslovakia, with some 2,250 different periodicals in 1920, ballooning to almost 4,000 by 1930.[24] Unlike countries such as Britain, where many of the largest newspapers, at least from 1914 onwards, were privately owned (albeit with political inclinations), the majority of the most popular periodicals in Czechoslovakia were directly run by political parties. As the Czechoslovak political system featured a multiplicity of parties and each one operated its own publication, these partisan newspapers dominated a large section of the press.[25] Most publications were upfront about their allegiances, but some, such as those published by the Melantrich publishing house, did not state their origins so openly.[26] Though freedom of the press was enshrined in the constitution, the state reserved the right to intervene in times of danger, to either fine or restrict the distribution

---

22 Andrea Orzoff, *Battle for the Castle: The Myth of Czechoslovakia in Europe, 1914–1948* (Oxford: Oxford University Press, 2011), 70–71.
23 Karel Čapek, *Hovory s T. G. Masarykem* (Prague: Fr. Borový a Čin, 1946). For more on Orbis, see Orzoff, *Battle for the Castle*, 4, 74.
24 Though there was some reproduction of content in smaller titles taking from their parent publication, these numbers remain impressive; see Jakub Končelík, Pavel Večeřa, and Petr Orság, *Dějiny českých médií 20. století* (Prague: Portál, 2010), 41.
25 For example, the National Democrats had several papers, including *České slovo,* and the Agrarians issued *Venkov,* as well as several local periodicals. In his extensive history of the First Republic, Zdeněk Karník suggested that, without their press presence, "political parties in this period had no hope of success," in *České země v éře První republiky (1918–1938)*, vol. 1, *Vznik, budování a zlatá léta republiky (1918–1929)* (Prague: Libri, 2000), 327. For more on the party political press, see ibid., 327–31.
26 Karník, *České země*, 1:329.

of publications that threatened the stability of the state or promoted criminal acts.[27]

Broadcasting was quickly popularised in the young republic and the political press soon expanded into this new medium. Regular broadcasting from Prague began in May 1923, and the broadcasting company Radiojournal was established in June of that year. Other stations grew up in Brno, Bratislava, Košice, and Moravská Ostrava throughout the 1920s, and the first simultaneous broadcasts, in which listeners across the country were able to listen to the same programme at the same time, began in December 1926.[28] By the end of 1933 there were over half a million radio licence holders in Czechoslovakia, with approximately 39 radio sets for every 1,000 inhabitants, largely concentrated in urban centres and more widely in central and northern Bohemia. This put Czechoslovakia on a par with countries such as Hungary (38 sets per 1,000 inhabitants) and France (33), but still far behind Great Britain (133) and Germany (77).[29] The number of radio sets in Czechoslovakia grew rapidly, however, almost doubling between 1933 and 1938, to approximately one million.[30] According to BBC intelligence, by the autumn of 1938 radio density in Czechoslovakia had reached the comparatively high level of 72.4 radio sets per 1,000 people – almost one in every other household – with the greatest density in Bohemia (83.2). It should be noted, however, that other regions had considerably lower levels of radio ownership: the BBC estimated there were 6 to 7 people per radio in Bohemia and Moravia, over 20 people per set in Slovakia, and approximately 65 per set in Subcarpathian Ruthenia.[31]

---

27 For more on the laws governing the press in this period, see Končelík, Večeřa, and Orság, *Dějiny českých médií 20. století*, 33–34; and Karník, *České země*, 1:337.
28 Although the broadcaster, Radiojournal, was a single company, the different stations did enjoy some programming freedom; see Končelík, Večeřa, and Orság, *Dějiny českých médií 20. století*, 56–57, 60.
29 Figures taken from A. J. Patzaková, ed. *Prvních deset let Československého rozhlasu* (Prague: Radiojournal, 1935), 684; radio density by region is shown in a foldout map (obr. 2) between pp. 672 and 673.
30 David Vaughan, *Battle for the Airwaves: Radio and the 1938 Munich Crisis* (Prague: Radioservis, 2008), 19; Briggs, *War of Words*, 737 (Appendix C).
31 "BBC European Audience Estimates: Czechoslovakia," 6 January 1944, pp. 1–2, EIP series 5, no. 6, E2/184, BBC WAC. The BBC paper notes the lack of precise figures for Subcarpathian Ruthenia, but these figures correlate with Končelík, Večeřa, and Orság's record of fewer than 10,000 radio licenses in the region by 1938 and Czechoslovak government sources putting the population at just over 700,000 in 1937; see Končelík, Večeřa, and Orság, *Dějiny českých médií 20. století*, 63; "Opis: Statistický lexicon obcí v republice československé," Ministerstvo vnitra Londýn [MV–L] 114: Referát pro Podkarpatskou Rus (RPR) 2-10-2, Czech National Archive [CNA], Prague.

The new technology was overseen by the state from the beginning, in the form of the Ministry of Post and Telegraphs (Ministerstvo pošt a telegrafů), which owned a fifty-one percent stake in Radiojournal from 1925.[32] There was further political influence in the radio as political parties exercised considerable control over broadcasts targeting their traditional support base: for example, the Agrarian Party held sway over broadcasting for agricultural workers, the Social Democrats over programmes for urban workers, and the Traders' Party over broadcasting for industry and trade.[33] Radio journalist and historian David Vaughan noted the complaints made by some at the time that political influence was stifling Czechoslovak radio, and concluded that "in Czechoslovakia, radio never quite managed to emerge as a strong, independent public institution."[34] However, although the state retained control in the management of Radiojournal, the appointment of speakers, and the right to censor programmes, the compliance shown by the broadcasting company meant that there was relatively little interference in actual programme content. This lack of conflict has been attributed more to Radiojournal's willingness to abide by the verbal agreement and do "what the state expected of it" than to any particular political constraint.[35] Vaughan criticised this political dominance for allowing "party political squabbles," which "overflowed into Radiojournal's management and into the bodies overseeing public broadcasting," creating "an atmosphere of caution and self-censorship." However, Czech histories of the media tend to be less critical of this political influence.[36] Končelík and his co-authors described Czechoslovak radio in this period as a successful tool of public *osvěta*, "enlightenment," while other studies view the increasing political interest in radio as a natural result of the medium's growing popularity.[37]

Given the important questions of language in the wartime broadcasts from London which will be discussed later, it should also be noted that radio in the First Republic was not a solely Czech affair. Regular

---

32 Vaughan, *Battle for the Airwaves*, 20.
33 See Vaughan, *Battle for the Airwaves*, 22–23; Karník, *České země*, 1:339; on the Czechoslovak Traders' Party (Česoslovenská živnostenská strana středostavovská), see Barbara Köpplová et al., *Dějiny českých médií v datech: Rozhlas, Televize, Mediální právo* (Prague: Karolinum, 2003), 25.
34 Vaughan, *Battle for the Airwaves*, 23, 85.
35 Končelík, Večeřa, and Orság, *Dějiny českých médií 20. století*, 58–59.
36 Vaughan, *Battle for the Airwaves*, 85.
37 Končelík, Večeřa, and Orság, *Dějiny českých médií 20. století*, 62; see also Lenka Čábelová, "Československý rozhlas a stát 1923–1945," in *Konsolidace vládnutí a podnikání v České republice a v Evropské unii*, vol. 2, *Sociologie, prognostika a správa. Média*, ed. Jakub Končelík, Barbara Köpplová, and Irena Prázová (Prague: Matfyzpress, 2002), 291–306.

broadcasting began from Bratislava in October 1926, and "Slovak hours" were introduced into broadcasting from February 1928.[38] Broadcasting in German began in October 1925, originally being broadcast three times weekly, before being extended to 25 minutes a day from December 1926 and 30 minutes a day from 1929.[39] It has been estimated, however, that less than eight percent of Radiojournal broadcasts were in German by 1935 (despite the fact that almost a quarter of the population was German-speaking), and many listened to broadcasts from Nazi Germany instead.[40] While some deem this a "wasted opportunity," Czech historians of the media have suggested that Czech and Slovak listeners in the First Republic would not have tolerated too much minority-language broadcasting.[41] There were other small-scale ventures: 1933 saw the first broadcasts for the Hungarian minority in Slovakia; and in 1934 broadcasting for Subcarpathian Ruthenia began from Košice in all the languages of the region – Russian, Ukrainian, and the local Rusyn dialect.[42] As will be discussed in later chapters, the exile government in London was eventually granted permission to broadcast to Subcarpathian Ruthenia in Russian and Ukrainian, in addition to its Czech and Slovak broadcasts, but its repeated requests to broadcast in German were always refused by the Foreign Office for political reasons.[43]

Radio: The Ideal Medium for Exile

Studies of radio as a medium often focus on its position in the background of listeners' lives, something they half listen to while they drive to work or do the washing up. These works often attribute much of radio's power to this position as a "secondary" entertainment which listeners have come to take for granted as part of their quotidian experience. The radio audience, these studies contend, is so accustomed to the seemingly

---

38 See Köpplová et al., *Dějiny českých médií v datech*, 23, 27.
39 See Köpplová et al., *Dějiny českých médií v datech*, 18–19, 28.
40 Vaughan, *Battle for the Airwaves*, 27.
41 Vaughan, *Battle for the Airwaves*, 27; Končelík, Večeřa, and Orság, *Dějiny českých médií 20. století*, 62.
42 On Hungarian broadcasts, see Köpplová et al., *Dějiny českých médií v datech*, 34–35; for Subcarpathian Ruthenia, see Paul Robert Magocsi, *The Shaping of a National Identity: Subcarpathian Rus', 1848–1948* (Cambridge, MA: Harvard University Press, 1978), 223.
43 The FO argued that the inclusion of broadcasts for German-speakers in the Czechoslovak programme would be interpreted as a sign that German-speaking territories would be included in post-war Czechoslovakia, and thereby contradict HMG's policy of not committing to any borders in Central Europe; see Chapter Two for more.

innocuous background entertainment that listeners do not stop to question it; the medium's very mundanity and ubiquity prevent its content and methods from being consciously analysed by its users and thereby facilitate its acceptance by the listener.[44] This study focuses on quite a different period in the history of radio, one in which listeners had to disobey police orders, secretly conceal or repair their radio sets, patiently try to work around the jamming of incoming broadcasts, post watchers outside the room, and mute the radio by setting it on a cushion, so that they could hear a few words from London without the risk of arrest; this is a study of a time when radio was not in the background.[45]

Broadcasting was also a high priority for exiled politicians, as they lacked the usual press and media routes to promote themselves among their home population. The Czechoslovaks in London were faced with a daunting task, as they were deprived of all the usual ways of communicating with their people at a time when the need to promote their cause had never been more urgent. By definition, exile governments lack the typical means of asserting their authority through public events and enacting legislation, and propaganda is all that is left to them; it is both the foundation of and the main forum for their leadership, as well as being their only means of promoting their plans for the future. In the wartime context, there was also a pressing need to encourage people at home to endure and resist, as well as to counter the propaganda attacks being made against the London exiles by the enemy authorities, all of which had to be carried out without any of the usual resources. Regular broadcaster Prokop Drtina wrote of the motivation behind some of his wartime talks, claiming he was guided by his sense of duty to "strengthen and constantly re-strengthen the faith of our people at home in victory," especially at times of difficulty for the Allied cause, such as following the fall of France in 1940.[46] He wrote of the urgency with which the exiled

---

44 Almost every study of radio as a medium asserts its ubiquity and mundanity as defining characteristics; see in particular Andrew Crisell, *Understanding Radio* (London: Methuen, 1986); Martin Shingler and Cindy Wieringa, *On Air: Methods and Meanings of Radio* (London: Arnold, 1998), esp. ix–x; Paddy Scannell, *Radio, Television and Modern Life: A Phenomenological Approach* (Oxford: Blackwell, 1996), esp. 4–5, 7. Some have suggested that this ubiquity has contributed to a lack of institutional interest in the archiving of radio; see Laura J. Treat and Shawn VanCour, "Introduction: The State of Radio Preservation," *Journal of Archival Organization* 17, nos. 1–2 (2020): 1–12.
45 Measures such as these were recommended by the BBC to ensure safety while listening to foreign broadcasts. They are recorded in intelligence documents such as SEA, EOCOTF, 17 November 1941, 47/41, EIP series 1c, E2/192/2, BBC WAC.
46 Drtina, *A nyní promluví*, 15, 21.

Czechoslovaks attempted to counter Nazi propaganda, their efforts to prove to listeners that they were receiving reliable information about events in the Protectorate without incriminating anyone, and their successful efforts at launching campaigns among listeners, such as the press boycott of 1941 (discussed later in this volume).[47]

In terms of contact with the general public in the Protectorate and Slovakia, the exile government was limited in the connections it could make. Although a variety of Czechoslovak periodicals were produced in Britain – from the pro-government weekly *Čechoslovák* (*The Czechoslovak*) to the pro-Communist *Nové Československo* (*New Czechoslovakia*) – these were not available to the home population.[48] The only way of transmitting written material was by organising leaflet drops with the Royal Air Force (RAF) which, because of Czechoslovakia's position in the centre of Europe, was impossible for much of the war. Even when leaflet drops became feasible from 1943 onwards, and the British Political Warfare Executive (PWE) produced both Czech- and Slovak-language leaflets for dropping, they were a low priority for an overburdened air force and frequently went out of date before a flight became available, leading them to be pulped. Although in these leaflets PWE often reproduced the texts of speeches that had been broadcast in the government programme, control of the leaflets' content remained firmly in British hands and, combined with the logistical difficulties in their delivery, this meant that leaflet drops never offered the exile government a viable alternative medium for its propaganda.[49]

Radio was therefore the only means for the exile government to communicate regularly and directly with the public it sought to represent, and as a medium it has many features that make it well-suited to those in exile. Radio enables speakers who have been forced from their countries and are based thousands of miles away to address their fellow

---

47 Drtina, *A nyní promluví*, 37, 42, 142.
48 *Čechoslovák* was first published in 1939 as *Čechoslovák v Anglii*, and advertised itself as an independent publication, despite its connections with the exile government. The shortened name was taken up from 1 January 1941 and the subtitle proclaiming independence was dropped in 1942. Beneš's nephew Bohuš Beneš was the paper's chief editor for several years. For more on the Czechoslovak press in Britain, see Bořivoj Srba, *Múzy v exilu: Kulturní a umělecká sktivity čs. exulantů v Londýně v předvečer a v průběhu druhé světové války, 1939–1945* (Brno: Masarykova Univerzita, 2003), esp. 395–96.
49 For more details on RAF leaflet drops, see the minutes of the meetings of the Leaflet Sub-Committee in FO 898/429, The National Archive [TNA], Kew. Examples of the leaflets produced, including the texts of many broadcasts, and details on the dates of drops can be seen in FO 898/506, 1942–45, TNA.

countrymen directly in their homes. Although efforts can be made to jam incoming broadcasts, normally by transmitting loud and disruptive noise on the same frequency, it is extremely difficult to block them out completely and broadcasts are capable of reaching anyone with a receiver. The British combated German efforts to jam their broadcasts by regularly increasing the number of wavelengths on which they transmitted, and incoming intelligence from the Protectorate suggested that jamming only occasionally made listening impossible, and then only in large cities such as Prague and Brno, where the Germans had erected jamming transmitters. Other reports suggested that there was usually at least one frequency that remained audible, sparking a rumour that it was kept open to aid the work of the German monitors.[50] Radio's ability to cross borders and the possibility for listeners to receive transmissions at a great distance from their source have been identified as key aspects of the medium's transnational nature, and these were vitally important characteristics for the isolated broadcasters in London.[51]

Another crucial characteristic of radio as a medium is the potential for the broadcaster's voice to be perceived by audiences as addressing them directly. Listeners have repeatedly been found to sense that a radio presenter is speaking to them personally, even when they are rationally aware that this cannot be the case, and broadcasting is therefore capable of creating an illusory feeling of proximity and intimacy between speaker and listener.[52] It brings would-be leaders into close (albeit one-way) contact with the people they hope to lead and, as an oral/aural medium, it enables speakers to use all the power of the human voice to appeal, persuade, entertain, and influence. The political and propagandist possibilities of the medium are therefore enhanced as broadcasters can play on listeners' emotions, appeal to their sense of humour, or challenge them by altering their use of language, and they can also use the airwaves to transmit extracts of poetry and music calculated to most affect their audience. Psychological experiments in the 1930s showed that not only did

---

50 "BBC European Audience Estimates: Czechoslovakia," 6 January 1944, EIP series 5, no. 6, E2/184; "BBC Monthly Intelligence Report," 16 August 1941, 33/41, EIP series 1a, E2/185; "BBC Bi-Monthly Intelligence Report, Europe," 18 June 1942, 25/42, EIP series 1a, BBC WAC. For more on methods and efficacy of jamming, see Edward Tangye Lean, *Voices in the Darkness: The Story of the European Radio War* (London: Secker and Warburg, 1943), 171–74.

51 For more on how radio both transcends borders and has been shaped by transnational processes and networks, see Suzanne Lommers, *Europe – On Air: Interwar Projects for Radio Broadcasting* (Amsterdam: Amsterdam University Press, 2012).

52 David Hendy looks at this intimate atmosphere of radio, in *Noise: A Human History of Sound and Listening* (London: Profile Books, 2013), esp. 290–91.

listeners tend to attribute the disembodied voice of the radio announcer with a personality which they felt they could identify from their voice alone, but also that listeners were much less critical of something they heard from another human voice than they were of the same information when presented in written form.[53] The human voice is naturally persuasive and compelling to other humans and radio allows this influence to be exerted over long distances.

The 1930s had seen a huge expansion in radio broadcasting, and during the Second World War it became the primary medium for national and international propaganda. The importance of radio in wartime has been highlighted in many studies, as it enabled both Allied and Axis countries to speak beyond their own borders and project their views into the homes of their enemies, as well as their own citizens. Writing of the late 1930s, David Vaughan has claimed that greater public access to radio and its increased use for political purposes made influencing the public attitude easier than ever:

> As never before, information and disinformation spread instantly, as access to radio grew exponentially. With old certainties melting into air, this was fertile ground indeed for propaganda and counter-propaganda [...] Radio's key role in both forging and unravelling public opinion in the run-up to World War II cannot be underestimated.[54]

In the British context, the war period marked a time of vast expansion in domestic and foreign broadcasting that was to establish the BBC as a world broadcaster, and it has been identified by historians as a definitive time for the corporation.[55] For the exiled European politicians gathered in London, however, gaining access to BBC microphones was not a simple matter and involved careful navigation of a complex propaganda structure.

Analysis of the political structure built up around British propaganda in the Second World War reveals an inefficient system which ensured the

---

53 See Hadley Cantril and Gordon Allport, *The Psychology of Radio* (New York: Harper & Brothers, 1935), 109–25, 259–60.
54 Vaughan, *Battle for the Airwaves*, 18.
55 The war period features prominently in histories of the BBC: Briggs's five-volume history of the corporation devotes an entire volume to the war years, in *War of Words*; and these six years take up one of the four sections in David Hendy's recent history of the first hundred years of the BBC, *The BBC: A People's History* (London: Profile, 2022); see also Gerard Mansell, *Let Truth Be Told: 50 Years of BBC External Broadcasting* (London: Weidenfeld and Nicolson, 1982).

Czechoslovak exile government was eventually able to broadcast with a significant degree of freedom, capitalising on British disinterest in its affairs and the autonomy afforded to the BBC. In contrast to states such as Nazi Germany, no single government department took control of state propaganda in Britain and responsibility was shared across several different authorities. The Ministry of Information, which had been largely responsible for propaganda during the First World War, was recreated immediately after the outbreak of war in 1939, but its clumsy attempts at press censorship early in the conflict earned it a poor reputation.[56] Unlike the Czechoslovaks, many in Britain held a very negative view of propaganda following experiences in the First World War, and its proponents faced a great deal of opposition in their efforts to utilise it to the utmost. An extreme example of the reluctance of several British politicians to engage in propaganda is a comment made by MP Stafford Cripps when he was shown secret propaganda material targeting Germany: "If this is the sort of thing needed to win the war, I'd rather lose it."[57] It was not until Churchill became prime minister in May 1940 that greater emphasis was placed on propaganda, under the new moniker of "political warfare," and its potential contribution to the war effort was recognised in its designation as the "fourth arm," working alongside air, sea, and land forces on the battlefield.[58] This did not eradicate the problems caused by the overlapping of responsibility between the Ministry of Information, the Foreign Office, and the intelligence services, but the creation of PWE in 1941 marked the establishment of a department with the specific remit of spreading propaganda in enemy and enemy-occupied countries.[59]

The Czechoslovak cause had an ally at the heart of this new department: prior to this appointment as director general of PWE in 1941, Sir

---

[56] See Charles Cruickshank, *The Fourth Arm: Psychological Warfare 1938–1945* (Oxford: Oxford University Press, 1981), 21.

[57] Quoted in Kenneth Young, ed., *The Diaries of Sir Robert Bruce Lockhart*, vol. 2, *1939–1965* (London: Macmillan, 1980), 26.

[58] The frustrated efforts of those who believed in the need for propaganda are documented in Cruickshank, *Fourth Arm*; David Garnett, *The Secret History of PWE: The Political Warfare Executive, 1939–1945* (London: St. Ermin's Press, 2002); a first-hand account is available in Robert Bruce Lockhart, *Comes the Reckoning* (London: Putnam, 1947); and Young, *Diaries of Lockhart*, vol. 2.

[59] The MOI, FO, Special Operations Executive, and Ministry of Economic Warfare were all also involved in propaganda policy and execution, and this confusion often obstructed decision-making. For more detail on the difficulties of this arrangement and efforts to overcome it, see Garnett, *Secret History of PWE*, 14–87; Lockhart, *Comes the Reckoning*, 125–218; Cruickshank, *Fourth Arm*, 9–43.

Robert Bruce Lockhart had been working as British representative to the as yet unrecognised Czechoslovak government-in-exile. Having already developed what he called a "genuine affinity" with the people of Czechoslovakia while based at the British Legation in Prague before the war, Lockhart had felt great frustration as he struggled to convince anyone on the British side of the importance of the Czechoslovak cause.[60] He had been warned when he took up the role of representative that progress was "bound to be slow" because "the Czechoslovaks were not in favour and were not regarded as very important."[61] "Even in my Czechs the FO take no interest," he complained in May 1940. "I feel that every time I raise some point by Beneš I am only boring the Central Department [of the FO]." In July 1940, Lockhart was "in despair" about this lack of attention; he wrote that Strang, head of the Central Department, which was nominally concerned with Czechoslovak matters, had never shown "the slightest interest" in them. "I insist always that the Czechs can help us during the war," Lockhart wrote, "but no one listens; no one cares."[62] The Czechoslovaks in London were a low priority for the British government, and research into their propaganda efforts supports the findings of Vít Smetana, that British policy towards this "minor ally" remained distinctly "reactive," with decisions only made when wider circumstances necessitated it.[63] Painful and embarrassing though this situation was for Lockhart, it is the contention of this book that this lack of interest actually benefitted the Czechoslovak exiles when it came to propaganda.

Less Trouble than the Rest: The Czechoslovak Government within the British Propaganda Structure

In the *BBC Handbook* of 1941, broadcasting by Allied governments-in-exile was presented as a natural part of the corporation's new wartime role:

> British broadcasting must present the British case to friendly foreign countries. It must carry the truth across the barriers erected against it in

---

60 Robert Bruce Lockhart, *My Europe* (London: Putnam, 1952), 92.
61 Lockhart, *Comes the Reckoning*, 59.
62 Young, *Diaries of Lockhart*, 2:58, 64.
63 Vít Smetana, *In the Shadow of Munich: British Policy towards Czechoslovakia from the Endorsement to the Renunciation of the Munich Agreement (1938–1942)* (Prague: Karolinum, 2008), 15.

enemy and enemy-occupied countries. It must provide allied but exiled governments, and others carrying on the struggle by Britain's side, with opportunities to speak to their peoples at home.[64]

Isolated as they were, exile governments were indeed keen to make use of the BBC's broadcasting power, but the above statement conceals the corporation's initial reluctance to allow access to its microphones and the fact that it eventually yielded only under pressure. The BBC had recognised its own importance in warfare, recording in a paper of December 1939 that "the Corporation regards the prosecution of the War as the most important objective of broadcasting at the present time"; but many of those employed in broadcasting were suspicious of any threat to the impartiality upon which the BBC's reputation had been built, from politicians of any country.[65] The BBC's relationship with the British government in wartime was undefined, despite attempts by former director general Sir John Reith to clarify the situation as far back as 1934, and the corporation had cause to fear for its independence early in the war, when it was threatened with outright takeover by the Ministry of Information.[66] After the appointment of Brendan Bracken as minister in 1941, however, an uneasy peace was established. Bracken frequently supported the BBC in its quarrels with government departments, and in a speech in December 1943 he claimed that "I am constantly advising my friends in the BBC of the desirability of being independent and of being very tough with anyone who attempts to put pressure upon you."[67]

Broadcasting in foreign languages, a field into which the BBC had first ventured only in 1938, was more closely scrutinised than domestic broadcasting, however, and the BBC was obliged to co-ordinate its efforts with various government departments. When PWE was formed in 1941, it was given the mission of directing and co-ordinating all British propaganda to enemy and enemy-occupied countries, with the Foreign Office taking responsibility for all allied and neutral states.[68] As the BBC's European broadcasts constituted the single largest source of

---

64 *BBC Handbook 1941* (London: BBC, 1941), 12. BBC handbooks and yearbooks are a review of the previous year, with the 1941 volume providing information on 1940, etc.
65 "BBC paper on War-time Propaganda, Dec. 1939," quoted in Briggs, *War of Words*, 29n113.
66 The threat was made by Britain's first minister of information, Alfred Duff Cooper, but he was replaced by Bracken almost immediately; see Mansell, *Let Truth Be Told*, 76–77. On Reith's efforts before the war, see ibid., 60–61.
67 Brendan Bracken's Speech, 8 December 1943, quoted in Briggs, *War of Words*, 32.
68 This mission was laid down in PWE's charter; see Garnett, *Secret History of PWE*, 78.

British propaganda to the continent, which included states in all four of the above categories, it was of primary interest to both departments.[69] Relations with the Foreign Office were slightly strained, but the BBC tended to receive complaints regarding particular programmes only after they had been broadcast. The relationship between the BBC and PWE, despite being more structured, also offered the former a great deal of freedom. PWE was housed in Bush House, alongside the BBC European Service, and produced a general directive on propaganda themes which the BBC was obliged to observe. Each of PWE's seven directorates (for Germany and Austria; France; Norway and Denmark; the Netherlands and Belgium; the Balkans; Italy; and a single directorate for both Poland and Czechoslovakia) also produced a weekly regional directive for their associated BBC section, but these were merely advisory and broadcasters were not compelled to comply with them.[70] In his history of PWE, David Garnett complained that the executive was only ever able to establish "partial and intermittent control" over BBC broadcasts; but BBC historian Asa Briggs praised the "very substantial measure of independence" retained by the BBC, noting that conflict between the two was not as frequent or severe as might have been expected.[71]

Following the fall of France in June 1940, London had become the final point of refuge for former politicians and government figures from Holland, Belgium, Norway, France, the Balkans, Poland, and Czechoslovakia, among others, and each wanted to connect with their respective publics at home. While political figures did occasionally contribute to BBC programmes via the relevant BBC service early in the war, it was not long before these allied governments, both recognised and unrecognised, began to push for more broadcasting time. The BBC was initially cautious, referring all enquiries to the Foreign Office and the Ministry of Information, citing political and security questions that it was

---

[69] This is the case for "white" propaganda at least. Britain's secretive efforts in the field of "black" propaganda, which aimed to deceive listeners and conceal its British origin, were entirely separate and neither the BBC nor any exiled governments were permitted any part in it. For more on "black" propaganda and the work carried out by Department EH/SO1, see Mark Seaman, ed., *Special Operations Executive: A New Weapon of War* (London: Routledge, 2006), esp. Eunan O'Halpin, "'Hitler's Irish Hideout': A case study of SOE's black propaganda battles," 201–16.

[70] Czechoslovakia did not get its own PWE regional director until the appointment of Godfrey Lias in September 1943; see Cruickshank, *Fourth Arm*, 32–33. For a more in-depth discussion of PWE's conflict with the BBC on the issue of regional policy, see Garnett, *Secret History of PWE*, 86–93, 185.

[71] Garnett, *Secret History of PWE*, xxiii; Briggs, *War of Words*, 31, 34.

not qualified to answer.[72] In addition to fears for national security and the potential for broadcasting coded messages without British knowledge, concern was expressed in some quarters that the exiles constituted a political liability and that openly supporting groups that might later fall from favour could compromise the reputation of Britain and British broadcasting.[73] The principal concern in both government and broadcasting circles, however, was that of conflicting policy. BBC intelligence showed that listeners across Europe tended to assume that anything they heard being broadcast from London, regardless of who was speaking, had been officially approved by the British government. In an undated BBC memo it was reported that "the evidence shows that in enemy-occupied countries many listeners confuse the voice of Britain with the voice of their own countrymen who have escaped to freedom," but also that attempts by the BBC to disassociate itself from Allied governments would be open to exploitation by enemy propaganda seeking to undermine public trust in Allied unity.[74] In order to prevent the damage that would be done to the BBC's reputation if it was perceived to be inaccurate, contradictions with British policy had to be avoided at all costs. The matter was complicated further by the polyglot nature of Europe and the potential for cross-listening as many people tuned in to multiple language programmes. To maintain its credibility, the BBC could not afford to broadcast contradictions in any combination of languages and the varied domestic and foreign policies of Allied governments had therefore to be reconciled not only with British policy but also with each other. This could only be achieved if the BBC was able to oversee and supervise the total output, but this raised difficult questions of censorship and authority.

Despite the potential risks, however, there was also a strong argument for allowing the exiles to broadcast, because they had something to offer the BBC in return; as well as being able to inform the BBC's broadcasting with intelligence from their own sources, they could also

---

72 "Exile Government Requests," 21 May 1940, E2/10, BBC WAC.
73 The Security Executive was formed to answer questions on the matter of allowing exile governments to broadcast and concluded that "it was contrary to the interests of national security" for the BBC to allow it, due to the possibility of them passing messages home in "plain language code." It recommended, therefore, that only high-ranking figures with FO approval should be allowed to broadcast and the names of all announcers on foreign-language services should be submitted to the security services; see "Security Measures," BBC memo to Director General, 29 June 1940, E2/10, BBC WAC. For more on the concerns relating to alliance with foreign exiles, see Chapter One.
74 "British Broadcasts and Allied Governments," undated, E2/15, BBC WAC.

lend the corporation something of their own authority and credibility.[75] In a BBC paper entitled "British Broadcasts and Allied Governments," written while German successes still filled the daily news, the situation was likened to governmental negotiation and recognition: "The British Government does not recognise refugees as a government for nothing: when it does so, it incurs a liability to gain an asset – the power to lead their people." The asset at stake was "radio leadership," which the writer defined as "the power to make men and women and children obey our broadcasts even when freedom is a long way off and danger near," suggesting the possible connections between such broadcasts and encouraging resistance to Nazi occupation. The message of the paper was that the BBC must make the most of the contribution Allied governments could make to building up British "radio leadership" and furthering "the projection of Britain." A certain amount of freedom had therefore to be granted in order to make the latter believable, and the unnamed writer felt that everything possible must be done to make listeners "take the broadcasters for the free voice of their own country."[76]

Exile governments continued to request greater and greater access to broadcasting, reflecting the high value attributed to radio propaganda. There was a consistent clash of priorities here, however, as the BBC wished to focus on delivering reliable, up-to-date war news, while Allied governments often wished to pursue specific themes of relevance to themselves and their own countries which were of little interest to British broadcasters. By mid-1940, exile interference in the making of BBC programmes was causing so much resentment and taking up so much time, both on air and off, that the BBC began to consider the idea of "free time." Although the policy would not allow the exiles "complete carte-blanche" to say what they wished (all programming remained subject to British censorship and scripts had to be vetted in advance), it did give them a much freer choice of topic and removed the constraint of having to observe British propaganda directives.[77] It also gave exile governments

---

75 It was noted that the Czechoslovak government in particular had valuable intelligence to offer the BBC and the British departments behind it; Garnett, *Secret History of PWE*, 185. František Moravec, head of the Czechoslovak intelligence services since 1937, escaped to Britain and spent the war working closely with Beneš and sharing intelligence with Britain. In his memoirs, he described this work as "our most positive contribution to the allied war effort"; see František Moravec, *Master of Spies: The Memoirs of František Moravec* (London: Bodley Head, 1975).
76 "British Broadcasting and Allied Governments," undated, E2/15, BBC WAC.
77 Mansell, *Let Truth Be Told*, 108; see "Memorandum on the co-operation between the BBC and Allied Governments in Great Britain," 29 May 1941, E2/15, BBC WAC.

their own distinctly separate programme, set apart from those produced by the BBC and openly attributed to the government in question. This privilege was first extended to the Dutch government, which launched *Radio Oranje* in July 1940 and, as many at the Ministry of Information had feared, it was indeed "the thin end of the wedge."[78] The BBC and the Foreign Office were soon besieged with requests from other Allies, and their frequency caused many at the BBC to believe that it would be less trouble to grant the time than it would to constantly explain why it was not possible. For example, a comment on the confidential European Service paper "'Free Time' for Allied Governments" warned that the Polish government ought to have free broadcasting time because "there will be conflict until they do."[79] Political tension was exacerbated by the fact that several of the exile governments had already broadcast freely from France before the German invasion (or had been given permission to do so), and they were therefore resentful of greater restrictions being imposed by Britain in the dissemination of their own news and propaganda. Efforts to keep all Allied governments on side also meant that, ideally, they should be treated equally in terms of broadcasting privileges, to prevent accusations of favouritism. The BBC found this almost impossible to implement to begin with, as it was bound by the guidance of the Foreign Office, which pursued different policies towards Britain's allies based on their varying positions in the conflict.[80] The changing relationship between the Czechoslovak government and the BBC in relation to the government's programme has not been documented elsewhere and is worth summarising to provide context to the broadcasts.

Officially, the Czechoslovak exiles came to "free time" much later than most of their European colleagues, preferring a more general collaboration with the BBC Czech Service to a single, separate programme and maintaining this arrangement for as long as possible. The Czechoslovaks were praised at the BBC for co-operating well, and there is an interesting parallel to be drawn with Radiojournal during the First Republic. Just as in the 1920s and 1930s broadcasters in Czechoslovakia had submitted to government control and thereby retained freedom in programme production, so too did the Czechoslovaks in London show a willingness to follow the British rules, which earned them a reputation at the BBC for

---

[78] Briggs, *War of Words,* 242–44; "Free Time for the Dutch Government," 26 June 1940, E2/10, BBC WAC.
[79] "'Free Time' for Allied Governments," undated, E2/15, BBC WAC.
[80] See Briggs, *War of Words,* 243.

reliability that, in turn, won them greater freedom in their broadcasts. In contrast to other exiles, such as the Poles, the Czechoslovaks enjoyed a significant degree of freedom at the BBC, and their respect for the importance of propaganda can be clearly seen in their commitment to co-operation with the corporation.

In discussions of exile government broadcasting at the BBC, the Poles were frequently, and unfavourably, compared to the Czechoslovaks and often cited as an example of the dangers of allowing foreign politicians to influence programming. Balancing the diplomatic problems of handling exile governments against the demands of the British propaganda structure and the BBC's own principles and interests presented no small difficulty, and European Controller Ivone Kirkpatrick described it in his memoirs as "our most difficult task."[81] Kirkpatrick frequently complained that, when the BBC was too lax with exile governments, it faced the censure of ministers and the Ministry of Information, but when it was too strict, the exiles complained of harsh treatment and the BBC was subject to remonstrance by the Foreign Office for complicating diplomatic relations. His dissatisfaction with the entire policy was clear as he referred to "free time" for Allied governments as "a constant source of embarrassment to our broadcasts," and admitted in 1941 that, should the Ministry of Information decide to "abolish or curtail Allied Free Time, I, for one, will be more relieved and grateful than anyone."[82] The Polish government's attempts to interfere in the BBC's Polish-language programming and even to win control over all broadcasts to Poland earned it a bad reputation at the corporation and created an atmosphere of "mutual suspicion."[83] When the Poles were granted their own programme, at the end of 1941, it was more limited in scope (solely to activities of the Polish government and troops in Britain) and more closely supervised than those of other Allied governments; while switch censors (supervisors checking announcers followed the approved script and able to switch off transmission if they deviated from it) worked during all such broadcasts, they were on special alert during the Polish ones.[84] Kirkpatrick was driven to complain of the Poles, that "they are constantly attempting to misuse their liberty in order to put over material which

---

81 Ivone Kirkpatrick, *The Inner Circle: Memoirs of Ivone Kirkpatrick* (London: Macmillan, 1959), 160.
82 Kirkpatrick to Foot, "Broadcast by Monsieur Vallin," 21 September 1941, E2/10, BBC WAC.
83 Briggs, *War of Words*, 424.
84 See Briggs, *War of Words*, 423–26.

is definitely embarrassing to us."[85] As will be discussed later, one of the most serious points of friction in relations between the Polish exiles and the British (both in government and at the BBC) was the thorny issue of Polish–Soviet relations.

In contrast, the Czechoslovaks were known at the BBC for being co-operative. In preference to taking on "free time" and thereby limiting their influence on broadcasting to a single time slot, the Czechoslovaks contributed content and assistance to all Czech and Slovak programme production at the BBC and their compliance won them many compliments. Even the prickly Kirkpatrick was obliged to admit that "there is no friction and we have less trouble with the Czechoslovaks than with any other allies [...] the situation is entirely satisfactory."[86] One BBC memo noted approvingly that the Czechoslovak government-in-exile was "anxious to secure the maximum possible co-operation with the BBC," and described the relationship between the Czechoslovak exiles and the BBC as "harmonious."[87] The BBC also hoped to gain something from this collaboration as the quest for "radio leadership" continued; it was recognised that, "to the Czechs, with the humiliations of Munich fresh in their minds, the voice of Czechs officially recognised by the British Government may well have extreme value" – that is, value to the projection of Britain.[88] In short, the voices of government figures were the best possible counter to Nazi claims that Britain had no interest in the fate of the people of Czechoslovakia.

Although *Hovory s domovem* was not officially a "free time" programme, the Czechoslovaks were able to express themselves relatively freely and government representatives took part in BBC planning meetings.[89] The lack of a firm British policy towards Czechoslovakia engendered a more relaxed approach to censorship and, although there were three switch censors appointed to monitor the Czechoslovak broadcasts, by some accounts their control was not very strict. In his article

---

85   Kirkpatrick to Foot, "Broadcast by Monsieur Vallin," 21 September 1941, E2/10, BBC WAC.
86   Kirkpatrick to Bracken (MOI), "Allied Broadcasting," 30 November 1942, E2/10, BBC WAC.
87   "Report on broadcasting by foreign Governments resident in London, the Greek Government and the Fighting French," undated, E2/10, BBC WAC.
88   "British Broadcasting and Allied Governments," undated, E2/15, BBC WAC.
89   It should be noted here that not all Czechoslovak exiles supported the government or approved of this co-operation. Poet and writer Ivan Jelínek worked at the BBC Czech Section and opposed intervention from Beneš and his allies. His personal opposition to Beneš and objection to the involvement of Josef Körbel in programme-making decisions led him to leave the BBC to rejoin the armed forces; see Ivan Jelínek, *Jablko se kouše* (Prague: Torst, 1994), esp. 498–502.

on wartime broadcasting from London, former radio editor Jiří Hronek described the level of comprehension of Czech by Messrs. Watson, Fields, and Patterson as "average to below average," and noted that the last of these three censors "very often slept during transmission."[90] The structure of the European Service, which concentrated considerable influence in the hands of a few individuals, also worked in the Czechoslovak government's favour, as it enjoyed the support not only of Kirkpatrick but also of European news editor Noel Newsome. Briggs claimed that Newsome "admired" the Czechs and encouraged Beneš and Hubert Ripka, head of the MZV Information Department, "to express general views on Europe's future which were far more comprehensive than those permitted to Polish speakers."[91] Newsome also had a personal connection with the Czechoslovaks after his marriage in 1942 to Czech Section editor Sheila Grant Duff (who had written several books sympathetic to the Czechoslovak cause), and Briggs notes that neither she nor her successor Reginald Betts felt "in any sense inhibited in programme policy by PWE."[92] This lack of inhibition, aided by the British political indifference to internal Czechoslovak affairs outlined above, took pressure off BBC broadcasters and, in turn, Czechoslovak exile broadcasters as well. The Czechoslovak government enjoyed extensive co-operation with the BBC for several years before it was forced to formalise its position and accept "free time" somewhat against its will.

The BBC had begun daily news broadcasts in Czech on 8 September 1939, when former Czechoslovak minister to Britain and future foreign minister Jan Masaryk gave a short introductory message. When the British government awarded the Czechoslovaks provisional recognition in July 1940, the Czechoslovak MZV set up an Information Department which contained a Radio Department, the former headed by Hubert Ripka and the latter by Josef Körbel. This section worked closely with the BBC in all programming and produced the daily fifteen-minute programme *Hovory s domovem,* first broadcast on 11 August 1940, in which they could broadcast talks and news commentaries, distinct from

---

90 Jiří Hronek, "Československý rozhlas v Londýně za války," in *Kapitoly z dějin čs. rozhlasu* (Prague: Studijní oddělení československého rozhlasu, 1964), 39.
91 Briggs, *War of Words*, 426–27.
92 Briggs, *War of Words*, 426n209. Grant Duff was the author of *Europe and the Czechs* (Harmondsworth: Penguin, 1938) and *A German Protectorate, the Czechs under Nazi Rule* (London: Macmillan, 1942).

the BBC's main contribution of news bulletins.[93] Despite this high level of influence, the programme itself was not explicitly attributed to the exile government – in the *BBC Handbook*'s review of foreign-language broadcasts in 1940, only the Dutch and the Free French are mentioned specifically as having their own transmission periods, while instead it is noted that "the Czechs also have a special period, which serves as a link between the Czech forces in this country and those who are carrying on the resistance at home."[94] To increase communication with the BBC, the Czech Service Meeting was also formed, which included members of the Czechoslovak government, the BBC Czech Section, and the Ministry of Information. The meeting was held weekly between September 1940 and October 1941, when it was discontinued.[95] The MZV Information Department also established an Advisory Radio Committee (Poradní rozhlasový sbor, PRS) to discuss any potential problems.[96] The PRS had over thirty members, including representatives from across the political spectrum, as well as radio editors and others with broadcasting experience.

By 1941, BBC memos had begun to circulate regarding the problems of "free time" for Allied governments, and they shed some light on the BBC's understanding of the Czechoslovak collaboration. Changes were being proposed to the system of "free time" in view of the fact that research showed that listeners were failing to distinguish between BBC broadcasts and those of exile governments. It had been established that it would be politically damaging for Britain to be perceived to be distancing itself from its supposed allies, and the BBC – as Britain's ambassador to occupied Europe – had to be cautious.[97] It was decided that the BBC should emphasise the freedom it was giving Allied governments in allowing them to broadcast, but that there should also be a clearer separation of BBC and non-BBC programmes, to be reinforced by announcers and the use of different signature tunes. The freedom

---

93 In February 1941 an extra fifteen-minute news commentary programme was added at 11:15 p.m. UK time, on which the Czechoslovak government collaborated with the BBC. For more on the structure of programming, including non-government BBC Czech broadcasting times, see Ondřej Koutek, "Zahraniční odboj na vlnách BBC: Československé vysílání z Londýna, 1939–1945," *Paměť a dějiny* 8, no. 1 (2014): 32–43.
94 John Salt (Director of the European Service), "The European Service," in *BBC Handbook 1941*, 41.
95 Czechoslovak Service, Meetings, 1940–1942, E1/638, BBC WAC.
96 Rozhlas – Poradní sbor, "Zřízení Poradního rozhlasového sboru," 18 November 1940, Londýnský archiv (obyčejný) [LA (O)] 353, Czech Ministry of Foreign Affairs Archive [*Ministerstvo zahraničních věcí*, MZV], Prague.
97 "Report on broadcasting by foreign Governments resident in London, the Greek Government and the Fighting French," undated, E2/10, BBC WAC.

the Czechoslovaks were enjoying, without officially being awarded "free time," was noted in BBC memos; one commentator suggested that "they do practically have the kind of 'free time' envisaged. It's only a question of making it official."[98] This comment also shows that there was little resistance from within the BBC (which was subject to external pressure from the Foreign Office regarding such matters) to the possibility of Czechoslovak "free time," suggesting that the Czechoslovaks were not thought likely to contravene the BBC's rules as the Poles had done. In his memo "Radio London and Free Time," Newsome's deputy Douglas Ritchie showed faith in the trustworthiness of the Czechs, by suggesting that, if they were given a freer hand, "it would not, in fact, make much difference to what is already broadcast" and it "would probably have an excellent effect on Anglo–Czech relations."[99] Apparently happy with the existing co-operation, there was no push for official "free time" from the Czechoslovak side, and it was only in 1943 that the exiles were forced to standardise their relationship with the BBC in line with those of other governments, having avoided doing so for as long as possible.

Following discussions with the BBC in late 1942 and early 1943, the MZV Radio Department had drawn up its own proposal for restructuring programming, which involved a new ten-minute early morning broadcast with a set daily theme (for example, Mondays would feature talks to Subcarpathian Ruthenia) and added time for expansive quotations, poetry, music, and discussions of Czechoslovak news in the international press during the existing evening broadcast.[100] This proposal was rejected by the BBC and Sheila Grant Duff, then Czech editor, who explained that, as far as the BBC was concerned, "the Czechoslovak transmission is an integral part of a European Service, the main purpose of which is political warfare in Europe." The proposed schedule of themed morning talks did not allow for the daily changes in propaganda directive and Grant Duff maintained that closer collaboration with the BBC was needed. Insisting it was important that "the broadcasts to Czechoslovakia be formed into one coherent whole, directed towards an agreed goal in concert with our other European broadcasts," Grant Duff offered the Radio Department two choices: either it could accept "free time" and therefore hold talks on whatever topics it saw fit, but lose its existing influence on the composition of BBC news and talks; or it would have to

---

98 BBC European Service, "'Free Time' for Allied Governments," undated, E2/15, BBC WAC.
99 Ritchie, "Radio London and Free Time," 3 June 1941, E2/15, BBC WAC.
100 Rozhlas – Poradní rozhl. sbor 1941–44, undated note, MV–L 271: 2-82-4, CNA.

agree to "complete concentration and complete amalgamation."[101] Negotiations on amalgamation came to nothing and the department were therefore compelled to accept "free time" and the associated limiting of its influence to the specified government programme.[102] When presenting the changes to ministers at a cabinet meeting, Ripka explained that he had opposed the changes on the grounds that, in effect, "we will actually have less time than we do currently," but that he had been able to secure fortnightly meetings between himself, Betts, and his team, "by means of which it will be possible to influence them."[103] Several ministers expressed their dissatisfaction but Ripka claimed to have secured the best possible deal in the circumstances and defended the BBC, reminding the group that broadcasters in Moscow had no such freedom. Jan Masaryk acknowledged that the BBC had a lot to contend with in seeking to balance so many requests, telling his colleagues that "The English have a hell of job sorting [broadcasting] for the whole world; we are just one small part of it and we think we're the most important [...] We're doing well out of it."[104]

The new government programme, *Hlas svobodné republiky*, began on 29 March 1943, and it was broadcast for ten minutes in the early morning and fifteen minutes in the late evening until August 1944, when an extra early evening programme was also added.[105] The Czechoslovaks were then free to pursue their proposed schedule, with the early morning programme generally targeting specific groups of listeners: Mondays for Subcarpathian Ruthenia, Tuesdays for workers, Wednesdays for younger listeners, Saturdays for women, and Sundays for religious programming and talks for farmers.[106] Total Czechoslovak broadcasting output increased from seven hours per week in September 1940 to just under seventeen by May 1945, and the last episode of *Hlas svobodné republiky*

---

101 Sheila Grant-Duff to Dr. Körbel, 9 March 1943, MV–L 271: 2-82-4, CNA.
102 Note from Dr. Körbel to Dr. Ripka, 29 March 1943, MV–L 271: 2-82-4, CNA.
103 Minutes from meeting, 2 April 1943, in *Zápisy ze schůzí československé vlády v Londýně*, vol. 3.1, *leden–červen 1943*, ed. Jan Němeček et al. (Prague: Pravnická fakulta Univerzity Karlovy, Historický ústav Akademie věd ČR, Masarykův ústav a Archiv Akademie věd ČR, 2012), 226.
104 Minutes from meeting, 2 April 1943, in Němeček et al., *Zápisy ze schůzí*, 3.1:229–30.
105 There was some fluctuation in broadcasting times, but the morning programme generally went out at 6:10 a.m., the early evening programme at either 5:15 p.m. or 6:15 p.m., and the evening programme at 7:45 p.m. or 8:45 p.m. All times are British.
106 This schedule was subject to change at need but was fairly standardised in this form from mid-1943.

was broadcast on 11 May 1945.[107] The most high-profile broadcasts were the speeches of President Beneš, and these were normally repeated several times at various hours of the day, to ensure they reached the maximum possible number of listeners. They were also often followed by associated commentaries from other speakers, to analyse and explain the significance of his words. Other ministers, such as Minister for Justice Jaroslav Stránský and Foreign Minister Jan Masaryk, were awarded their own regular broadcasting slots, while members of the National Council (Státní rada), such as Rudolf Bechyně and Prokop Maxa, also occasionally broadcast. In addition to political speeches, the broadcasts were an opportunity to promote the more tangible successes of the exile movement, such as diplomatic recognition and honours, and the work of Czechoslovaks in the military. The weekly military programme *Vojenská beseda* (*Military Talk*), broadcast on Wednesday evenings, kept listeners informed of the achievements of Czechoslovak units in the armed forces and air force, as well as broadcasting a number of short interviews and appeals from soldiers. Visiting speakers, from diplomats and sympathetic Britons to academics and priests, brought variety to the programme. There was also a core team of Czechoslovak broadcasters and writers, employed by the BBC but working closely with the MZV and contributing to both BBC and government broadcasts. Several of these young men, such as Ota Ornest, Josef Schwarz, and Pavel Tigrid, were also active in the wider Czechoslovak cultural scene in London, writing for newspapers and appearing in plays, and they would become well-known names both at home and in exile after the war.[108]

---

[107] As some countries had already been liberated before May 1945 and their broadcasting time correspondingly reduced, a comparison of hours and minutes allotted to each language/territory from September 1943 is perhaps more revealing of priorities overall. At this point, the BBC European Service was broadcasting 15 hours and 10 minutes per week in Czech/Slovak, placing it mid-table when compared to other languages; the greatest outputs were in French (39 hr., 30 min.), German (34 hr., 40 min., plus 8 hr., 45 min. of broadcasts specifically for Austria), Italian (29 hr., 45 min.), English (21 hr., 5 min.), and Dutch (17 hr., 30 min.). Polish was equal with Czech/Slovak on 15 hr., 10 min., with Norwegian and Greek just behind on 12 hr., 15 min. each, then "Yugoslav" (11 hr., 20 min.) and Spanish (10 hr., 30 min.). The other eleven European languages broadcast all received less than 10 hours per week. All figures for BBC European Service output taken from Briggs, *War of Words*, 440.

[108] These three, along with Leon Braun, joined the BBC in 1941 and were later joined by Karel Brušák, who went on to become a respected academic in Britain. Detailed information on the work of each can be found in Srba, *Múzy v exilu*, esp. 111–17, 324–26. An edited volume of Tigrid's writings from the period, including his radio talks, was published in 2017; Prokop Tomek, ed., *Pavel Tigrid: Volá Londýn. Ze zákulisí čs. vysílání z Londýna* (Prague: Ústav pro studium totalitních režimů, 2017).

The remaining chapters of this book will examine how the Czechoslovak government-in-exile used its radio broadcasts – both *Hovory s domovem* and *Hlas svobodné republiky* – to perform as a government, and how the dominant themes in these programmes reflected the political issues confronting the government-in-exile during its time in London. Although the level of freedom enjoyed by the Czechoslovak exiles was relatively high, especially in comparison to some other exile governments, it should not be forgotten that they were never totally free from the constraints of their British context and there were points at which their desires were thwarted by their hosts. These conflicts and the negotiation surrounding them will be discussed as and when they arise, as part of the contextualisation of each propaganda theme. The fact remains, however, that much of what was most important to the Czechoslovak exiles – those questions of what Czechoslovakia had been and should be after the war, which involved national, ethnic, personal, and political issues – was considered by the British to be an internal affair in which they had little interest. Once such content was restricted to the government's own programme and did not directly contradict any established British policy, the exiles were largely free to use the broadcasts to speak to and for a nation of their own design. This study therefore seeks to examine not only how the Czechoslovak exiles used the radio to further their own performance of authority, but also what their broadcasts reveal about their understandings of Czechoslovakia.

Chapter One focuses on the concept of Czechoslovakia as a state, one which may have been temporarily occupied and divided but was also represented by an internationally recognised government-in-exile and retained some kind of legal existence, even if this was not reflected in the practical experience of listeners. This chapter will demonstrate how the exiles used their broadcasts to establish their position as both the legal and ideological leaders of the Czechoslovak people. It will also show to what a significant extent both aspects of their leadership were associated with the memory of the First Czechoslovak Republic, a period upheld even today as "the gold standard by which all subsequent regimes are to be measured."[109]

---

[109] Mary Heimann, *Czechoslovakia: The State that Failed* (New Haven: Yale University Press, 2011), 48.

In contrast, Chapter Two addresses the idea of Czechoslovakia as a *nation*, a single national unit connected through a shared history and culture. This chapter argues that the London exiles used the government programme to design their own audience, to create an imagined community of "Czechoslovak" listeners and perform a specific interpretation of Czechoslovak national identity intended to simultaneously attract the support of listeners and complement their own wartime task of representing Czechoslovakia politically. The features of radio as a medium which make it well-suited to such acts of nation-building are analysed in this chapter. As will be demonstrated, however, the fundamental issue with the government's interpretation of the nation was that the future republic it was describing was to be a Czechoslovak one, but the cultural and historical material used to support the idea of this republic was almost entirely Czech.

The difficulty of promoting Czechoslovak unity in these broadcasts while simultaneously taking into account the specific needs of listeners in Slovakia was to prove insurmountable for the exile government and this struggle is examined in Chapter Three. Although by the end of the conflict none of the Allied powers considered any possible fate for Slovakia other than a return to the shared Czechoslovak state, this was not a victory that was won in the field of propaganda. The exiles faced multiple practical and ideological difficulties in planning wartime broadcasts to Slovakia, and this chapter argues that their efforts ultimately resulted in abrupt and negative propaganda which failed to address either the inherited national problems of the First Republic or the new questions raised by the first experience of Slovak statehood.

Broadcasting to another of Czechoslovakia's regions, Subcarpathian Ruthenia, is discussed in the final chapter of this study, which examines the dangerous consequences for propaganda once control over policy has been lost. In the context of increasingly close Czechoslovak–Soviet relations, Soviet desires became a dominant factor in policymaking and Czechoslovak exile propaganda became increasingly erratic, as previously promoted policies disappeared from the airwaves and never came to pass. Soviet opposition was the downfall of the proposed Central European Confederation and the reason behind the loss of Subcarpathian Ruthenia; the territory was forcibly annexed by the Soviet Union and made part of the Ukrainian Soviet Socialist Republic in 1945, but the broadcasts from London – the last communications between a Czechoslovak government and the population of the region – gave no warning of this, showing the dangers of broadcasting propaganda that is divorced from policy.

The Czechoslovak government programme from London was a crucial part of the performance of Czechoslovakia that the exiles enacted during the Second World War, and the motivation behind it was apparently straightforward; to the exiles themselves, it was simply work for "the Czechoslovak cause" and the broadcasts became "one of the most important weapons of the Czech and Slovak nation in resistance and in battle against Nazi Germany, and in the fight for liberation."[110] When studied as a whole, however, and read in the context of the diplomatic relations and cabinet discussions carried out off air, the texts of the broadcasts reveal the complexities of the exile mission. The primary task of the broadcasts was to convince listeners that there was a solid, cohesive, Czechoslovak population and that it was both officially and spiritually represented by a legitimate government-in-exile in London. To achieve this, the broadcasts therefore had to establish the idea of the state, convince listeners of the exiles' authority to lead it, and persuade their audience to perceive them as loyal members of that state, making the most of the capacity of radio to do so. When the exiles described the programme, however, they did not emphasise its political purpose. In his introduction to the first broadcast of *Hovory s domovem* on 11 August 1940, Minister Hubert Ripka presented it as an essentially cultural programme that would provide listeners with those products of their national culture of which they were being deprived:

> In these fifteen minutes, what we want to broadcast most of all are those products of the rich cultural output of our nation which the Nazis are forbidding at home. We will see to it that you hear the poems you are not allowed to read, we will recall those scenes of our history which they have torn from your books and textbooks, we will quote the literature which they have thrown out of your libraries [...] We will perform extracts of the plays which the Nazis fear to see on our stages, extracts from the operas which set fire to the heart and strengthen our unshakeable faith in a new life. We will keep you informed of everything that is happening in our

---

110 Prokop Drtina, *Československo: Můj osud: Kniha života českého demokrata 20. století* (Toronto: Sixty-Eight, 1982), 535–36.

army [...] We will give talks and interpretations about what is happening in the world and we will try in particular to keep you in permanent contact with the spiritual works and heroic political effort of this great country, of which we are guests and allies.[111]

Although cultural content such as music and poetry did play an important part in the exile government's propaganda, it would be highly disingenuous to present the government programme as anything less than political propaganda. Perhaps seeking to play down the important role the broadcasts played in persuading the audience of the government's authority, Ripka made no mention of the exile government itself or the political broadcasting that would go on to make up the majority of the programme, and indeed the remainder of that first broadcast. An announcer followed Ripka by reading a Czech translation of a radio talk given by British MP and Under Secretary of State for Foreign Affairs Rab Butler the day after Britain extended recognition to the provisional Czechoslovak government-in-exile. In this speech, Butler praised Beneš and the "outstanding men" who made up his government, who "previously held high offices in the Czechoslovak Republic." Butler's subsequent comment, that "in the last twenty years, the Czechoslovaks were a fine and living example of what a democratic government can do for its people," lent British support to the interpretation of the First Republic as a successful and admirable democracy upon which the wartime exiles founded their claims to legal and ideological legitimacy.[112]

Scope and Sources

This book touches on many different areas of study, and the following section outlines some of the existing literature consulted. The six years of the Second World War have been intensely studied from almost every angle, with tomes on the military, diplomatic, and cultural aspects filling many shelves. The neglect of Czech and Slovak history in much of the English-language historiography, and the long-term ideological restrictions on historical research in the former Czechoslovakia itself, mean that this period has, however, attracted renewed interest in the last

---

111 BBC Czechoslovak Programme, 11 August 1940, BBC Londýn – Zpravodajství [LN Z] 1940 – 1, Český rozhlas Archive [CRA], Prague.
112 BBC Czechoslovak Programme, 11 August 1940, LN Z 1940 – 1, CRA.

twenty years. Between 1948 and 1989, with only a brief respite during the liberalisation of the 1960s, the historiography of the wartime exile movement was limited by the constraints imposed by the Communist regime in Czechoslovakia. Access to archives and other sources was restricted, making it almost impossible for historians in Czechoslovakia and abroad to challenge the official narrative, which demonised the "conservative-bourgeois" London exile and celebrated instead the Communist exile movement, largely based in Moscow.[113] Since the end of Communist rule, historians of the region have sought to address what dissident historian Jan Křen termed the "white spaces" in Czechoslovak history, those topics which had been "concealed, obscured, made taboo or falsified" while a state-enforced ideology dominated academia – and the war period is one such topic.[114]

Parts of the story of the Czechoslovak exile government in Britain have already been told, both in the memoirs of those involved and by later historians. The government that coalesced around former president Edvard Beneš had its origins in the Czechoslovak National Committee (Československý národní výbor), which was formed in Paris and relocated to London following the fall of France in June 1940. Provisional recognition was awarded by Britain in July 1940 and full recognition followed in July 1941, when it was also announced by the Soviet Union. Memoirs from the period include those of Beneš, his close collaborator Prokop Drtina, Head of Czechoslovak Intelligence František Moravec, Communist Bohuslav Laštovička, and, from the British side, those of Robert Bruce Lockhart, British representative to the provisional government until the award of full recognition.[115] Researchers such as Vít Smetana, Martin Brown, and Detlef Brandes have examined the progression of the London exiles from Czechoslovak National Committee to fully recognised government-in-exile in the context of their relations with the British government. Smetana's work in particular highlights the difficulties of the

---

[113] Jiří Hronek, a former editor in the exile government's Radio Department, wrote of his experiences for Československý rozhlas's internal periodical, published in 1964. He attributed all positive achievements to the "progressive" Communist representation in London "without exception"; Hronek, "Československý rozhlas v Londýně," 33, 40.
[114] Jan Křen, *Bílá místa v našich dějinách?* (Prague: Lidové noviny, 1990), 16.
[115] See Edvard Beneš, *Memoirs of Dr. Eduard Beneš: From Munich to New War and New Victory*, trans. Godfrey Lias (London: George Allen & Unwin, 1954); Drtina, *Československo: Můj osud*; Moravec, *Master of Spies*; Bohuslav Laštovička, *V Londýně za války: Zápasy o novou ČSR, 1939–1945* (Prague: Státní nakladatelství politické literatury, 1961); Lockhart, *Comes the Reckoning*; Young, *Diaries of Lockhart*, vol. 2.

situation the exiles found themselves in, constrained by a British host for whom Czechoslovak issues were of minimal importance or interest.[116] The arguments advanced by Beneš for the legal continuation of the state and his presidency, based on his contention that the Munich Agreement and all subsequent changes had been carried out under threat of force, were one of several points of tension in the Czechoslovak–British relationship, and historians such as Jan Kuklík have sought to examine their legal basis.[117]

Any study of the Czechoslovak exile government demands an understanding of the context in which it was working, both in British and international terms. Beneš and his supporters were part of a much larger Czechoslovak exile community, complete with its own cultural life and diverse range of political opinion.[118] Although its representatives eventually established themselves as the unrivalled leaders of the exile movement, the exile government faced opposition from several sides early on, and, with Jan Němeček, Kuklík has also written the most comprehensive history of this opposition.[119] In international terms, the war period marked the pivotal transition in Czechoslovakia's foreign relations, as the westward-facing outlook of the First Republic shifted to the east and the Soviet Union became the state's dominant ally. Czechoslovak–Soviet relations is another field in which researchers are trying to move beyond the established interpretation of the Communist era, both by using previously unavailable sources – as Valentina Mar'ina did in her case study of Czechoslovak–Soviet approaches to Subcarpathian Ruthenia – or by working to make such sources more widely available to researchers.[120] Jan Němeček and a team of editors have compiled volumes of documents charting the development of Czechoslovak relations

---

116 See Smetana, *In the Shadow*; Martin Brown, *Dealing with Democrats: The British Foreign Office and the Czechoslovak Émigrés in Great Britain, 1939 to 1943* (Frankfurt am Main: Peter Lang, 2006); Detlef Brandes, *Exil v Londýně, 1939–1943: Velká Británie a její spojenci Československo, Polsko a Jugoslávie mezi Mnichovem a Teheránem* (Prague: Karolinum, 2003).
117 Beneš's argument for the legal continuation of Czechoslovakia and of his presidency met with resistance on the British side. For more on these arguments, see Jan Kuklík, *Londýnský exile a obnova československého státu, 1939–1945: Právní a politické aspekty obnovy Československa z hlediska prozatímního státního zřízení ČSR v emigraci* (Prague: Karolinum, 1998); Smetana, *In the Shadow*, esp. 136–76.
118 Bořivoj Srba offers an extensive, if not particularly rigorous, study of Czechoslovak cultural life in Britain, in *Múzy v exilu*.
119 Jan Kuklík and Jan Němeček, *Proti Benešovi! Česká a slovenská protibenešovská opozice v Londýně 1939–1945* (Prague: Karolinum, 2004).
120 See Valentina Mar'ina, *Zakarpatskaia Ukraina (Podkarpatskaia Rus') v politike Beneshe i Stalina: 1939–1945, Dokumental'nii ocherk* (Moscow: Novii khronograf, 2003).

with the USSR, which sit alongside earlier published volumes, such as those of Otáhalová and Červinková.[121] Efforts to make sources available to historians characterise a current movement in Czech historiography to open up previously unstudied topics. For future studies of the wartime government-in-exile, for example, the project publishing the minutes of its meetings will prove an invaluable source, and they are used here to give some insight into the political and propaganda discussions happening behind the scenes.[122]

The other side of the wartime story, of events in the Protectorate and Slovakia, was also complicated by ideological restrictions in the postwar period, and prominent works on the Protectorate, such as those of Detlef Brandes, have only recently been published in Czech.[123] While earlier historians sought to piece together evidence of what had taken place in the Protectorate – as Vojtěch Mastný did in his study of Czech resistance in the early years of the occupation – more recent works, like Chad Bryant's *Prague in Black*, seek to understand the period in a broader national context, tracing the impact of the wartime experience on Czech

---

121 Jan Němeček et al., eds., *Československo-sovětské vztahy v diplomatických jednáních, 1939–1945: Dokumenty*, vol. 1 (Prague: Státní ústřední archiv, 1998); vol. 2 (Prague: Státní ústřední archiv, 1999). Libuše Otáhalová and Milada Červinková, eds., *Dokumenty z historie československé politiky 1939–1943* (Prague: Československé akademie věd, 1966).
122 These minutes were previously inaccessible to researchers and several sections had been removed from the archive entirely, but they were unearthed as part of this project. It was a collaborative effort between the Law Faculty of Charles University and the Historical and Masaryk Institutes at the Czech Academy of Sciences, and involved a team of editors. Jan Němeček et al., eds., *Zápisy ze schůzí československé vlády v Londýně*, vol. 1, *1940–1941* (Prague: Historický ústav Akademie věd ČR, Masarykův ústav, a Archiv Akademie věd ČR, 2008); vol. 2, *1942* (Prague: Historický ústav Akademie věd ČR, Masarykův ústav a Archiv Akademie věd ČR, 2011); vol 3.1; vol 3.2, *červenec–prosinec 1943* (Prague: Pravnická fakulta Univerzity Karlovy, Historický ústav Akademie věd ČR, Masarykův ústav a Archiv Akademie věd ČR, 2012); vol. 4.1, *leden–červen 1944* (Prague: Pravnická fakulta Univerzity Karlovy, Historický ústav Akademie věd ČR, Masarykův ústav a Archiv Akademie věd ČR, 2014); vol. 4.2, *červenec–prosinec 1944* (Prague: Pravnická fakulta Univerzity Karlovy, Historický ústav Akademie věd ČR, Masarykův ústav a Archiv Akademie věd ČR, 2015); vol. 5, *1945* (Prague: Historický ústav Akademie věd ČR, Pravnická fakulta Univerzity Karlovy, Masarykův ústav a Archiv Akademie věd ČR, 2016).
123 One of the most thorough studies of the Protectorate is Detlef Brandes, *Češi pod německým protektorátem: Okupační politika, kolaborace a odboj 1939–1945* (Prague: Prostor, 1999). It was first published as two separate volumes in German, the first in 1969 and the second in 1975. Brandes had managed to gain access to the Czechoslovak archives before the period of "normalisation" set in and access was severely restricted. For the second volume, he relied on sources from elsewhere and the first Czech edition came out twenty-four years after the German. Václav Kural discusses the difficulties Brandes and other historians faced in the period of normalisation in his foreword to the Czech edition; ibid., 15–16.

nationalism and self-image.[124] Identity and national mythology were constant underlying themes in the London broadcasts, and this book will argue that the Czechoslovak identity devised and broadcast in London was strongly Czech-dominated, a persistent issue throughout the history of the joint state. The preponderance of Czech references and images in the broadcasts is reflected in this research, and Slovak broadcasting is treated in this work, as it was in London, as a subsidiary of Czech-centric Czechoslovak broadcasting. The term *Czechoslovak* is used in this work to describe the joint state and its representatives, and in a national sense when it was used that way by broadcasters. Some more recent work by scholars to examine *Czechoslovakism* as a concept omits the war period, a gap which this publication can go some way to filling.[125]

The history of wartime Slovakia was also limited to a single official narrative during the Communist period, and the history of the first Slovak Republic remains "complex and ambivalent" for Slovak historians.[126] As a fascist and strongly nationalist state which was allied with Nazi Germany, the first Slovak Republic was ideologically problematic in the post-war period and thus research into wartime Slovakia was limited prior to the 1990s. The exception was in regard to the Slovak National Uprising of August–October 1944, which was much promoted in the Communist era as an expression of the Slovak people's rejection of fascism and is still often cited as a source of Slovak national pride.[127] Since the end of Communism and the establishment of an independent Slovak state in 1993, some historians have introduced greater ambiguity into understandings of the period in their efforts to examine the more "positive" aspects of a time which represented the Slovak people's first experience of statehood. Such efforts are, however, often still associated

---

124 See Vojtěch Mastný, *The Czechs Under Nazi Rule: The Failure of National Resistance, 1939–1942* (New York: Columbia University Press, 1971); Bryant, *Prague in Black*.
125 In their collected volume of seventeen essays on Czechoslovakism, Adam Hudek, Michal Kopeček, and Jan Mervart examine three periods: pre-1918, 1918–1938, and post-1945. While one essay covers the war period, it focuses on national minorities in the military; see Hudek, Kopeček, and Mervart, eds., *Czechoslovakism* (London: Routledge, 2022).
126 Ivan Kamenec, *Slovenský stát* (Prague: Anomal, 1992), 1.
127 In a public opinion poll published in 1971, Slovaks voted the Slovak National Uprising to be the third greatest era of Slovak history, after the national revival of the 1840s and the period of liberalisation early in 1968; see Carol Skalnik Leff, *National Conflict in Czechoslovakia: The Making of the State, 1918–1987* (Princeton: Princeton University Press, 1988), 296. Of the many works on the uprising, one of particular use to this project is Vilém Prečan, *Slovenské národné povstanie: dokumenty* (Bratislava: Vydavateľstvo politickej literatúry, 1965). Kamenec, *Slovenský stát* was one of the earliest published efforts to compile an overall picture of the structure of the First Slovak Republic.

with a polemical nationalist approach.[128] This study does not offer a new history of Slovakia during the Second World War but rather seeks to examine the exile government's understanding of the Czech–Slovak relationship in this period, as it reflected on the First Republic and looked forward to the re-establishment of the state.[129] In this, it draws on works on Czech–Slovak relations which seek to assess the shared history of the two nations and acknowledge Slovak complaints without demonising the Czech side for dominating the state.[130]

The Czechoslovaks in London carried out their broadcasting in difficult political circumstances. Unlike some other exile governments sheltering in Britain, which had received a warm welcome and whose legitimacy was quickly accepted, it took the Czechoslovaks two years to win full recognition from the British.[131] The de facto recognition extended by Britain and others to the Protectorate and Slovakia made the exile government's task even harder and, although never expressly opposed to the recreation of a Czechoslovak state, British policy remained broadly apathetic towards the prospect for much of the first half of the war.[132] Even when the government had been recognised and the Munich Agreement renounced, Britain refused to guarantee any borders of the future state.[133] Added to the inherent unpredictability of wartime and concern

---

[128] Slovak collaboration with Germany in the name of the national "struggle for survival" is downplayed in, for example, Stanislav J. Kirschbaum, *A History of Slovakia: A Struggle for Survival* (New York: St. Martin's Press, 1996).

[129] The relationship between Czechs and Slovaks forms the basis for comprehensive works, such as Jan Rychlík, *Češi a Slováci ve 20. století: Česko-slovenské vztahy 1914–1945* (Bratislava: Academic Electronic Press, 1997); it also features prominently in histories of Slovakia, such as Dorothea H. El Mallakh, *The Slovak Autonomy Movement, 1935–1939: A Study in Unrelenting Nationalism* (Boulder: East European Quarterly, 1979); Leff, *National Conflict in Czechoslovakia*. Contrasting ideas of Czech and Slovak identity are examined in Robert B. Pynsent, *Questions of Identity: Czech and Slovak Ideas of Nationality and Personality* (Budapest: Central European University Press, 1994). More recent works on the topic include Josette Baer, *A Life Dedicated to the Republic: Vavro Šrobár's Slovak Czechoslovakism* (Stuttgart: Ibidem Press, 2014).

[130] See, for example, Rychlík, *Češi a Slováci*. See Chapter Three for more.

[131] There are many works devoted to other governments in exile, but one volume that devotes particular attention to Czechoslovakia is Vít Smetana and Kathleen Geaney, eds., *Exile in London: The Experience of Czechoslovakia and the Other Occupied Nations, 1939–1945* (Prague: Karolinum, 2017).

[132] Several countries, including Britain, extended de facto recognition to both states early in the conflict, through diplomatic channels such as consulates and legations. The legal position of Czechoslovakia was therefore called into question, although some Czechoslovak representation, such as the legations in France and Britain, did not submit to German control. For more, see Kuklík, *Londýnský exil*, esp. 46–48.

[133] The FO refused throughout the conflict to guarantee any post-war borders in Central and Eastern Europe until the war was over. As well as wishing to avoid commitments that might compromise relations with other countries in the region, the FO had made an agreement

over developments in the Protectorate and Slovakia, these issues created a climate of uncertainty from which the exiles had to broadcast with a clear and optimistic voice. They could not afford for their authority and standing to be questioned by listeners, or by enemy propaganda, so they were compelled to project an image of unity that could reach out to former Czechoslovak citizens now divided across the Protectorate of Bohemia and Moravia, the Slovak Republic, and the territories annexed to the German Reich, Poland, and Hungary in various stages between 1938 and 1939.[134] During their time in London, the exiles managed to maintain some lines of communication with the resistance at home, but their only way of consistently reaching the public at large was over the radio and their broadcasts therefore constituted an "immensely important part" of their connection with their home.[135]

Although the history of its development and structure is fairly well-documented, no in-depth study of the BBC Czech Service has yet been carried out. The early years of the BBC European Service, including the corporation's complex relationship with the various Allied exile governments gathered in London, are detailed in histories such as Gerard Mansell's work on BBC external broadcasting *Let Truth Be Told* and, most thoroughly, in Asa Briggs's *A History of Broadcasting in the United Kingdom*, the third volume of which is devoted exclusively to the war years.[136] While the BBC's centenary celebrations in 2022 have prompted the publication of several more recent studies, these have focused primarily on the social and cultural history of Britain and the corporation's position within that history, discussing international broadcasting more as part of Britain's projection of itself.[137] The position of Czechoslovakia as a minor ally, however, is reflected in the relatively scant attention Czechoslovak broadcasting receives in such works. The only book devoted solely to

---

with the USA to avoid border guarantees. In his note of 5 August 1942 which renounced the Munich Agreement, Foreign Secretary Anthony Eden merely assured the Czechoslovaks that Britain's future decisions on borders would in no way be influenced by "any changes effected in and since 1938"; Eden to Masaryk, 5 August 1942, C 7210/326/12, FO 371/30835, TNA. For more on border negotiations and their relation to the Munich Agreement, see Smetana, *In the Shadow*, 273–303.

134 Following the Munich Agreement of September 1938, Czechoslovak border territory to the west was ceded to Germany, the Těšín/Cieszyn region was ceded to Poland, and much of southern Slovakia to Hungary. On 15 March 1939, all remaining Czech territory was occupied by Germany, and Hungary occupied Subcarpathian Ruthenia.

135 Drtina, *Československo: Můj osud*, 510.

136 See Mansell, *Let Truth Be Told*; Briggs, *War of Words*.

137 See, for example, Hendy, *The BBC*; Simon J. Potter, *This Is the BBC: Entertaining the Nation, Speaking for Britain, 1922–2022* (Oxford: Oxford University Press, 2022).

the topic of the BBC Czech Service – Milan Kocourek's short work of 2013, *Volá Londýn* – briefly covers the entire history of Czech and Slovak broadcasting by the BBC from 1939 to 2004, but focuses more on the structure of programming and memories of former employees, the majority of whom worked during the Cold War period.[138] Ondřej Koutek successfully compiled an overview of the exile broadcasts and general trends within it, but the only academic study that actually analyses the content of the broadcasts is Jan Láníček's case study on the representation of Jews in the government programme.[139] This project therefore represents the first effort to study in detail the spoken content of the exile government's broadcasts and how it used the radio as part of its wartime mission.

Studies of other BBC services have been written and several pay particular attention to the war years, but most are based on entirely different approaches to this book. From the British side, Siân Nicholas's work on the BBC Home Service offers insights into British domestic propaganda and its impact on morale.[140] Individual European services have also attracted the attention of researchers, including the Polish, German, Danish, French, and Portuguese broadcasts. Krzysztof Pszenicki's history of the BBC Polish Service contains only short, anecdotal references to the establishment of the section and its work in the war, however, almost completely glossing over the troubled co-operation with the Polish government-in-exile. Pszenicki's focus is clearly on the Cold War period, devoting much more attention to the years in which he himself was director of the section (1980–88). As a short institutional history, Pszenicki's book is devoted more to charting changes in staff and explaining the BBC to Polish readers in its post-war context, alongside Radio Free Europe and the Voice of America.[141] Memories of wartime work in the BBC's German-language broadcasting are included in a 2003 collection of short essays on the subject and the recent work by Vike Plock, as well as shorter studies focusing on the presentation of the Holocaust or the bombing war,[142]

---

138 See Milan Kocourek, *Volá Londýn: Historie českého a slovenského vysílání BBC* (Prague: Ottovo nakladatelství, 2013).
139 See Koutek, "Zahraniční odboj"; Láníček, "Czechoslovak Service."
140 See Siân Nicholas, *The Echo of War: Home Front Propaganda and the Wartime BBC, 1939–45* (Manchester: Manchester University Press, 1996).
141 See Krzysztof Pszenicki, *Tu mówi Londyn: Historia Sekcji Polskiej BBC* (Warsaw: Rosner & Wspólnicy, 2009).
142 On Germany, see, for example, Charmian Brinson, "'Patrick Smith bei den Österreichern': The BBC Austrian Service in Wartime," and Lorle Louis-Hoffman, "My Years at Bush House, 1940–1945," in *"Stimme der Wahrheit": German-Language Broadcasting by the BBC*, ed. Charmian Brinson and Richard Dove (Amsterdam: Rodopi, 2003); Plock, *BBC German Service*; Stephanie

while the war period also forms the basis of specific studies of the French, Italian, and Danish services. Jeremy Bennett's *British Broadcasting and the Danish Resistance Movement* is a rigorously academic work and, although the emphasis clearly lies on connections with Danish resistance groups, Bennett touches on aspects of British–Danish negotiation that are also of relevance to this project.[143] Aurélie Luneau's comprehensive study of the BBC French Service during the war period traces changes in broadcasting alongside other military and political events in the conflict, and seeks to examine the relationship established with French listeners and how the broadcasts have been idealised in memory.[144] A contrasting account of BBC broadcasts to a neutral state can be found in Nelson Ribeiro's work on the BBC Portuguese Service, focusing on public reception of the broadcasts and trust in the corporation as a news provider, and Ester Lo Biundo's study of wartime BBC broadcasts to Italy offers a further interesting case study.[145] Few of the studies mentioned, however, attempt a close analysis of individual broadcasts, or make an effort to place the common themes of wartime programming in the wider historical and cultural context of the nation involved.

This work is based on my doctoral studies completed between 2011 and 2015 at the University of Bristol. The original impetus for this project was the discovery of a collection of uncatalogued vinyl records from the war period, which had been held by the Czech MZV since the end of the conflict. Negotiations for the transfer of these recordings began in 1992, but it was not until 2010 that they were eventually acquired by Český rozhlas (Czech Radio) and identified as material for a research project, set up in collaboration with the University of Bristol and the Arts and Humanities Research Council. The project was intended to produce

---

Seul, "'For a German audience we do not use appeals for sympathy on behalf of Jews as a propaganda line': The BBC German Service and the Holocaust, 1938–1945," and Emily Oliver, "Inventing a New Kind of German: The BBC German Service and the Bombing War," in *Allied Communication to the Public during the Second World War: National and Transnational Networks*, ed. Simon Eliot and Marc Wiggam (London: Bloomsbury Academic, 2019).

143 See Jeremy Bennett, *British Broadcasting and the Danish Resistance Movement 1940–1945: A Study of the Wartime Broadcasts of the BBC Danish Service* (Cambridge: Cambridge University Press, 1966).

144 See Aurélie Luneau, *Radio Londres: les voix de la liberté, 1940–1945* (Paris: Perrin, 2005). For a study of the use of sound in French cultural broadcasting in the BBC's domestic broadcasts during this period, see Claire Launchbury, *Music, Poetry, Propaganda: Constructing French Cultural Soundscapes at the BBC during the Second World War* (Oxford: Peter Lang, 2012).

145 See Nelson Ribeiro, *BBC Broadcasts to Portugal in World War II: How Radio Was Used as a Weapon of War* (Lewiston, NY: Edwin Mellen Press, 2011); Ester Lo Biundo, *London Calling Italy: BBC Broadcasts during the Second World War* (Manchester: Manchester University Press, 2022).

a catalogue of the recordings, later to be made available to the public, and to use them as the basis for a thesis examining the relationship between the Czechoslovak government-in-exile and the BBC. However, initial investigation revealed that the majority of the recordings were not, as had been assumed, recordings of programmes broadcast by the exile government, but specially commissioned programmes produced by the London Transcription Service (LTS).

The LTS was a branch of the BBC which produced records to be sent to subscribing radio stations abroad, but its work has not been notably studied. Originally formed as the Joint Broadcasting Committee early in 1939 and taken over by the BBC in July 1941, the LTS had its own separate staff and commissioned and produced its own programming, in addition to taking charge of all transcription of BBC programmes.[146] A memo of 1944 numbers the LTS's staff at around 120, with programmes being produced in nineteen languages for re-broadcasting in eighty-five different territories. However, this same memo also explains that "nearly all the output in foreign languages is specially originated by the LTS, and produced and recorded in their own studios."[147] Much of this output was devoted to feature programmes on aspects of the British war effort, such as RAF Coastal Command or a typical day in a British factory or school. These programmes often took the form of "soundscapes," made up of extensive recordings of sounds or speech from, for example, an airfield, with short explanations in between. These explanations could then be translated into many languages, including Czech, and re-edited for different audiences. Czech-language programmes produced by the LTS were sent out to Czechoslovak legations and radio stations to be played to expatriate communities in North America, Latin America, the Middle East, Australia, India, and South Africa.[148] The collection held by Český rozhlas includes some English-language programmes and some Czech translations, as well as a great deal of music, but the majority of the material comes from British sources and focuses on British topics. Although the LTS did communicate with the Czechoslovak government-in-exile

---

[146] Information on the wartime work of the LTS is hard to find and is hardly mentioned in Briggs, *War of Words*. Information can be found in the BBC Archives, in particular in R13/163; see "The Transcription Recording Unit of the London Transcription Service," undated [c. 1943], R13/163/5, BBC WAC; "The London Transcription Service," undated [before 1 July 1941], R13/163/1, BBC WAC.

[147] C. Conner, Director of Overseas Programme Services to several departments, "The Transcription Programmes," 27 January 1944, R13/163/4, BBC WAC.

[148] "London Transcription Service: Estimate for 1942/1943," June 1942, R13/163/2, BBC WAC.

and some political speeches do appear in the collection, including talks by President Beneš and Foreign Minister Jan Masaryk which do not appear in published volumes, very few of the records therefore represent original Czechoslovak content that was broadcast to Europe, and too little is known of the provenance for them to be used as a single corpus.[149] The broadcasts in the collection are far from being without value to researchers, but they do not accurately represent the broadcasting carried out by the exile government during the war. Consequently, although the catalogue was still produced and examination of the recordings has greatly informed this project in a general sense, the programmes have not formed a central part of my thesis as originally imagined.

Instead, it is the scripts of the government programme, the majority of which survive in the Český rozhlas Archive in Prague, which form the core of this study. The texts cover almost every broadcast made in the government's name as part of its programmes *Hovory s domovem* (August 1940 to March 1943) and *Hlas sovbodné republiky* (March 1943 to May 1945) and, due to BBC regulations regarding censorship, they offer a reliable account of what was broadcast. The Czechoslovaks were required to submit texts in advance and the BBC then verified them against an English translation that was approved by the censor. In the studio, announcers worked in the presence of switch censors who had the power to cut the broadcast in the event of a deviation from the approved text.[150] Broadcasting several times a day for nearly six years, these scripts chart the major events of the war from the exile government's unique perspective and, having never previously been studied as whole, offer a new insight into the relationship between the exiles and their listeners at home.

Additional primary material on the co-ordination of programmes and the associated political issues and negotiations is drawn from the Czech MZV Archive and the Czech National Archive in Prague, as well as in Britain, from The National Archives at Kew and the BBC Written Archives Centre at Caversham. In the case of the latter, however,

---

149 Communications between the LTS and the Czechoslovak MZV were nearly always carried out via Viktor Fischl of the MZV Information Department. This correspondence mostly comprises LTS requests for help in sourcing Czech and Slovak music, as well as finding speakers for programmes. The MZV in turn submitted requests for discs and sent contact details for stations interested in airing LTS programmes. This correspondence can be found in the MZV archive, mostly in LA (O) 1939–1945, Osvěta 254, 353, and 354.
150 For more on the work of censors within the BBC, see Briggs, *War of Words*, 423–24; Tangye Lean, *Voices in the Darkness*, 99–100.

the project faced an early obstacle in the discovery that the main files relating directly to the BBC Czech Service in this period have been lost and, despite appearing in the catalogue, are apparently untraceable. In terms of published sources, several broadcasters brought out collections of their talks after the war, and in these cases they provide an alternative source for texts as well as some comments from their writers on the context in which they were broadcast.[151] The minutes of the exile government meetings have also been of significant use to this project, revealing a great deal about the political ideas on which the programmes were based, through the discussions held behind the scenes. The body of primary material used in this project is large and much of it has not previously been studied in depth. This book places the primary material at the forefront, drawing out from it wider themes that can inform understandings of the Czechoslovak government-in-exile, how it interpreted its wartime task, and how it used radio to try and achieve that mission.

This study draws on a range of historiographical sources and approaches, combining elements of Czech and Slovak history and nationalism studies with diplomatic history and broadcasting theory. The most extensive literature with which this project engages is that of wartime diplomatic history – the history of Czechoslovak–British and Czechoslovak–Soviet relations – and the study of broadcasting has something new to offer here by revealing how these relationships, and changes in them, were represented to the listening public. The broadcasts will also be analysed in the specific context of Czech and Slovak history and nationalism studies, as a largely unexamined record of the exile government's interpretation of the Czechoslovak state in this eventful period. Exile broadcasters were very preoccupied with the idea of the state that they represented and they projected a very specific interpretation of its history and character in their broadcasts, both overtly in discussions of the topic and implicitly in their understanding of current events. The theme of Czech national identity and the form in which it is asserted within the broadcasts stem from the historical narrative standardised in the First Republic, and study of this period therefore informs research of

---

[151] Notable works of this kind include Edvard Beneš, *Šest let exilu a druhé světové války: Řeči, projevy a dokumenty z r. 1938–1945* (London: Týdeník Čechoslovák, 1945); Drtina, *A nyní promluví*; Jan Masaryk, *Volá Londýn* (Prague: Panorama, 1990); Jaroslav Stránský, *Hovory k domovu* (Prague: Fr. Borový, 1945). Some radio talks are also included in Vladimír Clementis, *Odkazy z Londýna* (Bratislava: Obroda, 1947); Jan Šrámek, *Politické projevy v zahraničí* (Prague: Výkonný výbor československé strany lidové, 1945).

the interwar era and the ideology of the Czechoslovak state. The wartime broadcasts also offer a useful case study in which to examine the problematic topic of Czechoslovakism, both as a state- and nation-building tool. Czech dominance of the projected Czechoslovak national identity and discussion of the Czechs and Slovaks as members of a single nation are both prominent themes in the wartime broadcasts. Discussion of these themes engages with wider questions of the Czechoslovak national project and relations between the Czechs and Slovaks which persisted throughout the history of the shared state and beyond its division in 1993.

This multilateral approach also offers something new to the study of broadcasting, by examining how radio can be used in the specific circumstances of political exile, as a means to communicate with an audience living in very different circumstances and whose listening is being obstructed. Studies of radio as a medium and how people listen to it, such as those by Paddy Scannell and Andrew Crisell, have greatly informed this project, but no work has yet been done which takes into account the unique listening environment in which occupied Europe heard the BBC.[152] As the first comprehensive study of Czechoslovak wartime radio, this project therefore makes a contribution to the study of broadcasting in general, while also filling a gap both in the history of British broadcasting and in the history of the Czech media. Though the study of the history of the Czech media is a growing area, works tend, for understandable reasons, to focus on the media operating within either Czechoslovakia or what is now the Czech Republic. In the wartime context, this involves a study of the press and radio in the occupied Protectorate but often pays minimal attention to radio propaganda from London.[153]

---

[152] See, for example, Paddy Scannell, *Broadcast Talk* (London: Sage, 1991); Scannell, *Radio, Television*; Crisell, *Understanding Radio*; Andrew Crisell, ed., *Radio: Critical Concepts in Media and Cultural Studies*, vol. 1, *Radio Theory and Genres* (London: Routledge, 2009).

[153] Though several histories of the Czech media have recently been written, they tend to be very broad in scope and, when they do address exile propaganda activities, they are focused on the broadcasting structure rather than programme content. Works of note include Končelík, Večeřa, and Orság, *Dějiny českých médií 20. století*; Petr Bednařík, Jan Jirák, and Barbara Köpplová, *Dějiny českých médií: Od pocátku do současnosti* (Prague: Grada, 2011).

Chapter One

"Legal, loyal, and internationally recognised": Legitimacy and the Performance of Government

> *"As the legal, loyal, and internationally recognised government, we must prepare the final judgements against the enemies and saboteurs of the nation."*
> Government Declaration, 18 June 1942[154]

The Czechoslovak exiles in London used their radio broadcasts as an arena in which they could perform as a government, seeking to convince the audience of their legitimacy and right to lead in the process. This performance was intended to compensate for the fact that they – like all governments-in-exile – could not exercise their authority in the manner of a typical government, by passing legislation or exerting control over state bodies such as the police. What they could do (if only for a few minutes a day) was give speeches, commemorate events, and discuss plans for the future, in the hope that establishing their legitimacy now would endow them with the authority to enact these plans at a later date. For this legitimacy to be accepted beyond challenge, they performed for both a domestic and international audience; exile governments need to be accepted as legitimate rulers both at home and abroad, and the two are mutually dependent, as foreign allies want to ensure the government they recognise will be accepted by the public, and the public are more likely to accept the rule of a government that is recognised internationally.

---

[154] BBC Czechoslovak Programme, 17 June 1942, LN Z 1942 – 14, CRA.

In a sense, every political speech is a public performance, and the development of modern media such as radio and television has enabled politicians to perform to a wider public than ever before. John Street argued that performance is at the centre of politics in the media age, and that all politicians are forced to adopt a celebrity role in which a successful "performance" convinces the audience that they represent their stated values, thereby hoping to win public support for their cause.[155] Each performance is thus intended to be a distillation of these values and is designed to leave the audience with a certain impression of the speaker, usually as a capable and trustworthy figure who is fit to lead them.[156] In addition to performing in this literal sense, however, by using its programme to promote its work and address its public on political and historical matters, the Czechoslovak exile government also used the platform offered by radio for a more figurative performance of power, as it both established and exercised its claim to legal and ideological authority.

Histories of exile governments often focus, understandably, on the legal arguments that are central to recognition of their legitimacy. These legal questions of legitimacy in exile can be addressed by winning international support and recognition as an exile government, representative of a state; but establishing the ideological and political credentials to lead a people is a more complex matter when the public is limited in its ability to express support for an external group or cause. In her study of the post-war Polish and Spanish governments-in-exile, Alicja Iwańska described the threat posed to exile governments by the perception of "psychological distance" between them and the people they claimed to lead as they were seen to fall out of step with public opinion at home, discrediting their claims of legitimacy.[157] The British authorities during the war also viewed this isolation from the experiences and opinions of the domestic population as an inevitable consequence of exile, and figures such as Minister for Economic Warfare Hugh Dalton argued against recognising European exile governments, on the grounds they

---

155 See John Street, *Mass Media, Politics and Democracy* (Basingstoke: Palgrave Macmillan, 2011), 256–57.
156 See John Corner, "Mediated Persona and Political Culture: Dimensions of Structure and Progress," *European Journal of Cultural Studies* 3, no. 3 (2000): 386–402.
157 Iwańska wrote specifically of the difficulties faced by the Spanish and Polish exile governments of the post-war period, both of whom left authoritarian regimes at home to live in the democratic states of France and Britain respectively; see Alicja Iwańska, *Exiled Governments: Spanish and Polish, An Essay in Political Sociology* (Cambridge, MA: Schenkman, 1981).

could later prove unpopular at home and thereby damage Britain's own standing by association.[158] An unsigned PWE draft paper on propaganda (dated 28 September 1941 and therefore postdating the recognition of many governments, including that of Czechoslovakia) showed how these fears persisted even as recognition was awarded. The writer advised that "it will not, I think, be good propaganda to boost too hard the various exiled Allied Governments. These may be found not to have much following when the storm breaks in their home lands." The inevitability of increasing isolation from the home population is expressed in the conclusion that "As the period of their exile lengthens, these Governments must tend to lose touch and become more and more unrepresentative."[159]

British intelligence sources, however, and notably those held at the BBC, show that there was believed to be extensive popular support for the Czechoslovak exiles at home. One BBC intelligence report from December 1941 warns of the dangers to British credibility posed by the use of unpopular émigrés as broadcasters, but makes a clear distinction for some figures: "That President Beneš, Queen Wilhelmina [of the Netherlands] and King Haakon [of Norway] are assets to our broadcasts is confirmed again and again."[160] Several intelligence reports sent by Lockhart to the Foreign Office in late 1942 cite a reliable source in claiming that listening to the BBC is very widespread in the Protectorate, that "the London government is very popular," and that "sympathy for Beneš is greater than it ever was during the Republic."[161] Despite such intelligence, the fear of a growing separation from the people at home is an innate problem of political exile, and the attention that the London Czechoslovaks paid to the matter in their broadcasting indicates that they felt it posed a serious threat to their legitimacy.

Political power is dependent on the mass acceptance of the legitimate right of a leader or government to rule over the masses; but as Conway and Romijn have highlighted, "there was no clear dividing line between regimes that were and were not considered legitimate in Europe in the

---

[158] Cruickshank, *Fourth Arm*, 56.
[159] "PWE Draft paper on propaganda," 28 September 1941, FO 1093/129, TNA.
[160] "BBC Intelligence Report: Europe," 3 December 1941, 49/41, EIP series 1a, E2/185, BBC WAC. A BBC European audience survey of 1942 also confirmed that "President Beneš is still regarded as the liberator"; SEA, EOCOTF (Central-Southern Europe), 19 September 1942, 38/42, EIP series 1c (b), E2/192/5, BBC WAC. Czechoslovak intelligence under František Moravec also shared intelligence with the British, albeit only that which was beneficial to the former's cause.
[161] Lockhart to Strang, 5 and 8 November 1942, file 13, "Czechoslovakia: Secret Reports, 1943, Robert Bruce Lockhart," FO 800/879, TNA.

1930s and 1940s."[162] In this context, multiple groups claimed authority over the same territory and population, and each – be they occupiers, local collaborators, or exiles – could be seen as legitimate by different people at different times. This was also a time of great political upheaval, with the conflicting ideologies of fascism, communism, democracy, colonialism, monarchism, and religious authority all proposing different means by which to legitimise power, and leaders of all different political stripes seeking to establish their authority with the audience at the cost of their rivals. Max Weber, still a touchstone in discussions of political authority, advanced three possible means by which claims to political power can be legitimised: the authority of legality, the authority of tradition, and the authority of charisma.[163] This chapter will demonstrate that these same three claims to authority were asserted by the Czechoslovak government-in-exile as it used its radio broadcasts to establish its legal and ideological legitimacy through a performance of authority, and then sought to exercise this authority over the domestic population by issuing instructions from London.

The exile government's legal arguments and its claims to be working within an established Czechoslovak tradition both hinged on the theme of continuity, as Beneš and his colleagues presented themselves as the heirs to the First Czechoslovak Republic in every sense. The legal argument for continuity formed the cornerstone of Beneš's campaign for recognition among the Allies and came up against a great deal of resistance. However, in the interests of presenting the exiles' authority as being unchallenged, this resistance was never acknowledged in the broadcasts, and the government's legal continuity was only ever presented as an established fact. The exile government's programming also drew heavily on the rhetoric and mythology established during the interwar period, to emphasise that the exiles were as much legal as ideological heirs to the First Republic and its founder, Tomáš Garrigue Masaryk. This continued to entrench a national myth that would be preserved in the next wave of Czechoslovak exile, following the Communist Party's ascent to power in 1948.[164] Broadcasters also positioned the government

---

[162] Martin Conway and Peter Romijn, eds., *The War on Legitimacy in Politics and Culture 1936–1946* (Oxford: Berg, 2008), 4.
[163] Max Weber discusses the three means and their expression in the structure of administration in *Economy and Society: An Outline of Interpretive Sociology* (Berkeley: University of California Press, 1978), 212–301.
[164] In his 1989 work on Masaryk, Robert Pynsent suggested that "Still today for the average Czech he is 'Daddy Masaryk', the great founder of Czechoslovakia, the enthroned philosopher

within a historical tradition of Czechoslovak exiles and emphasised its emotional and spiritual unity with the people at home, seeking to justify its claims to speak for them. Connections with the First Republic were also highlighted in the presentation of "charismatic" pre-war figures such as Beneš (presented as a natural leader), and broadcasters such as Jan Masaryk made the most of their personal charisma and the potential of radio as an intimate medium to build an emotional bond with listeners. Having identified themselves as not only the legal but also the ideological heirs to the First Republic, the exiles then had to ensure their broadcasts represented the period in a positive light, pushing back against criticisms levelled at the period not only in the Protectorate and Slovakia but also abroad.

"In the name of the Czechoslovak Republic": The Authority of Legality

Questions of legality are central to the work of exile governments as they seek to win recognition of their status as legally representative of their state or people, with the associated authority over a given territory or population once it can be wielded (that is, once the occupying power has been defeated). Without such recognition, there is nothing to differentiate them from other discontented groups of exiles and they have no platform from which they can work to bring about the revolution they seek in their home country. They are, as a consequence, entirely reliant upon their allies and their host state in their efforts to act as a government at all.[165] As such, efforts to address legal questions and assuage any doubts held by the hosting authorities generally form the basis of any exile government's early work and, as and when recognition is achieved, it progresses into establishing formal alliances and making plans to be realised on its assumption of power. As Weber argues, however, legal claims to

---

and the representative of the highest moral values. Indeed for the average Czech today he has become the representative of a mythical golden age"; Robert B. Pynsent, ed., *T. G. Masaryk, (1850–1937)*, vol. 2, *Thinker and Critic* (Basingstoke: Macmillan, 1989), 1.

165 Iwańska notes that, though some governments can maintain authority through illegitimate means, such as violence, these options are not available to exile governments. The importance of legitimacy and the legal basis for their authority therefore become highly significant and are stressed much more frequently and emphatically than in other exile organisations. She also argues persuasively that all exile governments are inherently idealistic and revolutionary, as they work for a complete change in political power in their home country; see Iwańska, *Exiled Governments*, esp. 14, 3.

authority also offer "rational grounds" on which the public recognise a political leader, and legal recognition elsewhere can therefore also be used to reinforce acceptance among the home population, which remains a key consideration for exile politicians.[166] In Weber's definition, legal authority is based on the public's belief in the legal system and the duty they feel to obey the law of the state and fulfil their own role within it.[167] Beneš's arguments for the legal continuity of the First Republic targeted the sense of duty the public felt towards their former state and sought to establish the legitimacy of his government-in-exile on a legal foundation.

Beneš's claims to legal legitimacy as the president-in-exile were based on his understanding of himself and his governments as the representatives of the First Czechoslovak Republic which had, he argued, been illegally brought to an end by the consequences of the Munich Agreement in September 1938. Beneš's argument hinged on the premise that all political and territorial changes from the Munich Agreement onwards had been carried out under threat of force and were therefore illegal. He argued that his own resignation from the presidency in October 1938 was invalid for the same reasons and, therefore, he continued to be president of the First Czechoslovak Republic.[168] The original British argument – that Beneš had resigned voluntarily and that the Munich Agreement was legal until the conditions had been violated by Germany in March 1939 – opposed Beneš's on almost every point, and the situation was further complicated by the fact that Britain had recognised both the Protectorate and Slovakia de facto within a few months of their creation.[169] The journey of the Czechoslovak exiles from national committee (accepted as representative only of a people) to provisional government and, finally, fully recognised government-in-exile, representative of a state and with a president at its head, was both more difficult and more complex than it was presented in their broadcasts. Having loudly proclaimed the victory of their claim of continuity at the first stages of recognition, however, the exiles could not then promote subsequent achievements as proudly. The quest for legal recognition, which was of primary importance to the exile government's wartime work, therefore features much less prominently in

---

166 Weber, *Economy and Society*, 215.
167 See Max Weber, *Political Writings* (Cambridge: Cambridge University Press, 1994), 312.
168 For a closer study of Beneš's legal arguments of continuity, see Kuklík, *Londýnský exil*.
169 On British recognition of Slovakia and the Protectorate and British arguments against continuity, see Brown, *Dealing with Democrats*, 115–36.

the broadcasts than it did in the actual diplomatic and political work the exiles carried out.

The official status of the Czechoslovak exile movement around Beneš during the Second World War changed several times as it edged closer towards winning full recognition from the British government. The Czechoslovak National Committee (Československý národní výbor) as formed in Paris in 1939, was recognised by Britain in December of that year as being "qualified to represent the Czecho-Slovak peoples." In July 1940, Britain recognised the "Provisional government established by the Czechoslovak National Committee" as being "a representative government of the Czech and Slovak peoples," but not of the Czechoslovak Republic itself. It was not until 18 July 1941 that the Czechoslovaks attained the position already held by other Allied governments in Britain, upon which the term "provisional" was dropped from official communications and full diplomatic recognition was extended in the appointment of a British minister plenipotentiary and envoy extraordinary to Beneš as president of the Czechoslovak Republic.[170] The Czechoslovak journey to full recognition was long and difficult, with the British imposing conditions and raising objections along the way.[171] Listeners to the government broadcasts, however, were presented with swift successes and heard no hint of British opposition.

Hovory s domovem had not yet begun when Beneš's government received provisional recognition from the British in July 1940, but listeners were informed of the event in talks by Prokop Drtina and by Beneš himself via the BBC Czech Service. In a programme on 23 July 1940, Drtina told listeners that "from mid-April President Dr. Edvard Beneš has been negotiating with the British government, the British Foreign Office, and with Lord Halifax regarding the full legal and political recognition of the provisional Czechoslovak government." Although he alluded to various "obstacles" on the route to recognition, Drtina did not go into detail and attributed all obstruction to the French government. The fall of France meant these obstacles had been removed and Beneš's negotiations, which touched on "a whole range of important

---

[170] Stefan Talmon, *Recognition of Governments in International Law: With Particular Reference to Governments in Exile* (Oxford: Clarendon Press, 1998), 151, 28, 152. The recurring references to the Czechoslovak exiles in this work show how complex the journey towards recognition was, touching on a variety of Talmon's themes.

[171] For details on how this journey progressed and how Czechoslovak and British views collided along the way, see Smetana, *In the Shadow*.

political, military, and other questions," could therefore "finally reach their goal."[172] Although there is no mention of the legal and political continuity of the First Republic in this broadcast, it is strongly implied that all Beneš's desires have been met and that, despite the use of the word "provisional," British recognition is essentially "full." Beneš's status as "our president" is also made clear, despite the fact that the British argued against Beneš's claims that his resignation was invalid and did not recognise him as president of the Czechoslovak Republic until a year later, in July 1941.[173]

In his own speech on the achievement of provisional recognition, Beneš assumed his old title for the first time when speaking from exile, beginning with the words, "As president of the Czechoslovak Republic, I turn to you today with this message: the first stage of our fight for liberation is over."[174] He then went on to outline the "legal and political foundations" of his argument for the continuity of the First Republic and consequent illegality of everything done by Germany and the Protectorate government, to which the Czech people should feel no obligation.[175] Beneš had begun promoting his theory of continuity in public talks from June 1939, but Britain continued to view his resignation of October 1938 as valid and frequently referred to it as such in correspondence. In the exchange of letters that preceded provisional recognition, British Foreign Secretary Lord Halifax had also laid out several conditions, including the Foreign Office's express rejection of Beneš's suggestion that, by not legally recognising the Protectorate after occupation, Britain therefore accepted the continuity of the Czechoslovak Republic.[176] The fact that such statements were not censored in the exile government's broadcasts once again shows the relative freedom it enjoyed.

British sources on the awarding of provisional recognition are less than flattering to the Czechoslovaks, and the reality was a world away from the expression of confidence presented in the broadcasts. As alluded to by Drtina, the fall of France had removed an obstacle to recognition in the form of a French government which had opposed Beneš and supported the rival authority of Stefan Osuský, former Czechoslovak ambassador

---

172 BBC Czechoslovak News, 23 July 1940, LN Z – 50, CRA.
173 See Kuklík, *Londýnský exil*, 98–100.
174 Beneš, *Šest let exilu*, 52.
175 Beneš, *Šest let exilu*, 53.
176 See Smetana, *In the Shadow*, esp. 162, 194.

to France.[177] This had in turn prompted the British to demand that Beneš make peace with those of his countrymen who opposed his claims to leadership before they would consider recognising him formally, a task that Beneš described as "superhumanly difficult."[178] Following the fall of France, French views were no longer a factor in British decision-making and a now isolated Britain was more attracted by the military and financial contributions to the war effort that the Czechoslovaks were in a position to make. Even so, the British did not have high hopes regarding what they stood to gain from the arrangement, and the opinion expressed by the deputy head of the Foreign Office's Central Department – supposedly the section most concerned with Czechoslovak affairs – shows a less than optimistic attitude: "our own position has changed for the worse and, having less to lose, we can perhaps afford to take on the Czechoslovaks."[179] Following provisional recognition, Czechoslovak army units were formed, the first Czechoslovak RAF squadrons appeared in July and August 1940, and frozen Czechoslovak assets of up to 7.5 million pounds sterling were made available to the war effort.[180] Once Britain found itself in need, the Foreign Office was thus prepared to accept what the Czechoslovaks had to offer, while expressly rejecting their arguments regarding continuity and the invalidity of Munich. This did not prevent government broadcasters from promoting the formalisation of their position as a provisional government as a great success for the Czechoslovak cause.

When full recognition was finally awarded, Britain's hand was again forced by outside events – in this case, the Soviet threat to Britain's position as leader of the Allies. After entering the war on 22 June 1941, the Soviet Union was quick to make connections with certain Allied governments, and Ivan Maisky, Soviet ambassador to exiled governments, made it clear to Beneš that the USSR was prepared to offer full legal recognition straight away. Beneš appealed to the Foreign Office to do the same and, though some on the British side complained at being threatened in this regard, Britain did not want to risk pushing Czechoslovakia

---

177 On French support for Osuský, see, for example, Smetana, *In the Shadow*, 168, 176–80.
178 Beneš, *Memoirs*, 121.
179 Makins, FO minute, 24 June 1940, quoted in Smetana, *In the Shadow*, 193. For more on opposition to Beneš, see Kuklík and Němeček, *Proti Benešovi!*
180 For more on the Czechoslovak armed forces and the political negotiations associated with them, see Alan Brown, "The Czechoslovak Armed Forces in Britain, 1940–1945," in Conway and Gotovitch, *Europe in Exile*, 167–82.

closer to the Soviet Union by withholding recognition any longer.[181] British recognition was secured within four hours of that of the Soviet Union, both on 18 July 1941. Early plans to stop short of full diplomatic recognition, simply removing the term "provisional" from their correspondence and appointing a "representative" rather than an ambassador, were abandoned as the Soviet position forced Britain, in the words of Foreign Secretary Anthony Eden, to go "the whole hog."[182] Although Eden noted that full recognition of the exile government still did not equate to British acceptance of Beneš's argument of legal continuity of both the state and his presidency, or of commitment to any future borders, Beneš was not perturbed and considered that the conferment of recognition "fully opened the way for a solution of both these questions in future discussions."[183]

Aiming to impress listeners at home with their diplomatic achievements, the London exiles let no trace of British reluctance enter their propaganda, and this meant that, when full recognition was achieved, there was little left to celebrate in the broadcasts. Having never used the term "provisional" after the original statements in July 1940, the change in title did not affect the way the exile government spoke about itself. In his announcement of full recognition, however, Foreign Minister Masaryk was at pains to stress the government's international position as representatives of the Czechoslovak state, not only its people: "from today, official communications will refer to the Czechoslovak Republic, the president of the Czechoslovak Republic, the government of the Czechoslovak Republic, the embassy of the Czechoslovak Republic, and so on. All agreements and documents from our side will, from today, be given in the name of the Czechoslovak Republic."[184] Lockhart's account of the awarding of full recognition describes the emotional reactions of both Masaryk and Beneš, and makes the significance of the event clear, suggesting that, though this did not mark the end of the Czechoslovak mission, "at any rate they were now on the right road, and a great

---

[181] FO documents from 1941 show the British considered it possible that Beneš was exaggerating Soviet willingness to recognise his government in order to put pressure on Britain, but Lockhart recommended recognition anyway; see Central, 1941, Czechoslovakia, file 7140, "Czechoslovak-Soviet Relations," FO 371/24610, TNA, esp. Lockhart to Eden, 28 June 1941 (C 7140/7140/12) and 14 July 1941 (C 7884/7140/12).
[182] Diary entry, 14 July 1941, diary no. 38, Lockhart Papers, House of Lords Record Office, quoted in Smetana, *In the Shadow*, 232n137. For more on full recognition, see ibid., 229–35.
[183] Beneš, *Memoirs*, 127.
[184] BBC Czechoslovak Programme, 18 July 1941, LN Z 1941 – 7, CRA.

wrong and much cruel indifference had been righted."[185] Although full recognition marked a substantial change in international standing and had been the focus of much of Beneš's London work up until this point, it was not strongly reflected in the government's propaganda and this was largely because the previous achievements in recognition had been overstated and listeners had accepted them. For example, one listener in Brno who avidly followed the London broadcasts simply summarised the "encouraging news" of full recognition in a single sentence of a diary entry, before returning to the topic of his recent holiday; having already accepted the exile government's version of events, this new development was a mere formality.[186] It was not in the interests of the Czechoslovak exiles to draw attention to the opposition they encountered on the British side and, consequently, the diplomatic negotiations and legal arguments that were so pivotal to the execution of their wartime work were less prominent in their propaganda.

In December 1942, however, government broadcasters felt the need to explain to the audience why the upcoming expiration of Beneš's seven-year presidential term – which had reinvigorated the anti-Beneš opposition-in-exile – did not change his legal position as president.[187] Following a brief report on the government statement that Beneš would continue to act as president, Prime Minister Jan Šrámek gave a short talk explaining the legal aspects of the question:

> Dr. Beneš's formal resignation from presidential office was enforced by the violence of Munich and is constitutionally and legally invalid, as is everything that the German attack has enacted against our national integrity and sovereignty. Dr. Beneš has therefore remained continuously as president from 18 December 1935, even though he was sometimes unable to fulfil his presidential role due to international political reasons.

---

185 See Lockhart, *Comes the Reckoning*, 120.
186 See Čestmír Jeřábek, *V zajetí antikristově* (Olomouc: R. Promberger, 1945), 149. Jeřábek was an interwar novelist and dramatist associated with the Moravian avant-garde, who had fought on both the Eastern and Italian Fronts in the First World War. His wartime diaries have been described by Robert Pynsent as the most representative source of their kind on the views of Czech intellectuals, in "Activists, Jews, the Little Czech Man and Germans," *Central Europe* 5, no. 2 (2007): 218.
187 Figures such as Osuský took this opportunity to push again for a change in leadership. For more, see Kuklík, *Londýnský exil*, 100–104.

Šrámek went on to explain that, although Beneš's term of office would theoretically end on 18 December 1942, having completed seven years in office, the Czechoslovak constitution clearly stated that, when there was no possibility of holding free presidential elections, the serving president would remain in office as long as necessary. This was followed by a talk from member of the National Council, Prokop Maxa, who on behalf of the group expressed confidence that its support for Beneš's continuance as president corresponded to the will of the people. According to Maxa, "if it were possible, Dr. Edvard Beneš would be re-elected as president not only by the National Assembly, but also by the public vote."[188] In general, the nuances of legal arguments do not make for particularly engaging propaganda, and highlighting British opposition to Beneš's claims would only have served to undermine the standing of the exiles in the eyes of their compatriots. The exile government's propaganda therefore presented the legal details of their legitimacy to their listeners as a fait accompli, leaving aside the messy details of the "thorny way" to full recognition, and focused instead on convincing listeners with ideological arguments.[189]

"We are the Masaryk nation": The Authority of Tradition

Weber's second proposed means of authority – the authority of tradition – focused largely on political systems in which a leader is chosen according to a long-held set of customs, such as a monarchy. However, his theory that rule can be legitimised by appealing to "an established belief in the sanctity of immemorial traditions and the legitimacy of those exercising authority under them" is also applicable in this context.[190] The London exiles presented themselves as inheritors and perpetuators of the nation's traditional values, and Beneš's arguments of continuity were to recur here. The particular interpretation of Czechoslovak political tradition and the nation's shared values that was constructed within the broadcasts was dominated by the figure of first Czechoslovak

---
[188] BBC Czechoslovak Programme, 4 December 1942, LN Z 1942 – 17, CRA.
[189] For a detailed account of this "thorny way," including the final steps to full recognition, see Smetana, *In the Shadow*, 214–39.
[190] Weber, *Economy and Society*, 215; also 226–41 (for further discussion of authority by means of tradition).

president, T. G. Masaryk, and drew heavily on his work and that of others in interpreting the nation's history during the First Republic. Rather than discussing the legal arguments for continuity that were employed in diplomatic negotiations, broadcasters focused on emphasising the traditional democratic values that had long been associated with the interwar republic and presenting themselves as the upholders of this tradition, in contrast to the ruling governments in the Protectorate and Slovakia. Jan Masaryk outlined his view in a characteristically concise way during a broadcast of 5 August 1942, in which he reminisced about the last time he saw Prague some four years previously and stated simply, "I represent that First Republic and no other."[191]

In order for the exiles' association with the First Republic to enhance their standing among listeners, it was necessary to project a positive image of the period in the broadcasts. Many early programmes promoted an idealised image of the interwar period and its political system, drawing favourable comparisons with the current conditions in the Protectorate, particularly regarding the rights of minorities and social justice. As the war progressed, this image underwent a slight change and broadcasters came to acknowledge that not every aspect of the First Republic would be welcome when it came to re-establishing the Czechoslovak state after the war, suggesting some improvements that would be made. No such transition was to be found in programming relating to Masaryk, however, whose name and memory continued to dominate the broadcasts until the very end. Beyond the totemic use of his name and discussion of his political and philosophical beliefs, Masaryk's presence can also be detected in the exile government's interpretations of Czechoslovak history, as the narrative that he had promoted in his lifetime continued unchallenged. The exile government's discussion of the First Republic also involved a robust defence of democracy, which was attracting much criticism as a weak political system that had buckled in the face of fascist strength. Exile broadcasters sought to counter this and reproduced familiar arguments about democracy as part of the national tradition.

It is important to examine the development of the exile interpretation of the First Republic presented in the broadcasts as much of it has been preserved in the public imagination up to the present day. In part, this is down to the crystallisation of this interpretation in opposition to the official pro-Soviet narrative that prevailed throughout the Communist

---

191 Masaryk, *Volá Londýn* (1990), 136.

period, entrenching in Czech self-perception the "romantic national narrative" of an innately democratic, westward-looking nation in the heart of Europe.[192] So prodigious were the efforts of state propaganda in the newly formed republic that the era was somewhat self-mythologising, and much that was said at the time concerning the success of a young democracy in a difficult period is still repeated by historians today, with contemporary opposition and criticism receiving less attention.[193] In his three-volume study of the First Republic, Zdeněk Karník concluded that the story of the First Republic as an "island of democracy," a cliché that frequently appeared in English-language propaganda of the interwar period, has a "real and indisputable foundation," and that the building of such a republic in such a difficult period constituted "a brave step."[194] The tradition of almost hagiographic biographies of T. G. Masaryk also persists in Czech historiography, though some historians such as Mary Heimann and Andrea Orzoff have sought to re-examine the interwar period and to challenge these myths.[195] These efforts have caused controversy, but some suggest it has done little to shift public attitudes overall; in an essay on Czech national identity, academic and former diplomat Pavel Seifter suggested that, "Although people are no longer as nationalistic as they once were, they tend to ignore their own historians in favour of a residual patriotic sentiment that has remained largely unchanged since the 'national revival' of the 19th century."[196]

The image of the interwar republic as an idyllic liberal democracy had been perpetuated in state propaganda from Czechoslovakia's foundation, so exile broadcasters in wartime London had a strong platform on which to build. They made the most of the audience's familiarity with

---

192 Pavel Seifter, "Czech Republic: National History and the Search for Identity," in *Histories of Nations: How Their Identities were Forged*, ed. Peter Furtado (London: Thames & Hudson, 2017), 105. The national narrative summarised by Seifter in this essay is one of an innately democratic and plucky Slavic people, repeatedly the victim of a series of national disasters at the hands of larger powers (often German-speaking), which would be comfortingly familiar to the wartime exiles.

193 The term *myth* in this book is not intended to be pejorative, or to imply to what extent the details upon which it was built were "true." The term is instead understood according to Orzoff's definition of a myth, as "a worldview based on identifiably ideological narratives or images claiming to be universally valid, yet only accepted as true by certain audiences at certain times"; Orzoff, *Battle for the Castle*, 15.

194 Karník, *České země*, 1:563–64.

195 Jiří Kovtun defends the achievements of the First Republic in the unfavourable context of interwar Europe, while simultaneously eulogising Masaryk, in *Republika v nebezpečném světě: Éra presidenta Masaryka, 1918–1935* (Prague: Torst, 2005). See Orzoff, *Battle for the Castle*; Heimann, *Czechoslovakia*.

196 Seifter, "Czech Republic," 105.

their theme, tacitly acknowledging that propaganda is at its most effective when it can exploit the existing opinions of the target audience, when it can "seek out and strike a chord that is already there."[197] The First Republic had seen the establishment of a government propaganda structure that produced a great deal of material promoting the political and ideological triumphs of the period, for both domestic and foreign audiences. The period began to be mythologised while it was still in progress. To legitimise the new state, government propaganda emphasised the innately democratic nature of the Czechs as a people and projected this back through history – for example, onto the fifteenth-century religious reformer Jan Hus and the Hussite rebels who later fought in his name. In a text published by the Foreign Ministry's own publishing house, Orbis, in 1929, one writer explained that,

> In the Czech lands, democracy had been the aim of national endeavours since the time of the national revival [...] It was therefore a foregone conclusion, both among the masses and also their political leaders, that Czechoslovakia would be a democratic republic and that the effort to build up a model democratic State where social justice should reign would animate all the laws establishing the political character of the country.[198]

The language used to describe the First Republic in the early wartime broadcasts is very similar. In November 1939, Beneš praised what he perceived as the fair and liberal nature of the period, telling listeners that "we are fighting again for our republic and we say that we will build it again, healthy and strong, progressive and democratic, fair and perfectly governed."[199] Much was made of the perceived liberal policy towards national minorities in the First Republic, and this served a dual purpose in the wartime context: firstly, it countered claims that Czechoslovakia's German population had been in any way unfairly treated; and secondly, it facilitated the drawing of stark comparisons with the current subjugation of Czechs and Slovaks to Germans, and Jews to non-Jews, in both the Protectorate and Slovakia. Beneš argued that even the most

---

[197] Charles Roetter, *Psychological Warfare* (London: B. T. Batsford, 1974), 188.
[198] Josef Borovička, *Ten Years of Czechoslovak Politics* (Prague: Orbis, 1929), 44–45. During the war years, Orbis remained under government control and became the voice of Protectorate propaganda.
[199] Beneš, *Šest let exilu*, 42.

objective statesmen would have to recognise "our very liberal system of public rights," which he described as "the most tolerant policy in all of Europe."[200] "There was no persecution of the Jews, there was no racial persecution of any kind," Beneš insisted, and he called on listeners to remember the opportunity that the republic had offered to Czechs, Slovaks, Germans, Hungarians, and Ruthenians alike.[201] Jan Masaryk claimed to be reminded of the social equality of the First Republic when describing the clear-up operation after the bombing of the Czechoslovak Red Cross building in London in May 1941. A range of people came forward to help – politicians, generals, workers, Jews, Christians – with no thought for their differences, "just as it should be, even when the bombs are falling, just as it was during the First Republic. Let us remember that."[202]

The topic of democracy, as both a political system and a significant feature of the national tradition, was discussed at length in the broadcasts. Justice Minister Jaroslav Stránský frequently engaged with more philosophical themes in his talks, and in February 1941, as part of his series of talks entitled "For a Better World," Stránský came out in defence of democracy. He asked listeners not to fall for the "cheap trick" that Nazi propaganda was attempting to pull, by presenting democracy as "an outdated system, old-fashioned and worn-out, which has played out its historical role and vainly stands against the young and fresh revolutionary movement of authoritarianism." He pointed out that authoritarian rule was many thousands of years older than parliamentary government, which was in fact the result of generations improving on the mistakes of their forebears: "Despotism and tyranny, the debasement of man to a mere instrument of another's will [...] that is nothing new but is, in fact, something terribly old. The history of the modern age is the history of attempts to liberate ourselves from this dead past."[203] This defence of democracy was founded on its ideological superiority to the alternatives. Stránský appeared to concede that the freedom of democracy had allowed movements to grow up which had destroyed it, but he argued that "if democracy is partially to blame for what came after it, then what came after it also vindicates it. It could also be said that dictatorship is a punishment for those who blunted democracy, or who doubted it, rather than perfecting it." Stránský claimed that even the harshest pre-war critic of

---

200 Beneš, *Šest let exilu*, 24.
201 Beneš, *Šest let exilu*, 24, 42.
202 Masaryk, *Volá Londýn* (1990), 96.
203 BBC Czechoslovak Programme, 14 February 1941, LN Z 1941 – 5, CRA.

democracy would support it over what has come to pass in its absence, and stated simply that "Democracy was peace, dictatorship is war."[204]

The image of democracy presented in the exile government's political broadcasts drew heavily on the works and legacy of T. G. Masaryk, and the two were inextricably linked in exile rhetoric. Beneš claimed that "what we are doing today is just that same international and European policy of Masarykian democracy and the twenty-year-long European policy of the First Republic," and assured listeners that it would triumph again, as it had in 1918.[205] Extracts from Masaryk's writings on democracy and even excerpts from some recorded talks on the subject were included in the government programme, and the broad scope of Masaryk's understanding of democracy was accepted and presented positively. Historian Andrea Orzoff has commented that "Masarykian democracy is less a political structure than a worldview, almost religious in scope," and this is borne out by comments made by Masaryk, describing democracy as a way of life and the moral meaning of the state.[206] In a talk marking the anniversary of Masaryk's birth, Minister Hubert Ripka tied the democratic rule extolled by the exiles to the nation's heritage, and he embraced Masaryk's broad interpretation of democracy when he summarised the former president's legacy:

> The most expressive and distinctive product of the politically creative genius of Masaryk is his conception of democracy. For him, it is not just a defined political and social system [...] To him, it is a declaration of faith, it is a practical expression of a philosophical and religious concept of the social destiny of the free man [...] This Masarykian conception of democracy [...] is in truth the founding and distinctive national concept of Czechs and Slovaks, in full agreement with the spirit and appeal of an ancient national tradition.[207]

The figure of T. G. Masaryk and the legend that had been built up around him formed an important element of the exile government's political broadcasts and he was a vital part of its attempts to establish its own ideological authority. It was also necessary to defend the symbol of Masaryk against Protectorate efforts to erase him from the public

---

204 BBC Czechoslovak Programme, 21 February 1941, LN Z 1941 – 5, CRA.
205 Beneš, *Šest let exilu*, 136.
206 Orzoff, *Battle for the Castle*, 30.
207 BBC Czechoslovak Programme, 7 March 1944, LN Z 1944 – 31, CRA.

memory: from August 1940, the Protectorate issued instructions for the removal of all pictures and memorials of Masaryk and the renaming of everything previously named in his honour.[208] Even the name originally chosen for the government programme, *Hovory s domovem*, recalled the image of Masaryk, by echoing the well-known title of Karel Čapek's published interviews with the then president, *Hovory s T. G. Masarykem*.[209] Masaryk's life and work had become mythologised during his lifetime, and the "personality cult" built up around him was not only perpetuated in the wartime broadcasts but formed a central tenet of the exile government's propaganda.[210] The introduction to a book on Masaryk, published to mark his eightieth birthday in 1930, is indicative of the style of the interwar period:

> In our history he lives and will always live as an unassailable political pioneer. As an enlightened social reformer, a progressively gifted revolutionary, as a wise founder of a new Europe and the first, immortal president of the Czechoslovak republican state [...] He was given to us as if by the will and choice of providence itself. In the eightieth year of his life, we hope for his sake, for that of our nation and state, that the days of his life will have no end.[211]

The legend of the "President Liberator" (as he was frequently referred to in the broadcasts) was a cornerstone of the exile government's political broadcasting, as announcers swore allegiance to him and used his name as shorthand for their entire policy. The patriotic and ideological heritage of the "father of the nation" was a constant theme as government broadcasters drew on their audience's familiarity with his works and shared respect for his achievements, to reinforce their own political legitimacy and ideological authority.[212] Beneš's work with Masaryk in

---

208 Čestmír Jeřábek noted receipt on 5 August 1940 of a Ministry of the Interior memo outlining these instructions at the institute at which he worked, in *V zajetí antikristově*, 95.
209 Čapek, *Hovory s Masarykem*. This formula was also used by later Czechoslovak president Václav Havel in his *Hovory z Lán* (*Conversations from Lány*, in reference to the Czech presidential residence), the name given to his weekly Sunday broadcasts beginning in 1990.
210 In the introduction to a collection of essays on Masaryk, Robert Pynsent explained that Masaryk had become a "legendary, even mythological figure" in Czechoslovakia since the First World War, and that "a personality cult of quite immense proportions came into existence immediately the Czechoslovak Republic was declared"; see Pynsent, *T. G. Masaryk*, 1.
211 František Soukup, *T. G. Masaryk jako politicky průkopník, sociální reformátor a president státu* (Prague: Ústřední dělnické knihkupectví a nakladatelství [Ant. Svěcený], 1930), 5–6.
212 Drtina, *A nyní promluví*, 163.

exile during the First World War and his direct inheritance of authority from his predecessor were central to his continuing authority, and other speakers – such as Masaryk's son Jan, Beneš's foreign minister for most of the war – also drew on their connection to him. Such was his dominance over the period that almost all discussion of the First Republic recalled the image of T. G. Masaryk. An excerpt of his writing was read in the very first broadcast of *Hovory s domovem*, and every March and September throughout the conflict saw a series of programmes devoted to marking the anniversaries of his birth and death respectively, ensuring his continued presence in exile propaganda. Masaryk's name, as a symbol of both an entire era and a system of political and philosophical values, was mentioned by speakers almost daily.

References to Masaryk within the broadcasts show that programme makers had complete confidence in the success of interwar propaganda and their audience's consequent familiarity with the man and his works. In an LTS programme made to mark the anniversary of his birth, the announcer remarked that celebrations of such historic figures always involved the repetition of the main dates and events of their lives, but

> I don't need to remind you of the important dates of his life, or of the works he wrote. Each of you knows them well. In fact, each of you probably saw T. G. Masaryk with your own eyes and many of you could probably recall memories or anecdotes from his life which history has forgotten.[213]

Loyalty to Masaryk's ideals was also upheld as a defining characteristic of every patriotic Czech and Slovak. One government broadcast claimed that "The best ideas in our history found new expression in the work of Masaryk [...] Loyalty to Masaryk's legacy today is the moral armament against the German usurper."[214]

So confident were the exiles in their audience's familiarity with and approval of Masaryk's political ideology that they had no reservations about tying their entire policy to his image:

> Masaryk is our programme. And because Masaryk is our programme, we cannot act differently during this war to how he acted during the last.

---

213 [Untitled], undated, 201, BBC Wartime Broadcasts Collection [WBC; working title], CRA.
214 BBC Czechoslovak Programme, 15 September 1943, LN Z 1943 – 24, CRA.

But Masaryk is not only our programme. He is also our example and our model. We follow him and so we will continue to whatever end, even if it is painful. For only that path, and no other, leads to victory.[215]

The exiles were not the first to treat Masaryk as a symbol rather than a mere politician. When Masaryk was unanimously re-elected as president in 1934, Karel Čapek wrote in the newspaper *Lidové noviny* that "Masaryk is a *principle*. Masaryk is for us and for the entire educated world the embodiment of certain moral and political ideals, which can be called *democracy*."[216] Statements of national unity under the banner of Masaryk appeared frequently in the broadcasts with no accompanying qualifying statements or arguments, suggesting speakers expected the logic behind them to be accepted without question: Masaryk embodied democracy, the exile government embodied the spirit of Masaryk, and that spirit connected the exiles to the nation at home. In September 1943, as part of a series of programmes remembering Masaryk's writings, one announcer stated simply, "We are the Masaryk nation," and called on listeners to "join together in his spirit."[217]

Beneš made frequent references to his work with Masaryk and often sought to emphasise his inheritance of the presidency (and associated authority) from his predecessor.[218] After the fall of France in June 1940, Beneš assured listeners that he would continue to fight for the reinstatement of Czechoslovakia and the furthering of Masaryk's legacy: "Whatever I may have to go through on this journey, whatever I may have to suffer and even if I should fall, I will not let drop from my hand that holy Czechoslovak banner which I received from Masaryk's hands."[219] He used a similar image in a speech in September 1940 marking the third anniversary of Masaryk's death, which Beneš concluded with a direct address to his predecessor, assuring him that his work was being continued:

---

215 25 October 1942, in Drtina, *A nyní promluví*, 268. Even the phrase "Masaryk is our programme" is a play on the former president's own statement "Tábor is our programme" in a speech of 1918, where he connected the founding on the Czechoslovak state with the reforming spirit of the Hussite movement that had settled at Tábor.
216 Karel Čapek, "Dvacátý čtvrtý květen 1934," originally written for *Lidové noviny*, 25 May 1934, reproduced in Karel Čapek, *Čtení o T. G. Masarykovi* (Prague: Melantrich, 1969), 67–70 (68). Emphasis in original.
217 BBC Czechoslovak Programme, 16 September 1943, LN Z 1943 – 24, CRA.
218 Masaryk recommended Beneš as his chosen successor and he was elected in December 1935 by 340 votes with only 100 against; see Zdeněk Karník, *České země v éře První republiky (1918–1939)*, vol. 2, *Československo a České země v krizi a v ohrožení (1930–1935)* (Prague: Libri, 2002), 572–74.
219 Beneš, *Šest let exilu*, 51–52.

"President Liberator, we remain faithful to the legacy that you passed into our hands!"[220] Masaryk's son Jan also drew on the authority of his family name in his broadcasts. In his first speech in September 1939, Jan Masaryk thanked listeners for taking such good care of his father's grave in Lány and combined the memories of Masaryk and religious reformer Jan Hus (1369–1415) in his promise that, "by the name which I bear, I hereby swear to you that we will win this battle and that truth will prevail."[221]

The exiles also sought to employ the authority of the Masaryk name in their efforts to encourage resistance – for example, during the boycott of the entire Protectorate press in September 1941. Vaunted as a successful demonstration of passive Czech resistance to German occupation, the government programme strongly promoted it, and not only on the exiles' own authority: "the general boycott of the Czechoslovak press will begin on Sunday 14 September 1941, the fourth anniversary of the death of the President Liberator, Tomáš Garrigue Masaryk. The general boycott will last for all of Masaryk week."[222] A few days after this announcement, the government programme featured several short patriotic rhymes promoting the boycott, and the image of Masaryk – and his continuing dominance over the republic – recurred again: "při památce Masaryka, slyšte heslo hodiny: celá jeho republika, nekupuje noviny" (In memory of Masaryk, hear the slogan of the hour: his whole republic is not buying newspapers).[223] The Gestapo reported a seventy percent drop in newspaper sales during the boycott, and the initiative won the support of the Central Leadership of the Home Resistance (Ústřední vedení odboje domácího, ÚVOD). This justifies the BBC's contemporary assessment of the boycott as "wholly successful," and the judgement of later historians that it marked "a great victory for the London radio," demonstrating the influence of the government programme on listeners.[224] In broadcasts such as this, the exiles overtly appropriated the authority that Masaryk's name carried with it, and used it to add weight to their own projects.

---

220 Beneš, *Šest let exilu*, 57.
221 Masaryk, *Volá Londýn* (1990), 11. "Truth prevails" was adopted as the presidential motto by T. G. Masaryk and remains on the banner of the Czech president to this day. It is drawn from religious reformer Jan Hus's writings on the importance of living in truth.
222 BBC Czechoslovak Programme, 12 September 1941, LN Z 1941 – 9, CRA.
223 BBC Czechoslovak Programme, 15 September 1941, LN Z 1941 – 9, CRA.
224 "BBC Intelligence Report: Europe," 3 December 1941, p. 11, 49/41, EIP series 1a, E2/185, BBC WAC. See Bednařík, Jirák, and Köpplová, *Dějiny českých médií*, 214; Koutek, "Zahraniční odboj," 38–39.

Although the spirit of the First Republic and of Masaryk's legacy was uniformly praised, the government programme did come to acknowledge some failings of the interwar state and promised to improve on them in the future. In a talk from October 1940, the announcer claimed that "the First Czechoslovak Republic [...] under the fatherly oversight of Masaryk, achieved a great deal to approach the ideal of human, economic, social, national, and religious justice." The programme went on to maintain that neither Masaryk nor the Czechoslovak nation were to blame for the fact that

> the promised development towards this ideal, which made [Czechoslovakia] into one of the foremost examples of a democratic state in which the people rule in the interests of the people, was interrupted before [Masaryk] could prove that a truly democratic system is the most successful system of state governance. God willing, the Third Republic, which will rise from the ruins left by the current storm, will prove this in the shining example of Tomáš Masaryk.[225]

As Stránský's talks in defence of democracy suggest, the government-in-exile was aware of the accusations that had been and continued to be levelled against the First Republic, in terms of its perceived weakness. Jan Masaryk suggested there were some aspects of the interwar system that could stand to be revised: in a talk also from October 1940 he hinted at known flaws, and in February 1941 he stated outright that, while the exact nature of the future political system was unclear, there could be no return to the inefficient stream of coalition governments that had been seen during the First Republic.[226] Beneš also acknowledged this failing of the interwar democracy, admitting that "all parts of our previous system that were party-political and especially coalition-based were unhealthy and have been rightly criticised."[227]

The legend of T. G. Masaryk was never to be revised, however. He remained an important symbol for the ideology of the exile government throughout the war and no attempt was made to either re-examine his legacy or reduce his prominence in the broadcasts. On the anniversary of his birth in 1945, *Hlas svobodné republiky* broadcast talks on Masaryk's life and heritage, as it had for the preceding five years, and Josef Kodíček

---

225 BBC Czechoslovak Programme, 18 October 1940, LN Z 1940 – 2, CRA.
226 Masaryk, *Volá Londýn* (1990), 74.
227 Beneš, *Šest let exilu*, 72.

explained to listeners that the President Liberator's foresight and understanding of what the future would bring had ensured his continuing relevance.[228] In one of the final talks to be broadcast from London, Head of the MZV Information Department Hubert Ripka spoke about the Czechoslovak people's liberation and the last skirmishes still taking place on home soil, and concluded that, "at this time, when the final fighting blows of our patriots welcome back our freedom, the thoughts of all of us turn to that grave in Lány so that we may all let our great deceased-but-eternally-living Masaryk know: President Liberator, we remained faithful, faithful we shall remain!"[229]

The Second World War marked an important stage in Czechoslovak national mythmaking that has significantly influenced how the state has been remembered both at home and abroad. The exiles carried out a concerted propaganda campaign in Britain, promoting the memory of the First Republic and their efforts to recreate it in public talks, books, and radio broadcasts. Books published in English by the MZV Information Department informed readers that the Czechoslovakia of 1918 was a new state, "but it was by no means a new or artificial product of the Peace Conference in Versailles," as Hitler had claimed it to be.[230] Instead, according to the MZV, the state was in fact "merely a return to a state of affairs which began to develop in its territory more than a thousand years before." It also left no doubt about the legacy of Masaryk, claiming that "the people loved and admired Masaryk, and when he died on September 14 1937, the whole nation mourned him as a father."[231] Talks were given in Britain by government-sponsored organisations such as the Czechoslovak Study Institute, and Czechoslovak figures also contributed to English-language radio programmes praising Masaryk and his legacy, such as the essay Jan Masaryk wrote for the series *The Eternal Torch: 20 Great Exiles of History Portrayed by 20 Great Exiles*

---

228 BBC Czechoslovak Programme, 7 March 1945, LN Z 1945 – 44, CRA.
229 BBC Czechoslovak Programme, 9 May 1945, LN Z 1945 – 46, CRA. These closing words also connect to resistance movements in the Protectorate, as there was a resistance group entitled Petiční výbor Věrní zůstaneme (The Petition Committee "We will remain faithful"). This group took its name from a manifesto by Czech writers, published in 1938, which pledged allegiance to T. G. Masaryk's ideals and called for national unity against the threat of German aggression.
230 Hitler made this accusation repeatedly and used it as justification for the destruction of Czechoslovakia; see, for example, Hitler's speech to the Reichstag, 28 April 1939, reproduced in Norman Baynes, ed., *The Speeches of Adolf Hitler: April 1922 – August 1939*, vol. 2 (London: Oxford University Press, 1942), 1620.
231 J. B. Heisler and J. E. Mellon, *Czechoslovakia: Land of Dream and Enterprise* ([London]: Czechoslovak Ministry of Foreign Affairs Department of Information, 1945), 13, 23.

of Today.[232] The acknowledgement of some minor failings – such as the multitude of political parties – was a small addition to a dominant narrative of democratic and tolerant values, which continues to this day. Much of the narrative established in the First Republic was entrenched during the war period and was preserved following the Communist takeover in 1948, as many former London exiles found themselves abroad again, often writing on national and historical topics. One prominent figure in both exile groups was Josef Korbel, head of the MZV Radio Department in London during the war and later founder of what is now the Josef Korbel School of International Studies at the University of Denver.[233] The understanding of the Czechs as an inherently democratic people had an obvious significance for Cold War era exiles, but it was also vital to exile government propaganda during the war period, as it offered a legitimising historical precedent which the exiles could use to cast themselves in the role of perpetuators of the Czech national tradition.

The London Czechoslovaks also portrayed their very presence in exile as further evidence of their perpetuation of national traditions. Government broadcasters both implicitly and explicitly connected themselves to historical examples of Czech exile movements, to legitimise their position and associate themselves with established national heroes. In his announcement on the award of "full recognition" by the British in the government programme on 18 July 1941, Jan Masaryk presented the achievement to listeners as a further step on the road towards the return of power to them, the public, with the promise that "Governance of your affairs will, slowly but surely, return to your hands, oh Czechoslovak people."[234] This paraphrasing of the well-known words of Comenius, an educational and religious reformer who left Bohemia during the Counter-Reformation of the seventeenth century, linked the work of Masaryk and his colleagues to that of previous exile movements that had also found refuge in Britain.[235] Parallels with Comenius were more

---

232 Details of this programme can be found in "Zaměstnanci: Masaryk, Jan," LA (O) 541, MZV. A typical example of a public talk is that of regular broadcaster and head of the Czechoslovak Study Institute Jaroslav Císař in Cambridge in 1941, entitled "TGM: Man and European"; see "Osvěta – Studijní ústav Londýn, Kulturní činnost v Londýně (Císař)," Doplňky (LA) 9, MZV.
233 Körbel was the father of US Secretary of State Madeline Albright and the academic mentor of later US Secretary of State Condoleezza Rice. He continued to write and reflect on the interpretation of Czechoslovak history in works such as *Twentieth-Century Czechoslovakia: Meanings of Its History* (New York: Columbia University Press, 1977).
234 BBC Czechoslovak Programme, 18 July 1941, LN Z 1941 – 7, CRA.
235 The text by Comenius (known in Czech as Komenský) reads, "vláda věcí tvých k tobě se zase navrátí, ó lide český!" (governance of your affairs will return to you, oh Czech people!)";

explicitly discussed by Prokop Drtina in a talk from 22 March 1942 marking the anniversary of the birth of "the greatest émigré in our history." In this programme, Drtina referred to Comenius and his colleagues as "our first exile movement in England," and claimed that "we here in England come upon the footprints of Comenius and all our Czech Brethren émigrés very often." In response to Protectorate propaganda condemning the exiles in London, Drtina used the anniversary to "set out the great political and moral meaning of exile for our nation," praising Comenius and his fellow exiles for keeping the national spirit alive when it was being suppressed at home. Geographical distance, Drtina argued, could have no impact on such spiritual closeness: "They never grew estranged from the spirit of their nation but instead became the bearers of her spiritual traditions."[236] The idea of a tradition of exile can also be seen behind Drtina's own pseudonym of Pavel Svatý, which played on the associations of St. Paul's epistles, written from far away to communities of Christians who were often suffering persecution.[237]

The exile work of T. G. Masaryk during the First World War was also used as an example of the tradition of exile with which Beneš's government sought to associate itself. For example, after the appointment of Reinhard Heydrich as deputy Reichsprotektor in September 1941 and the subsequent increase in arrests and intimidation within the Protectorate, Beneš spoke from London and sought to reassure listeners at home that the exiles understood what they were going through:

> I am with you and all of us here are with you in this time of suffering, repression, terror, and murder of our good, patriotic martyrs, so devoted to national issues. Our exiles during the Thirty Years' War, with Comenius at their head, went through similar times when the German mercenaries were murdering and executing our people at home; with Masaryk we went through similar times during the last war, when they were imprisoning those most dear to us and executing our legionaries.[238]

---

quoted in Jan Amos Komenský, "Kšaft umírající matky jednoty bratrské kterýmž (v národu svém a obzvláštnosti své dokonávjící) svěřené sobě někdy od Pána Boha poklady mezi syny a dcery a dědice své rozděluje, Léta páně 1650" (Private publication for participants at the conference of Skupina moravských knihomilů, Uherské Hradiště, 5 June 1938), 21.

236 Drtina, *A nyní promluví,* 194–96.
237 Drtina began using this pseudonym in his work in the domestic resistance, before leaving for London; see Koutek, "Zahraniční odboj," 33, 11.
238 Beneš, *Šest let exilu,* 81.

The exiles sought to stress that they were not enjoying the relative safety of their exile but were in fact suffering all the pain of the people at home, exacerbated by the additional pain of separation from them. Broadcasters claimed their thoughts were always with their compatriots at home, including statements that "we think of you a hundred times a day," and "every exile has some little corner of his native country which he remembers, wherever he goes. His last thought belongs to it, as he lays down to sleep, and his first, when he awakes."[239] The crackdown on resistance in the Protectorate following Heydrich's appointment encouraged the exiles to confront the issue of their relative safety. While Jan Masaryk felt driven to acknowledge the awkwardness of their position when he admitted in his broadcast of 1 October 1941 that "today I feel a little ashamed to speak to you from here, where I am safe," other broadcasters emphasised their own suffering.[240] In a radio speech on 25 November 1941, Beneš emphasised the difficulties of political isolation, likening exile to a physical illness: "political exile is discontent, pain, suffering – I would almost say a disease."[241] In March 1942, Drtina explained the self-sacrifice necessary to go into exile and emphasised the exiles' important role in working for the nation:

> There is no joy in exile. No one ever went into exile for their own enjoyment. Going into exile takes courage. There is also no shame in exile, it is just a difficult fate. He who can fight without going into exile does so. But when there is no other way to fight then the stronger and more numerous the exile movement is, the better for the state and the nation.[242]

Prime Minister Jan Šrámek also reflected on the nature of the relationship between exile speakers and their audience, concluding that they shared a bond of mutual understanding that the distance of exile could not influence: "We, you and we, are separated by a great distance and yet we are also joined together, because you hear our voices and understand them, and we note your silence and understand it."[243] In making more emotive statements such as these, broadcasters sought not only to validate their position in exile and excuse their distance from listeners, but

---

[239] Masaryk, *Volá Londýn* (1990), 12; Drtina, *A nyní promluví*, 199.
[240] Masaryk, *Volá Londýn* (1990), 125.
[241] Beneš, *Šest let exilu*, 197.
[242] Drtina, *A nyní promluví*, 198.
[243] BBC Czechoslovak Programme, 1 January 1943, LN Z 1943 – 18, CRA.

also to create a more personal connection through shared experience. Listeners were constantly told "we are with you," and some broadcasters emphasised their shared background with listeners. "I dare to touch on your pain, your hope, and your determination only because I am one of you," claimed Drtina. "I was on Wenceslas Square on October 28th with you, and on November 15th I accompanied the hero Opletal on his final journey with you."[244] While many broadcasters sought to convince listeners of this connection, none could rival the personal broadcasting style of Jan Masaryk, whose humorous and affectionate manner – combined with his success in distancing himself from his official position – made him one of the most effective and subtle propagandists of the entire Czechoslovak exile movement. The political possibilities of radio as an intimate medium, a way of establishing a personal connection with each listener, had been seen in the broadcasts of President Roosevelt in the 1930s, and Masaryk brought his own personal touch to the London broadcasts, drawing on what Weber termed the authority of charisma.

"We are close together at heart": The Authority of Charisma

While legal claims and the perpetuation of tradition both play significant roles in establishing legitimate authority, there is also an important individual factor in which the personality of political leaders comes to the fore. Weber defined charisma as "a certain quality of an individual personality, by virtue of which he is considered extraordinary," the figure in question being endowed with qualities "such as are not accessible to the ordinary person." Charismatic authority therefore rests on respect for these qualities among the governed population and "devotion to the exceptional sanctity, heroism or exemplary character" of the person displaying them.[245] The two most prominent individuals in the London broadcasts were President Beneš and Foreign Minister Jan Masaryk, and in their contrasting broadcast personalities they represent very different expressions of charismatic authority. Beneš, as the head of the

---

244 Drtina, *A nyní promluví*, 20. Here, Drtina refers to a public manifestation in defiance of the ban on celebrating the anniversary of Czechoslovakia's founding on 28 October 1939, and to the funeral of Jan Opletal, a Prague student killed during the anti-Nazi demonstrations.
245 Weber, *Economy and Society*, 241, 215. For further discussion of charismatic authority, see ibid., 241–45.

government and the leader of the London exiles, was revered in the government programme and presented by his colleagues as wise, universally respected, and almost infallible in his ability to predict the outcome of events. His speeches were high-profile broadcasting events, repeated several times throughout the day and analysed in great depth by commentators. Masaryk, in contrast, exemplified what might be considered a more traditionally charismatic style in broadcasts that established an emotional connection between himself and the listener. Weber argued that charismatic authority depended on such "strictly personal" relationships, and Masaryk used this bond, and the capacity of radio to act as an intimate means of communication, to promote the work of the government-in-exile in seemingly non-political broadcasts.[246]

Beneš's "extraordinary" quality was his foresight; he was presented in the broadcasts not merely as a wise leader but as a diplomat who had foreseen the entire course of the war.[247] In October 1941, in a talk on the executions of Czechs under the newly appointed Heydrich, Jan Masaryk told listeners that the president had foreseen the situation some three years previously but had decided to refrain from war with Germany until the rest of the world became aware of the danger posed by Hitler's regime.[248] On more than one occasion, Prokop Drtina returned to a speech given by Beneš on 22 September 1938, at the height of the Munich crisis, and quoted from it to illustrate how the president's prophesies were coming true. In July 1940, following the announcement of (provisional) recognition from Britain, Drtina opened his talk by quoting Beneš: "'I see things clearly and I have a plan.' Of course you remember where you heard these words." He cited Beneš's assertion that the crisis facing Czechoslovakia in 1938 would only be the beginning ("All of Europe, all of the world will undergo a great change: this is not only about us"), and that other countries would soon face similar challenges, noting that "not even two years have passed since those prophetic words were spoken," and listing the other European nations since occupied by Germany. In both this talk and the one that followed the announcement of full recognition in July 1941, Drtina quoted Beneš's claim that "I have

---

[246] Weber, *Economy and Society*, 246.
[247] Beneš's own efforts to convince the British of his powers of foresight drew much criticism from the FO. When Beneš sought permission to publish a book of speeches and documents in 1942, one FO official complained that his only motivation for doing so was "his own glorification and justification," and several others expressed doubts as to his prophetic ability; see September – October 1942, C 9103/9103/12, FO 371/30852, TNA.
[248] Masaryk, *Volá Londýn* (1990), 124.

a plan for every eventuality and I will be mistaken in nothing," presenting each stage of recognition as a further step in the president's successful plan. Having used the same words again when Britain renounced Munich in August 1942 and when Beneš left for Moscow in 1943, Drtina explained his motivations in returning to this theme: he used these moments of success to "dispel those remnants of doubt which remained among our people under the influence of Goebbels's propaganda," and to dismiss any lingering suspicions the public may have had regarding Beneš's conduct during the Munich crisis.[249]

The image of Beneš presented in the government broadcasts was therefore that of an experienced statesman, whose knowledge and almost professorial way of speaking could inspire confidence in the listener. Recording his thoughts on the London broadcasts in his diary, writer Čestmír Jeřábek described the President's voice as "calm, reliable and slightly lilting," eschewing oratorical techniques in favour of straightforward speech: "unsentimental like a doctor who has achieved his goal of combating death. After hearing him speak, one feels like a patient who has just been told that he has come through the worst of it and will soon be well again."[250] Around Beneš's birthday in May, the government programme often included a series of talks praising the man and his work, and a special feature programme was made to mark his sixtieth in 1944. "There are few men in the history of world politics who have lived greater lives, hardly any man whose life has been and still is so dramatic," listeners were told. "What strength, what self-deprivation and what faith must have been needed for this life not to falter in such a mission."[251] On the eve of his own return to Czechoslovakia in August 1944, Minister Němec expressed his confidence that the president's plans had never diverged from the wishes of the public, telling listeners that "It was our good fortune that we found in the figure of our president Dr. Beneš a man and a statesman who for six years led our shared struggle in such a way that it always corresponded to your opinions at home."[252] Beneš's speeches, much feted and given at fairly regular intervals throughout the war, were an important part of his persona as a leader. These speeches enabled him

---

249 Drtina, *A nyní promluví*, 37, 134, 244, 375. In the published collection of his talks, Drtina introduced the first broadcast quoting this speech with this explanation; ibid., 37.
250 Jeřábek, *V zajetí antikristově*, 80, 81.
251 BBC Czechoslovak Programme, 25 May 1944, LN Z 1944 – 32, CRA. Programmes on Beneš were regularly broadcast around his birthday; see, for example, BBC Czechoslovak Programme, 27 May 1941, LN Z 1941 – 6; 26 May 1942, LN Z 1942 – 14, CRA.
252 BBC Czechoslovak Programme, 20 August 1944, LN Z 1944 – 35, CRA.

to perpetuate traditions such as the presidential end-of-year address, and generally to perform as a president on the same platform that he had used at home, having regularly broadcast on Czechoslovak radio before the war.[253] The rise of radio listening in the 1930s had changed how politicians communicated with the people they governed, and public understandings of how political figures should speak were undergoing a shift in this period.

The Second World War marked an important change in the role of the media in politics and political oratory across the world, because it was the first conflict in which political speeches could be heard by the public at large. As radio ownership became more widespread in the 1930s, the new medium had taken up a central role in the dissemination of information and opinion, and its propaganda possibilities had been seized upon by governments across the political spectrum. While efforts to maintain radio as an "apolitical" medium in Weimar Germany had meant that National Socialist voices were almost never broadcast, the situation was swiftly inverted upon Hitler's seizure of power in 1933.[254] Just days after being appointed propaganda minister in Hitler's government, Josef Goebbels described radio as "by nature authoritarian" and told representatives from German broadcasting that "We make no bones about it: the radio belongs to us, to no one else! And we will place the radio at the service of our idea, and no other idea shall be expressed through it."[255] From then on, radio in both Germany and German-occupied territory would serve solely to provide a loud, unchallenged projection of the National Socialist perspective. Radio created new opportunities for the performance of authority and communication with the governed public for political leaders of all countries and orientations, but for the refugee European politicians gathered in London during the war, who lacked other means of exerting their authority, broadcasting gained extra significance. The inherent distance that exists between broadcaster and listener, described

---

253 In 1936, Beneš spoke on the radio thirteen times – more than once a month on average. The attention paid to these speeches in the radio yearbook shows the importance attributed to them; see Jaroslav Potůček, ed., *Ročenka čs. Rozhlasu 1937: Popisuje vývoj československého rozhlasu od roku 1934 do počátku roku 1937* (Prague: Radiojournal, 1937), 60.
254 In his history of German radio, Konrad Dussel suggests that programme makers in the Weimar period viewed radio as being primarily a cultural entity which should be above party politics. From 1932, greater efforts were made by government to centralise control over radio broadcasting and ensure the government had regular access to listeners, resulting in the nationalisation of radio later that year. See Konrad Dussel, *Deutsche Rundfunkgeschichte* (Cologne: Halem, 2020), 48, 67–71.
255 Ralf Georg Reuth, *Goebbels* (London: Constable, 1993), 176–77.

by Paddy Scannell as the "central fact" of radio communication, mirrors that between exile politicians and their public; both broadcasting and exile politics are characterised by efforts to "bridge the gap" and bring the audience closer, minimising that sense of distance.[256]

Academic studies of radio frequently touch on the intimacy of broadcasting and the potential for radio to make listeners feel a greater degree of involvement and engagement than consumers of other media.[257] One commonly identified contributing factor is the context in which people listen to the radio; broadcasts are often heard in a domestic environment, allowing "outside voices to enter the home" and giving broadcasters the chance to "speak to people as they relaxed."[258] This, in turn, influences the way in which people speak over the radio. Given that broadcasters cannot dictate how their programmes are received, they are forced instead to adapt their own speech to the listening environment if they hope to influence the listener. Scannell described the relationship between broadcaster and listener as "unenforceable," and suggested that early audience research by the BBC showed that "they did not, indeed could not, control what went on in the places of listening," leading the corporation to alter its output to meet the expectations of the listener, rather than expecting the audience to adapt its own behaviour.[259] Unlike the self-selecting audience members at a political event or rally, who have demonstrated their interest through their attendance, the average radio listener is likely to be less receptive to strident political rhetoric, and political broadcasters are therefore obliged to adapt their methods. Cantril and Allport suggested radio listeners in the comfort of their own home are "less suggestible" and "less well disposed" to political arguments than a mass audience at a rally, and therefore the speaker must adopt the tone "of the salesman rather than that of the spellbinder."[260]

---

[256] Paddy Scannell has argued that "the central fact of broadcasting's communicative context is that it speaks from one place and is heard in another," and that "the design of talk on radio and TV recognizes this and attempts to bridge the gap by simulating co-presence with its listeners and viewers"; see Scannell, *Broadcast Talk*, 1–2.
[257] So widely accepted is Andrew Crisell's description of radio as "an intimate medium" (Crisell, *Understanding Radio*, 12) that "Intimacy" features as one of the key concepts summarised in Hugh Chignell's handbook *Key Concepts in Radio Studies* (London: Sage, 2009), 85–87.
[258] David Goodman, *Radio's Civic Ambition: American Broadcasting and Democracy in the 1930s* (Oxford: Oxford University Press, 2011), 91.
[259] Scannell, *Radio, Television*, 12.
[260] Cantril and Allport, *Psychology of Radio*, 31.

Instead of long political speeches, a more persuasive and informal tone is needed, appropriate to this intimate setting.[261]

In addition to altering their tone, broadcasters wishing to influence their listeners must also consider how they address their audience. Paradoxically, although the audience for a radio broadcast may be huge, experiences in early broadcasting showed the effectiveness of making listeners feel that they were being personally addressed as small groups and individuals.[262] Scannell found that

> existing public forms of talk were inappropriate for the new medium of radio. The lecture, the sermon, the political speech, all had rhetorical styles that spoke to audiences constituted as a crowd, a mass. But radio must speak to each listener as someone in particular, with the attributes [...] of a person.[263]

This fact had also been identified in Czechoslovakia; in a pre-war study of radio audiences for the *Union Internationale de Radiodiffusion*, a Czechoslovak researcher noted how "sensitive the listener is to the talk that seems to be addressed particularly to him, where use is made of such expressions as 'I'm thinking of you,' or 'you, listeners in the Tatras,' or again 'you who are listening in Moravia.'"[264] As has already been seen in some of the above quotes, such direct addresses to listeners were common in the Czechoslovak government programme.

The very nature of radio as an entirely non-visual medium that permits the transmission of the human voice is also an important factor in its potential for intimacy. Crisell argues persuasively that the lack of any visual stimulus in radio broadcasting means that the listener is compelled to visualise the topics being discussed and engage their own imagination to do so, thereby taking the subject matter into their own internal

---

[261] In 1924, US Democratic candidate John W. Davis predicted that radio would mean the end of the long political speech, "Otherwise your audience might tune out without your knowing it. It's just a matter of turning a knob." Buhite and Levy noted that those political speakers who enjoyed greatest success with the radio microphone in the 1920s abandoned the style of formal speeches and adopted a more conversational tone; Russell D. Buhite and David W. Levy, eds., *FDR's Fireside Chats* (Norman: University of Oklahoma Press, 1992), xiv.
[262] For more on the paradoxical nature of radio as a mass-communication medium that addresses the individual, see Crisell, *Understanding Radio*, 13–14.
[263] Scannell, *Radio, Television*, 24.
[264] Goodman, *Radio's Civic Ambition*, 92n112.

world.[265] British listeners in the 1930s were even encouraged to try listening in darkened rooms, on the basis that "your imagination will be twice as vivid" in the absence of the distracting familiar objects around them.[266] The power of the spoken word to influence listeners has also been investigated by radio researchers, and Cantril and Allport concluded their study on the psychology of radio with the assertion that "time and again our experimental findings establish this point: the human voice is more interesting, more persuasive, more friendly, and more compelling than is the written word."[267] They identified the tendency of listeners to feel that they could identify the character of a broadcaster through their voice, imbuing disembodied voices with personalities, a consequence of the ostensibly "private" mode of speech being transferred to the "public" arena.[268] Gunther Kress argued that listeners naturally respond to public communication over the radio as a personal message because "that is what we understand (however implicitly) speech to be."[269] These characteristics humanised the disembodied voice of the wireless set, making it a facilitator for human communication rather than simply the projection of sound.

The political implications of radio's capacity for seemingly intimate communication could be seen before the war in the more personal broadcasts of US President Franklin Roosevelt. Radio had become an increasingly important political medium in the United States throughout the 1930s but, as David Goodman explains, this was accompanied by a deep suspicion of its propaganda power.[270] President Roosevelt's subtle and innovative use of radio for his more personal speeches, known as the "fireside chats," not only helped to win public support for his New Deal but also earned him a reputation as one of the most influential political

---

265 Crisell terms this another "paradox" of radio, as, although it is a long-distance mode of mass communication, it is also "an inward, intimate medium," because its messages can only be fully "realised" inside the listener's mind; Crisell, *Understanding Radio*, 13–14.
266 *BBC Yearbook 1930*, 60, quoted in Paddy Scannell and David Cardiff, *A Social History of British Broadcasting*, vol. 1, *1922–1939, Serving the Nation* (Oxford: Basil Blackwell, 1991), 371.
267 Cantril and Allport, *Psychology of Radio*, 260.
268 For David Hendy's discussion of this experiment, see *Noise*, 289–90. For Cantril and Allport's method and results, see *Psychology of Radio*, 109–26.
269 Gunther Kress, "Language in the Media: The Construction of the Domains of Public and Private," in Crisell, *Radio*, 47. This chapter is based on a paper from *Media, Culture & Society* 8 (1986): 395–419.
270 David Goodman discusses the contemporary arguments that surrounded the political use of radio in America in the 1930s and links them to the development of the commercial radio system. National broadcasters like the BBC were perceived as being state-controlled and therefore not sufficiently "free" for American audiences; see Goodman, *Radio's Civic Ambition*, 69.

broadcasters in US history.[271] Addressing listeners as "my friends," Roosevelt adopted a friendly and paternal tone that circumvented fears of overt propaganda, reassured the anxious American public, and appealed to them to engage personally in the major political events of the time.[272] Studies of the fireside chats, such as that of David Ryfe, have used these transmissions as an example of how broadcasting made engagement in political debate a possibility for a wider public than ever before. Ryfe described them as the first "transformative media events" in history, forcing listeners to reflect on a social issue and inviting them to "see themselves in new ways and to adopt new roles."[273] The natural intimacy of radio was enhanced by Roosevelt's personal tone, making listeners to the fireside chats feel like they were individually being addressed "as particular people who matter."[274] There is ample evidence for the intimate connection the president established with listeners in the letters they wrote to the White House, in which they assumed a familiar relationship with him, viewing him as almost a member of the family.[275] As well as changing the American public's perception of the presidency forever, Roosevelt also demonstrated the potential for personal and intimate broadcasting to make people feel invested in a political cause.[276] Although the audience conditions were drastically different for the wartime exiles – addressing listeners already accustomed to political topics and voices on

---

271 The term "fireside chat" was first used to describe one of Roosevelt's national radio addresses in a CBS network press release in 1933 and was quickly adopted by the press, public, and the president himself. Their popularity at the time and the significance attributed to them in changing the image of the American presidency have ensured the chats have been widely studied; see, for example, Buhite and Levy, *FDR's Fireside Chats*; David Michael Ryfe, "From Media Audience to Media Public: A Study of Letters Written in Reaction to FDR's Fireside Chats," *Media, Culture and Society* 23 (2001): 767–81.

272 William Leuchtenberg likened Roosevelt's style to that of "a father discussing public affairs with his family in the living room"; *Franklin D. Roosevelt and the New Deal, 1932–1940* (New York: Harper & Row, 1963), 330.

273 Ryfe, "From Media Audience," 767. In this study, Ryfe is drawing on the work of Dayan and Katz in *Media Events: The Live Broadcasting of History* (Cambridge, MA: Harvard University Press, 1992).

274 Ryfe, "From Media Audience," 769.

275 One letter explained that, "If I am addressing you too informally, it is only because you have brought yourself so close to us, the people. You may believe me that as I listened to you last night your every cough made me wince, and prompted me to admonish you, as I would one of the family, to take good care of yourself, for the country's sake, as well as your own"; quoted in Gerd Horten, *Radio Goes to War: The Cultural Politics of Propaganda during World War II* (Berkeley: University of California Press, 2003), 52n28.

276 Leuchtenberg argues that Roosevelt "gave people a sense of membership in the national community" and, by means such as his broadcasts, encouraged the public to feel personally engaged in political affairs. He also claims that every presidency since Roosevelt's has been affected by his reinterpretation of the role; see Leuchtenberg, *Franklin D. Roosevelt*, esp. 331.

the radio but largely living under occupation – broadcasters such as Jan Masaryk also made use of radio's potential as a personal and intimate medium to establish a bond with their audience.

After making his broadcasting debut in the very first Czech-language broadcast by the BBC on 8 September 1939, Masaryk became one of the most famous and popular voices of the exile movement. Son of the previous president and a pre-war diplomat who had spent a great deal of time in Britain and the USA, Masaryk was known as a charismatic and well-connected man, and he built up a friendly radio persona for which he is still remembered. Various collected volumes of Masaryk's talks have been published since the end of the war, one of the most recent being the 1990 Panorama Czech edition, and they remain the most prominent examples of wartime radio in Czech popular memory. Masaryk's early death in March 1948 and the controversy surrounding it have also done much to romanticise his life and cement his position in history.[277] Beginning with monthly appearances, Masaryk claimed his own weekly slot on Wednesday evenings from March 1940. Despite occasional interruptions by travel to the United States and elsewhere, he then broadcast weekly for much of 1940 and 1941, before fluctuating between fortnightly and monthly talks from then on. His sense of humour and personal charm earned Masaryk a position as one of the most popular broadcasters on the BBC Czechoslovak Service (and regular appearances on BBC Home Service programmes such as *The Brains Trust*), but, despite being appointed foreign minister to the provisionally recognised Czechoslovak government-in-exile in mid-1940, Masaryk continued to broadcast separately from his political colleagues and presented himself in such a way as to distance himself even further from his official role. His authority was therefore based on his personal charisma and name, and his broadcasts lent further credence to the exile government's work, by appearing to listeners as the opinion of a friend. In this way, his broadcasting technique was not dissimilar to that of Roosevelt, whose rhetorical skills he

---

277 Masaryk died shortly after the Communist Party took over the government, in a fall from his bathroom window, and his position as an early victim of the Communist regime – whether by means of psychological pressure or of outright murder – is widely accepted. Post-1989 biographies such as Pavel Kosatík and Michal Kolář's *Jan Masaryk: Pravdivý příběh* (Prague: Mladá fronta, 1998) perpetuate a romanticised image of Masaryk, and public discussions at events such as the symposium held by the Czech Embassy in London to mark the sixty-fifth anniversary of Masaryk's death in 2013 reveal how emotive and important a figure he continues to be.

praised, though Masaryk's tone was less paternal and more jocular.[278] Masaryk's broadcasts, and their continuing popularity, are testament to the political possibilities open to broadcasting that exploits the inherently intimate character of radio.

The friendly and personal atmosphere of Masaryk's broadcasts was established very early on, and he played on the idea of speaking to people in a domestic setting, as though he were a member of the family. When informing listeners that he was to begin broadcasting weekly, he told them "I'll always be at your place for a while on Wednesday evenings," using the Czech construction *u vás*, which indicates joining someone in their space, usually their home, rather than simply *s vámi*, "with you."[279] In his second speech, broadcast on Czechoslovak Independence Day on 28 October 1939, Masaryk furthered this familial tone by addressing his listeners as his "dear brothers and sisters" and assuring them that, though the exiles were physically distant from their listeners, "we are close together at heart."[280] When considering the first Christmas under occupation, Masaryk used references to festive traditions to again imply an almost familial relationship with his audience: "I wish I could eat a bit of fried fish with you in peace and comfort, and then go to St. Vitus Cathedral at midnight."[281] He began one of his weekly talks in February 1941 by musing, "And so, another Wednesday – how many will there be before we will be able to chat on Masaryk Embankment?," as though he were personally acquainted with every listener and bumped into them frequently on the streets of Prague.[282]

Masaryk further reinforced the intimacy between himself and his audience by speaking about his own emotions and sharing personal anecdotes. In his broadcast from 6 November 1940 he referenced All Souls' Day and told listeners of everything he was missing: from his mother who used to tuck him in at night, to childhood swimming in the Vltava ("by some miracle we didn't contract typhus") and skating on Prague's Shooter's Island (Střelecký ostrov) with his first love (hoping that she "was thoroughly thrilled with the English scarf [I'd given

---

[278] In a talk from 3 March 1943, Masaryk criticised prominent Protectorate Nazi official K. H. Frank for attempting to mimic Hitler's style of speaking, drawing unfavourable comparisons between it and the "individual" styles of Churchill and Roosevelt; Masaryk, *Volá Londýn* (1990), 172.
[279] Masaryk, *Volá Londýn* (1990), 19.
[280] Masaryk, *Volá Londýn* (1990), 12.
[281] Masaryk, *Volá Londýn* (1990), 16.
[282] Masaryk, *Volá Londýn* (1990), 75.

her], stolen from my late brother Herbert").[283] He often talked of how he missed his compatriots and feared for them, ending a broadcast on the recent appointment of the notoriously brutal Reinhard Heydrich as deputy Reichsprotector of Bohemia and Moravia with a plea to listeners not to provoke Heydrich and a forlorn sign off: "I find it hard to wish you goodnight tonight."[284] After a nine-month trip to America, Masaryk returned to the microphone in July 1942 and told listeners with great affection that he had carried them in his heart all that time, "like a mother with a child," and that he looked forward to victory so he could return and "kiss your hand."[285]

Jan Masaryk also made great use of his relationship with his father in his broadcasts. As well as contributing to the general effort to link the exile government to the legacy of T. G. Masaryk, the son also used this family connection to further the seemingly personal relationship between himself and his audience. His close relationship to the legendary figure of the "President Liberator" enabled Jan Masaryk to endorse the exile government's actions in his father's name, confidently asserting his approval of its work in London and predicting he would have been particularly satisfied with certain events, such as the resignation of Mussolini.[286] This close relationship with the most prominent figure in the birth of Czechoslovakia gave Jan Masaryk an authority that no other speaker could boast, but he also made it personal. He spoke of his father with sentiment and shared family anecdotes that portrayed T. G. Masaryk with both affection and reverence; for example, he shared stories of how his father had started to ice-skate again in his fifties, putting his children to shame with his skills, or how he would make great jumps on horseback in his eighties, teasing Jan for his caution.[287] The son thereby invited listeners to join in this familial feeling and made them feel closer both to himself and to his father, who was simultaneously presented as a symbol of the exile government and its ideals. This connection between the past and future Czechoslovakia was extremely important to the exiles and, as the son of the President Liberator, Masaryk was a huge asset to them.

---

[283] Masaryk, *Volá Londýn* (1990), 53–54.
[284] Masaryk, *Volá Londýn* (1990), 125.
[285] Masaryk, *Volá Londýn* (1990), 133.
[286] Masaryk, *Volá Londýn* (1990), 188.
[287] Masaryk, *Volá Londýn* (1990), 148–49.

The informal atmosphere that Masaryk created in his broadcasts was also evident in his playful use of language and sense of humour, which distinguished him from his fellow government commentators. While all Czechoslovak exiles emphasised the cruel character of the German leaders, for example, Masaryk was the only one to openly poke fun at them in his talks. He labelled Göring an "out of breath gangster-marshal, fat as a eunuch," he mocked Goebbels as a celibate, and he referred to Hitler as *"Ersatzchickelgruber"* (mocking a family name) and "that Viennese upholsterer."[288] He frequently ridiculed Nazis and collaborators for their speeches and propaganda, but claimed to read transcripts rather than listen to the radio, not being able to bear the sounds of *"quislingčata."*[289] In a typical play on words, rather than using the standard Czech plural of *quislingové* (Quislings), Masaryk here used an irregular plural ending that often refers to young animals, presenting the simultaneously grotesque and humorous image of a litter of "baby quislings." When commenting on one of Hitler's speeches in November 1942, Masaryk noted dismissively that "I listened to it for a while – I couldn't have lasted a whole hour," on the grounds that the speech was *"hitlerovsky nechutné,"* using an adverb meaning "in the style of Hitler" to express that the talk was "distasteful" in a way only Hitler could be.[290]

The personal manner in which Masaryk spoke and the individual style that he brought to his talks implicitly distanced him from his official political role, but he also sought to do this explicitly. When he was occasionally obliged to impart government news and statements as part of his talks, Masaryk was at pains to differentiate between them and his normal, friendly chats. When he introduced a talk on the signing of an agreement with the Free French in 1942, Masaryk explained, "I am speaking to you today as the foreign minister of the Czechoslovak Republic and not simply as Jan Masaryk, which I do more gladly."[291] This separation of Masaryk the friendly broadcaster and Masaryk the foreign minister was perpetuated in other broadcasts too, such as a retrospective programme on the success of Masaryk's talks, produced by the LTS. In this programme, the announcer recalled Masaryk's broadcasts:

---

[288] Masaryk, *Volá Londýn* (1990), 169, 170, 172, 29.
[289] Masaryk, *Volá Londýn* (1990), 111.
[290] Masaryk, *Volá Londýn* (1990), 150.
[291] Masaryk, *Volá Londýn* (1990), 143.

We say simply Jan Masaryk because he did not speak only as the minister of foreign affairs but as a good Czechoslovak, a good European, the son of the eternal Tomáš Garrigue Masaryk, and simply as the man we came to know and love as Jan Masaryk.[292]

Even the BBC did not classify his talks as part of the official government programme for several years. Despite having held his ministerial post for several months, Masaryk did not broadcast in *Hovory s domovem* when he returned to London from the USA in September 1940. Instead, he resumed his Wednesday night slot that had become established before he left in June and continued to pass his own individual comment on the week's events. Given the difficulty in communicating changes in the broadcasting schedule to those forced to listen in secret, it is perhaps understandable that Masaryk was not rescheduled, but it is interesting to note that even the BBC Czech Section did not classify Masaryk's talks as government talks, perhaps indicating the status he enjoyed as a prominent broadcaster. It was not until the entire department was restructured in March 1943 that Masaryk's talks, which were much less regular by this point, were incorporated into the government's new programme, *Hlas svobodné republiky*.

By denying his official role for all but the most formal of announcements, the majority of Masaryk's talks were presented as purely personal, belying their political motivations and implications. As a government minister for all but the first few of his talks, Masaryk became one of the best-known voices of the exile government and his words were therefore not simply those of a private individual. Despite the perception of his talks by himself, by many of his listeners, and even by the BBC, as something separate from the official government programme, Masaryk was a senior minister who spoke on the same topics as his colleagues and voiced many of the same opinions. By doing so in his own words and in his own personal style, Masaryk appeared to recommend these views personally, and not by virtue of his official position, thereby lending the government line his own individual credibility.

Evidence of the positive reception of Masaryk's broadcasts, combined with their continued popularity today, would suggest this subtle approach to propaganda was successful. Early on, resistance groups inside the Protectorate reported to the London Czechoslovaks that "Jan

---

292 "Jan Masaryk mluví k lidu doma," undated, 202, BBC WBC, CRA.

Masaryk's Wednesdays are having a significant effect," and that "what the shepherd's [T. G. Masaryk's] son is saying is much liked."[293] Čestmír Jeřábek discussed Masaryk's broadcasts in his wartime diary, likening them to "conversations with a trusted friend who sits down at the table with us and speaks from heart to heart, letting out a joke or a quotation here and there, clapping us on the shoulder." Convinced that this informal style brought Masaryk closer to his listeners, the writer suggested that "his words are as easy for them to understand as Aleš's pictures or folk songs [...] They are simple and yet wise. You get the impression that Jan Masaryk gets the same joy from them as those to whom they are addressed, probably because they are sincere."[294] In the introduction to the 1948 Czech edition of Masaryk's published talks, Josef Kopta also concluded that listeners were won over by Masaryk's sincerity, suggesting that he opened his heart at the microphone – speaking "as if he were at confession" – and they opened their hearts to him in return.[295] Historians of propaganda have noted that subtle and indirect approaches can appeal to an audience, particularly when a saturation of direct propaganda leads to resentment.[296] Jeřábek's comments also suggest that Masaryk's personal tone was perceived by some as being pitched at exactly the right level for his audience, showing the deep understanding of his listener's context and background that characterises truly effective propaganda.[297]

---

293 Otáhalová and Červinková, *Dokumenty z historie*, 2:514–16.
294 Jeřábek, *V zajetí antikristově*, 59. Mikoláš Aleš (1852–1913) was a Czech painter, known for portraying national themes and supporting Czech causes in Austria-Hungary, such as the Czech National Theatre.
295 Josef Kopta, "Domov děkuje," in *Volá Londýn*, by Jan Masaryk (Prague: Práce/Lincolns-Prager, 1948), 11. The introduction by Kopta, a First World War legionary, was written in the spring of 1946 and included in editions of *Volá Londýn* published in 1947 and 1948. The 1948 edition makes no reference to Masaryk's death in March, so was presumably published very early in the year. Following the Communist takeover in February 1948, no further editions of *Volá Londýn* were published until 1990, and the work of the domestic resistance was strongly promoted over that of the London exiles.
296 In his 1940 book on propaganda, John Hargrave described this as the "Drop it in his tea" approach, indirectly propagating an idea in the audience's minds; see Hargrave, *Propaganda*, 111–16.
297 In his ground rules for effective propaganda, Charles Roetter listed "a clear idea and knowledge of the target which is being aimed at" as being of critical importance; Roetter, *Psychological Warfare*, 14. An effective propagandist, according to Roetter, bases their arguments on the opinions of their audience, not their own.

Exercising Authority: The *odsun* and "Rabble-rousing" from London

By the various means outlined above, the representatives of the government-in-exile under President Beneš sought to establish themselves as the legitimate legal and ideological leaders of Czechoslovakia, who understood the suffering of the home population and shared with them a common view of the world and the war. A study of the wartime broadcasts also shows how they then strove to exert this authority from abroad by issuing orders and instructions to listeners. Early in the conflict, these orders were often immediate reactions to events taking place at home: for example, in spring 1941 Beneš's government broadcast a warning that any Czech student who obeyed the calls to attend a high school in the German Reich would be barred from Czech higher education once the occupation ended; and at the end of the year the government reminded the public that it did not respect the transfer of any state or government property that had taken place since September 1938.[298] The above-mentioned press boycott of September 1941 is an example of a more extensive campaign that was broadly successful, but, as the end of the conflict approached, the government programme featured more specific instructions to prepare the ground for liberation. From 1944 onwards, broadcasters issued appeals and directions on topics such as the formation of national committees to take over power once occupying and collaborationist authorities had been deposed. Despite the success of some of these appeals from London, study of one of the most significant postwar policies, that of the transfer of Czechoslovakia's German population, raises questions about the moral implications of exercising this authority from a distance.

In promoting the press boycott of 1941, the exiles had relied upon the authority of the name of T. G. Masaryk, but they had grown more assertive by April 1944, when they broadcast a declaration on the formation of national committees. Though the topic had been mentioned previously, as a way to ensure that "it is the Czechoslovak people who will, from the very beginning, be the bearers and executors of state power in the liberated Republic," the declaration differed by giving a list of

---

[298] BBC Czechoslovak Programme, 5 April 1941, LN Z 1941 – 6; 19 December 1941, LN Z 1941 – 11, CRA.

clear instructions on the formation of the committees and their duties.[299] The announcement ended with an authoritative call to "Citizens of the Republic!" and encouraging words issued in the government's own name:

> the government announces the organisational principles of the national committees at this time with the conviction that the leadership of the state can only be protected on the road from slavery to freedom by the devotion and loyalty of the sons and daughters of the nation.

The declaration then concluded with a reminder of the government's unity with the people at home: "to end the battle and build peace, to drive out the tyrants and renew and perfect social order in the Republic, this is now the duty of us all."[300] Listeners to the broadcasts to Subcarpathian Ruthenia were repeatedly urged to form national committees from then on, and there were also appeals to young people, workers, and, as liberation approached, residents of western Bohemia.[301]

Despite having made the declaration in its own name, the government-in-exile was keen to show listeners that the concept of national committees had support elsewhere: listeners heard quotations from *The New York Times* in favour of the plans and were told that Czechoslovakia would probably be liberated early to serve as a "positive example" to others.[302] The exiles were also careful to present the proposed system of national committees as being approved of across the political spectrum, re-broadcasting the message of support from Klement Gottwald, the Moscow-based leader of the Czechoslovak Communist Party (Komunistická strana Československa).[303] The word of the exile government was therefore reinforced by association with other authoritative sources

---

[299] From a talk by Communist Vilém Nový; BBC Czechoslovak Programme, 11 April 1944, LN Z 1944 – 31, CRA.

[300] The government declaration was broadcast on 16 April 1944 in Czech and repeated the following day in Slovak and Ukrainian; BBC Czechoslovak Programme, 16 April 1944; 17 April 1944, LN Z 1944 – 32, CRA.

[301] Examples of Ukrainian-language appeals can be found in BBC Czechoslovak Programme, 24 April 1944, LN Z 1944 – 31; 1 May 1944, LN Z 1944 – 32; 6 November 1944, LN Z 1944 – 37, CRA. An appeal to youth was made on 19 April 1944 (LN Z 1944 – 31), to western Bohemia on 20 April 1945 (LN Z 1945 – 45), and to workers in the last few days of the war (7 May 1945, LN Z 1945 – 46, CRA).

[302] BBC Czechoslovak Programme, 24 April 1944, LN Z 1944 – 32, CRA. In fact, Czechoslovakia was one of the last countries in Europe to be liberated and fighting continued in Prague until after the official announcement of peace on 8 May 1945.

[303] BBC Czechoslovak Programme, 5 May 1944, LN Z 1944 – 32, CRA.

in the USA and USSR, suggesting that London alone was perhaps not considered to be influential enough. The formation of national committees was not the only pressing issue for the post-war settlement, however, and the "German question" was also raised in the exile government's broadcasts.

It has been estimated that approximately seven million German-speaking people were expelled from Czechoslovakia, Poland, Romania, Yugoslavia, and Hungary between 1945 and 1948, in addition to the approximately five million who had already moved westwards from Germany's easternmost territories in the face of the Soviet advance from 1944 onwards. This remains the greatest movement of displaced persons in modern European history.[304] The post-war "transfer," both managed and "wild," of Czechoslovakia's German population remains a contentious issue to this day and has been described as "one of the most sensitive topics in modern Czech history."[305] Even the choice of terminology used to discuss it can be divisive, as the most commonly used Czech term – *odsun* (transfer) – is deemed to be too passive and neutral by some, who suggest that *vyhnání* (expulsion) or *nucené vysídlení* (forced resettlement) would more accurately denote the violence that was involved.[306] The *odsun* and its consequences recur in discussions of mod-

---

[304] Figures are taken from Mark Mazower, *Dark Continent: Europe's Twentieth Century* (London: Allen Lane, 1998), 220.
[305] Mark Cornwall, *The Devil's Wall: The Nationalist Youth Mission of Heinz Rutha* (Cambridge, MA: Harvard University Press, 2012), 7. The ongoing sensitivities were made clear by the outcry from several quarters following the 1992 signing of the Czechoslovak–German Treaty on Good Neighbourliness and Friendly Co-operation, and the subsequent wrangling about its successor following the split of Czechoslovakia (a Czech–German declaration confirming the treaty was finally signed in 1997). Some on the Czech side warned it contained clauses which would undermine the post-war settlement, and Sudeten German organisations complained that there "could be no friendship or co-operation until their grievances were settled." So pivotal is this period in Czech–German relations that Jürgen Tampke referred to this controversy in his introduction to *Czech-German Relations and the Politics of Central Europe: From Bohemia to the EU* (Basingstoke: Palgrave Macmillan, 2003), xiii; discussed in detail on ibid., 145–50.
[306] Tomáš Staněk notes the different terminology used on different sides of the historical debate, commenting that "West German literature rarely uses the terms 'transfer' or '*odsun*' (Abschub) to describe the forced post-war migration of Germans from Central and Eastern Europe, but rather expressions which are intended to emphasise the violent element of these acts (*vyhnání* [expulsion], *zapuzení* [banishment], *vypovězení* [eviction] and others – *Austreibung, Vertreibung, Ausweisung*, etc.)"; Tomáš Staněk, *Odsun Němců z Československa, 1945–1947* (Prague: Academia/ Naše vojsko, 1991), 384n8. A study by Václav Smyčka on the terms used in the hypertext of the German and Czech Wikipedia pages related to the subject suggests that debate over terms continues (see Smyčka, "Dějiny zachycené v síti," *Dějiny-Teorie-Kritika* (January 2014): 93–107), as does the title of a 2021 PhD thesis by Simon Ullrich at the University of Graz, "*Odsun/ Vyhnání*: The Eviction of the German-Speaking Minority from the Republic of Czechoslovakia 1945/46 and Its Reception in Austrian Newspapers." In terms of the violence of the process,

ern Czech–German relations, and historians such as Benjamin Frommer have sought to examine the crimes committed in the process, overlooked at the time and for decades afterwards.[307] Plans for the transfer of the German population of Czechoslovakia began well before the end of the conflict, however, and received tacit approval from the Allies from 1942.[308] The progression of Beneš's policy towards Czechoslovakia's German minority from one of territorial concessions to enforced transfer is documented elsewhere but, given the prominence of the topic in studies of twentieth-century Czech and European history, and its strong association with the exile government, it would be remiss to omit to examine references to the topic in the wartime broadcasts.[309]

Beneš's name remains closely associated with the fate of Czechoslovakia's German population, immortalised in the shorthand term for the orders authorising the transfer: the "Beneš decrees." However, in comparison with what was to come, Beneš's early proposals were very lenient, involving population exchanges, a possible canton system, and even the cession of some territory to the post-war German state. These plans immediately met with strong opposition from home resistance organisations such as ÚVOD, who criticised Beneš for his "damned cantons" and warned that "the people will tear you to pieces."[310] Since the end of Communism in Central Europe, scholarly works on the *odsun*

Tampke notes the widely variable estimates of deaths caused during or as a direct result of the transfer (West German estimates from the 1950s to 1980s put the figure over 200,000), but he feels recent figures of approximately 30,000 to be more plausible; see Tampke, *Czech-German Relations*, 93.

307 See Benjamin Frommer, *National Cleansing: Retribution against Collaborators in Postwar Czechoslovakia* (Cambridge: Cambridge University Press, 2005). Czechoslovak President Václav Havel officially apologised for the *odsun* in 1990, causing considerable outcry, but no German government has sought to pursue compensation or other claims on behalf of displaced persons or their descendants; see Tampke, *Czech-German Relations*, esp. 143–45. A project by the group Antikomplex to map the changes in the Czech border regions before and after the transfer of the German population resulted in a book and a travelling photography exhibition that was on tour from 2002. Comments collected from visitors show a wide range of responses and reveal the continuing divisive nature of the topic; see Antikomplex et al., *Zmizelé Sudety/Das verschwundene Sudetenland* (Domažlice: Český les, 2004).

308 Britain agreed to the "general principle of a transfer" by September 1942 and officially informed the Czechoslovaks of this agreement; see C 11244/9894/12, FO 371/34355, TNA. There was a fear, expressed by Lockhart in a letter of June 1945, that seeming to oppose population transfers could push Czech public support away from Britain and towards the USSR, which openly supported the plans; Lockhart to J. B. Clark, 28 August 1945, FO 898/220, TNA.

309 In his study of resistance in the Protectorate, Vojtěch Mastný attributed the radicalisation of Beneš's policy to increasing pressure from ÚVOD from August 1941; see Mastný, *Czechs under Nazi Rule*, 175. For an outline of Beneš's attempts to compromise on the Sudeten German question, see Brandes, *Češi pod německým porotektorátem*, 483.

310 Communications from ÚVOD quoted in Bryant, *Prague in Black*, 100.

have sought to show how Beneš's view was radicalised by the domestic resistance movement, and he was indeed forced to become increasingly radical in his approach in order to protect his own authority and keep up with public opinion at home.[311] The tone of Beneš's speeches also underwent a profound change, and there is plenty of evidence in his wartime broadcasts to justify Robert Pynsent's description of him as "something of a rabble-rouser."[312] The language and arguments used in many of the government's broadcasts encouraged the dehumanisation of the German population and revenge upon individual Germans for the crimes committed by Nazi Germany as a whole.

Beneš's early speeches acknowledged that not all of Czechoslovakia's German population had allied themselves with the fascist movement, but his tone changed quickly. In November 1939 Beneš referred to the "wise and progressive Germans among us" who "stood united with us against Nazism," and he included German citizens within his imagined audience of Czechoslovak listeners.[313] In his speech of 24 July 1940, Beneš explained that the illegality of everything carried out since Munich applied equally to "all of us here and for all members of our state and our nation, for Czechs, Slovaks, Germans, Carpathorusyns, and others at home."[314] After the appointment of Reinhard Heydrich and the associated increase in oppression in the Protectorate, Beneš began to take a more anti-German stance, and the idea of collective German responsibility for Nazi crimes was expressed by many different speakers across the broadcasts. Beneš warned as early as October 1941 that Heydrich's crimes "only serve to seal his own fate, that of his masters and helpers, and – no matter how various people excuse what is happening – that of

---

311 In the introduction to her book of documents relating to the transfer, Jitka Vondrová expressed a desire to support a more "objective" explanation of the circumstances that led to the transfer, noting that Beneš is often unfairly attributed with almost sole responsibility for the hardships suffered by the Germans who were forced to leave Czechoslovakia; Vondrová, *Češi a sudetoněmecká otázka, 1939–1945: Dokumenty* (Prague: Ústav mezinárodních vztahů, 1994), 5. Chad Bryant notes that the first suggestions for the expulsion of the German population came from ÚVOD. On the influence of the home resistance on Beneš's view, see Bryant, *Prague in Black*, 97–103. For examples of communication between London and the home resistance on this matter, see Vondrová, *Češi a sudetoněmecká otázka*, esp. 77–80, 264–65.
312 Pynsent, "Activists, Jews," 314. Here, Pynsent is referencing Tomáš Staněk, *Poválečné "excesy" v českých zemích v roce 1945 a jejich vyšetřování* (Prague: Ústav pro soudobé dějiny Akademie věd České republiky, 2005); and Staněk and Adrian von Arburg, "Organizované divoké odsuny?," *Soudobé dějiny* 3–4 (2005): 465–533.
313 Beneš, *Šest let exilu*, 40. This speech can also be heard in "Beneš: Proč bojujeme," undated, 43–45, BBC WBC, CRA.
314 Beneš, *Šest let exilu*, 53.

the German nation. It is and will be the judgement of history: *the retribution which is coming will be terrible.*"[315] Jan Masaryk presented the idea of military aggression as being inherent to all Germans in a broadcast of 1941, in which he drew historical parallels with the military campaigns of previous Germanic states: "the entire German population has been overtaken by that animalistically egotistical Prusso-Nazi mentality." In 1942 he predicted a punishment that would not discriminate between active and passive participants, warning that "not only the Nazis but the whole German nation" would pay for the invasion of Czechoslovakia.[316]

One of the earliest references to population transfers in the government programme was in a talk by Prokop Drtina on 24 October 1943. In this programme, Drtina claimed that "Munich proved what a dangerous instrument Germans in Bohemia and Moravia always are in the hands of Berlin's militaristic Pan-Germanism," and cautioned that the Czechoslovak German minority was "dangerous for European equilibrium, European peace, and European freedom." Citing recent statements from the Protectorate to support his argument, Drtina went on to explain that the German population had been well-treated in the First Republic but had become determined to destroy the state regardless. A new solution was now necessary, Drtina suggested, and he indirectly introduced the possibility of transfer when he stated that the Czech population could not leave the territory because "we have no other, and because it belongs to us historically, politically, and morally," implying therefore that the territory did not belong to the Germans and that they did have somewhere else to go. Without directly recommending the transfer of the German population, Drtina strongly insinuated his support for the idea by quoting the phrase of nineteenth-century writer Karel Havlíček Borovský, "Germany is yours, but Bohemia is ours." Since the "whole world" knew that "this new world war broke out because of them," it was "only fair that they bear its consequences,"[317] Drtina concluded.

Though Beneš was somewhat more circumspect in his speeches, his references to the question of the German minority do reveal an increasingly extreme policy, possibly in response to the hard line he knew was demanded by the home resistance. The president told listeners that allies such as the United States considered the question to be an "internal

---

315 Beneš, *Šest let exilu*, 81. Emphasis in original.
316 Talks given on 10 September 1941 and 23 December 1942, quoted in Masaryk, *Volá Londýn* (1990), 120, 161.
317 Drtina, *A nyní promluví*, 369–72.

matter" which would be left for Czechoslovakia to decide, and that the Soviet Union hoped for the post-war republic to be "as nationally homogenous as possible."[318] On 27 October 1944 he argued that "the German nation is guilty like no other in the world, the German nation therefore deserves punishment and the German nation and state will receive this punishment." Beneš concluded that accounts would be settled with "our Germans, who stabbed our state in the back in 1938," and that all those who were guilty – which he had thus expanded to include all Germans – "must go."[319] In his Christmas speech of 1944, Beneš promised listeners a "radical" solution to "the problem of our Germans," but offered no details on what that would involve.[320] In February 1945, before the legal structure for the transfer was put in place, Beneš's choice of words in promising listeners a "final solution to the questions of our Germans and Hungarians" carried chilling connotations of Nazi rhetoric.[321]

As the war progressed – and notably after the *Heydrichiáda*, the wave of violent repression in the Protectorate following the assassination of Reinhard Heydrich – Germans were increasingly dehumanised within the broadcasts, and violence against them was praised. After seeing a Soviet film in December 1942, Masaryk admitted that though he "didn't used to like seeing dead people," he "couldn't have imagined how pleasant it would be to look on a dead German."[322] Masaryk told his listeners in January 1943, "you must work day and night and beat the German wherever you can," assuring them that they had every right to take the law into their own hands.[323] During his speech on the 25th anniversary of the founding of Czechoslovakia in October 1943, Beneš told listeners that "For us, the end of this war will be written in blood. There will be fighting in our country just as everywhere else on the European continent and the Germans will be paid back mercilessly and many times over for every deed they have committed in our lands since 1938."[324] In the last days of the government programme, on 9 May 1945, head of broadcasting Josef Kodíček offered this pre-emptive justification for anti-German action: "[The Germans] forgot that the Czech nation has the right to consider every German in the Czech lands a violent criminal and an

---

318 Speeches given on 24 June and 21 December 1943, quoted in Beneš, *Šest let exilu*, 134, 144.
319 Beneš, *Šest let exilu*, 152, 154.
320 Beneš, *Šest let exilu*, 158.
321 Beneš, *Šest let exilu*, 162.
322 Masaryk, *Volá Londýn* (1990), 161.
323 Masaryk, *Volá Londýn* (1990), 166.
324 Beneš, *Šest let exilu*, 139.

invader (if they are a soldier), a looter and an invader (if they are a civilian), and an invader and a killer (if it is a member of the Gestapo or the SS)."[325] Although the "organised" population transfer was not to officially begin until January 1946, the "wild" transfers from May 1945 onwards saw widespread vigilante violence against Czechoslovak Germans for which many perpetrators were not held accountable.[326] The language used by politicians when referring to the German population continued to grow more radical once they returned to liberated Czechoslovak territory, but the foundations had been laid with the already aggressive rhetoric of their wartime broadcasts, which condoned violence against any and all Germans as representatives of a guilty nation. The leader of the Czechoslovak-German Social Democrats in London, Wenzel Jaksch, later accused the Czechoslovak exiles of using speeches like that of Beneš to make "frank appeals to bloodshed," and Benjamin Frommer has suggested that the exiles "consciously desired, planned, and executed" the wild transfer, whipping up vigilante feeling that would drive out much of the German population, thereby obviating the need for organised transfer.[327] Although Frommer mostly cites the work of Czechoslovak leaders after liberation, a study of the wartime broadcasts reveals an increasingly savage and vengeful tone in all mentions of the Czechoslovak Germans that began well before the transfer itself and later contributed to the apparent legitimisation of public acts of aggression.

* * *

The Czechoslovak government-in-exile relied on its wartime propaganda to perform its authority and establish its legitimacy as a government. Once established, this claim to authority was used to encourage the listening public to participate in acts of resistance (such as the boycott of the Protectorate press), to prepare themselves for the post-war settlement through the formation of national committees, and to assert their right to revenge against Czechoslovakia's German population. Although the arguments for legal authority that featured prominently in the exile government's diplomatic work were less frequently referred to in its

---

[325] BBC Czechoslovak Programme, 9 May 1945, LN Z 1945 – 46, CRA.
[326] For a discussion of the events of the *divoký odsun*, "wild transfer," see Frommer, *National Cleansing*, 33–62. See also Tomáš Staněk, *Odsun Němců z Československa*.
[327] Wenzel Jaksch, *Europe's Road to Potsdam* (London: Thames & Hudson, 1963), 373, 441n6; Frommer, *National Cleansing*, 40, 61.

propaganda, the same theme of continuity played an important role in the establishment of its ideological authority. By presenting listeners with an idealised image of the pre-war period and tying the ideals and successes of that era with their own political agenda, the exiles sought to win the support and loyalty of listeners, and to legitimise their own position as part of an established tradition of exile in Czech history that stretched back several centuries. Much of the wartime propaganda on the legacy of the First Republic served to further entrench the myth that had already been established in the interwar republic, and the image of T. G. Masaryk as the embodiment of Czechoslovak principles was important to the exile government's extrapolation of its own authority as a perpetuation of his. The charismatic authority of President Beneš was enhanced by repeated assertions of his wisdom and foresight, encouraging listeners to feel that the Czechoslovak cause was in safe hands. Some of the most effective propaganda produced by the exiles was less overtly political, however, and broadcasters such as Jan Masaryk sought to appeal to listeners on a personal level and create a sense of unity between the government and the people. In his final talk from London, Ripka characterised this connection between government and public in a new way, as he claimed that *Hlas svobodné republiky* had never hoped to be more or less than "the interpreter of the feelings and wishes of its people, whom the enemy deprived of the freedom of speech and expression."[328] Ripka sought to present the government programme as the mouthpiece of the public rather than politicians, repeating Körbel's assertion from the first broadcast of *Hlas svobodné republiky*, that the voice the audience heard was "your voice, the voice of the Czechoslovak people."[329] In reality, however, the exiles spoke *to* listeners more than they spoke *for* them, using the radio to shape their audience into a willing public.

---

[328] BBC Czechoslovak Programme, 11 May 1945, LN Z 1945 – 46, CRA.
[329] BBC Czechoslovak Programme, 29 March 1943, LN Z 1943 – 19, CRA.

Chapter Two

Populating the "Free Republic": Performing Nationhood over the Radio

The "free republic" of the Czechoslovak government programme was an alternative Czechoslovakia, an aural space impervious to enemy occupation and the setting for a performance of Czechoslovak nationhood intended to win the loyalty of listeners, the imagined citizens of this space. In the creation of different national services and huge efforts in the field of foreign-language broadcasting, the wartime BBC facilitated the creation of an alternative Europe in the words of her exiles, an imagined continent made up of free nations which listeners in occupied territories could figuratively inhabit as they listened to London.[330] For the duration of a given programme, divided and oppressed populations could hear themselves once more being addressed as a united, national whole, and join together in an "imagined community" of listeners.[331] These imagined countries were governed by different leaders and, within them, the music, literature, and national celebrations suppressed under occupation could once again be honoured. In order to persuade their audience to identify as members of these alternative national communities and obey the instructions they received from London, broadcasters had to ensure their programming felt authentic to listeners. This chapter will argue that the medium of radio is well-suited to this national

---

[330] See Hilary Footitt and Simona Tobia, *War Talk: Foreign Languages and the British War Effort in Europe, 1940–1947* (Basingstoke: Palgrave Macmillan, 2013), 71–80. Between 1938 and 1942 the BBC established broadcasting in twenty-two different European languages; see Mansell, *Let Truth Be Told*, 57, 122.

[331] For more on "imagined communities," see Benedict Anderson, *Imagined Communities: Reflections on the Origin and Spread of Nationalism* (London: Verso, 2006).

purpose and that the exiled Czechoslovaks used their broadcasts to present a carefully crafted version of Czechoslovak nationhood. To this end, they employed an established national narrative and familiar cultural products to attract their audience at home and populate their figurative "free republic" with self-identifying Czechoslovak citizens who were willing to follow their lead.

From the British point of view, popular and convincing foreign-language broadcasts were a useful means of promoting the Allied cause and inciting resistance in occupied Europe; but for the exile governments gathered in London, there was much more at stake.[332] In the case of Czechoslovakia, in addition to the challenge made to the state's legal existence by Slovakia's secession and the German occupation, the very concept of the state was under attack from enemy authorities in both the Protectorate and Slovakia. While the campaign to ensure legal recognition of the continuation of Czechoslovakia as a state formed the centre of President Beneš's wartime diplomatic work, all the exile government's propaganda, both that aimed at its allies and at its own population, intended to perpetuate the *idea* of Czechoslovakia. The only way in which this idea could be preserved was by ensuring that people continued to identify with it, by the willing participation of former Czechoslovak citizens in an imagined community of Czechoslovaks. The ability to broadcast over long distances on short wave meant that exiled politicians did not lose contact with their publics when they lost access to newspapers and printing presses, but could instead transmit their ideas to a huge audience across international borders. Broadcasting from London, the exile government could transmit simultaneously to listeners across Europe a united national message in the form of a speech, a piece of music, or a poem, reaching out to anyone who identified with it, regardless of their location at the time.

The imagined community has become something of a cliché in studies of both nationalism and media, but its relevance to both exile politics and exile broadcasting is striking. Exile governments, lacking as they do any executive or legislative power, depend on recognition and belief, both on the part of their allies and their subjects. Winning recognition from allies is the most effective way to be sure of taking power once the territory has been liberated, but, in order to earn that recognition and

---

[332] For more on the BBC's approach to using exile governments for the establishment of "radio leadership," see the Introduction; and "The Role of Free Time," undated, E2/10, BBC WAC.

to hold power beyond the immediate aftermath of conflict, exile politicians – and their authority – must be accepted by the home population too. The former citizens of Czechoslovakia were not being "governed" by the exiles in London in any legal sense, and any authority the exile government wielded was based entirely on the willingness of listeners to mentally align themselves with and imagine themselves to be citizens of the "free republic" which was created in its programming. In their broadcasts, exile politicians interpreted historical and cultural themes that were familiar to their audience and drew parallels with the present time, to build up a conception of national identity which listeners could use to interpret the current conflict and their place within it. Nineteenth-century traditions of nation-building were thus re-deployed via the twentieth-century technology of radio.

The experience of the Second World War mounted a challenge to existing national perceptions, and memories of the conflict continue to influence national discourse across the world today. In some states, as in 1930s' Germany, the status quo had come under attack and the Nazi Party presented a radical new interpretation of what it meant to be German, eliminating all culture it deemed to be "degenerate."[333] Elsewhere, in countries such as Britain, the experiences of the war have been adopted into stereotypes that continue to influence popular understandings of national identity long after the conflict itself, emerging again in references to national characteristics such as the "Blitz spirit."[334] In the Czechoslovak context, authorities in the Protectorate and the newly declared Slovak government both began a rigorous reinterpretation of Czech and Slovak identity, which attempted to discredit the concept of a shared identity that had been promoted during the First Czechoslovak Republic. Through administrative changes and directives, the Germans

---

[333] An interesting recent study of Nazi interpretations of what German culture was and should be is Jost Hermand, *Culture in Dark Times: Nazi Fascism, Inner Emigration, and Exile* (New York: Berghahn Books, 2013).

[334] The lingering influence of the Second World War on British, and particularly English, national identity has continued to the present day. As Richard Weight wrote, "the comforting warmth of Churchillian legends and myths appealed to all classes, sexes and ages, including millions who were not even born during the conflict"; Weight, *Patriots: National Identity in Britain 1940–2000* (Basingstoke: Macmillan, 2002), 15. Historians since the end of the Cold War have sought to re-examine the way the war has been remembered. A range of interesting studies are contained in Lucy Noakes and Juliette Pattinson, eds., *British Cultural Memory and the Second World War* (London: Bloomsbury Academic, 2014). These include Penny Summerfield's examination of the impact that memory of the conflict has had on later generations; see "The Generation of Memory: Gender and the Popular Memory of the Second World War in Britain," in ibid., 25–45.

prohibited any public reference to Czech culture as something distinct and separate from German culture, and to historical conflicts between the Bohemian crown lands and Germanic states. German propaganda offices across Europe instead sought to emphasise the Czech region's political and cultural reliance on Germany, presenting Bohemia and Moravia to the home population and to the world as a natural, historical part of Germanic Europe.[335]

Much German propaganda involved the reinterpretation of Czech history and legends in a pro-German light, and the Czechoslovak government programme sought to counter these attacks by reminding listeners of the Czechoslovak identity that had been popularised in the interwar period, also drawing on nineteenth-century symbols and narratives to do so. This identity was defined in many ways by its opposition to all things Germanic, and the war gave ample opportunity to trace a narrative of German aggression back through history.

The Czechoslovak government-in-exile did not explicitly discuss its own work in terms of nation-building; its goal was simply the unification of the listening audience and the strengthening of their will to resist the Axis powers. However, exile governments all work towards a different future for their nation, a more favourable situation in which they can return from exile, and this chapter argues that the exiles participated in the creation and curation of an imagined community, mindful of their place in a tradition going back at least to the Czech National Revival and most recently evoked during the establishment of the First Republic. As well as actively guiding listeners in how best to interpret their own history and nationhood, they also sought to provide the audience with programming they believed they wanted: cultural content such as music and poetry, as well as humorous content like dramatised dialogues. These programmes also played on shared ideas and experiences, reminding listeners of the ties that connected them both with the broadcasters themselves and with the rest of the audience. The fact that the idea of a unified national identity can be found behind such a diverse range of

---

335 In late 1941, German propaganda offices in Oslo, Prague, the Hague, Brussels, Paris, and Krakow received instructions to suppress any and all references to Czech culture (as distinct from German culture), any ties between different Slav nations, and any references to historical conflict between Czechs and Germans (such as the Hussite wars and the legions of the First World War), and to promote the idea of the territory belonging to the Germanic cultural sphere; see Eva Ješutová, ed., *Od mikrofonu k posluchačům: Z osmi desetiletí českého rozhlasu* (Prague: Český rozhlas, 2003), 163.

programming shows how fundamental it was to the propaganda work of the exile government.

Efforts to create a sense of unity can be seen in the smallest details of the government programme. After the exile government was awarded "free time" in March 1943, the programme was relaunched as *Hlas svobodné republiky* (*Voice of the Free Republic*), with Josef Suk's *V nový život* (*Towards a New Life*) as its introductory music. Listeners were told that both the title and the music had been chosen to "symbolically express the political task of our broadcasts." Suk's march was dedicated to the patriotic athletics organisation Sokol and had been played at its large-scale festivals in the First Republic, and it was the feeling of these events that broadcasters hoped to conjure up:

> All Czechoslovak people, from Prague to the remote villages of Subcarpathian Ruthenia, connect Suk's glorious march with unique memories of the united formations along the ramparts at Strahov, when the entire nation – without any differences in political thought – followed with awe and wonder the Sokol recruits of the republic.

Reminding listeners of the national solidarity shown at the last Sokol festival in July 1938, radio editor Josef Körbel claimed the music would "resonate in the spirits of all loyal Czechoslovaks," and he drew a parallel between the synchronised mass aerobic displays of the Sokol and the spiritual unity of the nation as a whole, in the phrase "one body, one spirit." [336]

Czechoslovak government broadcasters made use of established historical interpretations and cultural products to reinforce a feeling of unity in their audience and associate both themselves and their listeners with a continuing sense of Czechoslovak national identity; but this approach was not without its difficulties. The identity projected in the broadcasts drew heavily on the inherited traditions of the First Czechoslovak Republic, both in terms of historical narrative and in the dominance of everything Czech over anything Slovak in the cultural field. Part of this can be explained by the differing political situations in the Protectorate and in Slovakia; for the former, propagandists in London had to combat the German reinterpretation of Czech history and its appropriation of elements in Czech culture as signs of Germanic influence; while in

---

[336] BBC Czechoslovak Programme, 29 March 1943, LN Z 1943 – 19, CRA.

Slovakia, the Bratislava government had taken on the mantle of Slovak nationalism. As will be discussed in Chapter Three, broadcasting to Slovakia favoured political themes over cultural topics, and the Slovaks were to enjoy considerably fewer references to their poetry, music, and literature than Czech listeners. Specific references to Slovak history were also rare and, when it did feature in the broadcasts, it was only ever to reinforce the idea of the Slovaks' political unity with the Czechs. While the various opportunities provided by radio were exploited in the creation of a unifying national image, both its historical and cultural elements were almost totally dominated by the Czech identity.

Radio as a Medium for Nation-Building

By its very nature as a medium of mass communication, radio helps to form communities. In the first instance, radio unites listeners in a single aural experience; by the act of listening to a broadcast, whether individually or in a group, the audience enters into a community of "listeners" and gains an awareness of the existence of other members of this community. There was a second unifying factor among listeners in the wartime context, however, since they were all also taking a risk by tuning into London. Listening to foreign broadcasts was banned in the Protectorate from 1 September 1939, and cards were issued to be attached to the front of wireless sets, reminding listeners that the crime was punishable by imprisonment or even death.[337] Given this danger, listeners not only had to make the conscious effort to listen, but also had to take security measures while listening. They also had to overcome certain technical difficulties in order to listen, such as Nazi attempts to jam incoming broadcasts and, in 1943, to disable short-wave receivers.[338] The greater effort

---

337 Ješutová, *Od mikrofonu k posluchačům*, 158. Listening to banned broadcasts was included in the lists of charges used in some cases of execution but it was rarely a principal charge. The BBC considered such charges more as efforts to remind the increasingly disobedient population of the ban; SEA, EOCOTF (Central-Southern Europe), 2 November 1942, p. 2, 44/42, EIP series 1c (b), E2/192/6, BBC WAC.

338 BBC intelligence reports provided information of the ordered confiscation and disabling of all shortwave receivers in the Protectorate; "BBC Bi-Monthly Intelligence Report: Europe," 28 April 1943, 18/43, EIP series 1a, E2/185, BBC WAC; SEA, EOCOTF (South East Europe), 10 May 1943, 20/43, EIP series 1c, E2/192/6, BBC WAC. The BBC also issued instructions on how to repair disabled sets to continue listening to London, congratulating itself that "The BBC advised the Czechs how they might circumvent these measures, and there is evidence that the Germans have not succeeded in appreciably decreasing listening to London"; *BBC Yearbook*

invested in listening and the greater danger associated with doing so meant listeners had a larger-than-average emotional stake in the broadcasts they listened to. Listeners claimed to sit by the radio with bated breath and to rely on the broadcasts for support; in the words of one listener in the Protectorate, "London is the only thing to feed the soul."[339] It is possible that the sense of community among listeners was heightened as a consequence of this greater emotional investment, enhanced by the knowledge that others were taking the same risks to listen. BBC intelligence reports on listening habits in Europe gathered testimony from Czech listeners who were confident that "all Czechs" were listening to London.[340] This assertion, which at most could be based on a small amount of anecdotal evidence, highlights this sense of community, since it shows the assumption that other people perceived to share some common ties – fellow Czechs – must have the same listening habits and be of one mind when it came to propaganda from London.

Media such as radio can thus be used to engender a sense of community among users but also to form or reinforce association with wider groups, such as nations. When listening to, reading, or viewing media, consumers gain an awareness of other people within the audience, and therefore of themselves as part of a community, bonded by shared interests. Benedict Anderson identified a linguistic element to this characteristic when he traced it back to the very beginning of the print media and the earliest production of written texts in local vernaculars, arguing that those who could read them became aware of other readers and writers who shared the same language.[341] Any broadcast message thus promotes a sense of community on the basis of inclusion; it includes those who understand and identify with the message and excludes those who do not. Discussing wartime broadcasts (or acknowledging secret listening) often required an additional level of coded language that may have furthered a feeling of in-group camaraderie among listeners, excluding non-listeners and Germans. British intelligence reported advertisements for "The Tale of Honza" in Žižkov windows in 1941, noting that "it took

---

1944 (London: BBC, 1944), 77. Stories of resourceful listeners repairing sets with homemade *čerčilky* dials, named in honour of Churchill, are recorded in Koutek, "Zahraniční odboj," 37; Bednařík, Jirák, and Köpplová, *Dějiny českých médií*, 214.
[339] Jeřábek, *V zajetí antikristově*, 80; "BBC Bi-Monthly Intelligence Report: Europe," 16 September 1941, 38/41, EIP series 1a, E2/185, BBC WAC.
[340] "BBC Bi-Monthly Intelligence Report: Europe," 18 June 1942, 25/42, EIP series 1a, E2/185, BBC WAC.
[341] Anderson, *Imagined Communities*, 40–44.

the German authorities some time to discover that the placards were an advertisement for M. Masaryk's broadcasts in Czech from London."[342] Ernest Gellner has argued that this creation of a community and the inherent associated exclusion of those outside that community is an intrinsic feature of the mass media which helps to further the sense of the national community. While this argument is persuasive, especially in reference to a time before the commercialisation of radio, where much broadcasting carried out in Europe was state-sponsored, Gellner's emphasis on the comprehension of the message, rather than its content, distracts attention from other interesting areas of study.

Gellner argues that "abstract, centralized, standardized, one to many communication," as part of the wider changes in society in the modern era, "automatically engenders the core idea of nationalism," and that this effect is achieved "quite irrespective of what in particular is being put into the specific messages transmitted."[343] As well as seeming to disregard the fact that all products of the media are designed by individuals who draw on their own inherited sense of national identity in formulating their messages, Gellner's argument also overlooks the significance of the decisions behind the chosen message. National identity and a sense of national community are not concepts that can be spontaneously generated in the wake of new technology; they are subjective and shifting collections of myths, associations, and symbols which appeal to historical linguistic and ethnic ties.[344] In order for a particular national consciousness or identity to become established, it must be based on a proximity among peoples which already exists and is accepted as genuine. As Karl Deutsch put it,

> If Ruritanians do not communicate more easily with each other than with outsiders, if they cannot understand more readily each other's behaviour, and if they do not experience more quickly or drastically the effects of

---

342 Honza is a common Czech nickname for people called Jan, and Czech folk and fairy tales often feature a character called Honza; "Intelligence Report," 27 January 1941, Intelligence Reports: Czechoslovakia, C 52/52/12, FO 371/26380, TNA.
343 Ernest Gellner, *Nations and Nationalism* (Malden, MA: Blackwell, 2006), 121–22.
344 Although nationalism as a political movement is a relatively modern development, it must also be acknowledged that the idea of kinship among ethnic and linguistic communities which already existed provided a basis for later nationalist movements in many instances. On nationalism as a modern notion, see Eric Hobsbawm, *Nations and Nationalism since 1780: Programme, Myth, Reality* (Cambridge: Cambridge University Press, 1991), 3–10; for a discussion of pre-existing ethnic kinship behind nationalism, see Anthony D. Smith, *The Ethnic Origins of Nations* (Oxford: Blackwell, 1986), esp. 1–17.

one another's political or economic actions, then all attempts to cultivate among them a sense of "Ruritanity" [...] will retain an artificial flavour.[345]

The Protectorate and the London exiles were, after all, targeting their propaganda at the same people, in the same language, and via the same medium of radio; but the desired effect of the Protectorate's broadcasting – encouraging listeners to accept the place of Czechs as part of the Germanic world, subordinated to German rule – was entirely different, and therefore so was the national identity that was projected. The image of Czechoslovakia transmitted in the London broadcasts reveals a great deal about how the exiles understood their nation.

Radio offered new possibilities for the generation and transmission of national messages and also enabled a wider section of the public than ever before to participate in elements of contemporary national culture. Broadcasters could now project a single, unified image of national identity, and its attendant symbols and cultural products, directly to listeners in their homes all over the country, without them having to attend an event or a political rally. In the interwar period, the BBC played a key role in the moulding of national British culture, by enabling the majority of the population to jointly access civic, royal, and sporting events from their own homes and thereby gain a sense of shared experience on a national scale.[346] By bringing these large-scale expressions of national culture into the domestic sphere, broadcasting had the potential to both homogenise national myths and symbols into a single narrative, and to make them part of the "everyday" existence of listeners. Due to its unrivalled position as a broadcaster, the wartime BBC has also been credited with having helped to bring the conflict to civilian listeners and make it part of their everyday lives, whether they were children, housewives, or workers.[347] In the context of broadcasting to occupied Europe, radio similarly brought news of the war to listeners, but the term *everyday* needs some clarification.

Everyday implies a sense of ubiquity but also of mundanity, in keeping with the understanding of listening to the radio as a "secondary" or ancillary activity which people often perform while simultaneously engaged

---

[345] Karl W. Deutsch, *Nationalism and Social Communication: An Investigation into the Foundations of Nationality* (Cambridge, MA: MIT Press, 1966), 173.
[346] See Scannell and Cardiff, *Social History*, 277–86.
[347] Nicholas, *Echo of War*, 108.

in doing something else, such as cooking or working.[348] When listening to foreign radio could carry heavy prison sentences or even the threat of execution, however, the broadcasts from London could not become part of the mundane background of listeners' lives. The sense of ubiquity does apply in this context, however, as the repetition of familiar stories and images kept the chosen national symbols at the forefront of peoples' minds and reinforced the exile government's understanding of Czechoslovak nationality and history as the only accepted interpretation. It has been suggested that the successful creation of a national identity among a community requires a level of cultural homogeneity, and it is logical that a single, unified representation is easier to present than a nuanced debate.[349] On a similarly practical level, propaganda is often most effective when it can play on an idea that the listener has already had, and the various uncertainties and instabilities of wartime exile would encourage the use of tried and tested arguments and interpretations.[350] Listeners were therefore united not only by a shared ability to understand what was being broadcast to them, but also by their shared familiarity and common associations with the music, literature, and historical references arriving over the airwaves. The occupying German forces in the Protectorate and the government of the new Slovak state had set about reinterpreting the very nature of what it now meant to be Czech and Slovak, leaving their opposition in London with the task of rebutting these claims and attempting to remind listeners what it *had* meant to be Czechoslovak.

The presentation of the Czechoslovak nation as a discrete national unit sharing common bonds of history and identity was implied in all programming made by the Czechoslovak exile government during the war, and it can be heard even in small details of the exiles' speech. In his book *Banal Nationalism,* Michael Billig suggested that, in established nations, the idea of the nation as a distinct community is constantly reasserted in almost unnoticeable ways throughout daily life. In addition to

---

[348] Radio is thus presented in, for example, Crisell, *Understanding Radio*, 14; Michele Hilmes, "Rethinking Radio," in *Radio Reader: Essays in the Cultural History of Radio*, ed. Michele Hilmes and Jason Loviglio (New York: Routledge, 2002), 1. Hugh Chignell's 2009 handbook for students of radio includes an entire entry for "Secondariness," incorporating both the above definition and the subjugation of radio to television within Media Studies; see Chignell, *Key Concepts in Radio Studies*, 99–102.
[349] For more on the connections between cultural homogeneity and nationalism, see Gellner, *Nations and Nationalism*, 38.
[350] On building propaganda on established ideas, see Roetter, *Psychological Warfare*, esp. 14, 188.

days of national celebration, when the nation is "consciously flagged," the nation is "reproduced" on a daily basis, particularly by the media.[351] Billig draws examples from the British press, in which journalists refer to "the nation" as opposed to "this nation" or "the British nation"; the implication is that journalists can have confidence in the ideological basis already laid among their readership, which means *the* nation can only be their nation. The same structure is used for titles such as "the prime minister," and this places the nation in question, in this case Britain, as the context for all subsequent information. Billig summarises it thus: "The definite article accomplishes the deixis, indicating Britain as the centre of reader's and writer's ('our') shared universe." Members of this nation are thereby indirectly identified in the piece: "'we' are unmindfully reminded who 'we' are and where 'we' are. 'We' are identified without even being mentioned."[352] This feature of definite articles is characteristic of English, but examples of similar structures and assumptions can be identified in the Czech- and Slovak-language broadcasts made by the government-in-exile.

The Czech and Slovak word *národ* is most commonly translated into English as "nation," and it was frequently used in the broadcasts without any accompanying adjectives. It is possible that, in a similar manner to the British examples identified by Billig, broadcasters were confident that their listeners knew which nation was being referred to without any definition being necessary, but this ambiguity also sidesteps the difficult issue of defining the limits of the "nation" to which they referred. As will be discussed in Chapter Three, the matter of the "Czechoslovak nation" – as opposed to the separate but related Czech and Slovak nations – was highly contentious, and, rather than highlighting this division, broadcasters sought to project unity. The single *národ* implies both the existence of that nation and a common understanding of unity among its members; listeners were assured of the imminent "freedom of the nation," that war criminals would face "the wrath of the nation," and that Protectorate president Emil Hácha was guilty of "crimes against the homeland and the nation."[353] When an additional word was used, this nation was also commonly identified as "our" nation, thereby connecting those broadcasters in London with the listeners at home and

---

[351] Michael Billig, *Banal Nationalism* (London: Sage, 2010), 6–12.
[352] Billig, *Banal Nationalism*, 107–9.
[353] BBC Czechoslovak Programme, 19 November 1940, LN Z 1940 – 3; 6 January 1941, LN Z 1941 – 4; 1 December 1943, LN Z 1943 – 28, CRA.

associating both with a shared sense of nationhood. As well as generic references to "our people," "our beautiful lands," and "our capital city," broadcasters were also able to emphasise the shared task in references to "our struggle" and "our victory."[354] They associated themselves with events within the occupied territory when they referred to "our sacrifices" and "our liberation" taking place on "our land," but, once established, this connection was also used to associate listeners with activities taking place in London: the workings of "our state structure in exile" and "our government."[355] A sense of association and shared ownership of territory can also be seen in broadcasters' use of pronouns in references to events within the Protectorate and Slovakia. For instance, by employing the phrase *u nás* – here meaning "in our country," but which can be translated literally to mean "around us" or "near us" – broadcasters incorporated the London exiles into the events at home.[356] Not only were listeners therefore consistently encouraged to identify themselves as sharing a common bond with the exiles in London, but also to associate the government-in-exile with the hardships being suffered under German occupation and any expressions of resistance against it. The implication was that both broadcaster and listener belonged to a certain group which had historic claims on a certain territory and considered it to be "theirs."

"Faithful to the spirit of our history": Reading the War into the National Narrative

The Czechoslovak government programme made frequent historical allusions and comparisons, seeking to present the German occupation as the latest in a long history of (largely Germanic) challenges to the nation, doomed to fail in the face of the indomitable national spirit. Every national group creates its own historical narrative, combining myth with selective memory to create a framework within which the nation can orient itself. Myths of shared ancestry and a tradition of shared communal

---

[354] See, for example, BBC Czechoslovak Programme, 1 February 1944, LN Z 1944 – 30; 8 May 1945, LN Z 1945 – 46; 10 May 1945, LN Z 1945 – 46; 4 July 1944, LN Z 1944 – 34; 5 January 1941, LN Z 1940 – 4, CRA.
[355] BBC Czechoslovak Programme, 8 October 1940, LN Z 1940 – 2; 6 June 1944, LN Z 1944 – 33; 21 April 1943, LN Z 1943 – 20; 19 October 1943, LN Z 1943 – 26, CRA.
[356] See, for example, references to "Germans and traitors *u nás*" and the promise that "everyone *u nás* will receive what they deserve for their work since 1938"; in BBC Czechoslovak Programme, 19 August 1943, LN Z 1943 – 23; 3 May 1945, LN Z 1945 – 46, CRA.

life bring together the members of the national community and engender a feeling of unity, as well as providing a means to interpret both the nation's past and its present. A historical tradition is then built up which can be passed on to subsequent generations, providing "the means of collective location in the world and the charter of the community which explains its origins, growth and destiny."[357] This serves a dual purpose because, in addition to perpetuating the sense of community through future generations, this tradition also lends the nation a sense of historical legitimacy, to protect it from accusations of artificiality. It has even been suggested that

> myths and memories provide a kind of immortality by identifying individuals and groups with a society which has existed from time immemorial and which, through the memories and examples of each generation's sacrifices and achievements, will extend indefinitely into the future. They thereby supply a means of overcoming death.[358]

This national myth can then be interpreted within a particular historical narrative to identify supposed shared characteristics that continue to be expressed in the present. In his study of national identity as part of everyday life, Michael Skey highlighted how

> past events are carefully written into national histories, connecting "great" wars, leaders, empires and inventions with contemporary social actors and processes, thereby demonstrating the *eternal* essence (and power) of the nation over time.[359]

As Robert Gildea argued, however, these "collective constructions of the past" are never universal or objective, different constructions being favoured and promoted by different political communities in support of their own legitimacy. A comparison of wartime propaganda produced in London with that produced in the Protectorate supports Gildea's claim that the same events can be interpreted very differently by rival

---

[357] Smith, *Ethnic Origins of Nations*, 24. For a wider discussion of the use of mythology in nation-building and the legitimising function of national myths across generations, see ibid., 15–25. For examples of multiple national narratives, including the Czech Republic and Britain, see Furtado, *Histories of Nations*.
[358] John Hutchinson, *Modern Nationalism* (London: Fontana Press, 1994), 18.
[359] Michael Skey, *National Belonging and Everyday Life: The Significance of Nationhood in an Uncertain World* (Basingstoke: Palgrave Macmillan, 2011), 25.

groups, with these interpretations used to support their own favoured narrative.[360] In the Czechoslovak context, belief in this narrative was also used to reinforce the position of the London exiles; their cause was the historic cause of the nation and all loyal Czechoslovaks should therefore follow. Speaking on the eve of Czechoslovak Independence Day in 1940, Beneš did not ask listeners to be loyal to him and his government but instead appropriated a higher authority: "I ask you to be faithful to our thousand-year tradition, faithful to the spirit of our history, and faithful to all our great people, from the earliest Přemyslids to Masaryk."[361]

Every national movement contains an element of this historical myth-making and the Czechs are no exception; Ernest Gellner wrote of his own nation, "there can be few nations in Europe [...] which live on terms of quite such constant intimacy with their own history as do the Czechs. For Czechs, historicism is virtually a way of life."[362] There had been so much discussion of what lessons should be learned from Czech history in the last years of Austrian rule and throughout the First Republic that the debate earned itself a name: the "argument over the meaning of Czech history" (*spor o smyslu českých dějin*). A new generation of historians used newly available sources and applied modern methods to historical writing, bringing with them "a new spiritual stream in historiography." This debate brought historical discussion to the public's attention in the last years of the Habsburg Empire and contributed significantly to the establishment of a Czechoslovak academic sphere which both relied on and supported the independent state.[363] The ongoing polemic featured many different contributors in its various waves, but from the start T. G. Masaryk was at the very centre.[364] Contemporary critics of Masaryk, who was then working as a university professor, concluded that he had "invented a national mythology," though in fact his writings drew heavily on the work of nineteenth-century historian and intellectual František

---

360 See Robert Gildea, *The Past in French History* (New Haven: Yale University Press, 1994), 11, 340. For a recent study of radio propaganda and policy in the Protectorate, see Peter Richard Pinard, *Broadcast Policy in the Protectorate of Bohemia and Moravia: Power Structures, Programming, Cooperation and Defiance at Czech Radio 1939–1945* (Frankfurt: Peter Lang, 2015).
361 Beneš, *Šest let exilu*, 60. The Přemyslids were a Bohemian royal dynasty, first documented in the ninth century but with legendary origins associated with the foundation of Prague.
362 Ernest Gellner, *Encounters with Nationalism* (Oxford: Blackwell, 1994), 131–32.
363 Karník, *České země*, 1:529. For more on the contributions of historians in this period to the formation of national identity, see ibid., esp. 529–31.
364 For an introduction to the debate and opposition to Masaryk, see René Wellek, introduction to *The Meaning of Czech History by Tomáš G. Masaryk*, ed. René Wellek (Chapel Hill: University of North Carolina Press, 1974); see also Körbel, *Twentieth-Century Czechoslovakia*, esp. 18–22.

Palacký (1798–1876) and adopted his interpretation of the Hussite period as a defining moment in the history of the Bohemian crown lands.[365]

The historical narrative extrapolated from this interpretation is one of the intrinsic democracy and humanism of the Czechs, developed in opposition to a hostile, authoritarian, and militarist Germanic culture. In Masaryk's narrative, Hussitism and the nineteenth-century National Revival were both expressions of these same innately Czech characteristics, and this national spirit had asserted itself again when Czechoslovakia won independence in 1918. In the last years of Austria-Hungary and in the interwar period there had been much-publicised opposition to Masaryk's view from figures such as historian Josef Pekař, historian and later politician Kamil Krofta, and academic and future Communist minister for education Zdeněk Nejedlý. However, despite this debate regarding the interpretation and significance of various events in Czech history, only one viewpoint was presented in the wartime broadcasts.[366] This Masarykian interpretation, which placed Hussitism, democracy, and opposition to all things German at the centre of the Czech national idea, has had an enduring legacy, although scholars have recently sought to challenge some aspects which had gone unquestioned for decades. While the modern academic environment allows for nuance and compromise, however, and some have highlighted the positive impact of the German influence on Czech life, no such accommodation was open to wartime broadcasters and the strongly anti-German tone of the exile government's propaganda involved a projection of the current Czech–German conflict back through the shared history of the two nations.[367] Masaryk's interpretation of the national spirit and the influence of his historical and national thought were prominent in the broadcasts, and the London exiles built on the foundation established in the First Republic, finding evidence to support this narrative in the wartime context and retracing it back through several centuries.

---

365 Wellek, *Meaning of Czech History*, xxi; for more on Masaryk's views of Palacký, see Tomáš Masaryk, "Palackého idea národa českého," *Naše doba* 5 (1898): 769–95.
366 For more, see Josef Pekař, *O smyslu českých dějin* (Prague: Rozmluvy, 1990); Kamil Krofta, *Dějiny československé* (Prague: Sfinx, 1946); Zdeněk Nejedlý, *O smyslu českých dějin* (Prague: Svoboda, 1952).
367 Miroslav Hroch described the German influence as "an inspiration and never a threat," in *Na prahu národní existence: Touha a skutečnost* (Prague: Mladá fronta, 1999), 155. Hroch identified a new trend in research seeking to re-examine the established interpretation of the Czech national movement and the National Revival from the late 1980s onwards, in ibid., 5.

Broadcasters in the Czechoslovak government programme made frequent historical references which reinforced the approved narrative of innate Czech democracy maintained throughout a thousand years of conflict with German-speaking peoples, and broadcasters selected examples from history to illustrate the indomitable Czech spirit. In January 1941, a series of programmes and talks recounted the persecution of members of the Czechoslovak Legions – army brigades that had been formed abroad in the First World War, fought on the side of the Allies, and been celebrated as patriotic heroes. After many comments by his fellow broadcasters on the so-called "legionary spirit," former legionary-turned-playwright František Langer told listeners that "this was just one name for something eternal which is among us and within us, as an entire nation." Echoing Masaryk's interpretation, Langer described this "something" as "that which was once called Hussitism, at another time revivalism, and which will in the future be called something else again."[368]

Later broadcasters also alluded to this eternal "Czech spirit." Explaining why the Germans were seeking to attack it, regular broadcaster Pavel Tigrid declared that "Czech culture, the Czech spirit, is the arch enemy of their intentions." Defining it as "principally the ideal of freedom, the ideal of moral integrity, the ideal of humanity, democracy," he then named representatives of the Czech spirit throughout the last six centuries of Czech history: "it is Hus, Chelčický, Žižka, George of Poděbrady, Palacký, Masaryk."[369] Tigrid concluded that, despite German efforts to force Czechs to accept "Reich culture," they would never give up "their unique, tried and tested weapon against the invader," and that they "will continue to draw hope and strength for the fight from the inexhaustible well of the Czech spirit."[370] The dominance of Hussite figures in Tigrid's interpretation was typical of the government broadcasts which often ranked Jan Hus prominently in lists of national heroes and described him as "the symbol of resistance for us," due to his "uncompromised Czech spirit and his active resistance to the enslaving power." Hus's

---

368 BBC Czechoslovak Programme, 21 January 1941, LN Z 1940 – 4, CRA.
369 Jan Hus and Petr Chelčický (1390–1460) were religious and political leaders in fifteenth-century Bohemia; Jan Žižka (1360–1424) was a renowned military leader and follower of Hus in the Hussite Wars after Hus's death in 1415; George of Poděbrady (1420–71) was elected king by the Bohemian estates in 1458 and was also a follower of Hus; František Palacký was a nineteenth-century historian who was very influential in the period of the National Revival and is strongly associated with interpreting the Hussite period as a high point in Czech history.
370 BBC Czechoslovak Programme, 26 March 1943, LN Z 1943 – 19, CRA.

proposed reforms for the Catholic Church, which included giving sermons in the local vernacular and curbing corruption, were identified as examples of Czech democratic and humanistic ideals, in contrast to the Catholic establishment, who were labelled German occupiers and "natural enemies of the Czechs."[371]

In the wartime context, there were many opportunities for broadcasters to add further German crimes against the Czechoslovaks to the historical narrative of opposition that (they argued) had been established centuries before. The presentation of German-speakers as the eternal enemies of the Czechs considerably predates the Second World War, with probably the earliest examples being the fourteenth-century text known as Dalimil's Chronicle and later sources from the Hussite period of the fifteenth century.[372] During the period of the National Revival in the nineteenth century, the Germans were again presented in opposition to the much-vaunted virtues of the Slavs. In contrast to the peaceful and industrious nature of *slovanství* (Slavness) there was *neslovanství* (non-Slavness), "which, in the realm of Czech culture, is personified by Germanness, therefore the negative evaluation of German culture and language was almost obligatory."[373] The historical struggle of the Czechs against this "Germanness" was referenced frequently in government broadcasts as an accepted truth. For example, in a dialogue one speaker marvelled that the British were ever fooled by Hitler's lies about only seeking to protect the German population of Czechoslovakia, and his companion responded, "Don't be so surprised, they haven't lived through what we have for the last thousand years."[374] Historical parallels were drawn with previous conflicts, and particularly with the period after the Battle of White Mountain of 1620, at which the largely Protestant Bohemian army was defeated by the forces of Holy Roman Emperor Ferdinand II, with the Bohemian estates subsequently losing religious freedom and elements of regional independence.[375]

---

371 BBC Czechoslovak Programme, 6 July 1942, LN Z 1942 – 15, CRA.
372 See František Šmahel, *Idéa národa v husitských Čechách* (Prague: Argo, 2000), 25 (on Dalimil), 251 (summarising anti-German trends).
373 Vladimír Macura, *Znamení zrodu: České národní obrození jako kulturní typ* (Jinočany: H&H, 1995), 49.
374 BBC Czechoslovak Programme, 9 September 1940, LN Z 1940 – 1, CRA.
375 For more on the outcomes of the battle and their significance in Czech historiography, see Josef Petráň and Lydia Petráňová, "The White Mountain as a Symbol in Modern Czech History," in *Bohemia in History*, ed. Mikuláš Teich (Cambridge: Cambridge University Press, 1998), 143–63.

In a broadcast marking the 320th anniversary of the Battle of White Mountain on 8 November 1940, historian Gustav Winter claimed that the present day was a time at which "our nation is particularly able to understand the significance of that fateful day and learn from it." Then as now, Winter argued, "Czech independence" had been crushed and "the Czech language had been made a Cinderella in her own land," but neither the language nor the nation had died out. Winter refrained from explaining how he understood "Czech independence" in the context of the seventeenth century, allowing him to draw an ambiguous and sweeping parallel between the limited regional freedom of the time and interwar Czechoslovak statehood, both ostensibly lost to German aggression.[376] In a broadcast for the Battle of White Mountain anniversary the following year, former academic Vladimír Klecanda spoke of the meaning of the battle, which represented "German oppression [...] absolutism and Germanisation" and "became a symbol of all the evil that our German neighbours could ever bring us." Klecanda asked his listeners to consider the parallels: "Does it not sometimes seem to you, when you cross Charles Bridge towards the Old Town, that you see again the heads of executed martyrs on the bridge tower?" Many themes are interwoven in talks such as this, where distant historical events are conflated with modern ones in order to link listeners with their past; here, Klecanda even implied that a lingering collective memory of the seventeenth century would enable listeners to "see" such things "again." He also used historical imagery to explicitly assert national unity: "Today we stand on White Mountain in unbreakable ranks as an entire nation, all loyal Czechoslovaks, against Hitler's Germany and against fascism itself."[377]

Part of the historical preoccupation of the London broadcasts can be explained, however, by the nature of the Protectorate propaganda which they were opposing; many of the historically themed government radio programmes were direct rebuttals of Protectorate interpretations of Czech and Czechoslovak history which the exiles considered intolerable. For instance, Klecanda explained the flaws in the German representation of the Holy Roman Empire as a precursor to the German Reich, even though the London broadcasts essentially drew the same parallel in their interpretation of the Battle of White Mountain. Klecanda argued that the Bohemian crown lands had a special relationship with the empire, and

---

376 BBC Czechoslovak Programme, 8 November 1940, LN Z 1940 – 2, CRA.
377 BBC Czechoslovak Programme, 8 November 1941, LN Z 1941 – 10, CRA.

that "the relationship of the Bohemian crown lands to the Empire was never as the Nazi propaganda tries to depict it – that of a German part of a German Empire." He added a quote from Palacký on the Frankfurt Parliament of 1848, praising him for his foresight in his statement that "anyone who asks the Czechs to join the German Empire in a national sense is asking them to commit suicide."[378]

In July and August 1944, seven weekly programmes targeting younger listeners were devoted to a "holiday course" in Czech history. In the Wednesday morning slot reserved for broadcasts to young people, Professor Otakar Odložilík of Charles University explained to listeners in the Protectorate why the interpretation of their history being presented there was wrong.[379] Most of the programmes were constructed as question and answer discussions that once again focused on two key topics: František Palacký, whom Odložilík said the Germans had always hated for his arguments of historical Czech–German conflict, although "what is a crime in German eyes we see not only as honourable but also as excellent proof of Palacký's insight and political wisdom"; and Hussitism, with Odložilík claiming that the Germans sought to deny "this period of complete independence and national strength" as they knew Czech national consciousness was a threat to their occupation.[380] The appropriation of historical figures and reinterpretation of events within the Protectorate was part of a wider strategy to present the Bohemian crown lands – both to the Czechs and to the rest of the world – as being culturally and historically part of the Greater German lands, and both notions were dismissed by Odložilík as merely the latest manifestation of the German desire to profit from undermining the national unity among Czechs and Slovaks.[381]

In addition to figures such as Palacký and Hus, one of the historical names most frequently discussed in the broadcasts was St. Wenceslas (c. 907–35), the tenth-century Duke of Bohemia and later patron saint of Czechoslovakia and, today, the Czech Republic. The image of St.

---

378 BBC Czechoslovak Programme, 26 January 1941, LN Z 1941 – 4, CRA. Emphasis in original.
379 BBC Czechoslovak Programme, 19 July 1944, LN Z 1944 – 33, CRA. This series of programmes is similar in its intention to Pavel Tigrid's *Kapesní průvodce inteligentní ženy po vlastním osudu* (Toronto: Sixty-Eight Publishers, 1988), which describes a series of conversations with a young Czech girl on holiday, in which she learns how her understanding of Czech history has been limited by Marxist-Leninist interpretations.
380 BBC Czechoslovak Programme, 26 July 1944, LN Z 1944 – 33; 16 August 1944, LN Z 1944 – 34, CRA.
381 BBC Czechoslovak Programme, 9 August 1944, LN Z 1944 – 34, CRA.

Wenceslas, already a prominent national symbol, had become a familiar part of the iconography of the Czechoslovak state during the First Republic, and his millennial celebrations in 1929 had revealed how differently his memory was interpreted by the various national groups within Czechoslovakia. There was already an established German tradition associated with Wenceslas which focused on the theme of Catholic co-operation, and this dominated discussion of the millennium's significance in Czechoslovakia's German community, detaching Wenceslas from his Hussite-era interpretation.[382] In the Protectorate interpretation over a decade later, Wenceslas featured as a supporter of Czech–German co-operation and as an example of the wisdom of not attempting to resist Germany's will, based on his acceptance of demands from Bavaria that he pay tribute to their king without resistance. Rejecting all alternative interpretations of what they perceived to be their own national tradition, Czech broadcasters in London mocked the German idea that "St. Wenceslas is not the patron saint of Czech existence and Czech freedom but rather the patron saint of Czech extinction and Czech oppression," and expressed their incredulity that Germans could expect the population to accept this, commenting that it showed "that they think they are cunning and that we are weak in the head." The Christian spirit of the St. Wenceslas story had, broadcasters argued, been overlooked by the Germans, who could not be expected to understand such things, and this theory of his pro-German beliefs was felt to be "so stupid, it is harmless," as proven by the fact that "our princely saint" lives in the memories and minds of the nation "atop a horse, not as the groomsman of foreign lords."[383] The broadcast intentionally recalled familiar national images to the listener's mind through the reference to Wenceslas as "our" saint and the invocation of his image astride his horse, as he is presented in the statue on the Prague square which bears his name.

The wartime broadcasts also represented Wenceslas in his mythical role as eternal protector of the Czech lands. According to one legend, Wenceslas sleeps beneath the Bohemian mountain of Blaník with his

---

[382] Petr Placák examines national relations within Czechoslovakia through the 1929 celebrations, showing that different interpretations were used to encourage state-wide support for the festivities, and concluding that divisions between Czechs and Germans were not always as clear cut as they are represented now, with class and religious factors featuring as important points of difference, as well as the language question; see Placák, *Svatováclavské milenium: Češi, Němci a Slováci v roce 1929* (Prague: Babylon, 2002). For German interpretations of the St. Wenceslas tradition, see ibid., esp. 122–34.
[383] BBC Czechoslovak Programme, 26 September 1943, LN Z 1943 – 25, CRA.

army of knights and, when the need of the nation is greatest, the mountain will open and they will ride forth in defence of the Bohemian crown lands. Jan Masaryk invoked the spirit of Wenceslas in his broadcast for Czechoslovak Independence Day on 28 October 1939, linking the saint with ideas of resistance when he told listeners they would have to wait "for the moment when Blaník, that mountain of our opposition, will open again at the given signal and you, his knights, will expel the hated occupier forever from our lands, flowing with milk and honey."[384] The legend was also brought into the present day in the form of a children's story, when the sword of St. Wenceslas – used as a coronation sword in Bohemia since the fourteenth century and held as part of the crown jewels – appeared in a radio play written by František Langer that was broadcast at Christmas 1940. In Langer's play *The Children of Prague and the Sword of St. Wenceslas*, a group of Czech children find the sword after attending Christmas Eve Mass at St. Vitus Cathedral. They know they must hide it from the Germans – who are in Prague because "after all, there is no fairy tale without the baddies and the monsters" – and take it upon themselves to look after it until the time is right for Wenceslas to come and claim it.[385] Once the children have hidden the sword, Langer concludes that "here somewhere our salvation and hope are hidden for the darkest times," and the playwright then links the idea of national salvation with the next generation of Czechs: "whenever we meet a Czech child, we will say of them, 'Here it is!'"[386] Langer plays on the ubiquity and familiarity of the legend to invoke a renewed sense of national identity, whilst encouraging endurance and patience in the wartime struggle.

A further expression of the importance of historical allusions in the broadcasts can be seen in the use of anniversaries and national celebrations. A shared knowledge of their common history was an assumed characteristic of listeners, and the historical narrative outlined above was reflected again in the choice of anniversaries that were marked within the government programme. The celebration of important anniversaries also furthered the creation of an imagined Czechoslovakia over the airwaves, as events that had previously been celebrated in public – such as the anniversaries of the founding of the state on 28 October and of the death of first president T. G. Masaryk – had disappeared from the daily lives

---

[384] Masaryk, *Volá Londýn* (1990), 13.
[385] Broadcast as part of *Hovory s domovem*, but also published in František Langer, *BBC Londýn* (Prague: Fr. Borový, 1947), 11.
[386] Langer, *BBC Londýn*, 17.

of Czechs and Slovaks. The broader Czechoslovak exile community in Britain, beyond the immediate circle of politicians, continued to mark important national anniversaries with public events but, for those at home, they could only be celebrated over the radio.[387] Mass events such as national holidays are often associated with rituals and traditions that make the national group highly visible and can be used to reinforce the previously identified national characteristics and virtues, thereby linking the current celebrating population with those who had marked it in the past.[388] Michael Skey has suggested that, in addition to the everyday reinforcement of the nation in small ways, occasional "ecstatic nationalism" is necessary to "concretise the idea of the nation moving through history."[389] Though these celebrations could not be held in reality, the government programme was able to perpetuate this aspect of national life over the airwaves and thereby recreate – aurally, if not physically – some of the key rituals that define citizenship and participation in the state, encouraging listeners to continue to engage in such celebrations.[390]

The historical allegiances of the exile government were clearly reflected in its chosen anniversaries. The national day of 28 October and the associated anniversary of the founding of Czechoslovakia in 1918 were of primary importance, and celebratory programmes were broadcast every year, usually continuing for several days. As well as addresses from prominent exile figures such as Beneš and Jan Masaryk, there were also often messages of greeting and solidarity from prominent British figures, such as "our old friend" Robert Bruce Lockhart, British representative to the Czechoslovak exiles until 1941, and Philip Nichols, British envoy to Czechoslovakia from 1941 onwards.[391] The day was also sometimes marked in other language services of the BBC and various Czechoslovaks would contribute to the production of feature programmes.[392] The exile government's devotion to T. G. Masaryk's legacy was also evident:

---

[387] For more on the marking of anniversaries among Czechoslovak exiles in Britain, see Srba, *Múzy v exilu*, 175–77.
[388] Gabriella Elgenius, *Symbols of Nations and Nationalism: Celebrating Nationhood* (Basingstoke: Palgrave Macmillan, 2011), 131.
[389] Skey, *National Belonging*, 25, 117 (on "ecstatic nationalism").
[390] For more on the roles of national events and ceremonies in the performance of national identity, see Eric Hobsbawm and Terence Ranger, eds., *The Invention of Tradition* (Cambridge: Cambridge University Press, 1992), 10–12.
[391] For example, Lockhart spoke in 1941 and Nichols in 1943; BBC Czechoslovak Programme, 30 October 1941, LN Z 1941 – 10; 30 October 1943, LN Z 1943 – 26, CRA.
[392] Scripts for programmes for many different language services can be seen in Czech Editor's Papers, 1943–45, Countries: Czechoslovakia, E1/1323, BBC WAC.

while some anniversaries went in and out of favour and were only marked in certain years, the birth (in March) and death (in September) of the first Czechoslovak president were marked every year without fail, often by a whole week of programming known as "Masaryk Week." The only other figures to have their anniversaries marked in at least three separate years were Jan Hus, prominent First Republic writer Karel Čapek (1890–1938), and T. G. Masaryk's Slovak colleague in the foundation of the Czechoslovak state, Milan Rastislav Štefánik (1880–1919).[393] It is telling that the only Slovak to have his life marked so prominently was principally known for his dedication to the joint state, and that other prominent Slovak anniversaries that were marked included the signing of the Pittsburgh Agreement and the Martin Declaration, two important documents in the union of Czechs and Slovaks.[394] Most of the pre-1918 anniversaries that were marked – such as the aforementioned Battle of White Mountain and the fifteenth-century Battle of Grunwald – were presented as historic expressions of anti-German sentiment.[395] Anniversaries of wartime events were also commemorated, such as the attacks on Czech students and the closure of the universities on 17 November 1939, and the formations of the various Czechoslovak squadrons in the RAF throughout 1940.[396] More modern traditions, such as the Christmas radio address made by the president, were also continued, so that, though the

---

[393] Hus's death was marked on 6 July in the years 1942, 1943, and 1944; Čapek's death on 25 December in 1940, 1942, and 1944; Štefánik's death was marked on 4 May 1942 and on 3 May in 1943 and 1944.

[394] The Pittsburgh Agreement was signed on 31 May 1918 in the US city of Pittsburgh, Pennsylvania, by representatives of American Czech and Slovak groups, and by Tomáš Garrigue Masaryk. It supported the creation of a joint state of Czechs and Slovaks, with the latter retaining some autonomy. The Martin Declaration was signed by two hundred Slovak representatives on 30 October 1918 in Turčiansky Svätý Martin, now Martin, Slovakia. Its expression of support for union with the Czechs is disputed; see Chapter Three for more.

[395] The anniversary of the Battle of White Mountain was marked on 8 November in the years 1940 and 1941; the Battle of Grunwald on 15 July 1941. Both were referred to in other programmes as well. See BBC Czechoslovak Programme, LN Z 1940 – 2; LN Z 1941 – 10; LN Z 1941 – 7, CRA.

[396] The attacks of 17 November 1939 were marked in the annual celebration of Students' Day, now an internationally celebrated occasion. The anniversary of the Czechoslovak RAF fighter squadron no. 310 was marked on 12 July 1943 and 11 July 1944, and squadron no. 313 on 11 May 1943. The Czechoslovak RAF bomber squadron no. 311 was celebrated on 2 August 1943, 4 August 1943, and 31 July 1944. There was a third Czechoslovak fighter squadron, no. 312, and a significant Czechoslovak presence in the RAF night fighter squadron, no. 68. See BBC Czechoslovak Programme, LN Z 1943 – 22; LN Z 1944 – 34; LN Z 1943 – 21; LN Z 1943 – 24; LN Z 1944 – 34, CRA. For more on Czechoslovaks in the RAF, see Alan Brown, "The Czechoslovak Armed Forces in Britain, 1940–1945," in Conway and Gotovitch, *Europe in Exile,* 167–82; Zdeněk Hurt, *Czechs in RAF Squadrons of World War II in Focus* (Walton on Thames: Red Kite, 2004).

state to which these occasions belonged no longer existed, an aspect of Czechoslovak life was able to continue over radio. Czechoslovak cultural life, perpetuated in exile through concerts and lectures, was also celebrated in the "free republic" of the radio as government broadcasters used their programme to remind listeners of their shared cultural heritage, linking music, literature, and poetry to their political cause.

"Anything that is dear to their hearts": The Mobilisation of Culture

The mobilisation of cultural content such as music, literature, and poetry for propaganda purposes was a prominent element of the Czechoslovak government programme, playing on the audience's familiarity with certain popular works and their shared feeling of attachment to this cultural heritage. The associated theme of language, which had always been prominent in the Czech national movement, was also used by broadcasters as a rallying point for Czech listeners against the Germans. Just as the government programme celebrated historical events with anniversary programmes, so too did it mark the births and deaths of composers such as Antonín Dvořák (1841–1904) and Bedřich Smetana (1824–84), as well as events such as the opening of the National Theatre in Prague and premieres of popular and now banned works, including Smetana's *Braniboři v Čechách* (*The Brandenburgers in Bohemia*).[397] The emotional significance of such occasions for listeners was much promoted, as shown in František Langer's introduction to his programme on the National Theatre:

> the sixtieth anniversary of the National Theatre is a most precious celebration for us. This beautiful monument has such meaning for us, it is both symbol and witness of so many ideas, efforts, and events in our national life that its celebration is a ready-made festival of everything which is sacred to the Czech soul.[398]

---

397 The centenary of Dvořák's birth was marked on 8 September in 1941 and 1942; Smetana's birth on 2 March in 1942 and 1943; the opening of the National Theatre on 18 November 1943; and the 79th anniversary of Smetana's premiere and its political significance on 5 January 1945. See BBC Czechoslovak Programme, LN Z 1941 – 9; LN Z 1942 – 16; LN Z 1942 – 12; LN Z 1943 – 19; LN Z 1943 – 27; LN Z 1945 – 40, CRA.
398 BBC Czechoslovak Programme, 18 November 1943, LN Z 1943 – 27, CRA.

Broadcaster Anna Patzaková's comments on Smetana's opera were no less emotionally charged, as she claimed it was banned because its theme of "Germanic barbarity and wicked avarice" could not be reinterpreted in a positive way for the Protectorate. She described Smetana as "a foremost fighter for the freedom of the nation and justice against brutal violence," whose work "embodied the national idea and therefore became the property of the entire nation," before going even further: Patzaková said that with this opera, depicting a thirteenth-century Prague rebellion against Brandenburg forces, Smetana had given the Czechs "their first patriotic manifesto," and she described the work as "a call to patriotic and underground battle, the battle for liberation which must end in the driving out of the invader."[399]

Although the use of cultural material as propaganda was not new, the Second World War and the circumstances of the German occupation of the Czech lands were particularly conducive to its use. T. G. Masaryk had written about the importance of culture in making effective propaganda in the 1920s, arguing that a propagandist could not rely simply on enthusiastically stating their case when attempting to win their audience to a particular political cause. Warning that "political agitation often puts people off or fails to win them over," Masaryk advised would-be propagandists accordingly:

> There is one important lesson in the psychology of propaganda: Do not think that people are won over to a political programme solely and principally by having its various points energetically and enthusiastically laid out to them – the thing is to catch their attention by any means, perhaps indirectly. Talk about art, about literature and so on, about whatever the other person is interested in, and you will win him.[400]

For Masaryk, the interest that people felt for cultural subjects made them the perfect indirect means for winning the audience's attention and preparing their ears for the required propaganda message, without wearying them with overt political arguments. In the context of the occupied Protectorate, where censorship and the imposition of German cultural dominance had outlawed many works of Czech literature and culture, this was likely to carry even more weight, as broadcasters could offer

---

[399] BBC Czechoslovak Programme, 5 January 1945, LN Z 1945 – 40, CRA.
[400] Masaryk, *Světová revoluce*, 100.

their audience a chance to hear a favourite poem or piece of music that was now banned or out of favour.

The BBC had also recognised the value of using cultural and historical elements in its efforts to win the loyalty of listeners, especially those in the former Czechoslovakia. A European intelligence report from a correspondent of the BBC Overseas Intelligence Department in early 1940 proposed the use of more cultural material in the broadcasts to Czechoslovakia, explaining that "only those who know the people well and who have experienced the pleasure they receive from hearing anything that is dear to their hearts being broadcasted from London or Paris, will fully understand the value of this suggestion."[401] By offering the "pleasure" of being able to hear references to familiar and popular works of Czechoslovak culture, the BBC could win the attention of a wider audience for its broadcasts, and an affectionate familiarity with national cultural classics was an assumed characteristic of all Czechoslovaks, without regard to class or profession. The Czechoslovaks had a reputation in Britain for being highly educated, and government speakers had confidence in the cultural education of their listeners.[402] In response to the attempts of the Protectorate authorities to separate the "workers" from "the intelligentsia," Jan Masaryk responded scathingly that, "For us, the intelligentsia means workers, farmers, professors, priests, office workers, and teachers; we are an intelligent nation that cannot be divided."[403]

Cultural material was therefore universally seen as a useful facilitator of political propaganda, and the Czechoslovak government-in-exile mobilised literary and musical works for its own campaign of political warfare. The use of cultural elements within its broadcasts was a means to simultaneously counter German attempts to discredit Czechoslovak culture, unify the divided home population, and promote the image of a cultured, independent Czechoslovak nation to an international audience. The desire to use cultural references in propaganda is logical; when speaking to a national audience, broadcasters can use the attachment listeners feel to certain familiar works to encourage them to associate with a political idea – in this case, the rejection of German occupation and loyalty to the government-in-exile. When addressing an international audience, Czechoslovak cultural works and the people behind them

---

401 Briggs, *War of Words*, 162–63.
402 "Zpráva o poměru anglického veřejného mínění k Československu," October 1940 – March 1941, MV–L 271: 2-82-10, Tisk-rozhlas 1944, CNA.
403 Masaryk, *Volá Londýn* (1990), 145.

could be presented as positive ambassadors for their nation, and the inherently Czechoslovak nature of these works was emphasised in the hope that the Allies would come to respect the Czechoslovak nation as culturally (and, by extension, politically) valid in its own right. German censorship of certain cultural products within the Protectorate gave programme makers an opportunity to tempt listeners to defy German laws forbidding listening to foreign radio broadcasts, in the hope of hearing something comfortingly familiar being broadcast from London. Great cultural works of the past were then upheld as aspirational patriotic examples when broadcasters sought to encourage a feeling of national unity. By reminding listeners at home of the music and literature that they held "dear to their hearts" – and of the fact that they were being denied it by the occupying Germans – programme makers sought to strengthen cultural identity in opposition to all that the occupiers represented, and to promote themselves as its true representatives.

Literature featured prominently in the Czechoslovak government programme, primarily in the form of poetry. Though prose and fiction writers such as Karel Čapek were often referred to, it was rare for extracts of their work to be read out, possibly due to the limitations of the fifteen-minute programme slot. One of the most prominent literary figures discussed in the broadcasts was the nineteenth-century writer Božena Němcová (1820–62), whose works were presented as a much-loved symbol of Czech national feeling. In an early broadcast, Jan Masaryk concluded an otherwise unrelated broadcast with the statement that he was going to go home to re-read Němcová's novella of 1855, *Babička* (*Grandmother*), and he identified the eponymous matriarch as an example of the strength of Czech national spirit: "A nation which has such grandmothers will not die out – God bless them!"[404] In the early morning broadcast on 22 January 1944, *Hlas svobodné republiky* also marked the anniversary of Němcová's death the previous day in an overtly nationally minded way. Communist member of the National Council Anežka Hodinová-Spurná gave a talk in which she described Němcová as "a truly national writer," who "is still teaching us to love the motherland and to strive for the home country to provide joy, happiness, and beauty for all her children." She also maintained that generations of Czech mothers had learned from Němcová how to protect their children from

---

[404] Masaryk, *Volá Londýn* (1990), 32. The first film version of *Babička* was released in 1940, directed by František Čapek, and widely understood as an expression of Czech patriotism.

Germanisation. This was followed by an extract from *Babička* in which the grandmother told her granddaughter that even the very young can do something to help the motherland. This extract was introduced (in Slovak, suggesting that not only a Czech audience was expected for the programme) as "something every one of us knows well." The audience was encouraged to "listen well and read *Babička* yourself again and again, because today, in these times of unhappiness and suffering, it speaks to us in a clear and beautiful language that every one of us understands better than in times of good fortune and prosperity."[405]

There was also some original fiction and poetry written specifically for the government programme. Very early on in the government's broadcasts, between August and November 1940, Jaroslav Hašek's famous character Josef Švejk appeared in his own short series of eight programmes set in the Protectorate. The programmes were written by Václav Panský-Solský, read by Josef Kodíček, and imitated Hašek's characteristic humour as Švejk constantly got into trouble with the authorities (in this case German, where they had formerly been Austrian). As in Hašek's stories, Švejk was outwardly obliging and approving towards the authorities but satirised their ideology in his own obscure and absurd explanations for the world around him.[406] For example, when comparing life in the First Republic to life in the Protectorate, Švejk appealed to his fellow drinkers in the *U kalicha* pub:

> Only remember Czechoslovakia. What kind of a life did we have when we were still a free country? We had a wretched life. We were like pigs or even worse. We ate and we boozed, and everybody wrote in the newspapers whatever came into his head, so that it was really a terrible state of affairs. And what do we see today? In the newspapers there is order. They all write the same thing, and we have not anything to eat either, and every day we get slimmer and happier [...] Such a bestial life as we used to live will not come again. And whom have we to thank for that? It is Adolf Hitler that we have to thank.[407]

---

405 BBC Czechoslovak Programme, 22 January 1944, LN Z 1943 – 28, CRA. Němcová remains a high-profile figure in the history of Czech literature, featuring on the current 500-crown banknote.
406 The Švejk stories were broadcast weekly on Thursday evenings between 15 August and 5 September 1940, with subsequent programmes on 13 September, 11 and 18 October, and 28 November; see BBC Czechoslovak Programme, LN Z 1940 – 1-3, CRA.
407 BBC Czechoslovak Programme, 22 August 1940, LN Z 1940 – 1, CRA. This quote uses the BBC's English translation.

The character of Švejk had a complex symbolism in terms of resistance, however. The word *švejkovina* (defined in one BBC intelligence report as "resourceful resistance even in small matters") had come to represent the minor acts committed on a large scale by Czechs in resistance to Austrian rule before and during the First World War.[408] Švejk's version of resistance had been rejected in the 1920s, however, in favour of a wave of heroic literature describing the Czechoslovak legionaries who had fought abroad against the Central Powers. The reception of Hašek's work underwent a further cyclical turn during the Second World War, as *švejkovina* was at first praised and then again rejected in favour of more intensive action where possible. The term appears in BBC intelligence reports where acts of *švejkovina* were applauded and resistors carrying out small acts, such as advertising the incorrect dates for Protectorate-backed events, were described as "local Švejks."[409] While Jan Masaryk urged listeners to "act like Švejk [*švejkujte*] discreetly, slack off where you can get away with it and fight where you can," other broadcasters took a harder line.[410] Prokop Drtina (as Pavel Svatý) told listeners that "we" in London agreed with the words of Zdeněk Nejedlý in Moscow, that "now is not the time for Švejks" and small acts of resistance were not enough – listeners must also imitate the soldier and First World War legionary Josef Švec.[411] The Czechoslovak government newspaper in Britain, *Čechoslovák*, promoted a similar interpretation with the words, "For us, Švejk is dead." Such tactics as his were no longer appropriate, the paper argued: "We will remember him with a smile and with gratitude. He did his job well. Today's task is different and harder. The conditions of the contest have worsened."[412]

In terms of poetry, verses by established writers featured alongside original work by programme writers and broadcasters Ota Ornest and Pavel Tigrid.[413] In addition to traditional poems and rhymes, three poets

---

408 SEA, 9 June 1941, 24/41, EIP series 1c, E2/192/1, BBC WAC.
409 "SEA: EOCOTF (Central-Southern Europe), 2 November 1942, 44/42, EIP series 1c (b), E2/192/6, BBC WAC.
410 Masaryk, *Volá Londýn* (1990), 161.
411 BBC Czechoslovak Programme, 17 August 1941, LN Z 1941 – 8, CRA.
412 "Kdo na místo Švejka?," *Čechoslovák* 3, no. 18 (2 May 1941): 6. Radko Pytlík, who has written extensively on Švejk and his reception, complained that the concept of *švejkovina* predates the character and has little to do with the texts themselves. He also charts the criticism surrounding the work, both from literary and ideological perspectives, in *Kniha o Švejkovi* (Prague: Československý spisovatel, 1983).
413 Ornest (born Ota Ohrenstein) and Tigrid (born Pavel Schönfeld) were young actor-directors who went into exile and joined the BBC Czech Service in 1941. While Ornest returned to

appeared with particular frequency: Antonín Sova, Viktor Dyk, and Jan Neruda. Sova and Dyk, respected writers of overtly patriotic verse in the late nineteenth and early twentieth centuries, were both quoted on several occasions, the chosen works reflecting the needs of the times. In May 1943, with victory still a distant prospect, Sova's words encouraged listeners to "have strength: you will see that long-lost freedom resurrected"; while Dyk's poem "Země mluví" (The Country Speaks) reassured listeners that "I will not die out, I am eternal," but also warned them of the dangers of treason.[414] On 9 May 1945, however, once victory was won, Sova was quoted again, to tell the audience that "we always knew that it is beautiful to endure."[415] The single most frequently broadcast poem was Jan Neruda's "Jen dál!" (Only Forward!), which was quoted on three separate occasions, including in the first broadcast of the government programme after its restructuring as *Hlas svobodné republiky*. The poem's opening stanza illustrates its relevance to the war situation as the Czechoslovak state was threatened:

> We were born of a stormy time,
> And step by step we walk in stormy clouds,
> Proudly towards our noble goal,
> Bowing our heads only before our nation.
> We knew what awaited us on our journey,
> Although thunder crashed and frost blew into our bones,
> It is to that ancient Czech music,
> That we will go forwards – on, ever on! [416]

Works of Czech literature, like events and figures of Czech history, were presented as being deeply linked with the "Czech spirit" and the Czech language, both of which were equally incomprehensible to the Germans. In response to a speech made by Goebbels at a gathering of cultural workers, the government programme reported that the Reich's

---

Prague after the war, Tigrid was to become a prominent figure in the anti-Communist exile after 1948. For more information on their work in London, see Srba, *Múzy v exilu*, 94, 111–17. Ornest described some of his experiences in London, in *Hraje váš tatínek ještě na housle? Rozhovor Marie Valtrové s Otou Ornestem* (Prague: Primus, 1993), esp. 60–70.

414 BBC Czechoslovak Programme, 16 May 1943; 9 May 1943, LN Z 1943 – 21, CRA.
415 BBC Czechoslovak Programme, 9 May 1945, LN Z 1945 – 46, CRA.
416 The poem was read on 29 March 1943, 8 April 1944, and 6 May 1945; see BBC Czechoslovak Programme, LN Z 1943 – 20; LN Z 1944 – 32; LN Z 1945 – 46, CRA. Translation is author's own.

propaganda minister had "sacrificed himself so much that he recently read a few Czech books and watched a few Czech films."

Which books were they? We doubt that he would read Palacký, Neruda, Masaryk, or Čapek. If his brain, ravaged by Nazi nihilism, was at all capable of understanding the great works that the small Czech nation has given the world, works filled with a deep humanity, Dr. Goebbels would never be able to lower himself to the superficiality of his speech to Czech cultural workers.[417]

The occupiers were therefore excluded from the best of Czech culture, unable to understand the spirit that influenced the nation's language and cultural works. There is a certain parallel here with British domestic propaganda which often also emphasised the brutal and uncultured nature of Nazism, sometimes reverting to First World War rhetoric about "the Hun" to broaden these criticisms to the wider German population.[418] In the Czechoslovak context, however, government broadcasters could also draw on the political significance of the Czech language, as established in earlier expressions of Czech nationalism.

National languages are often identified as a defining characteristic of a nation and in the ethnically mixed communities of Central Europe this has been particularly true. Historians such as Jaroslava Pečírková and Robert Pynsent have shown that, in the medieval period, the terms *jazyk* (language, tongue) and *národ* (nation) were used synonymously, and Czech grammars and textbooks of the Baroque period, such as Václav Rosa's *Čechořečnost seu Grammtica linguae Bohemicae* (1672), also used the promotion of the Czech language as a means of furthering the Czech national idea.[419] A later "linguocentrist" trend in Czech nationalism was inspired by thinkers such as Herder and began at the end of the eighteenth century, coming to the fore in the nineteenth-century national movement as a clear point of difference with German-speakers.[420] Following

---

417 BBC Czechoslovak Programme, 7 December 1940, LN Z 1940 – 3, CRA.
418 Nicholas, *Echo of War*, 154–55.
419 See Pečírková, "Staročeská synonyma jazyk a národ," *Listy filologické* 92 (1969): 126–30; Robert B. Pynsent, "Die Dalimil-Chronik als polymythischer Text (Dalimil – Fichte – Havel)," in *Geschichtliche Mythen in den Literaturen und Kulturen Ostmittel- und Südosteuropas*, ed. Eva Behrig, Ludwig Richter, and Wolfgang Schwarz (Stuttgart: Franz Steiner Vg, 1999), 199–231, 205.
420 For more on the importance of language to the Czech national movement, see Hugh LeCaine Agnew, *Origins of the Czech National Renascence* (Pittsburgh: University of Pittsburgh Press, 1993), 55–91; Macura, *Znamení zrodu*, 42–60.

the dissolution of the multilingual Austro-Hungarian Empire after the First World War, the designation of a specific language became accepted as an important ethnonational characteristic of successor states, including Czechoslovakia.[421] As a spoken medium, radio perhaps encourages a focus on language and the topic was often discussed by broadcasters in London.

The government broadcasts used the Czech language as a point of national pride, though the tone of their programming shifted from one of defiance to one of increasing sentimentality. Early on, the Švejk broadcasts mocked the Protectorate's attempts at Germanisation, asserting the superiority of Czech over German through satire. In his apparently pro-German way, Švejk referred to the Czechs as a "backward nation" and claimed that Hitler, "in his goodness, lets us speak Czech privately and only corrects us on our grammar and closes the universities." He then went on to criticise the Czechs for hanging onto their language:

> The word is that the Führer is going to simplify our grammar even further, when he's already corrected our spelling, and now we write Führer with a capital F, and we say we're going to *Prag* and to the *Protektorat Böhmen und Mähren* on the *Böhmisch Mährisch Eisenbahn*. Why should we go on putting on airs and using seven cases and expressing male and female gender in the verb? Are four cases not enough for us, when they are enough for the great German nation?[422]

This humorous take on German efforts to influence and suppress the Czech language soon gave way to a more emotive approach, however, reminiscent of some nineteenth-century nationalist writings on the topic. Josef Jungmann (1773–1847), one of the most influential figures in the Czech National Revival from the first half of the nineteenth century, placed the Czech language at the very centre of his philosophy, describing it as "the most precious treasure left to us by our ancestors."[423] Palacký also viewed the Czech language as a vital aspect of Czech

---

421 For an extensive study of the links between language and nationalism in the region, see Tomasz Kamusella, *The Politics of Language and Nationalism in Modern Central Europe* (Basingstoke: Palgrave Macmillan, 2009).
422 "Švejkův komentář," 29 August 1940, LN Z 1940 – 1, CRA.
423 Josef Jungmann, "Slovo k statečnému a blahovzdělanému Bohemariusovi," 1814, reproduced in Felix Vodička, ed., *Výbor z díla Josefa Jungmanna* (Prague: F. Kosek, 1948), 57.

national heritage and wrote of the importance of preserving it in the face of the Germanising influence of Vienna:

> The national language is undeniably the most fundamental and dearest aspect of our Bohemian ancestors' legacy to future generations. It was through this medium that the Czechs were able to form an independent nation and acquire a history which shall forever occupy an illustrious place in the annals of the world [...] It is therefore crucial for our generation to preserve this language.[424]

When Prokop Drtina claimed in 1941 that, by imposing the German language on the Czechs, the Germans had robbed the people "of that which is dearest and most sacred to the nation – its language, its mother tongue," he was, therefore, hearkening back to an established trope.[425] Speaking in October 1942, Jan Masaryk wanted to address Nazi Secretary of State for the Protectorate Karl Hermann Frank in one of his broadcasts, but refused to do so in Czech: "For the guy who christened Masaryk Embankment Heydrich Embankment and simultaneously allowed innocent women and children to be imprisoned, I believe Czech is too good. I will not speak with Frank in the language of Hus, Palacký, and Čapek."[426] In Masaryk's interpretation, the Czech language was an important spiritual treasure of the nation and enemies of that nation were unworthy even to hear it. Czech listeners were, however, intrinsically linked to the Czech language, as he indicated at the end of his broadcast:

> And now, a word of good night to you all, you dear, sacred, and innocent ones, whether you are already in Terezín or a concentration camp. I thank you in our sweet mother tongue. I think of you in Czech, I pray for you in Czech and, in the name of all free Czechoslovaks, I thank you in Czech.[427]

It is interesting to note that, in this passage, Masaryk appears to conflate the suffering of all Czechs with the particular persecution of Czechoslovakia's Jewish population, who made up by far the largest group among

---

[424] Quoted in Monika Baár, *Historians and Nationalism: East Central Europe in the Nineteenth Century* (Oxford: Oxford University Press, 2010), 138.
[425] BBC Czechoslovak Programme, 2 March 1941, LN Z 1941 – 5, CRA.
[426] Masaryk, *Volá Londýn* (1990), 145.
[427] Masaryk, *Volá Londýn* (1990), 147.

those imprisoned in camps like Terezín. There is a parallel here with the established post-war narrative of the occupation and Holocaust, which highlighted the nationality of the victims and either underplayed or outright ignored their Jewish ethnicity. There have even been accusations that this was done deliberately, to "embellish portrayals of Czech suffering." Whatever his intentions – and it should be noted that he did speak out against anti-Semitism in his wartime broadcasts – Masaryk was clearly using language here as a common and unifying factor, and endowing it with an emotional significance that listeners were assumed to share.[428]

The spiritual and emotional significance of the language to the nation were also discussed in a broadcast by Minister Jaroslav Stránský. He criticised the German understanding of nationhood which limited itself to "*Blut und Boden*" (blood and soil), maintaining that the most important factor for the Czechoslovak nation was language. According to Stránský, Czechs understood that a language was "the soul of the nation" and "part of every one of us": "We say 'our language' but we are more hers than she is ours." For him, language was not merely a means of communication, it was "the wisdom, experience, feeling, taste, and humour of countless generations [...] the inexhaustible treasure of the nation." Stránský argued that it was the duty of the nation to retain this connection with its language in the face of German opposition, and to ignore the Protectorate press and radio as they reproduced their translations "from bad German into bad Czech."[429]

The idea that Germans were incapable of speaking or writing good Czech was another established theme of the wartime broadcasts. Language errors were highlighted and presented to listeners as a sign of the low intelligence of the Germans behind the text, and the implication was that any content which went against the Czech "spirit" could not be written in "good" Czech. Speaking in condemnation of the magazine *Moravská volnost* (*Moravian Liberty*) in January 1941, Drtina complained that "The magazine goes after the president of the republic and the Czechoslovak army abroad, and it is written in horrible Czech which

---

[428] Eva Schmidt-Hartmann, "The Enlightenment that Failed: Antisemitism in Czech Political Culture," *Patterns of Prejudice* 27, no. 2 (1993): 122, quoted in Alena Heitlinger, *In the Shadows of the Holocaust & Communism: Czech and Slovak Jews Since 1945* (New Brunswick, NJ: Transaction Publishers, 2006), 50n11. Heitlinger discusses this Communist-era narrative in Chapter 3, "(Non)Remembering Jews and the Holocaust," 47–66. In addition to other, shorter references, Masaryk focused particularly on denouncing anti-Semitism in his talk of 29 March 1943; *Volá Londýn* (1990), 194–96.
[429] BBC Czechoslovak Programme, 8 August 1941, LN Z 1941 – 8, CRA.

is teeming with all the most primitive grammatical errors."[430] Anything said in Czech in support of Germany was judged to be in bad Czech, contaminated by a German mentality, even when it was written by native Czech speakers; when condemning the Protectorate press in a speech in 1941, Prokop Drtina dismissed it as being "written in Czech but thought up in German."[431] When Protectorate Prime Minister Alois Eliáš released a statement following his conviction for crimes against the Protectorate, the London broadcasts questioned its validity on linguistic grounds. The bilingual text contained not a single error in the German version, even though "it is known" that Eliáš's command of German was not sufficient for him to have composed it himself. The Czech version, by contrast, contained "several errors against the spirit of the Czech language" and gave "the impression of being a translation from German."[432]

In stark contrast to this lack of comprehension, the writers behind the government programme were keen to show their own familiarity with the intricacies of the Czech language. In a series of comedic dialogues, two apparently typical Czechs, Pepík and Vašek, discussed recent events and Protectorate politics and, just as Švejk had, mocked the absurdity of German propaganda claims and arguments by seeming to take them literally. The dialogues were written and performed by Josef Schwarz and Ota Ornest and appeared sporadically from 1941, before becoming a regular feature of *Hlas svobodné republiky* between April and December 1943. The conversations between Pepík and Vašek (familiar forms of two very common Czech first names, Josef and Václav, respectively) were prefaced with the promise, "you will hear the voice of Prague's streets." In them, Schwarz and Ornest sought to recreate the familiar language and atmosphere of a chance meeting in Prague, demonstrating their familiarity with it while appealing to the audience's own knowledge.[433] The language of these dialogues was very different to that normally heard in the government programme, as they were performed in highly informal spoken Czech, known as *obecná čeština,* and were full of slang phrases and non-standard grammar.[434] These dialogues are an example of how

---

430 BBC Czechoslovak Programme, "Politický pokyn," 6 January 1941, LN Z 1941 – 4, CRA.
431 Drtina, *A nyní promluví*, 144.
432 BBC Czechoslovak Programme, 18 October 1941, LN Z 1941 – 9, CRA.
433 See, for example, the opening of a dialogue from August 1943: "Těbuh, Pepíku, seš nějakej přepadlej, hochu, copak tě trápí?"; BBC Czechoslovak Programme, 10 August 1943, LN Z 1943 – 23, CRA.
434 For example, terms such as *brácha* instead of *bratr*, "brother"; replacing the long *-ý* with *-ej*; adding a *v-* to the beginning with o (*voni* rather than *oni*), etc.

a sense of community can be perpetuated over the radio in a unique way, without referring to already established historical works or figures. The programmes were predicated on intimate knowledge of the spoken dialect of Prague and, though they can be read, they are intended to be spoken aloud and listened to as an example of everyday, informal communication. The audio nature of radio made it uniquely well-suited for this kind of performance, at this particular time.

Czech music was felt to be just as incomprehensible to German ears as the Czech language. In 1944 Jan Masaryk spoke with disgust at hearing that Germans in the Protectorate were celebrating the 120th anniversary of the birth of Bedřich Smetana, and felt that their performance of *Z českých luhů a hájů* (*From Bohemia's Fields and Groves*) was so bad as to seem almost deliberately poor. "I can imagine though," he added, "that, for the German *Horst Wessel Lied* generation, playing Smetana is difficult. Smetana – pure, clear, Slavic, optimistic, and unyielding in the face of suffering – is the absolute antithesis of everything the former so-called Germany has done, is doing, and will continue to do for a little while yet." He then suggested that love of great Czech music should inspire listeners to greater acts in defence of the nation, predicting that, over the next few months, "Czechs and Slovaks will show, must show, the world that they are worthy of Bedřich Smetana."[435] Smetana's *Má vlast* (*My Country*) was a highly patriotic set of symphonic poems devoted to Bohemia that was, unusually, not immediately banned in the Protectorate. This prompted Josef Kodíček to explain to listeners that

> Even if they generously allow you to play Smetana's *Má vlast* and actually applaud it, even in Berlin, then it is only because in their limitless stupidity they do not understand that *Tábor* and *Blaník* speak in just the same way as Palacký, Neruda, Třebízský, Jirásek, Holeček, Sládek, and all Czech culture. You understand though and you know that the noble conclusion of Libuše's prediction will help you to overcome all the evils of hell.[436]

---

[435] Masaryk, *Volá Londýn* (1990), 203.
[436] BBC Czechoslovak Programme, 27 April 1941, LN Z 1941 – 6, CRA. *Tábor* and *Blaník* are two movements of *Má vlast* which take their names from sites associated with the Hussite movement and St. Wenceslas, respectively. Václav Beneš Třebízský (1849–84) was a novelist, Alois Jirásek (1851–1930) was a writer of historical plays and novels, Josef Holeček (1853–1929) was a ruralist writer, and Josef Sládek (1845–1912) was a writer and poet of the same period. Libuše was a mythical Czech princess remembered as the founder of the Přemyslid dynasty and of the city of Prague, predicting it would be a city whose glory would touch the stars.

Movements from *Má vlast* and other works by Smetana, such as the opera *Prodaná nevěsta* (*The Bartered Bride*), were among the most frequent choices of music played on the government programme, and listeners were assured that "you will once again listen to his music without the Gestapo at the door."[437] Music was often played in the Wednesday morning broadcasts for young listeners from mid-1943 onwards, and folk songs and music also appeared both in the government programme and in the discs produced by the LTS and sent to Czechoslovak expatriate communities overseas. Songs with a historical significance also appeared, such as the Hussite anthem "Kdož jsú boží bojovníci" (Ye Who Are Warriors of God).[438]

When Protectorate propaganda emphasised the influence of German writers and musicians on their Czech counterparts in order to support Nazi claims that much of Czech culture was merely derivative of German culture, London broadcasters came to their culture's defence. Kodíček argued that German music affected Czech music in form only, in "tone" it remained entirely Czech, and a staged debate broadcast from London reached similar conclusions.[439] Several speakers assured each other that no Czech was deceived by this pathetic attempt at Germanisation, before an extract from Dvořák's *Slovanské tance* (*Slavonic Dances*) was played. The announcers concluded that this music represented a certain "Czech truth" that was both "ungermanised and ungermanisable," predicting that "it will win out in the end."[440] Similar statements were made in reference to the power of music to convince members of other Allied nations of the truth of the Czechoslovak cause. In an LTS programme entitled "Czech Music in England," the narrator noted the admiration on the faces of the British audience when they heard a Czech trio's performance of a piece by Josef Suk, and suggested that the music was capable of winning people over: "This music was born in Bohemia," he commented, "the freedom of the nation that gave the world that music is worth fighting for."[441] Drtina expressed a similar idea in his talk of 14 Decem-

---

437 This comment was made during a programme for the anniversary of Smetana's birth on 2 March 1943, in which the *Vltava* movement was played. Excerpts of *Vltava* were also played on 25 October 1942 and *Vyšehrad* and *Tábor* on 4 April 1943. *Prodaná nevěsta* was played on 4 February and 3 October 1943.
438 This song was included in the military programme on 1 October 1943 and following instructions for the formation of national committees on 16 April 1944; BBC Czechoslovak Programme, "Vojenská beseda," 1 October 1943, LN Z 1943 – 26, CRA; BBC Czechoslovak Programme, 16 April 1944, LN Z 1944 – 32, CRA.
439 BBC Czechoslovak Programme, 18 July 1942, LN Z 1942 – 15, CRA.
440 BBC Czechoslovak Programme, 4 March 1941, LN Z 1941 – 5, CRA.
441 "Česká hudba v Anglii," 101, BBC WBC, CRA.

ber 1941, in which he suggested that Antonín Dvořák was an effective propagandist because his work was not limited by any constraint of language. Dvořák had written music "in his mother tongue," leaving a legacy of works in which "he spoke Czech, but he was speaking a language that is understood in England and America as well as in Kralupy."[442]

By linking culture and history to the linguistic difference between themselves and the Germans, the Czechs in London continued in the established tradition of defining themselves in opposition to the "other." These arguments relied on an acceptance of the idea that there was a fundamental and intrinsic difference between Czechs and Germans that could be neither denied nor overcome. All national groups perceive themselves to be limited groups and therefore exclusive (no nation imagines itself to be "coterminous with mankind").[443] By definition, therefore, there is always another community excluded from the national group, and this could be on the basis of a variety of criteria, be they ethnic, religious, or linguistic. Some have argued, such as Linda Colley in her work on the formation of British national identity, that the definition of the "other" often precedes the definition of the nation: "Men and women decide who they are by reference to who and what they are not. Once confronted with an obviously alien 'Them,' an otherwise diverse community can become a reassuring or merely desperate 'Us.'"[444] Others have suggested that the existence of any natural geographic divisions or objective linguistic or cultural differences is not necessary for the construction of oppositional national identities – it is merely the perception of difference that is vital.[445]

Although the representation of Germans as the alien "other" was already an established trope in Czech nationalism, their position as occupiers and enemies in wartime facilitated an intensification of this representation. While British domestic propaganda tended to present Nazism as the main enemy, rather than the German people as a whole, Czechoslovak broadcasts were often less discerning.[446] The narrative of

---

442 Drtina, *A nyní promluví*, 169–70.
443 Anderson, *Imagined Communities*, 7.
444 Linda Colley, *Britons: Forging the Nation, 1707–1837* (New Haven: Yale University Press, 1992), 6.
445 Peter Sahlins, *Boundaries: The Making of France and Spain in the Pyrenees* (Berkeley: University of California Press, 1989), 270–71.
446 Siân Nicholas argued that, although British propaganda sometimes generalised its insinuations about the enemy to include all Germans, rather than just the Nazi leaders, this was done "more by implication than by design," and thus did not display the concerted effort at

historical German aggression was already established in the national story, and increasing evidence of German violence made the production of propaganda which dehumanised the German people relatively straightforward. As happens frequently in wartime, the perceived negative qualities of the enemy were hugely magnified and relied on stereotyped images. Just as the British did with the French throughout the eighteenth and early nineteenth centuries, the Czechoslovaks defined themselves against the Germans "as they imagined them to be" – in this case, barbaric, militarist, and cruel.[447] The language used by broadcasters in the government programme furthered this impression of the Germans as inhuman invaders. Germans were frequently referred to as *vetřelci* – a word which can be translated as "invader," but also as "imposter" or "alien" – and occasionally as *násilníci* (violators, criminals), *okupanti* (occupiers), and even, mimicking the vocabulary of National Socialism itself, as *národ palidí* (a nation of sub-humans).[448] Few broadcasters were capable of rivalling the vitriol and disdain that Jan Masaryk reserved for discussions of the German character and, in his calls for violence against Germans, he played upon an established Czech historical theme. Given what cultural giants like Beethoven and Bach had achieved, Masaryk asked, "how in God's name is it possible for the German nation to have fallen so low?" There were no exceptions, as far as Masaryk was concerned; the entire nation had been "taken over" by the "Prusso-Nazi mentality" and the punishment would be terrible – "a hundred Germans for every Czech, and that won't be enough!"[449] Here, Masaryk seemed almost to mimic the call of Soběslav, a twelfth-century Bohemian prince who is reputed to have offered rewards to men who presented him with the noses they had cut from the faces of defeated Germans.[450]

The other principle "enemy" to be featured in the broadcasts was Hungary, generally cast into the same role of "eternal foe" and "other," but for the Slovaks and Subcarpathian Ruthenians to define themselves against, rather than the Czechs. One broadcast for Subcarpathian Ruthenians claimed that "the Hungarian overlords, just as much

---

generalisation that I argue can be seen in the Czechoslovak exile government's broadcasts; see Nicholas, *Echo of War*, 155.
447 Colley, *Britons*, 5.
448 BBC Czechoslovak Programme, 2 July 1944, LN Z 1944 – 33; 20 August 1944, LN Z 1944 – 35; 7 December 1940, LN Z 1940 – 3, CRA.
449 Masaryk, *Volá Londýn* (1990), 81, 120, 125.
450 The story appears in Dalimil's Chronicle; see Jiří Daňhelka et al., eds., *Staročeská kronika tak řečeného Dalimila*, vol. 2 (Prague: Academia, 1988), 179.

as the Germans, are the ancient enemies of the Slavs," and there were frequent references in both Slovak- and Russian/Ukrainian-language programmes to the historical oppression inflicted by the Hungarian kingdom on its non-Hungarian subjects.[451] In particular, the kingdom's policy of "magyarisation" – the suppression of other languages and cultures in favour of Hungarian – was highlighted as oppression of national culture from which life in the shared Czechoslovak Republic had offered "salvation."[452] The Hungarians were not discussed as aggressively or as frequently as Germans, however, and there are two likely reasons for this. Firstly, negative mentions of Hungary were not permitted to be broadcast early in the conflict, as Britain wished to avoid raising tensions which might push Hungary to declare war.[453] In fact, British broadcasting to Hungary was seen by the Czechoslovak exiles as overly sympathetic even after the two were officially at war from late 1941.[454] A possible secondary reason is simply that the topic pertained more to Slovakia and Subcarpathian Ruthenia than the Czech lands and, as with other themes, therefore received less airtime.

* * *

Cultural, linguistic, and historical arguments were thus deployed by the Czechoslovak government-in-exile to support the idea of the "free republic" that its programme represented, and the medium of radio provided the exiles with useful means by which to further this concept. Broadcasting enabled them to play patriotic music, recite poems, read humorous short stories, and perform informal, slang-laden sketches, all of which demonstrated the cultural ties they shared with their listeners. The exile government also used its programme to discuss Czechoslovak history

---

[451] BBC Czechoslovak Programme, 18 October 1943, LN Z 1943 – 25, CRA.
[452] BBC Czechoslovak Programme, 25 October 1943, LN Z 1943 – 25, CRA.
[453] British caution in this area can be seen in discussions following a speech given by Beneš in Aberdeen in November 1941, which made reference to specific territorial claims and was later repeated in part on the BBC, despite a ban. The FO informed the BBC Czech Section that it must broadcast a statement saying Beneš's views were not the views of the British government, and Hungarian specialists at PWE supported the suggestion, but there was opposition from the exiles, Lockhart, and Strang, who admitted he did "not very much care what the Hungarians think or do" at this stage. Roberts of the FO noted that such a statement "would be a public rebuke, however well merited, to Dr. Benes, and it might convey rather too apologetic an impression if we are intending within the next few days to declare war on Hungary," which Britain was to do on 5 December that year; see Roberts, FO minute, 13 November 1941, Broadcasts to Czechoslovakia, C 13319/10893/12, FO 371/26418, TNA.
[454] Němeček et al., Zápisy ze schůzí, 1:378, 400, 835.

and perpetuate the already established narrative of an innately democratic and cultured people continually suffering at the hands of their aggressive, uncultured, and ignorant German neighbours. The much-discussed but only loosely defined "Czech spirit" was held up to listeners as an example, appealing to all of those who shared some kind of identification or familiarity with any of the many historical, cultural, or linguistic allusions made in the broadcasts. The fundamental issue with nationalist propaganda within the government-in-exile's radio programme, however, was its Czech-centric approach.

Throughout the twenty years of the First Republic, the complexities of the "Czechoslovak" national identity had been the focus of much emotionally charged debate, which continues today when historians of the period sometimes become preoccupied with the question of whether the Czechoslovak state, with its mixture of nationalities, was doomed to fail from the start.[455] With regard to Slovakia, the war period – during which Czechs and Slovaks had very different experiences of occupation and resistance – marks a difficult chapter in the long history of Czech–Slovak relations. Although a significant amount of Slovak-language broadcasting was carried out from London (and will be discussed in more detail in Chapter Three), Slovak cultural and historical content was never featured to the same extent as its Czech counterpart. Although there were several occasions on which Slovak poems and sometimes Slovak folk music were broadcast, they were often uncredited. No Slovak writers had their anniversaries marked and no literary works were held up for their national significance, despite the boom in Slovak-language publishing since 1918.[456] Part of the problem – in addition to the lack of attention and respect accorded to Slovak culture in the preceding two decades – was that the government in Bratislava held something of a monopoly over Slovak nationalism, leaving relatively little for the exiles to include in their united Czechoslovak identity that was specifically Slovak.[457] The

---

455 In his introduction to Placák's book on the St. Wenceslas millennial celebrations, for example, Petr Pithart states, "We need to know whether all the efforts of the founders and builders of the state were or were not ridiculous and pointless from the start," and he concludes from Placák's slim volume that "what happened [i.e., the break-up of Czechoslovakia in 1938–39] need not have happened"; Placák, *Svatováclávské milenium*, 8.
456 On the development of Slovak literature in the First Republic, see Štefan Krčmery, "Slovak Literature," in *Slovakia Then and Now*, ed. Robert Seton Watson (London: George Allen & Unwin, 1931), 141.
457 Jan Rychlík has estimated that Slovak culture had "almost no impact on the Czechs" during the First Republic, but that "the Czech cultural impact on Slovakia was considerable"; Rychlík, "'Czech-Slovak Relations in Czechoslovakia, 1918–1939," in *Czechoslovakia in a Nationalist and*

points on which the London broadcasts challenged the ruling Hlinka Slovak People's Party (Hlinkova slovenská ľudová strana, HSĽS) were in relation to political and religious legitimacy and the idea of unity among Slavs. It is impossible to judge from the surviving sources whether this was a conscious decision based on what was thought to make the most effective propaganda, or the result of a lingering lack of interest in works of Slovak high culture, but the Czech-centrism of both the government apparatus in London and its broadcasting is indisputable.

The Czechoslovak government in London was also somewhat limited in its efforts to address the German-speaking population of Czechoslovakia. Early on, political figures such as Beneš included German-speaking citizens in their references to the Czechoslovak population and efforts were made to include some German-language programming in the Czechoslovak broadcasts. The Czechoslovak Germans were represented in London by Social Democrat émigrés under the leadership of Wenzel Jaksch; as a native German-speaker politically opposed to Nazism, the British made use of him in the early years of the war in programmes broadcast on both the Austrian and German services of the BBC. The Czechoslovak government argued that Czechoslovak German-speakers should broadcast via the BBC Czechoslovak Service, on the grounds that doing otherwise suggested the German-speaking regions were not considered by Britain to be part of Czechoslovakia. The Foreign Office denied this request on the grounds that including broadcasts for German-speakers in the Czechoslovak programme would be interpreted as a sign that German-speaking territories *would* be included in post-war Czechoslovakia, thereby contravening the British government's policy of refusing to commit to any borders in Central Europe. The Foreign Office thereby acknowledged the potential political significance of a speaker appearing on a particular BBC service while simultaneously denying the fact that including such speakers on the German and Austrian services also implied British plans for post-war borders. Attempts by the Czechoslovak government to either incorporate Jaksch into the Czechoslovak Service or to organise its own German-language broadcasts were repeatedly refused. However, as news of Nazi brutality increased, both the Czechoslovaks and the British lost interest in enabling further broadcasts by Czechoslovak Germans. Sympathy for the victims of atrocities

---

Fascist Europe, 1918–1948, ed. Mark Cornwall and R. J. W. Evans (Oxford: Oxford University Press, 2007), 21.

such as the massacre at Lidice in 1942 hardened British public opinion and Jaksch's broadcasts – which had been as frequent as fortnightly – were no longer felt to be appropriate; his post-Lidice talk on the BBC German Service was his last speech before the Foreign Office put a stop to them in June 1942.[458] Unable (or unprepared) to incorporate Slovak and German themes into their projected national identity, Czechoslovak broadcasters from London instead perpetuated the heavily Czech-centric image that had developed in the First Republic, and limited membership of their imagined community to those who were prepared to identify with it.

---

458 Negotiations between Jaksch and Beneš broke down later that year and, in April 1943, the German Social Democrats publicly declared their break with the exile government. Jaksch did not broadcast again and, though he continued to campaign for the rights of Sudeten Germans and oppose the principle of population transfer, he fell from favour and lost what British support he had enjoyed. British arguments against Beneš's requests for German-language broadcasting can be seen in documentation held in FO 371/26418, TNA – for example, December 1941, C 13993/10893/12. For more on Jaksch's broadcasts, see Brown, *Dealing with Democrats*, 290–305; for more on the wider movement, see Anthony Glees, *Exile Politics in the Second World War: The German Social Democrats in Britain* (Oxford: Clarendon Press, 1982); and Tampke, *Czech-German Relations*.

Chapter Three

Idiots and Traitors? Addressing Slovakia from London

"Anyone talking about an independent Slovakia is either an idiot or a traitor."
Jan Masaryk, 6 January 1943[459]

Broadcasting a message of Czechoslovak unity to listeners in the wartime Slovak Republic caused many problems for the exiles in London, as they struggled with both practical and ideological challenges throughout the conflict. In the context of war, all issues came second to the exile government's fundamental aim of ensuring the post-war recreation of Czechoslovakia. In their determination to present a united front to the Allies, the exiles continued to emphasise Czechoslovak unity in a way that diminished Slovak demands for recognition of their nationhood and their need for autonomy. This chapter will examine the practical factors that limited the exile government's propaganda work in regard to Slovakia and then analyse the most prominent themes selected for Slovak broadcasts. Analysis of this programming shows that, after an early defence of the Czechoslovak nation as a concept, the London exiles were forced to at least partially acknowledge Slovak nationhood in response to accusations from Slovakia itself, but that the rest of their propaganda remained distinctly negative. The primary objective of propaganda to Slovakia was to discredit the Slovak state and even the idea of Slovak political independence in the future, and all subsidiary propaganda themes reinforced this same message: broadcasters played on Slovak affection for America

---
459 Masaryk, *Volá Londýn* (1990), 165.

by highlighting US opposition to the state; religious arguments were used extensively to discredit Slovak leaders' claims of defending Catholicism; and historical and ethnic ties with Russia were used to encourage support for the USSR (and to discourage fighting against Soviet forces). Rather than a "positive" approach of trying to attract Slovak listeners to align with their arguments, programming was instead designed to make them feel guilty for any deviation from the London line. The negative propaganda produced in London for Slovak audiences failed to address the concerns being raised by Slovak representatives in exile, leaving existing problems of Czech–Slovak relations from the First Republic to continue, unresolved, into the post-war period.

Czech–Slovak relations within the shared state is an area of Czechoslovak history which continues to draw attention from scholars, and studies range from condemnations of Czech imperialism to associated defences of the Czech strategy towards Slovakia.[460] The recent publication of a collection of seventeen essays on the topic of "Czechoslovakism" shows ongoing interest in the topic, with the volume's editors positing that only now, after nearly thirty years of separation, have emotions cooled enough to enable frank academic discussion.[461] It is not the intention of this project to seek out and apportion blame, but study of the exile government's work in London and its propaganda reveals that not only were the exiles aware that they were not successfully engaging with much of the Slovak public in their broadcasts, but also that they did little to combat this. Although few speakers used the terse language of Masaryk quoted above, the negative broadcasting to Slovakia from London did nevertheless seek to discredit and condemn any faith in the possibility of Slovak independence, leaving all Slovaks who did not consider themselves to be either idiots or traitors to accept the inevitable return of the Czechoslovak Republic. This state, listeners were told, would learn from the mistakes of the past and ensure total equality between Czechs and Slovaks, but the practical realities of the government's position in exile meant that it could offer few of the concrete promises that Slovak audiences were hoping for.

---

460 Of the former, Kirschbaum's *History of Slovakia* offers an example of an extremely unsympathetic portrayal of the Czech administration, both in the First Republic and throughout the war. Of the latter, Rychlík's *Češi a Slováci* attempts to evaluate the charges most frequently made against the First Republic, generally concluding that they are not supported by evidence.
461 Hudek, Kopeček, and Mervart, *Czechoslovakism*. The editors made these comments at the roundtable session "A Century and a Half of Czechoslovakism" at the 2022 BASEES Conference, held in Cambridge, UK, on 9 April 2022.

The exile government brought with it to London a long legacy of Czech–Slovak tension, and all of the most prominent national issues of the First Republic raised their heads again in the microcosm of exile. The longevity of these arguments – relating to Slovak representation within the state and the status of the Slovak language – has ensured their continuing attraction for historians. As Carol Skalnik Leff noted, the Slovak nationalist movement had consistently sought to capitalise on times of national crisis, to attempt to "reap from the whirlwind" some tangible advance in its affairs.[462] As these crises – the Munich Agreement of 1938, the German invasion of 1939, the Second World War, the Soviet invasion of 1968 – have become the milestones that mark different eras in Czech and Slovak history, the theme of Czech–Slovak relations is relevant to many areas of study.

Jan Rychlík has traced the various peaks and troughs of this relationship throughout the First Republic, but he did not address the war in detail and concluded that, following negotiations between the Slovak National Council (Slovenská národná rada, SNR) and the government-in-exile at the end of the war, the Slovaks "approached the renewal of the Czechoslovak Republic under entirely different conditions" to those of 1918.[463] Conversely, a study of the wartime broadcasts shows just how little progress was made among the exiles on the questions of representation and language left unresolved since the First Republic, suggesting their understanding of shared nationhood had not undergone such a shift as Rychlík identifies. One of the principal practical issues often asserted in defence of the First Republic – that Czechoslovak unity had to be emphasised above all to protect the state against the claims of the German minority – is also of clear relevance to the war period, and the exiles worked so hard to convince the Allies of this unity that subsequent efforts to address specifically Slovak issues were dismissed by the British as an internal linguistic matter, not worthy of broadcasting resources. The exile government was therefore faced with the difficult task of balancing recognition of Slovak issues while simultaneously emphasising unity, and a study of its wartime propaganda reveals a commitment to the latter that was to the detriment of the former.

Exile broadcasters thus found themselves facing two distinct audiences but trying to address them as one. Listeners in the Protectorate were

---

[462] Leff, *National Conflict in Czechoslovakia*, 3.
[463] Rychlík, *Češi a Slováci*, 255–56.

living under German occupation, had seen their state invaded, and faced the threat of death if caught listening to banned foreign broadcasts. Slovak listeners, by contrast, were living in the first Slovak state, exposed to all the propaganda of that state which claimed to be the pinnacle of their national development, and were generally subject to less direct oppression (for example, a ban on listening to foreign radio was only introduced in March 1943).[464] While historical grievances against the First Republic were much promoted in the Slovak press, the broadcasts of the government-in-exile struggled to balance the need to acknowledge certain Slovak specificities with simultaneously presenting Slovakia as an "integral part" of the Czechoslovak state.[465] In an attempt to target Slovak listeners more effectively, various distinct themes were pursued in the exile government programme – principally those of Slovak patriotism, Christianity, and solidarity among Slavs – which appropriated long-standing elements of Slovak national identity. These were then deployed in a negative sense, intended to elicit the guilt of Slovak listeners for betraying their traditional values. Support for any aspect of the "so-called independent Slovakia," as it was often called, was condemned as both unrealistic and shameful, since the subservience of the Slovak state to Nazi Germany tainted it with crimes against the Slovak national tradition.[466] Anyone continuing to support such a state after hearing the evidence laid out in the broadcasts was, the speakers implied, not only a bad Czechoslovak but a bad Slovak, a bad Christian, and a bad Slav.

As well as ideological issues, there were also certain practical matters complicating the exile government's attempts to broadcast effective propaganda to Slovakia. The two most significant of these were the difficulties in allocating specific Slovak programming time, and the lack of appropriate Slovak representatives in London to write and present broadcasts. The Slovak language did not feature in the very earliest broadcasts from London, beginning only at the very end of 1939.[467] Slovak talks then appeared at irregular intervals before becoming a regular

---

[464] "BBC European Audience Estimates: Czechoslovakia," 6 January 1944, EIP series 5, no. 6, E2/184, BBC WAC. It must, of course, be noted that this relative freedom did not extend to persecuted minorities, such as Slovak Jews and Roma peoples. For more on the persecution of these groups in the Slovak state, see Ivan Kamenec, *Po stopach tragedie* (Bratislava: Archa, 1991); Eduard Nižňanský, *Politika antisemitismu a holokaust na Slovensku v rokoch 1938–1945* (Banská Bystrica: Múzeum SNP, 2016).
[465] Minister of the Interior Juraj Slávik described it as such at a cabinet meeting of 16 December 1941; Němeček et al., *Zápisy ze schůzí*, 1:820.
[466] For example, BBC Czechoslovak Programme, 18 February 1941, LN Z 1941 – 5, CRA.
[467] See Ješutová, *Od mikrofonu k posluchačům*, 173.

component of BBC news broadcasts in the second half of 1940.[468] In mid-June 1941 an effort was made to improve the broadcasts to Slovakia when a series of changes were agreed upon: two short Slovak talks were scheduled for broadcast on Mondays and Thursdays every week, the BBC requested the appointment of new Slovak announcers, and Ján Čaplovič (member of the National Council and PRS) volunteered to work with the MZV Radio Department to oversee broadcasts to Slovakia and recruit more Slovaks to help in their production.[469] Those advocating the devotion of greater time and resources to programming specifically for Slovakia, however, faced opposition from those unwilling to accept an administrative division between Czech and Slovak broadcasting which they felt would be an acknowledgement of disunity.

Other international broadcasters had no such qualms; the Soviet Union had launched programmes in Czech (*Za národní osvobození*, "For National Liberation") and Slovak (*Za slovenskú slobodu*, "For Slovak Freedom") in the summer of 1941 and the two had always been entirely separate, a fact which did not go unnoticed in London.[470] In fact, programme makers became increasingly concerned by the rival broadcasts; at a PRS meeting in late June, State Minister Hubert Ripka told members, "We have a new competitor in Moscow." Having heard both the Czech and Slovak broadcasts, Ripka felt that "both were very good" and he advised the PRS that "in light of this, we must raise the level of our broadcasts."[471] At the next meeting, held a month later, Josef Körbel reported that Moscow was broadcasting four Czech and four Slovak programmes per day, for a total of 4.5 hours. Körbel also told members that, prior to the signing of the agreement with the Czechoslovak government-in-exile on 18 July 1941, Moscow had "addressed the Czech and Slovak nations separately," with Prokop Drtina responding that they now "mostly" addressed the "Czechoslovak nation." Multiple committee

---

[468] See Karel Brušák, "Notes on the Czechoslovak Section," undated, E1/1323, BBC WAC.
[469] PRS, 19 June 1941, MV–L 271: 2-82-4, CNA.
[470] See Bednařík, Jirák, and Köpplová, *Dějiny českých médií*, 213. Zdeněk Nejedlý published a collection of his radio talks from Moscow in *Hovoří Moskva: Rozhlasové projevy z let 1939–1945* (Prague: Odeon, 1977); and Zdeněk Fierlinger, who spent time in both Moscow and London during the war, published "Několik vzpomínek na činnost Československého rozhlasu v době války," in *Kapitoly z dějin čs. rozhlasu* (Prague: Studijní oddělení československého rozhlasu, 1964). Moscow also broadcast programmes targeting German-speakers in Czechoslovakia; for more information, see Mark Cornwall, "Stirring Resistance from Moscow: The German Communists of Czechoslovakia and Wireless Propaganda in the Sudetenland, 1941–1945," *German History* 24, no. 2 (2006): 212–42.
[471] PRS, 30 June 1941, MV–L 271: 2-82-4, CNA.

members pressed Körbel to meet with Zdeněk Fierlinger (Czechoslovak envoy to the Soviet government) before he left for Moscow, in the hope of aligning the Moscow and London broadcasts more closely.[472] Over a year later, however, the situation was still apparently unresolved, when Slovak State Minister Ján Lichner raised the issue at a cabinet meeting on 28 August 1942, complaining that the Czech and Slovak broadcasts from Moscow were still separate and "if they recognise the Czechoslovak Republic, then that should be reflected in the broadcasts too." General Sergej Ingr explained that the system had been established when Slovakia still had a separate consul in Moscow. Although efforts had been made to address this issue via prominent Czechoslovaks in Moscow, such as Zdeněk Nejedlý, Ingr advised that Czechoslovak broadcasters "do not have the same standing as here" and were largely powerless to influence what was, in reality, "Soviet radio in foreign languages," rather than radio run by any Czechoslovaks themselves.[473]

Many of the London exiles refused to differentiate between Czech and Slovak broadcasting as a matter of principle, but this became increasingly impractical in the face of growing criticism of the Slovak-language programmes. At a PRS meeting on 9 July 1942, which included many members of the government and the National Council, Pavol Macháček advised that, despite not wishing to differentiate between Czech and Slovak radio (insisting that "it is in fact Czechoslovak radio"), he was forced to agree with the "majority" of Slovaks that Slovak broadcasting was failing in its mission. Arguing that the Slovak "mentality" was fundamentally different to the Czech, Macháček insisted that those who did not truly know the Slovak people should not broadcast to them, labelling such attempts as "impudent." Macháček warned that he didn't want Slovak listeners addressed by "some Vopršálek or Čecháček," using pejorative names that implied Czech everymen. The sensitive nature of these comments can be seen in the immediate indignant response from Jan Masaryk. Sensing an attack, Masaryk – who regularly referred to his Slovak heritage and spoke fairly frequently in Slovak in his broadcasts, while remaining predominantly a Czech-speaker – replied defensively, "I am a Slovak."[474] Although Macháček's comments were couched in the necessary Czechoslovak-minded terms which a meeting with government figures required, he was suggesting that, in order to be truly effective, Slovak

---

[472] PRS, 24 July 1941, MV–L 271: 2-82-4, CNA.
[473] Němeček et al., *Zápisy ze schůzí*, 2:567, 569.
[474] PRS, 9 July 1942, MV–L 271: 2-82-4, CNA.

broadcasts needed to be designed specifically to appeal to a different audience. In a subsequent meeting of 30 September that year, Minister Ripka informed the PRS that discussions were underway with the BBC to change the late-night broadcasts to increase "broadcasting for Slovaks," admitting reluctantly that "those who listen to the radio irregularly and don't follow everything have the impression that there is not enough Slovak propaganda broadcasting." Further division of the broadcasts would not be acceptable, however: "Slovak broadcasting cannot be separated from other broadcasting, it is Czechoslovak broadcasting."[475]

While no formal split was made, action was taken to improve Slovak representation within the broadcasting structure towards the end of 1942. Four Slovak members of the PRS and National Council (Macháček himself, Jozef Valo, Ján Paulíny-Toth, and Pavol Viboch) formed a committee and requested that they take it in turns to attend the daily meeting of the MZV Radio Department. They also wanted another Slovak member of staff appointed to the department itself.[476] Having admitted the inadequacies of the propaganda to Slovakia and confirmed that the possibility of expanding the Slovak broadcasts by ten minutes in the late-night slot was soon to be discussed with the BBC, Ripka invited the group to attend a Radio Department meeting in mid-November.[477] At this meeting, the four Slovaks were told that their request for a regular afternoon broadcast dedicated to Slovak issues was being refused, on the grounds that these high-profile slots had to be reserved for current events and were required to follow the propaganda directive for the day (this was the same argument that the BBC later used to reject the MZV's plans for changing the government programme, resulting in the reluctant acceptance of "free time"). Instead, the already established short Slovak broadcasts on Mondays and Thursdays would continue and the upcoming change to the late-night broadcasts would also include two five-minute slots per week for Slovak talks, with other Slovak programming to be arranged "whenever it proved to be necessary." The principle issue, however, was that the BBC considered news and accuracy to be of primary importance and viewed "the language question" (from the BBC perspective, the matter of Slovak-specific broadcasting was viewed solely

---

475 PRS, 30 September 1942, MV–L 271: 2-82-4, CNA.
476 PRS, 30 November 1942, MV–L 271: 2-82-4, CNA.
477 PRS, 30 September 1942, MV–L 271: 2-82-4, CNA; Ripka to Viboch, 13 November 1942, Londýnský archive [LA] 25: 61-20-6, CNA.

in terms of the language spoken) as a secondary matter.[478] As for the appointment the committee had requested, their nominated candidate, Jozef Prídavok, was rejected on the grounds that his brother publicly espoused views on Slovak issues that clashed with those of the exile government.[479] Ignoring protests that Prídavok was not influenced by his brother's work and that improvement in the Slovak broadcasts would demand the appointment of the best possible candidates, Ripka advised the Slovaks to find an alternative.[480] Ministers Lichner and Slávik doubted the likelihood of finding another similarly qualified Slovak journalist in London and Minister Bečko commented succinctly that, when it came to appointing Slovaks, "there simply aren't the people."[481]

The number of Slovaks working within the Czechoslovak government apparatus in London was an issue raised both behind the scenes and within the broadcasts to Slovakia. The general shortage of Slovaks available in the London exile community was a problem for many branches of the exile government and it also revived memories of the long-standing problem of representation in administration that had plagued the First Republic.[482] The fourteen-member exile government as formed on 21 June 1940 contained five Slovaks: Ján Bečko (minister of social welfare from 12 November 1942), Ján Lichner (minister of agriculture from 12 November 1942), Štefan Osuský (who stopped attending meetings early in 1941 after conflict with other members and was officially removed from government on 31 March 1942), Juraj Slávik (minister of the interior from the government's inception), and General Rudolf Viest (state secretary and the state minister in the Ministry of National Defence).[483] There were also approximately ten other Slovaks who served in the National Council at various times, one of whom also broadcast

---

- 478 Körbel summarised the meeting at the following session a week later; PRS, 30 November 1942, MV–L 271: 2-82-4, CNA.
- 479 Peter Prídavok was being monitored by PWE, and Lockhart had noted that he was "violently anti-Beneš" in a letter of October 1941 to the controller of the BBC European Service, Ivone Kirkpatrick; Lockhart to Kirkpatrick, 29 October 1941, PWE "Contacts with Slovakia [Petr Priedavok]," E1/641/2, BBC WAC.
- 480 Němeček et al., *Zápisy ze schůzí*, 2:723–4.
- 481 Němeček et al., *Zápisy ze schůzí*, 2:724, 725.
- 482 Jan Rychlík offers a comprehensive history of the *personální otázka* in his history of Czech–Slovak relations, *Češi a Slováci*, 84–89, 154–57. The lack of qualified Slovak officials in 1918 had caused an influx of Czechs into the administration in Slovakia and Rychlík outlines the various arguments as to whether or not the numbers of Czechs were excessive and obstructed the development of a Slovak administrative class. Debates on this matter continue today.
- 483 For details on the composition of the exile government, see Němeček et al., *Zápisy ze schůzí*, 1:60–61.

(Alexander Vido) and five of whom both broadcast regularly and sat on the PRS: Čaplovič, Macháček, Paulíny-Toth, Valo, and Viboch. Even among these Slovak figures, however, the topic of Slovak representation remained contentious.

At a cabinet meeting on 13 January 1941, the issue was raised of a request by Minister Štefan Osuský for information regarding the employment of Slovaks in the Ministry of Social Welfare (Ministerstvo sociální péče, MSP). The sensitive nature of this issue is clear from the first response, as Ján Bečko, then state secretary in the MSP, testily retorted that there would be more Slovaks in London to employ if Osuský (previously Czechoslovak ambassador to France) had helped more of them to evacuate before France fell.[484] Jan Masaryk was also defensive on the issue of Slovak employees, sharing his regret that "there are not enough Slovaks here," but asserting that everyone knew his family connection with Slovakia and he would not stand for anyone telling him how many Slovaks to employ in his office.[485] Minister Ján Lichner offered a conciliatory voice, saying that, although it was a "petty question," he understood why it mattered to Osuský "as a Slovak," who he maintained had a right to know who was working where. Lichner followed this comment with a word of warning, however: "I would just like to note that this question has caused us difficulties for twenty years. Today we must be aware that we should share a single common goal, that of a united Czechoslovakia."[486] Juraj Slávik returned to the ideological implications of Osuský's question and expressed his resistance to the division of employees into Czechs and Slovaks, claiming that, if he were to receive such a request regarding his staff, he would simply reply "that I employ only Czechoslovaks."[487]

It was acknowledged, however, that listeners in Slovakia were interested in the numbers of Slovak representatives in London. An undated report on Slovak student opinion from the latter end of the conflict advised that "Slovak ministers in London always attracted great attention, with the greatest notice taken of their numbers."[488] An awareness of this interest can be clearly seen in broadcasts, such as that in which Slávik

---

[484] Němeček et al., *Zápisy ze schůzí*, 1:280. Accusations of this kind would later contribute to Osuský's resignation from the government; see ibid., 1:603 (Appendix B).
[485] Masaryk's paternal grandfather had been a Slovak; Němeček et al., *Zápisy ze schůzí*, 1:280.
[486] Němeček et al., *Zápisy ze schůzí*, 1:280–81.
[487] Němeček et al., *Zápisy ze schůzí*, 1:281.
[488] "Názor slovenského studentstva na slovenskou vládu a čs. zahraniční vládu," undated, LA 2: 61-2-5/1-78, CNA. Although this document is undated it refers to events in "the first years of

refuted Slovak propaganda claims of divisions in London. Emphasising the prominent positions held by Slovaks in London, Slávik insisted that all Slovaks in the government ("Ján Bečko, Ján Lichner, Rudolf Viest, and I"), as well as all Slovaks in the National Council ("in which sit 12 Slovaks from a total of 40 members and where in the 6-member presidium there are two deputy chairmen: Dr. Ján Čaplovič and Dr. J. Paulíny-Toth"), were "united in fundamental matters and all working hard for the return of the Czechoslovak Republic to our native Slovakia."[489] Perhaps to make these numbers sound more impressive, Slávik appears to be counting the Slovak government ministers again in his figures for the National Council, even though they did not have voting rights there. On 15 July 1943, speaking in response to a Slovak propaganda attack on a declaration made by the government-in-exile, Slávik again took pains to name prominent London-based Slovaks and commented that, in trying to undermine the impact of the declaration,

> Šaňo Mach attempted a deception: he said that the declaration had been signed by two Slovak ministers – Slávik and Lichner – and just happened to forget that there is also State Secretary General Viest, and that Ján Bečko also had a role to play. Slovaks know very well that there are four Slovaks in the Czechoslovak government who all signed the declaration: Bečko, Lichner, Slávik, and Viest.[490]

The declaration in question, which expressed unanimous Slovak support for the exile government, was accused by Slovak propagandists of proving that the exiles did not recognise the Slovaks as a separate nation, including as it did references to "the sovereign Czechoslovak nation."[491] The debate over whether the Czechs and Slovaks constituted a single nation is another example of an issue that went unresolved in the First Republic and returned to trouble the exiles in London.

---

the war" in the past tense and the reformation of Czechoslovakia in the future tense, placing it in the second half of the conflict.
489 BBC Czechoslovak Programme, 3 April 1943, LN Z 1943 – 20, CRA.
490 BBC Czechoslovak Programme, 15 July 1943, LN Z 1943 – 23, CRA. Šaňo (Alexander) Mach was a member of the HSĽS and served as both Slovak minister of the interior and head of the party's militia, the Hlinka Guard.
491 BBC Czechoslovak Programme, 11 July 1943, LN Z 1943 – 23, CRA.

"The admirable and loyal Czechoslovak nation"

The "national question" and references such as those made in the declaration of 11 July 1943 to "the admirable and loyal Czechoslovak nation" were problematic for exile broadcasters, as unresolved arguments about what this term represented resurfaced in London.[492] In seeking to establish Czechoslovakia's rights as a nation-state, the First World War-era exiles under T. G. Masaryk had carried out a successful propaganda campaign abroad to convince the Allies of the existence of a Czechoslovak nation hitherto unknown to them, and debate on this "foundational concept" of the state had continued throughout the First Republic.[493] The 1920 Constitution proclaimed itself to be that of "the Czechoslovak nation," and the term became increasingly common in government rhetoric thereafter, shown in legislation, political speeches, and official publications such as school textbooks.[494] The drive to present Czechs and Slovaks as a single nation, as was commonplace in statistics and census data, has been accurately described as "tactically motivated," ensuring as it did that the single Czechoslovak nation made up the absolute majority of the population, significantly outnumbering the German minority and thereby justifying Czechoslovak rule.[495] Challenges to the official narrative, according to which the Czechs and Slovaks were two "tribes" or "branches" of a single nation, were most often made by advocates for greater Slovak autonomy and were generally perceived by the administration in Prague as efforts to undermine the

---

492 BBC Czechoslovak Programme, 11 July 1943, LN Z 1943 – 23, CRA. For more on the problems caused in Czech–Slovak relations by debate over the doctrine of Czechoslovakism, see Rychlík, *Češi a Slováci*, esp. 126–29. For a more detailed study of Czechoslovakism with specific reference to Slovakia, see Elisabeth Bakke, "Czechoslovakism in Slovak History," in *Slovakia in History*, ed. Mikuláš Teich, Dušan Kováč, and Martin Brown (Cambridge: Cambridge University Press, 2011), 247–68. Josette Baer's recent study, A *Life Dedicated to the Republic: Vavro Šrobár's Slovak Czechoslovakism*, offers an analysis of the doctrine as part of the work of Šrobár, long-time Slovak minister in the First Republic.
493 Hudek, Kopeček, and Mervart, introduction to *Czechoslovakism*. For more on Czechoslovakism in First World War propaganda, see Bakke, "Czechoslovakism in Slovak History," 249–51.
494 See Elisabeth Bakke, "The Making of Czechoslovakism in the First Czechoslovak Republic," in *Loyalitäten in der Tschechoslowakischen Republik 1918–1938: Politische, nationale und kulturelle Zugehörighkeiten*, ed. Martin Schulze Wessel (Munich: R. Oldenbourg Verlag, 2004), 24–28.
495 Bakke, "Making of Czechoslovakism," 25. "Czechoslovaks" made up over 65% of the population. Division into Czechs and Slovaks would have made Czechs the single largest group (50.8%), Germans the second largest (23.4%), and Slovaks the third (14.7%). See *Sčítání lidu v republice československé ze dne 15. února 1921* (Prague: Státní úřad statistický, 1924), 60, 66, quoted in Bakke, "Making of Czechoslovakism," 25n3.

state.[496] T. G. Masaryk himself was also outspoken on the subject and attributed such challenges to hostile foreign interests, telling a French newspaper in 1921 that "there is no Slovak nation [...] it is the invention of Magyar propaganda."[497] Jan Rychlík's argument that Czechs in the First Republic accepted this shared nationhood as the basis for the state but that, for Slovaks, "it was more a matter of calculated construction which would be abandoned once it had fulfilled its purpose," is borne out by the fact that these two opposing views continued to be expressed by Czechs and Slovaks in London after the end of the First Republic.[498]

Though the question of dual or shared nationhood was not omitted from the exile government programme on the BBC, broadcasters initially sought to move debate on from that single recurring issue. Jaroslav Stránský was the only broadcaster who directly raised the question of two nations in his talks, and the progression of this theme shows the changing approach to the idea in the government programme over time. In a talk of 1941 on the question of Slovak autonomy within Czechoslovakia, Stránský began by stating that "we do not want to return and we will not return to the question of whether Czechs and Slovaks are two nations or two tribes of a single nation. It need only be added that even the Slovaks themselves are not of one mind on this matter." Suggesting that some had viewed the "Czechoslovak nation" not as an existing entity but as something that would develop within the joint state, Stránský emphasised that it did not matter whether this view was correct or not: "maybe they and the Czechs who thought the same were mistaken."[499] He stressed that opinion was divided on this issue, but that those who believed in Czechoslovak state unity saw autonomy as a Czechoslovak

---

496 Bakke points out that the views on the "national question" tended to coincide with views on the structure of the state, since pro-Czechoslovak parties favoured a centralised system and Slovak autonomists a dual federation. Political and national questions were therefore closely intertwined. See Bakke, "Making of Czechoslovakism," 23–24.
497 "Une heure chez Masaryk," *Le Petit Parisien* (14 September 1921), quoted in Tomáš Masaryk, *Cesta demokracie: soubor projevů za republiky*, vol. 2, *1921–1923* (Prague: Čin, 1934), 78.
498 Rychlík, *Češi a Slováci*, 54.
499 Rychlík and Bakke both suggest that this belief was in fact very prominent in the First Republic, but that it was generally interpreted as an expectation that Slovak identity would be subsumed into a Czech-dominated Czechoslovak identity. Rychlík attributed the view that "Slovaks were, or at least would be, Czechs" to the majority of Czechs and a small minority of Slovak Czechoslovakists; Rychlík, *Češi a Slováci*, 128. Bakke argues persuasively that the national identity developed by Czechoslovakists in the First Republic was sufficiently Czech-dominated as to be "complementary" to the existing Czech national identity, but represented a challenge to existing Slovak identities; see Bakke, "Making of Czechoslovakism," 35.

(rather than a Slovak) issue, to be discussed within the shared state which was beyond question.[500]

Despite apparently refusing to countenance the question further, Stránský returned to this question twice in 1943, demonstrating the importance of the issue. On 6 March, the night before the anniversary of T. G. Masaryk's birth, Stránský described the former president as "Slovak by blood, Moravian by birth, Bohemian by language and education, and a Czechoslovak in his work as a statesman," claiming that "he represents Czechoslovakia as a political and nationally unified entity." He went on to dismiss the two nations question again, maintaining that

> whether someone views the Czechs and Slovaks as two national tribes or two branches of one national tribe, after Masaryk no propaganda can drown out and no violence can wipe out the fact that the mutual relationship of Czechs and Slovaks is not a coincidental and changeable result of political conjecture and speculation, but an indivisible fateful and spiritual unity.[501]

On 20 July 1943, in defence of the same government declaration of Slovak ministerial support that Slávik had referenced five days previously, Stránský devoted an entire talk to the question of two nations. He flatly denied the claim that the London exiles were asking Slovaks to replace their Slovak national consciousness with a Czech or Czechoslovak one ("No member of our government thinks or behaves so unwisely") and argued that Czechoslovakia was the joint product of both Czech and Slovak national consciousness. "Any decent and sensible Czech can therefore see Slovak national consciousness only as a condition of Czechoslovak political cohabitation and not an obstacle to it," Stránský argued, claiming that many Czechs and Slovaks already felt a dual national consciousness. "Whether Czechs and Slovaks are two branches of a mutual national tribe or two nations is a question which only the future will reliably answer," he continued, arguing that this was a "scientific question" and pleading, "let's not seek to bicker about it." No government could dictate national consciousness, Stránský stated, suggesting that the only course was to see whether national consciousness developed separately or mutually. Stránský sought to divide the political and national issues

---

500 BBC Czechoslovak Programme, 10 January 1941, LN Z 1941 – 4, CRA.
501 BBC Czechoslovak Programme, 6 March 1943, LN Z 1943 – 19, CRA.

that had caused so much conflict in the First Republic by insisting that the key issue was the importance of Czechoslovak *state* unity, as distinct from the *national* unity that may or may not come.[502]

The Slovak National Uprising, which took place between August and October 1944 and ended with Slovak troops retreating to fight a partisan war, is often cited as a pivotal moment in Slovak and Czechoslovak history, and it offers another example of how the assertive and confident tone of the government broadcasts concealed anxieties behind the scenes.[503] Despite struggling to win guarantees of support from the Allies and worrying about the impact which a German victory could have on both the population and the future of the state, the London exiles not only remained optimistic in updating their listeners on events but also made sure to drive home their message that the uprising was an expression of Slovak commitment to the shared state.[504] "The most fundamental and most important fact is that Slovakia has risen to fight in the name of the Czechoslovak Republic," Ripka told listeners, claiming that the Slovak people had thereby "of their own free will repudiated all the consequences of Munich, of their own free will rejected the so-called independent Slovak state and the traitorous Tiso regime, of their own free will claimed allegiance to the Czechoslovak Republic."[505] Vilém Nový suggested that, as "brothers," the Czechs and Slovaks were "imbued with the same values and fighting for the same thing against the same enemy," and that "this unity for our shared cause – for the Czechoslovak Republic – must show itself most strongly at this very moment."[506]

While the uprising did much to raise the status of Slovak concerns in the recreation of Czechoslovakia, the exile government felt the need to bind the event closely to its cause – both in its own broadcasting and outwardly to its allies – and Stránský felt prompted to return to the shared nation question one last time. On 22 October Stránský broadcast

---

502 BBC Czechoslovak Programme, 20 July 1943, LN Z 1943 – 23, CRA.
503 Slovak historian Vilém Prečan titled his chapter "The Slovak National Uprising: The Most Dramatic Moment in the Nation's History," in Teich, Kovač, and Brown, *Slovakia in History*.
504 On the exile government's struggles, see Jan Němeček, "Československá exilová vláda a počátky Slovenského národního povstání," in *Slovenské národné povstanie – Slovensko a Európa v roku 1944*, by Marek Syrný et al. (Banská Bystrica: Múzeum Slovenského národného povstania, 2014), 239–46. The minutes of the cabinet meetings during the period are also of relevance, and many related documents have been published; see, for example, Prečan, *Slovenské národné povstanie: dokumenty*.
505 BBC Czechoslovak Programme, 8 October 1944, LN Z 1944 – 38, CRA. Jozef Tiso was a member of the HSĽS and president of the Slovak Republic from 1939 to 1945.
506 BBC Czechoslovak Programme, 31 August 1944, LN Z 1944 – 35, CRA. Emphasis in original.

his final discussion of the topic and proclaimed "the argument is over." Following a visit to London by members of the SNR and an agreement being reached, it was clear to Stránský that internal politics of the future republic would "not founder on the one-time question of whether Czechs and Slovaks are separate nations." However, certain notes and marks on the surviving text of the talk challenge the confidence of this assertion. In general, the surviving scripts from the government programme tend to be unmarked, beyond the occasional addition of commas or similar. Stránský's final comments in defence of Czechoslovakism have been edited, seemingly by another hand. His original description of the national question as "non-political" has been obliterated from the Czech text and his statement that it would not recur in the future was highlighted with both an exclamation mark and a question mark. A further obliteration followed his comment that "politically the Slovaks are a distinct nation, as soon as they want to be one and for as long as they want to be one. Just like the Czechs," removing the promise that "no one will obstruct those Slovaks or Czechs who feel Czechoslovak not only in political terms but also nationally." Despite these edits, Stránský offered one last defence of Czechoslovakism: "The concept of national Czechoslovakism was intended, in its beginning, to unite in love and with love what the ages had separated, and not to impose itself on anybody violently, or by means of majority rule." He outlined Slovak support for the foundation of the state and drawing up of the constitution in the name of "we, the Czechoslovak nation," but also acknowledged that "what was suitable then may not be suitable today." Stránský concluded that, while no one could predict what the future would bring, no national argument could affect the fact that "these nations are so close to each other, like no two other nations in the world, nations that are – let us promise this irrevocably – eternally inseparable."[507]

In broadcasting terms, the "national question" often also manifested in arguments over terminology. It was not uncommon for broadcasters to refer to "the Czech nation," the "Slovak nation," and "our nation," though references to "the Czechoslovak nation" also appeared occasionally. Beneš himself was both personally and politically committed to a single Czechoslovak national idea, stating in a Bratislava speech of 1933 that "I speak as a Czechoslovak because [...] I do not feel solely Czech and

---

[507] BBC Czechoslovak Programme, 22 October 1944, LN Z 1944 – 38, CRA.

my Czech feeling is subjugated to my Czechoslovak feeling."[508] This commitment was reflected in the language of government statements, such as the aforementioned controversial statement of 11 July 1943. However, the recollections of Jiří Hronek, who worked as an editor in the MZV Radio Department, suggested the president was not inflexible on the matter. Hronek reported that, following criticisms from Valo in November 1942 that the Slovaks should be given a clear promise that they would be guaranteed equal rights in the renewed republic, Beneš told a meeting of radio workers on the topic of terminology that the Czechoslovak nation existed for him, but that he would not force this view on others. Hronek claimed that Körbel tried to encourage use of the phrase "the Czechoslovak nation" in broadcasts but most staff, with the exception of Kodíček, were resistant and preferred to say "the Czechoslovak people" as a compromise. Writing in the 1960s, Hronek claimed to still possess the text of his report on the signing of the Czechoslovak–Soviet agreement of 18 July 1941, in which he described the treaty as having been written "in Russian and in Czech." Körbel had apparently crossed out "Czech" and replaced it with "Czechoslovak," but Hronek read "Czech" regardless.[509] This attempted correction connects to another controversial aspect of Czechoslovakism: the concept of a single Czechoslovak language.

In addition to the difficulties apparent when actually discussing the national question, there were also political implications involved in the language of the broadcasts. Czech and Slovak are linguistically very close and mutually comprehensible in almost all circumstances, but the experience of the First Republic had shown the emotional and political significance associated with the "language question." Slovak linguists in the eighteenth and nineteenth centuries had advanced various theories on the Slovak language (some suggesting it was a dialect of Czech and others that it was a distinct language of its own), and these theories had become closely bound up with the question of nationhood.[510] Calls for Czechoslovak unity leading up to the creation of the republic had often emphasised the close relations between the Czech and Slovak languages;

---

508 Quoted in Rychlík, *Češi a Slováci*, 134.
509 Hronek, "Československý rozhlas v Londýně," 51–52. It should be noted that Hronek rose to become editor-in-chief of Czechoslovak Radio after the war and retained this high position after the Communists took power in 1948. The tone of his writing in this period is strikingly pro-Communist and, consequently, anti-Beneš.
510 For an overview of the history of Slovak and changing interpretations of it as a language, see Kamusella, *Politics of Language*, 131–35.

the National Slovak Council said of Bohemia, Moravia, and Slovakia in 1848 that "one language resounds throughout these countries," and the Declaration of the Slovak Nation, signed at Turčiansky Svätý Martin on 30 October 1918, proclaimed that "the Slovak nation is a part of the Czechoslovak nation, both in language and in culture and history."[511] Within the First Republic, however, accusations of attempts to "Czechify" Slovak caused outcry, and the conflict over use of Czech and Slovak within the state meant that, by the time the war broke out, the status of Slovak as a distinct language was widely accepted.[512] Although there is certainly no evidence in the sources used for this project to suggest any classification of Slovak as less than a distinct language in its own right, the unresolved "language question" was another problem of the First Republic which returned to haunt the exiles in London.

Despite mutual comprehensibility, efforts by figures such as Jan Masaryk and President Beneš to speak Slovak on air and various discussions held behind the scenes show deference to the emotional significance of the language used in broadcasting. The issue was raised at a PRS meeting on 30 June 1941, when Paulíny-Toth called for political talks to sometimes be broadcast in Slovak. Assuming that Paulíny-Toth meant for the political figure who had written the talk to deliver it in Slovak, Stránský expressed concern that, while this might work for figures such as President Beneš, it was uncertain "what effect it has when someone speaks Slovak badly." This discussion evinces an awareness of the emotive power of language among Slovak listeners, and Paulíny-Toth's response – that he actually envisioned Slovak announcers reading translations of political talks originally written in Czech – suggests that he felt there was political capital to be gained by addressing major political themes in Slovak, even if the original content would have been understood by Slovak listeners without translation.[513] Translations from Czech into Slovak were very rare within the broadcasts, however, and generally appeared as translated quotes within a Slovak-language commentary

---

511   Ivan Markovič, "The Cooperation of Slovaks and Czechs in War and Revolution," in Watson, *Slovakia Then and Now*, 92.
512   Jan Rychlík argues that the term "Czechoslovak language," as used in official documents in the First Republic, was interpreted in practice to mean either Czech or Slovak. While there was some Czech influence on Slovak (and none the other way), Rychlík rejects the suggestion that Czechs didn't accept Slovak as an official language and finds that even those Czechs who originally considered it a dialect of Czech rather than a distinct language were eventually convinced "under pressure from the objective reality"; Rychlík, *Češi a Slováci*, 79–84.
513   PRS, 30 June 1941, MV-L 271: 2-82-4, CNA.

on an originally Czech-language speech or document; for example, in a commentary on the speech given by Beneš after his arrival in Košice in April 1945, an announcer read, in Slovak, a section on the equality of Czechs and Slovaks within Czechoslovakia.[514] Meanwhile, in a talk on Protectorate President Emil Hácha, Interior Minister Slávik made an unusual departure from speaking in his native Slovak: "Since I am speaking primarily to listeners in the Czech lands today, so that there may be no opportunity to manipulate and distort what I say, I will speak Czech."[515] This suggested that, at the very least, he felt the potential for misunderstanding and distortion to be greater if he were to speak Slovak.

The importance of the Slovak language to listeners in Slovakia is also evident in the wartime intelligence received by the Czechoslovak government-in-exile and the BBC. One BBC survey report from January 1942 quoted an edition of *Slovák* (*The Slovak*), the newspaper of the HSĽS, from 26 November 1941, as saying that "Beneš's neglect of the Slovaks is illustrated by the fact that the broadcasts are in bad Slovak. Macháček's Slovak is not very good but it is nerve-racking to listen to Bečko, Vallo [*sic*] and Vido." The compiler of the intelligence digest accepted that such criticism was "not necessarily without effect" but also "not necessarily well-founded (since no Slovak seems to think that any other Slovak can speak good Slovak)."[516] Indeed, the repeated contradictory complaints that BBC intelligence gathered, relating to the quality of Slovak spoken in the broadcasts, meant that the compilers ceased to take such comments seriously: in another digest the author commented that "Previous experience has shown that few Slovaks agree about the way their language should be spoken."[517] The emotional impact of the language remained important, however. A further report quoted a letter from Slovakia which also suggested that, despite being able to understand what was said in Czech, Slovak listeners were more likely to be engaged in the exile cause if they could identify with the broadcasts they heard in their own language: "More Slovak should be spoken and more attention be paid to Slovakia because the Slovaks need more prodding than the Czechs, who do their bit anyway."[518] The effect that such a measure could also

---

514 BBC Czechoslovak Programme, 10 April 1945, LN Z 1945 – 44, CRA.
515 BBC Czechoslovak Programme, 4 December 1943, LN Z 1943 – 28, CRA.
516 SEA, EOCOTF, 26 January 1942, 3/42, EIP series 1c, E2/192/3, BBC WAC.
517 SEA, EOCOTF (South East Europe), 10 March 1943, 11/43, EIP series 1c, E2/192/6, BBC WAC.
518 SEA, EOCOTF, 2 November 1942, 44/42, EIP series 1c (b), E2/192/6, BBC WAC.

have on Czech listeners was referenced in a report which described the comments made by a "Czech forestry student" who had left the Protectorate a year earlier. The student reported that Czechs would be happy to hear more Slovak on the radio as "they understand it perfectly well" and "this would indicate to them that efforts to win back the Slovaks were considered more promising."[519]

This comment touches on the final – but by no means the least significant – practical consideration which limited the potential of the exiles' broadcasting to Slovakia; due to their status as an exile government, the Czechoslovaks in London were limited in what they could promise regarding the post-war arrangement of the state, and they feared making guarantees that could not then be met. The principle of equality between Czechs and Slovaks was of great significance to Slovak representatives and featured in many of the government's radio commentaries, but always in general terms.[520] In February 1941 a programme was broadcast which insisted that the Slovaks were very aware of how much better off they had been in the First Republic than they were at the present time, but added a hint of future change:

> When we boldly declare that under the Czechoslovak Republic Slovakia fared much better than at present, that it made great progress in the economic sphere, in agriculture and in industry, and when we further add that Slovakia, in order to advance, needs an organic connection with the Czech lands, this does not yet mean that we envisage the restored Czechoslovakia exactly as it was before Hitler destroyed it. The Slovak people at home, as well as the Slovaks abroad, are united in thinking that Slovakia must fare better in the restored and improved Czechoslovakia. It will be necessary to change and improve much in the restored Republic [...] Never again must the time return when there are thousands of unemployed in Slovakia. Here we must be well aware that a common life with the Czech people is the best guarantee of the economic and industrial reconstruction and social progress of Slovakia.[521]

---

519 SEA, EOCOTF (Central-Southern Europe), 24 December 1942, 51/42, EIP series 1c (b), E2/192/6, BBC WAC.
520 The principle of *rovný s rovným* (equal with equal) was repeated a great deal in communications with the SNR, the co-ordinating body behind the 1944 uprising. When an SNR delegation came to London to negotiate with Beneš in October 1944, one of their demands was that the future republic be built on this principle. See Rychlík, *Češi a Slováci*, 247.
521 BBC Czechoslovak Programme, 15 February 1941, LN Z 1941 – 5, CRA. This quote uses the BBC's English translation.

Details relating to possible Slovak autonomy could not be given, however, as the government-in exile made no final decisions on this matter, and this limited the reassurances it was able to provide in its propaganda. Ripka told the PRS of the dangers of speaking too soon on such an important topic:

> Until the Government or the National Council can reach an agreement on these fundamental political matters [...] we cannot allow such topics to be discussed in our radio propaganda [...] We will do nothing in radio propaganda which could prejudice the future resolution of affairs at home.[522]

This left the propagandists in a hopeless position, as they could make no strong claims – either encouraging and positive, or threatening and negative – that could be supported by clear government policy. At the final PRS meeting of 1942, Valo raised the awkward question of why their propaganda had such limited influence in Slovakia. He felt that the broadcasts from London were doing little to encourage Slovaks to rise up against their leaders, and told his colleagues that "we must ask ourselves whether we here in London are really addressing the Slovak people's greatest concerns." Unanswered questions regarding Slovakia's status in a future Czechoslovak state were open to exploitation in Slovak propaganda, and Valo argued that if the government-in-exile wished truly to win the confidence of the majority of Slovaks, rather than merely to undermine the claims of the current leaders, promises needed to be made on topics such as legal decentralisation in post-war Czechoslovakia. Čaplovič, however, dismissed this argument, by maintaining that the situation in Slovakia was not as bad as Valo suggested, and, moreover, added that it had been the exile government's policy from the beginning that the relationship between Czechs and Slovaks would be decided at home, "as the majority of Czechs and Slovaks will wish it to be." Čaplovič then ended the meeting with a statement that was unlikely to calm Valo's fears, and reveals a certain fatalistic approach to propaganda: "If the Slovaks don't believe that, then they won't believe anything we say to them from here."[523]

---

[522] PRS, 29 January 1942, MV–L 271: 2-82-4, CNA.
[523] PRS, 31 December 1942, MV–L 271: 2-82-4, CNA.

"Do not betray yourselves": A Policy of Negative Propaganda

In contrast to some of the more inspirational propaganda intended for Czech listeners, the propaganda produced in London and aimed at Slovak audiences was broadly negative, in the sense that it did not offer an ideal to which listeners should aspire but sought instead to tear down any alternative view. Propagandists in London did not so much seek to win (or win back) Slovak support for the Czechoslovak state as to force Slovaks to accept the situation by discrediting all alternatives, and they did this on both practical and ideological grounds. Slovak patriotic feeling, including the tradition of solidarity among Slavic peoples, was appropriated alongside the Christian faith to discredit the Slovak Republic in the eyes of its people, and listeners were repeatedly told that the only safe future was within a re-formed Czechoslovak Republic: "the stronger Czechoslovak state unity is, the safer the Slovaks will be."[524] The primary target was the Slovak government and its claims of independence for the Slovak people; broadcasters repeatedly emphasised Slovakia's subservience to Germany, the state's lack of international recognition, and the impossibility of Slovak independence from the Czech lands. This was supported by historical and religious arguments presenting any support for the Slovak state as being entirely incompatible with Slovak patriotism. The result was a clear message of the impossibility and undesirability of Slovak independence, and the inevitability of Czechoslovakia's return.

"There is no free Slovakia": Political Arguments

It was of primary importance for the exile government that the Slovak population at large did not believe that the Slovak state was truly independent, nor that it could maintain independence from the Czech lands after the war, and broadcasters did not mince their words in their efforts to communicate this to listeners. At the first session of the Czechoslovak government-in-exile on 23 July 1940, President Beneš set the tone in his opening speech, declaring that "there was never any doubt here about the unity of the Czech lands with Slovakia; neither an independent

---

[524] BBC Czechoslovak Programme, 22 January 1944, LN Z 1944 – 38, CRA.

Slovakia, nor her joining to any other state, was ever seriously spoken of or considered."[525] The legitimacy of the state was also never accepted in the London broadcasts, referred to from the start as the "so-called Slovak state" with its "self-proclaimed" government of "traitors" and its subservience to Hungarian "feudal lords" and German "slavers."[526] Jan Masaryk mocked the suggestion of Slovakia's new-found freedom in independence ("a fine freedom this is!"), and Macháček maintained that the Slovak people knew full well that "the Slovak state is nothing but a toy in the hands of Adolf Hitler."[527]

In a strongly worded broadcast, Paulíny-Toth informed listeners that "this state, occupied by Germans, is not independent [...] it is not even a state, but a German province." "Slovakia cannot in fact be an independent or self-contained economic unit," Paulíny-Toth continued, "without lowering the living standards of Slovak workers, those in the country and in the towns – i.e., the entire Slovak people." He claimed that Slovakia was not economically, militarily, or politically viable on its own and would always depend on a larger neighbour, concluding that "only the Czechs have the means and the honest intention to protect Slovakia politically as well," with no desire to use Slovakia in "shady international political dealings."[528] When Slovakia declared war on the Allies in December 1941, Slávik explained to listeners that the Allies would not be making a retaliatory declaration against Slovakia, because "in the eyes of the world there is no free Slovakia [...] For the free world, there only exists the Czechoslovak Republic."[529] Slovak member of the National Council Alexander Vido sought to present the shared state as beneficial to the Czech lands but vital to Slovakia, predicting that "the Czech lands would lead a difficult life without Slovakia" but that "a Slovakia that wasn't joined to this natural unit would be an organ without blood and would quickly die out." He continued this biological imagery in his description of the state's disintegration as "the tearing of Slovakia from its natural organism," and described the separation of Czechs

---

525 Němeček et al., *Zápisy ze schůzí*, 1:88.
526 For example, BBC Czechoslovak Programme, 18 February 1941, LN Z 1941 – 5; 9 December 1943, LN Z 1943 – 28; 31 July 1943, LN Z 1943 – 23; 10 January 1943, LN Z 1943 – 18, CRA.
527 Masaryk, *Volá Londýn* (1990), 31; BBC Czechoslovak Programme, 2 January 1941, LN Z 1941 – 4, CRA.
528 BBC Czechoslovak Programme, 14 August 1941, LN Z 1941 – 8, CRA.
529 BBC Czechoslovak Programme, 7 December 1941, LN Z 1941 – 10, CRA. Slovakia had signed the Tripartite Pact in November 1940 and declared war on the Allies on 12 December 1941, along with other minor signatories of the pact: Hungary, Romania, and Bulgaria.

and Slovaks almost as a crime against nature: "Nature itself has already destined the Czechs and Slovaks to inseparable co-existence. There are no natural barriers between them [...] only those created by the Nazis." Vido expressed his confidence that his listeners accepted this obvious fact, asserting that "you have all come, as we have, to the conclusion that the Slovak people belong inseparably to the shared state with the fraternal tribe of the Czechs, to the Czechoslovak Republic." Slovakia could not survive independently in the long term, Vido concluded: "you have known this since the first days of so-called Slovak independence."[530] The fate that Slovaks could expect outside the protection of the Czechoslovak state was hammered home to listeners repeatedly: that of a German province facing the wrath of the victorious Allies. Listeners were reminded that their redemption depended on their unity with the Czechs: Slovakia would not be on the list of guilty states at the peace conference, they were told, "only because all warring states and America recognise the Czechoslovak Republic."[531] That the London exiles achieved some minor success by propagating this view among the British can be seen in BBC documents of the war period where mentions of Slovakia (which are admittedly rare) are always included in sections on "Occupied" nations, rather than "Satellite countries" or "Germany's former allies."[532]

In an attempt to combat the propaganda of the Slovak Republic which presented itself as the realisation of the Slovak national tradition and claimed that in the new state "the Slovak nation has reached the pinnacle of all its desires," broadcasters in London sought to recast Slovak patriotism in a Czechoslovak mould, presenting it as being inherently linked with the joint state.[533] In addition to bald statements about the Slovak Republic's lack of international standing and the impossibility of its continuation – and threats regarding its dark future without the protection offered by the Czechs – broadcasters also presented the state's very creation as an act of treachery not just against the Czechoslovak government in Prague, but against the Slovak national tradition itself and some of its most popular proponents. As Slávik proclaimed on 15 July 1943, "the Slovak people know that the current sad situation is

---

530 BBC Czechoslovak Programme, 8 September 1941, LN Z 1941 – 9, CRA.
531 BBC Czechoslovak Programme, 5 November 1941, LN Z 1941 – 10, CRA.
532 See, for example, *BBC Yearbook 1944*, 77; *BBC Yearbook 1945* (London: British Broadcasting Corporation, 1945), 118–99.
533 Pauliny-Tóth attributed this claim to the Slovak government; BBC Czechoslovak Programme, 14 August 1941, LN Z 1941 – 8, CRA.

slavery, a betrayal of Slovakia's past, and of the Czechoslovak Republic, the only thing that can guarantee Slovak freedom."[534] The pro-Russian leanings of cultural figures were also highlighted in defence of the Soviet Union, and the political legacies of prominent Slovaks such as Andrej Hlinka and Milan Rastislav Štefánik were used to further discredit the concept of an independent Slovak state.

Andrej Hlinka (1864–1938), Catholic priest and founder of the Slovak People's Party (Slovenská ľudová strana), was the single most dominant figure in the Slovak national movement prior to the Second World War, and he remained a totemic figure for the wartime state. Bearing his name was not only the ruling party, the Hlinka Slovak People's Party (Hlinkova slovenská ľudová strana, HSĽS) – as it was renamed in 1925 – but also its militia, the Hlinka Guard (Hlinkova Garda). Rather than attempting to discredit Hlinka himself and risk alienating those Slovaks who felt loyalty to him, Slovak broadcasters in London sought instead to counter the Slovak government's claims of association with him and to emphasise that Hlinka had advocated Slovak autonomy within Czechoslovakia rather than full independence. In one of the first Slovak talks featured in *Hovory s domovem,* Macháček (himself former general secretary of the HSĽS) accused the "so-called president of 'independent' Slovakia" of playing up his connection with Hlinka, insisting that all of the current party leaders were "unworthy of even tying his shoes." Claiming that Hlinka had never wanted Slovakia to leave the Czechoslovak state, Macháček asserted that "all true Slovak nationalists" had "looked at this national hara-kiri, carried out by people who had nothing in common with true Slovak nationalism, with bleeding hearts and the greatest grief."[535]

As with other historical figures, anniversaries associated with Hlinka were marked with related government programming and efforts to reclaim his legacy. In August 1943 the government programme marked the fifth anniversary of Hlinka's death with a compilation of quotes in which Hlinka expressed support for Czechoslovak unity; and in 1944 a programme by regular Slovak broadcaster and Communist Vladimír Clementis suggested that the HSĽS had not made Hlinka's final testament public because it reflected his belief that Czechoslovakia was the

---

534 BBC Czechoslovak Programme, 15 July 1941, LN Z 1943 – 23, CRA.
535 BBC Czechoslovak Programme, 21 October 1940, LN Z 1940 – 2, CRA.

only safe home for the Slovak nation.[536] Hlinka was not the only figure from the interwar HSĽS that the London broadcasts quoted in their efforts to prove that a desire for political autonomy for Slovakia did not equate to a desire for independence: one programme presented excerpts from a selection of statements made by various members of the HSĽS during the 1920s, in which they denied accusations that they sought to separate Slovakia from the joint state. A quote from Ferdiš Juriga in 1927 expressed a similar theme to that of Macháček, by suggesting that no true Slovak patriot could want independence: "Anyone who thinks that we want autonomy in order to break away from the Czechoslovak Republic is mistaken. Not at all. We know this and anyone who doesn't is not a Slovak but, under his skin, a Magyar or a German."[537]

Milan Rastislav Štefánik, as a colleague of T. G. Masaryk and Slovak co-founder of the Czechoslovak state, was a natural symbol for broadcasters in London to promote, and they made the most of his continued popularity. Štefánik had died in a plane crash on his way back to Slovakia on 4 May 1919, and he therefore remained strongly associated with the founding ideal of Czechoslovak unity rather than the actual workings of the state that established itself more fully after his death. As with Hlinka and Masaryk, the anniversary of his death was marked with regular programming, much of which positioned Štefánik as a national hero and allied him firmly with the government in London. Speaking in 1942 on the 23rd anniversary of Štefánik's death, General Viest reminded listeners of the inscription on the Štefánik monument that had been unveiled three years earlier: "He who would destroy what Štefánik built, tread not here, for this place is sacred for every loyal Slovak." According to Viest, this inscription had "beautifully, clearly, and exactly expressed the thoughts of the Slovak people," but had then been condemned by "those in foreign, German and Hungarian service who betrayed the Czechoslovak Republic."[538]

London broadcasters argued that Slovak propaganda claims on Štefánik – whom Viest described as an "uncompromising advocate" of Czechoslovak unity – brought shame on his memory and it was in fact the exiles in London who were fighting "in the spirit of Štefánik," a man who would always remain "in the heart of every loyal Czech and Slovak

---

536 BBC Czechoslovak Programme, 2 August 1943, LN Z 1943 – 23; 16 August 1944, LN Z 1944 – 35, CRA.
537 Quoted in BBC Czechoslovak Programme, 2 August 1943, LN Z 1943 – 23, CRA.
538 BBC Czechoslovak Programme, 4 May 1942, LN Z 1942 – 13, CRA.

as a representative of Czechoslovak national and state unity."[539] In 1944 Lichner marked the 25th anniversary of Štefánik's death with the claim that, if he were alive, he would be working in exile again as he had in the first war: "We are where he would be, if he had lived. We are working as he worked and we want to achieve what he achieved." Lichner added that Štefánik's patriotism could be seen in his choice of allies; he had worked to protect the nation with British, American, French, and Russian help, while "today's masters of Slovakia – Tiso, Tuka and others – are working at the whim of Hungarian lords."[540] The implication of these broadcasts was, therefore, that anyone supporting a political future for Slovakia outside the Czechoslovak state was not a true follower of Hlinka and was a traitor to the ideals of Štefánik, who had sought to ally the Slovaks with democratic states such as the USA.

"The most blatant ingratitude": The Slovak State and the USA

References to the United States were used in the government programme to appeal to the consciences of Slovak listeners, and broadcasters exploited the ties created by mass Slovak emigration to the USA – and the respected status of America among Slovaks – to discredit the Slovak state.[541] An early Slovak-language broadcast by Čaplovič told of a meeting between representatives of Slovak-American groups and President Roosevelt, in which even those who had formerly expressed support for the Slovak regime were revising their opinions. "Soon there will be no Slovak left in America who will still approve of the present Hitlerite regime in Slovakia," Čaplovič declared; "all Slovakia must know this today in order to be confirmed in its resistance to Hitler's Nazism and his Slovak instruments."[542] In a strongly worded broadcast in December 1940, Lichner condemned Slovakia for making the state subservient to Germany by joining the Axis Tripartite Pact, warning that this would trap Slovakia into fighting America, should the USA enter the conflict.[543]

---

539 BBC Czechoslovak Programme, 4 May 1942, LN Z 1942 – 13, CRA.
540 BBC Czechoslovak Programme, 3 May 1944, LN Z 1944 – 32, CRA. Vojtech Tuka was a member of the HSLS and prime minister of the Slovak Republic from 1939 to 1944.
541 Some have estimated that almost twenty percent of the Slovak population emigrated to America in the last fifty years of Hungarian rule, and that emigration continued post-1918; see Karen Henderson, *Slovakia: The Escape from Invisibility* (London: Routledge, 2002), 3.
542 BBC Czechoslovak Programme, 25 October 1940, LN Z 1940 – 2, CRA.
543 BBC Czechoslovak Programme, 5 December 1940, LN Z 1940 – 3, CRA.

When Slovakia joined other Axis countries in declaring war on America a year later, on 12 December 1941, Slovak broadcasters in London responded first with mockery, before returning to the theme of guilt.

The next day, Pavol Macháček suggested that the Slovak declaration of war had left the combined populations of the British Empire and the United States "dumbfounded," forcing them to carefully study a map in order to locate "that jumped-up pretend mini-state, recognised by no one besides Schickelgruber-Hitler and his vassals." Macháček described the declaration as "a real farce" which made Slovakia the laughing stock of the rest of the world, but also as a cause of "profound shame and pain" for "all of us who sincerely love our Slovak nation." While he considered the US entry into the war as an opportunity for "our American brothers" to fight for "the victory of the Czechoslovak Republic" and to amend the damage done to "the good name of Slovakia," he also condemned the "Slovak quislings" for showing their "darkest and most blatant ingratitude towards America." Macháček reminded listeners that the USA had, even in times of economic difficulty, "offered not only hospitality to those sons and daughters of the Slovak nation who were forced to flee before the inhuman persecution of their oppressors and enslavers, but also gave them all bread."[544] The ties between Slovakia and the USA produced by years of Slovak emigration were further emphasised two days later when Clementis (broadcasting under his pseudonym of Petr Hron) claimed, "to be sure, there is no country on earth to which Slovakia is bound by as many family ties as it is to America. There is perhaps no hamlet in Slovakia which doesn't have its own 'American' over the ocean." According to Clementis, one third of "the members of the Slovak nation" were then "preparing for war in America," but, like Macháček, he also felt that Slovak Americans were contributing to the Slovak cause, fighting "in aid of their nation."[545] The idea of a debt of gratitude owed to the USA for taking in Slovak émigrés appeared again in a talk by Vendelín Platek of the Slovak National Union, a Slovak-American association. He told listeners of the disgust felt in the United States at the "ingratitude" of Slovakia, when the former country had given both shelter and opportunity to so many fleeing Hungarian oppression.[546] Broadcasters implied that supporting the Slovak state and its decisions, such as going to war against the USA, brought shame on all Slovaks in American eyes and betrayed

---

544 BBC Czechoslovak Programme, 13 December 1941, LN Z 1941 – 10, CRA.
545 BBC Czechoslovak Programme, 15 December 1941, LN Z 1941 – 10, CRA.
546 BBC Czechoslovak Programme, 18 January 1942, LN Z 1942 – 11, CRA.

those who had made their homes there. In a programme featuring the views of two American soldiers of Slovak origin, one said that the news of Slovakia's declaration of war on the USA had caused the greatest stir and asserted that "such a crime could only be committed by people who never felt Slovak and who do not know what America means for Slovaks."[547]

Opposition to the Slovak state among Slovak-American representatives was proclaimed repeatedly in government broadcasts, despite the exiles receiving intelligence to the contrary. After a visit to the USA, Minister Ján Lichner reported to the government-in-exile in February 1942 on the state of Slovak opinion in America and noted that, among the groups he had met with, some openly opposed the exile government and others excused Slovak president Jozef Tiso's actions as attempts to protect Slovakia against German aggression.[548] This difference in opinion did not prevent Lichner from assuring listeners in a broadcast a month later that all Slovak Americans had been opposed to Slovak secession from Czechoslovakia.[549] Similarly, when Jan Masaryk returned from the USA in July 1942, he reported to the government-in-exile that it had the definite support of approximately 40% of Slovak Americans (as opposed to 90% of Czech Americans), whereas 25% was definitely against it and 30% [sic] remained unsure. Masaryk said he had not pursued the "Slovak question" too openly, because he had not wanted to encourage Americans to consider it if they had not already, and he insisted that it was time for the London exiles to take a definitive line on the Slovak "pseudo-government."[550]

Despite these doubts behind the scenes, broadcasters in London were keen to stress the lack of support for the Slovak state among Slovak-American groups, and to emphasise their important work in winning Slovakia classification as an ally, rather than an enemy. Lichner presented a programme on the work of the US-based Slovak Catholic Sokol movement, which was promoting Czechoslovak unity by pre-emptively campaigning against Slovakia being classed as an enemy once the war was inevitably lost by the Axis powers.[551] This point was driven home further in a broadcast by Clementis (attributed to Hron and read by another announcer), which asserted that Slovak Americans and the

---

547 BBC Czechoslovak Programme, 27 June 1943, LN Z 1943 – 22, CRA.
548 27 February 1942, Němeček et al., *Zápisy ze schůzí*, 2:139–41.
549 BBC Czechoslovak Programme, 5 March 1941, LN Z 1942 – 12, CRA.
550 10 July 1942, Němeček et al., *Zápisy ze schůzí*, 2:444–45.
551 BBC Czechoslovak Programme, 16 April 1942, LN Z 1942 – 13, CRA.

London exiles had successfully counteracted the initial progress made by Slovak state-sponsored propaganda to convince Americans that the Slovak Republic represented the Slovak nation. Apparently, the "decisive majority of Slovaks in America" had always seen through the "treachery" of the Bratislava government, and the universally friendly and respectful reception of President Beneš on his recent trip to the USA clearly showed American support for a united Czechoslovakia.[552]

A further Clementis/Hron talk responded to Slovak propaganda aimed at Slovak Americans by quoting Josef Husek, a former supporter of Bratislava who had defected to the Allies: "I am ready to tell the Slovak nation that its so-called government is not its government but Hitler's puppet government, and that this government will lead the nation to ruin." Clementis claimed that Husek's warning showed that even former Slovak-American proponents of Slovak independence were now abandoning the cause: "Anyone can tell from this what loyal Slovaks in America think of the Bratislava lords and their crimes."[553] Clementis reported further on the shame Slovak-American associations felt towards Tiso's government; and the unity of opinion among them was emphasised again when Jozef Valo returned from North America in July 1944 and reported on the firm opposition among Slovaks in both the United States and Canada.[554] Exile broadcasters thus emphasised respected US opposition to the Slovak state to encourage listeners to question the HSĽS and its rule.

"Your Catholic, Christian, and Slovak conscience compels you": Religious Arguments

Another important point of opposition highlighted in the London broadcasts was that of the Church, challenging the Slovak leaders on their claims of representing Catholic Slovaks. Religious arguments and appeals featured very prominently in the broadcasting to Slovakia and listeners were frequently confronted with the many offences against religion perpetrated by Nazi Germany and, by extension, the Slovak state. While religious broadcasting in Czech did occur and religious holidays

---

[552] BBC Czechoslovak Programme, 17 May 1943, LN Z 1943 – 21, CRA.
[553] BBC Czechoslovak Programme, 22 May 1943, LN Z 1943 – 21, CRA.
[554] BBC Czechoslovak Programme, 16 October 1943, LN Z 1943 – 26; 24 July 1944, LN Z 1944 – 34, CRA.

were marked, the majority of religious references were historical ones, associated with the tradition of Hussitism, for example. Like the Czechs, the population of Slovakia was mostly Catholic, but, unlike in the Czech crown lands, religion was much more closely involved in Slovak politics, and the HSĽS had long been committed to having the Church play a leading role in government.[555] The Christian foundation of the state was expressed in the preamble to the constitution of 21 July 1939, which declared that "the Slovak nation, under the protection of Almighty God, has stood for aeons on the land intended for it, where, with His help, from which comes all power and right, it has established its own free Slovak state." The constitution also asserted that "the Slovak state unites according to the natural law all the moral and economic strength of the nation in Christian and national fellowship."[556] Both the inherent importance of religion to the Slovak people, and its appropriation by the Slovak government, contributed to making it a key theme in propaganda broadcast to Slovakia from London.

Religious themes and terminology permeated the language of the programming intended for Slovakia. In a broadcast on Good Friday of 1942, Juraj Slávik assured listeners of Slovakia's approaching resurrection and "eternal life for the Czechoslovak republic," while Ján Lichner suggested on New Year's Eve that the Slovaks had already experienced one miracle in their national life: "the Slovaks were resurrected and brought forward in their national development in the Czechoslovak Republic."[557] Slovak president and Catholic priest Jozef Tiso was labelled a "satanic devil," and acts of the Slovak government were often criticised for contravening the Christian principles they claimed to uphold.[558] Speaking in January 1941, Macháček, also a Catholic priest, quoted an American archbishop's claim that the Slovak regime, under Tuka and Tiso, had brought shame on Catholicism as a whole.[559]

---

[555] On the HSĽS, see Nadya Nedelsky, *Defining the Sovereign Community: The Czech and Slovak Republics* (Philadelphia: University of Pennsylvania Press, 2009), 70–71. In the Czech crown lands, the association of Catholicism with Habsburg rule had prevented it playing a "national role," but religious leaders in Slovakia had been active in nationalist work before the creation of Czechoslovakia. For more on the different roles of religion in Czech and Slovak political society, see Rychlík, *Češi a Slováci*, 76–77.

[556] "Ústavný zákon zo dňa 21. júlia 1939 o ústave Slovenskej republiky," 21 July 1939, Ústav pamäti národa, accessed 8 December 2014, https://www.upn.gov.sk/data/pdf/ustava1939.pdf.

[557] BBC Czechoslovak Programme, 3 April 1942, LN Z 1942 – 12; 31 December 1942, LN Z 1942 – 17, CRA.

[558] BBC Czechoslovak Programme, 10 January 1943, LN Z 1943 – 18, CRA.

[559] BBC Czechoslovak Programme, 28 January 1941, LN Z 1941 – 4, CRA.

According to broadcasters, one of the most shameful acts of this government was the persecution of Slovakia's Jewish population, and on this topic frequent appeals were made to the Christian conscience of listeners.[560] Anti-Jewish decrees had been steadily proliferating from the earliest days of the Slovak state; laws limiting the right of Jews to own land and businesses were introduced throughout 1940, and in September 1941 the Act on the Legal Standing of Jews was signed by the Slovak government, based on Nazi Germany's Nuremberg laws.[561] Mass deportations of Jews to camps in German-occupied territories began in March 1942 with the knowing consent of the Slovak authorities.[562] That June, Slávik condemned the persecution of Jews as disgraceful and unchristian, urging listeners to take a more brotherly attitude.[563] Slovak priest Father Varga came to the microphone for a morning broadcast the following May to express the Church's rejection of anti-Semitism and to emphasise that all races are equal before God.[564] In June 1943, following the broadcast of excerpts on Vatican radio, the content of the open Pastoral Letter of Slovak Catholic bishops provided broadcasters in London with the ideal rallying call.

The Pastoral Letter of 21 March 1943 was presented as irrefutable proof that the Catholic Church did not support the anti-Jewish measures being carried out in Slovakia. Recalling a similar letter by Slovak Evangelical bishops the previous year, Clementis wrote in a commentary of June 1943 that "the Slovak conscience has made itself heard," and that "Christians are speaking via the mouths of the Slovak bishops, Catholic and Evangelical." He refuted the claims made in *Gardista (The Guardsman)*, the daily paper of the Hlinka Guard, that the Catholic Church in Slovakia did not oppose the "so-called definitive solution of the Jewish question," with its associated implication that church circles supported the deportation and slaughter of Slovak Jews. According to Clementis, the "clear, biblical speech" of the letter showed the fallacy of that claim and the Slovak government was now trying to suppress news that

---

560 For a detailed study of the representation of Jews and the Holocaust in the BBC Czechoslovak broadcasts, see Láníček, "Czechoslovak Service."
561 Kirschbaum, *History of Slovakia*, 197; "Nariadenie zo dňa 9. septembra 1941 o právnom postavení Židov," 9 September 1941, Ústav pamäti národa, accessed 8 December 2014, www.upn.gov.sk/data/pdf/vlada_198-1941.pdf.
562 Ivan Kamenec, "The Slovak State, 1939–1945," in Teich, Kovač, and Brown, *Slovakia in History*, 189.
563 BBC Czechoslovak Programme, 15 June 1942, LN Z 1942 – 14, CRA.
564 BBC Czechoslovak Programme, 16 May 1943, LN Z 1943 – 20, CRA.

"Catholic believers" had accepted the words of their pastors. Clementis proclaimed that every voice raised "at a time when both human law and divine law are brutally crushed under foot" constituted "an act in service of the nation," and he expressed confidence that "all Czechs and Slovaks who sincerely care for the fate of Slovakia" had gratefully welcomed the letter. Without such voices, Clementis warned, and without support being shown by increased resistance within Slovakia, a "hard fate would threaten the Slovaks."[565] This commentary was followed by excerpts from the Pastoral Letter itself, as broadcast by the Vatican, and then further commentary which addressed listeners directly: "Slovak Catholics: Not one of you can remain inactive. You must all do what your spiritual pastors are calling on you to do." The broadcast followed the example of the letter by citing the story of the "good Samaritan" and urging help to "all victims of anti-Christian measures, whether they are Jews or Christians." The tone of the broadcast was insistent and the demands clear: listeners must support their bishops in demanding these laws be suspended. "You can be quiet no longer," the broadcast stated, "this is only the smallest of duties which your Catholic, Christian, and Slovak conscience compels you to perform."[566]

The London broadcasters further appealed to the listeners' Christian sensibilities on the topic of Slovak allegiance to Germany, by seeking to educate them on Nazi Party policy towards religion. Macháček outlined the persecution of Catholics in Poland, while Clementis encouraged listeners to question how Tiso and other Slovak leaders could work with a party which was actively persecuting church leaders in other occupied countries.[567] Following the signing of a German–Slovak cultural agreement in May 1942, Clementis quipped that looking to Germany for cultural guidance made even less sense than buying holy water from the Devil.[568] When comments by Martin Bormann (Hitler's personal secretary) on the nature of Christianity were published in a Swedish newspaper later that year, a government evening programme began with a request for Slovak listeners to have a pen and paper ready to take down what he had said. Programme makers were confident that Bormann's statement that religion and National Socialism were irreconcilable, that the Church

---

[565] BBC Czechoslovak Programme, 14 June 1943, LN Z 1943 – 22, CRA.
[566] BBC Czechoslovak Programme, 14 June 1943, LN Z 1943 – 22, CRA.
[567] BBC Czechoslovak Programme, 28 January 1941, 4 February 1941, LN Z 1941 – 4; 20 April 1942, LN Z 1942 – 13, CRA
[568] BBC Czechoslovak Programme, 11 May 1942, LN Z 1942 – 14, CRA.

was based on people's ignorance, and that its influence must be crushed, would be of significance to the Slovak audience.[569] The Germans were described as "barbarians" and the involvement of Slovak troops in wars against other Catholic countries on Germany's behalf was also stressed.[570]

The British shared the view that war with fellow Catholic countries could be an effective propaganda theme, with one weekly directive produced by PWE in April 1943 encouraging broadcasters to give special attention to reports from neutral countries of persecution of the Catholic Church in Poland, "especially for the benefit of our audience in Slovakia."[571] PWE also encouraged the presentation of the Pastoral Letter, with one of its directives from June 1943 instructing that British propaganda should "show that genuine Catholic Christianity is the antithesis of National Socialist ideology and practice."[572] The message here was clear: no true Christian could support the actions of Nazi Germany or its allies in the Slovak government.

Religious arguments also arose when broadcasters in London sought to debunk Axis claims that soldiers participating in the war against the Soviet Union were fulfilling their Christian duty. The involvement of Slovak troops in the Nazi invasion of the USSR, which was launched in June 1941, caused significant political problems for the Czechoslovak government-in-exile, as some of its citizens were then in direct conflict with a country that, as a result of the invasion, became one of the Allied powers. Čaplovič broadcast a condemnation of the agreement to send Slovak troops to join the invasion, describing it as the greatest crime yet committed by the Slovak government, and other propagandists quickly mobilised to defend the Soviet Union.[573] A month into the invasion, code-named Operation Barbarossa, Macháček suggested at a PRS meeting that religious issues could be a "rewarding area" for the London broadcasts, as "the Germans are bragging about religious issues just like the Slovak government" and "the Russians cannot very well answer this propaganda on their own."[574] The issue of religion appeared again at a PRS meeting a year later, in which Slovak State Minister Ján Bečko

---

[569] BBC Czechoslovak Programme, 7 September 1942, LN Z 1942 – 16, CRA.
[570] BBC Czechoslovak Programme, 23 December 1940, LN Z 1940 – 3, CRA.
[571] PWE Regional Directive for BBC Czech Service, 15–21 April 1943, C 194/194/12, FO 371/34333, TNA.
[572] PWE Regional Directive for BBC Czech Service, 10–16 June 1943, C 194/194/12, FO 371/34333, TNA.
[573] BBC Czechoslovak Programme, 26 June 1941, LN Z 1941 – 7, CRA.
[574] PRS, 24 July 1941, MV–L 271: 2-82-4, CNA.

argued along similar lines to Macháček, claiming that "the best weapon against an enemy is the one he himself uses," urging his colleagues to further the religious theme: "We must look for means of political-religious propaganda. Proper attention must be devoted to this sphere of propaganda. I would put real emphasis on this area."[575] In the final PRS meeting of 1942, Čaplovič commented that "the only thing working for the regime in its battle against the Russians is the introduction of the conviction that Bolshevism means the ruin of religion," concluding that the exile government's own Slovak propaganda should focus on religious matters to thwart this success.[576]

The counter-attack began in 1943, as Stalin took an apparently more sympathetic policy towards religion. Several Slovak-language broadcasts from London then seized on the opportunity to argue against the claims being made in German and Slovak propaganda that the Orthodox Church was under threat in the USSR.[577] In January 1941 Ján Čaplovič had said that no one believed Germany's claims to be fighting the Soviets in defence of Christianity, and he claimed that church leaders of all denominations across the USSR were calling on their congregations to help drive out the German "neo-pagans."[578] Two years later, while quoting Martin Bormann, Macháček refuted the claims of religious persecution as "lies," maintaining that "in the Soviet Union the suppression of religion is a severely punished crime. Freedom of faith and confession is guaranteed by the Soviet constitution." According to Macháček, church services in the USSR were still drawing large congregations, praying for victory, but those churches on the territory taken by German troops were being desecrated.[579] The appointment of the new Patriarch in September 1943 provided propagandists with the ideal evidence to support their claims of Soviet support for the Church. In a Czech-language broadcast, Jaroslav Stránský said the appointment of the first new Orthodox leader since the banning of church elections following the death of Patriarch Tikhon in 1925 showed "progress in the

---

575 PRS, 9 July 1942, MV–L 271: 2-82-4, CNA.
576 PRS, 31 December 1942, MV–L 271: 2-82-4, CNA.
577 This change in policy has been attributed to multiple causes, including Stalin's desire to induce the other Allies to open a second front, to help mobilise public support for the war effort, and to begin incorporation of the Church into state structures for greater control after the war; see Adriano Rocucci and Élise Gaigenbet, "Le tournant de la politique religieuse de Stalin: Pouvoir Soviétique et Église Orthodoxe de 1943 à 1945," *Cahiers Du Monde Russe* 50, no. 4 (2009): 671–98.
578 BBC Czechoslovak Programme, 18 January 1943, LN Z 1943 – 18, CRA.
579 BBC Czechoslovak Programme, 16 February 1943, LN Z 1943 – 18, CRA.

internal consolidation of Soviet Russia." He also expressed understanding for the difficulties the Soviets had faced in balancing the needs of a church structure that had been so closely associated with the Tsarist regime with those of the revolution, associated with traditional Marxist "distrust" of religion. He predicted the move would settle discord within the USSR and declared that "reconciliation of the government with orthodoxy is a new victory for Stalin."[580]

While Stránský emphasised the political stability that the Patriarch's appointment would bring, other broadcasters focused more on the religious issues involved. In a Sunday evening broadcast, Father Hala said the appointment was a sign of a brighter future, and he reminded listeners that, just like the Slovaks, the Russians shared the Christian heritage of St. Cyril and St. Methodius, missionaries from Byzantium in the ninth century. Seeking to remind listeners of this shared religious heritage rather than emphasising the current political state of the Soviet Union, Hala described the October Revolution as "a fight against need, disease, and ignorance" that was "only temporary." Recalling his visit to an exhibition of gold and jewelled Russian icons in Paris some years previously, Hala said his mind had turned to "those icons that had remained in Russia: primitive, simply painted, without gold or jewels; gloomy pictures of the saints, passed from father to son." Thinking of these icons, Hala was "convinced that in the hearts of Russian men and women they had not disappeared and would not disappear." According to Hala, the Russians had never ceased to be Christians and now "all the material and ideological elements of the Russian resistance are united," with the Church becoming "a leading element of that great struggle, which the Soviet people are fighting for their own freedom and for the freedom of other nations."[581] Meanwhile, a talk written by an Orthodox clergyman serving in the Czechoslovak army in Russia confirmed that "the Orthodox Church never disappeared in Soviet Russia," declaring that the agreement between Church and state was "very important for the development of the Soviet Union and for Slav unity."[582]

---

[580] BBC Czechoslovak Programme, 7 September 1943, LN Z 1943 – 25, CRA.
[581] BBC Czechoslovak Programme, 12 September 1943, LN Z 1943 – 25, CRA.
[582] BBC Czechoslovak Programme, 25 June 1944, LN Z 1944 – 33, CRA.

Russians, Not Monsters: Tackling the Bolshevik Bogey

The theme of unity among Slavs was prominent in the broadcasts to Slovakia, and it formed the second prong of the fightback against anti-Soviet propaganda that attempted to whip up fear and hatred of the USSR by evocations of the so-called "Bolshevik bogey." By labelling the Soviet Union a threat to Christianity, Axis propagandists sought to cast their troops in a heroic light, as defenders of the faith. As was outlined above, these efforts were dismissed by the London broadcasters and publicity of Stalin's apparent reconciliation with the Orthodox Church did much to support their argument. When it came to the Soviet Union, however, one theme overwhelmingly dominated all propaganda on the subject, and that was the theme of *slovanstvo*, "Slavdom," or the idea that, as fellow Slavs, the Slovaks shared a kinship with the Russians that overrode all other ties.

One of the earliest references to this theme appears in a broadcast from 1940, in which Ján Bečko condemned the Slovak government for involving Slovak forces in battle with their "Slav brothers," the Poles; but it was not until the participation of Slovak units in the German invasion of the Soviet Union in June 1941 that discussions of Slavdom became more prevalent in the broadcasts from London.[583] Days after the launch of Operation Barbarossa, Ján Lichner read the "manifesto of free Slovaks in the Czechoslovak struggle abroad," which claimed to represent the "united opinion" of "Slovak political representatives of all orientations." In this manifesto, it was asserted that the Slovak nation had been forced into war with Russia against the will of the people, as they had first been turned against their "closest brothers" the Czechs, then their "Polish brothers," before they helped Germany in intrigues against "Yugoslav unity." "Now continuing in their treachery, they besmirch the Slovak name and national tradition anew, they dirty the cradle of Slovak thought," the manifesto proclaimed. The document ended with a call to Slovak listeners: "We are calling out to you, brothers under the Tatras: do not desecrate your beautiful history, do not betray yourselves!" Listeners were reminded of those Slovaks who had fought in the First World War and chosen to desert rather than fight their "Russian brothers," and they were now encouraged to turn their weapons on "the eternal enemy,

---

[583] BBC Czechoslovak Programme, 6 October 1940, LN Z 1940 – 2, CRA.

Germany."[584] At several points in the broadcasts Germany was referred to as the historic enemy of all Slavs – the "eternal enemy of Slavdom" and "the executioners of Slavdom," who had "mercilessly massacred tens of thousands of Czechs, hundreds of thousands of Yugoslavs, two million Poles, and still uncounted millions of Russians, Ukrainians, and Belarusians."[585]

The participation of Slovak troops in the war on the Eastern Front was presented in the broadcasts as contrary to Slovak principles and traditions but, in addition to ideological arguments, broadcasters also employed more direct tactics to discourage listeners from either fighting or fearing the Soviet Union. Soldiers were frequently encouraged to desert, both by political figures and by fellow soldiers from Britain, who urged them to be "worthy followers of the example of [their] fathers and older brothers" who had deserted from the Austro-Hungarian army during the First World War and joined the Czechoslovak Legions.[586] The exile government in London had intelligence of pro-Russian feeling in Slovakia early on, and received reports that this was increasing as the military conflict continued.[587] One BBC intelligence report from late 1942 suggested that "German brutality and admiration for Russian resistance are described as reviving feelings of Slav solidarity," and a report from Slovakia received by the MZV in 1944 confirmed that "Russian successes which showed the dishonesty of anti-Bolshevik propaganda have greatly increased pro-Russian sympathies, although not necessarily to the detriment of sympathy for a new Czechoslovak Republic."[588] Confirmed reports of troops deserting to join the Russians were of great value in propaganda terms, and the broadcasts remained encouraging, despite some concern among members of the exile government early on that the numbers of deserting soldiers had been exaggerated and that in reality the welcome they had received from the Soviet troops (mistrustful of anyone who had previously fought against the USSR) had been less than enthusiastic.[589]

---

584 BBC Czechoslovak Programme, 27 June 1941, LN Z 1941 – 7, CRA.
585 BBC Czechoslovak Programme, 22 June 1944, LN Z 1944 – 33; 21 June 1943, LN Z 1943 – 22, CRA.
586 BBC Czechoslovak Programme, 28 June 1941, LN Z 1941 – 7, CRA.
587 Němeček et al., Zápisy ze schůzí, 1:170.
588 SEA, EOCOTF (Central-Southern Europe), 2 November 1942, 44/42, EIP series 1c (b), E2/192/6, BBC WAC; Zprávy ze Slovenska, 1944, Archiv Huberta Ripky [AHR] 181: 1-49-14, CNA.
589 Němeček et al., Zápisy ze schůzí, 2:567.

The regular Wednesday evening military programme in mid-1941 featured interviews with Slovak soldiers who had defected to the Russian army during the First World War, who were said to have always understood that Russians were their "brother Slavs" and therefore their friends.[590] From the late summer of 1941 until the last months of the conflict, the London broadcasts regularly congratulated deserting units and applauded this expression of the "true character" of the Slovaks and the will of the Slovak people, which supported the exile government's claims that Slovaks could be relied upon to fight for the Allied cause.[591] Following the recruitment of fresh troops in Slovakia in October 1943, Slovak General Rudolf Viest broadcast an appeal for them to follow in the footsteps of their predecessors from the previous year by deserting.[592] Moscow radio occasionally broadcast talks by some Slovak deserters who had joined the Soviet side, in addition to lists of names, some of which were re-broadcast from London.[593] As well as providing an impression of great numbers and support for their claims of desertion, these broadcasts also targeted families waiting for news of relatives in the Slovak units and called on them to further disrupt the military effort. Appeals from Moscow radio, urging the families of soldiers to encourage their relatives to allow themselves to be taken prisoner by Soviet troops, and to demand that the Slovak army be recalled, were re-broadcast from London.[594] This was followed by a talk which thanked the mothers and wives of Slovak soldiers for campaigning for their withdrawal from the front and urged the continuance of these activities.[595] Later in the conflict, in November 1943, a series of appeals was broadcast that called on the families of Slovak soldiers to demand information on the Slovak units fighting on the Eastern Front, putting pressure on the Slovak government to reveal how they were being deployed.[596]

---

590 BBC Czechoslovak Programme, "Vojenská beseda," 16 July 1941, LN Z 1941 – 7, CRA.
591 BBC Czechoslovak Programme, 29 September 1941, LN Z 1941 – 9; 10 June 1942, LN Z 1942 – 14; 8 October 1944, LN Z 1944 – 38, CRA.
592 BBC Czechoslovak Programme, 8 October 1943, LN Z 1943 – 26, CRA.
593 SEA, EOCOTF (Central-Southern Europe), 2 November 1942, 44/42, EIP series 1c (b), E2/192/6, BBC WAC. Beyond the re-broadcasting of select programmes, British-Soviet co-operation in broadcasting was not extensive. Soviet suspicion of British motives prevented the creation of a BBC Russian Service and co-operation was limited to a weekly fifteen-minute newsletter in collaboration with TASS, the Soviet news agency. See Briggs, *War of Words*, 360–62.
594 BBC Czechoslovak Programme, 28 January 1942, LN Z 1942 – 11, CRA.
595 BBC Czechoslovak Programme, 5 February 1942, LN Z 1942 – 12, CRA.
596 For example, BBC Czechoslovak Programme, 19 November 1943, LN Z 1943 – 27, CRA.

Russians were frequently referred to as the "brothers" of the Slovaks, and the familial imagery in the broadcasts sometimes went even further. From the announcement of the invasion of the Soviet Union onwards, broadcasters frequently referred to the "fratricidal war" being waged, and General Viest claimed that the Germans wanted the Slovak people to "betray its soul and go to kill its brother, as Cain did Abel."[597] In a broadcast to Slovak workers, Jozef Valo expressed his confidence that "you will not betray yourselves, your birth, and your Slavonic family" by supporting the Axis cause.[598] The exact role that each country played within this family was characterised in one of the later broadcasts, from April 1945, following the liberation of Bratislava by the Red Army. The freedom of Slovakia was to be "an eternal freedom, which was won with great sacrifices and brought by the older and powerful Russian brother to his Slovak sister."[599] This representation of Slovakia as a small girl, reliant on her strong older brother for protection, carries with it connotations of subservience and gratitude, and is rather different to the image of the adult brothers Cain and Abel.

The expectation that Slovaks should honour the relationship they shared with their Russian protectors had been reinforced from the entry of the Soviet Union into the war. One of many appeals to Slovak soldiers not to fight against their fellow Slavs came from Sub-lieutenant Korda of the Czechoslovak forces in Britain, who spoke in the name of "soldiers of the Czechoslovak Republic, loyal sons of the Slovak nation":

> We are calling you, brothers, we beseech you at this sad time not to forget that: honour and loyalty are the only assets of a small nation, and a life without honour is worse than death; that the Russians against whom you march today are your God-given brothers, in language and blood, battle against them is not battle but fratricide; that a Slovak has never taken up arms against a Russian by his own will.

The broadcast continued with references to the Czechoslovak Legions established on Russian soil during the First World War and presented the war with Russia as being only in the interests of cowardly alien powers.[600] In relation to the war with the Soviet Union, Slovak-language broadcasts

---

597 BBC Czechoslovak Programme, 28 June 1941, LN Z 1941 – 7, CRA.
598 BBC Czechoslovak Programme, 14 January 1943, LN Z 1943 – 18, CRA.
599 BBC Czechoslovak Programme, 5 April 1945, LN Z 1945 – 45, CRA.
600 BBC Czechoslovak Programme, "Vojenská beseda," 28 June 1941, LN Z 1941 – 7, CRA.

drew a stark contrast between honourable loyalty and shameful betrayal. But this was not limited to a supposed ethnic betrayal of fellow Slavs: the pro-Russian and pan-Slav elements of early Slovak nationalism were frequently recalled, to cast current opposition to the Soviet Union as a betrayal of Slovak thought and patriotism itself.

The Slovak cultural and historical figures that appeared most frequently in the wartime broadcasts were all actively associated with pro-Russian sentiment, in order to encourage listeners who admired them to support the Soviet cause by association. The three most prominent figures were Pavol Jozef Šafárik, Ján Kollár, and Ľudovít Štúr. Šafárik (1795–1861), known in Czech as Pavel Josef Šafařík, was a writer and ethnographer, while Kollár (1793–1852) was known primarily for his pan-Slavist poetry and linguistic work. Both were Slovaks who worked a great deal in Bohemia and promoted the idea of "Slav reciprocity," according to which Slavs of all regions would mutually benefit by studying the languages and literatures of their fellow Slavs. Štúr (1815–56) represented the next generation of ethno-linguistic nationalists in the Slovak National Revival who worked to create a single written language that united all Slovaks. Štúr differed from Kollár in his insistence that the Slovaks constituted a separate nation within the wider family of Slavs. While Šafárik and Kollár had promoted Slav unity within a purely literary and cultural context, Štúr promoted the idea of a pan-Slav political union too.[601] The idea of affinity among Slavs had not disappeared from Czech and Slovak discourse in the twentieth century, however, and had continued to interest academics during the First Republic.[602] The fellow feeling between Slavs had already been politicised as early as the eighteenth century, but the Second World War brought about a surge in interest in the topic, which broadcasters specifically directed towards the promotion of affection for the Soviet Union.

In a special broadcast to Slovak listeners on 13 March 1943, President Beneš called on them to "imagine how our great Ján Kollár, the Slovak creator of Slav solidarity, Šafařík and Štúr, two great sons of Slovakia who spoke out at the anti-German and anti-Hungarian Slavonic

---

601 For more on Kollár and Šafárik's interpretation of Slavdom, see Pynsent, *Questions of Identity*, 43–94. For an overview of changes in Slovak pan-Slavism, see Ľudovít Haraksim, "Slovak Slavism and Panslavism," in Teich, Kovač, and Brown, *Slovakia in History*, 101–19. For more on Kollár and Šafárik's work on the Slovak language, see Kamusella, *Politics of Language and Nationalism*, 537–42; on Štúr, see ibid., 543–50.
602 See, for example, Miloš Weingert, *Slovanská vzájemnost: Úvahy o jejích základech a osudech* (Bratislava: Academie, 1926).

Congress of 1848 in Prague, are spinning in their graves."[603] When reporting on Beneš's trip to the Soviet Union in December 1943, Prokop Drtina described the co-operation between the two nations as the laying of "real and solid foundations for a practical Slavonic policy" which had been the dream of alternating Czech and Slovak historical figures: "Dobrovský, Kollár, Čelakovský, Šafařík, Palacký, Štúr, Havlíček, Rieger, Vajanský, Neruda, Hviezdoslav and Štefánik."[604] In his talk on the Czechoslovak–Soviet agreement signed on that trip, Hubert Ripka repeated a similar alternating list, and added several more names to emphasise the Russian connection. While the agreement marked the completion of "the hundred year old tradition of Czechoslovak ideals," involving the ideas of "Dobrovský and Kollár, Havlíček and Šafařík, Palacký and Štúr, Rieger and Hviezdoslav," Ripka stated that it was also "accompanied by the spirit of Herzen, Bakunin, and Shevchenko" and, once freed, a reunited Czechoslovak Republic would "lean on the powerful and progressive Slavonic empire to the east."[605]

When preparing his talk on the Czechoslovak–Soviet treaty, Prokop Drtina had felt the need to respond to German attempts to use Beneš's trip to the Soviet Union to "scare the Czech public with a description of the horror of Bolshevism." Drtina's broadcast presented the agreement with the USSR as "an agreement against a German *Drang nach Osten*," as he attempted to persuade Czechs and Slovaks that it was necessary and nothing to fear.[606] The "Bolshevik bogey" was a key feature of German propaganda across Europe and was used to encourage support of Germany as Europe's protector against the sinister forces of Bolshevism, as embodied in the Soviet Union. To this end, the Czech League against Bolshevism (Česká liga proti bolševismu) had been founded in the Protectorate. In a broadcast from 26 March 1944 Drtina mocked the idea of anyone fearing the imagined threat of Bolshevisation while suffering in

---

603 Beneš, *Šest let exilu*, 125.
604 Drtina, *A nyní promluví*, 380. Josef Dobrovský (1753–1829) was a Czech historian and philologist; František Čelakovský (1799–1852) was a Czech writer; František Rieger (1818–1903) was a Czech politician; Svetozár Hurban-Vajanský (1847–1916) was a Slovak writer and journalist; Pavol Országh Hviezdoslav (1849–1921) was a Slovak poet and writer.
605 BBC Czechoslovak Programme, 14 December 1943, LN Z 1943 – 28, CRA. Alexander Herzen (1812–70) was a Russian writer and social philosopher; Mikhail Bakunin (1814–76) was a Russian anarchist and activist; Taras Shevchenko (1814–61) was a Ukrainian poet and political figure.
606 Drtina, *A nyní promluví*, 378. *Drang nach Osten* (Drive to the East) is the term for German expansion and settlement into Central and Eastern Europe, first used in the 19th Century but strongly associated with National Socialism.

a fascist reality, and commented that "no nation that still has the desire and will to be a nation can have any liking for this kind of defence."[607] Slovak broadcasters highlighted the similarities between this German threat and the old arguments of the Hungarians during the Austro-Hungarian Empire, with Clementis claiming that Germany was merely recycling the old Hungarian lie that failure to submit would result in domination by Russia: "The Slovak nation does not fear a Soviet military victory. On the contrary, [...] it will be their victory as well, and it will mean the end of German and Hungarian rule over Slovakia."[608] Soon after, Clementis gave a talk on the growing falsification of Slovak history by the Slovak and German authorities, and insisted that they knew full well that Kollár and Štúr had looked away from Germany, towards Russia, and had "planted in Slovak hearts a faith in the great Russian nation" which was still bearing fruit. The true followers of Kollár and Štúr, according to Clementis, "look at Russians and see Russians, not the monsters painted by German propaganda."[609] Broadcasts on this topic show a concerted effort to appeal to historical and ethnic associations with Russia, rather than dwelling on the current political regime in the Soviet Union, but some felt more could have been done. One comment recorded during a seminar in December 1942 criticised the terminology used in the broadcasts:

> It is a mistake for us to say "Soviet" and not "Russian." The Bratislava radio talks constantly about Bolsheviks and never about Russians and we help them if we avoid the word "Russian." We like Russians and it doesn't matter to us who is sitting in Moscow.[610]

In his response to this comment, Josef Körbel indicated that broadcasters were following the Soviet Union's own guidelines for terminology, but the content of the broadcasts would suggest that a conscious effort was made to promote the ethnic Russian heritage of the Soviet Union.

In a strongly worded broadcast two years later, Ján Paulíny-Toth linked the Slovak National Uprising to the theme of Slav unity and portrayed this act of defiance as the pinnacle of the pro-Slav tradition in

---

607 Drtina, *A nyní promluví*, 400.
608 BBC Czechoslovak Programme, 22 February 1943, LN Z 1943 – 18, CRA.
609 BBC Czechoslovak Programme, 25 May 1943, LN Z 1943 – 21, CRA.
610 "Report on Slovak seminar," 12 December 1942, Londýnský archiv (důvěrný) [LA (D)] 42, MZV.

Slovakia. "We have always maintained that the Slovak tradition has been the tradition of co-operation of Slav nations," Paulíny-Toth began, arguing that "we can boldly state that conviction in the fellowship of the Slavs gradually spread among the masses simultaneously with the growth of Slovak national consciousness and self-confidence." For Paulíny-Toth, "this development reached its peak in the Slovak uprising," in which the Slovaks had shown "the strength of their idealism," "the strength of the Slovak Slav tradition," and "the desire for freedom and a free life within the Slav family." He then outlined Hitler's disgust for all Slavs and warned listeners that "the gas chambers used against Jews would, after the victorious war, have been used for the liquidation of the leading classes of all the Slav nations."[611] The fact that the Soviet Union – Slovakia's Slav big brother – failed to provide the military support that could have enabled the uprising to succeed outright, and thereby ensured that only the Red Army would be in a position to liberate the country, is likely to have undermined feelings of Slav solidarity among those who hoped Slovaks would be able to secure their own liberation.[612]

* * *

The Czechoslovak government-in-exile was committed to the recreation of the Czechoslovak Republic and was therefore bound to refute any and all claims to the independence and political viability of the Slovak state. This theme made up the bulk of the government's radio propaganda to Slovakia, which repeatedly condemned the Slovak state as a Nazi puppet and presented Czechoslovakia as the only safe political home for the Slovaks. It was claimed that those who took up arms as part of the Slovak National Uprising did so to show their desire to return to this shared state, and broadcasters sought to shame listeners for any residual positive feelings they felt for a state which was unanimously opposed by the United States, the Christian world, and all loyal Slavs. Propaganda efforts were occasionally hampered by practical limitations – such as the limited amount of broadcasting time available, the short supply of

---

611 BBC Czechoslovak Programme, 16 December 1944, LN Z 1944 – 39, CRA.
612 As Jan Němeček notes, we lack the sources to know precisely the reasons for Soviet delays in responding to Czechoslovak calls for armed support, but Jan Masaryk suggested at the time that the Soviet Union feared a recurrence of the anti-Soviet sentiments expressed in the recent Warsaw Uprising, and later historians have supported this interpretation; see Němeček, "Československá exilová vláda," 244. Masaryk's comments were made during a cabinet meeting on 1 September 1944; see Němeček et al., *Zápisy ze schůzí*, 4.2:187–88.

Slovak personnel, and the BBC's resistance to letting domestic politics dominate European Service broadcasts (itself a testament to the success of the exiles' claims of authority over Slovakia) – as well as suspicions raised by any suggestion of dividing the Czech and Slovak audiences too overtly. Divisions among even the London staff can be seen in the wartime scripts: where one scriptwriter asserted in a talk of April 1945 that "we are addressing all loyal Czechoslovaks," an unknown editor has struck out the final word and replaced it with "Czechs and Slovaks."[613]

Although the Czechoslovak shared state was recreated in 1945, the lack of political alternatives available to Slovaks meant they had little choice in the matter. Carol Skalnik Leff has suggested that the waning of support for the Slovak regime had more to do with the fact that its existence was too obviously limited by that of Nazi Germany than it did with any particular desire to recreate the lost Czechoslovak Republic, and this study of the wartime broadcasts provides evidence that the exiles in London knew and accepted this.[614] The exile government was not in a position to negotiate the details of a restructured republic that would please those Slovaks who had been dissatisfied with the old system, and its distinctly negative wartime propaganda presented Slovak listeners with the inevitable return of the Czechoslovak state, whether they liked it or not. In this matter, the exile government perpetuated political tactics from the First Republic whereby Czechoslovak governments pressed for unity and often did not directly address Slovak concerns, hoping that integration would eventually cause such dissent to die out.[615] The confidence with which the experience of independence had endowed Slovak national consciousness, however, would mean the continued failure of such tactics.

Archive sources on opinion in the newly liberated Slovakia suggest widespread listening to broadcasts from London, but also show the problems caused by the exile government's failure to provide these listeners with a clear plan for the future. In his report on the return of the Czechoslovak government delegation to Czechoslovak territory in 1945, František Uhlíř was generally very positive about its reception in Slovakia, assuring those still in London that the delegation was greeted everywhere with cries of "the Londoners are here!" and questions about

---

613 BBC Czechoslovak Programme, 19 April 1945, LN Z 1945 – 45, CRA.
614 Leff cites the writings of later Czechoslovak president Gustav Husák in her comments; see Leff, *National Conflict in Czechoslovakia*, 90
615 See Leff, *National Conflict in Czechoslovakia*, 176–77.

the wellbeing of popular broadcasters like Slávik, Bečko, and Čaplovič. Uhlíř said that "every word spoken from London was an object of consideration, investigation, and debate," and that all Slovak people "want the Republic, the President, a Czechoslovak government." However, Uhlíř reminded his colleagues that it was important to bear in mind that "Slovak national self-confidence has markedly increased" and there were suggestions that it had not developed along purely Czechoslovak lines. Uhlíř met Slovaks who thought Slovakia should join the USSR, and others hoping for a confederation of independent Czech, Slovak, and Subcarpathian Ruthenian states. "It is not possible to say with a clear conscience that the state-political and national-political problem in Slovakia was presented unequivocally and clearly," Uhlíř concluded. While he drew comfort from the fact that all were united in their desire for the recreation of Czechoslovakia within its pre-Munich borders, his claim that people "differed only in their opinions on how that republic would look internally" suggested that the fundamental issue of equality between Czechs and Slovaks remained unresolved and hinted at further Czech–Slovak strife to come.[616] This was not the only difficult relationship facing the future Czechoslovak state, however, as its relationship with its "Slav brothers" in the Soviet Union was also to become much more intimate in future.

---

616 MZV Vládní delegace – F Uhlíř, 1945, Zprávy z Podkarpatské Rusi, AHR 194: 1-53-5-2, CNA.

Chapter Four

"We will manage our own affairs": The Soviet Union and Broadcasting the Future of Czechoslovakia

"No one is going to push us around any more. We will manage our own affairs, in the most intimate co-operation with the great Allies, of course..."
Jan Masaryk, 31 March 1943[617]

The Second World War marked a turning point in Czechoslovakia's foreign relations. The First Republic-era conception of the state as "the heart of Europe" and as a bridge that, "by its mission, links up West and East" was overwhelmed by a shift fully into the orbit of the powerful Soviet Union to the east.[618] From being distant but friendly nations before the conflict, joined by a treaty of 1935, Czechoslovakia and the USSR became both close allies and neighbours by the war's end. As a consequence of these closer relations, the Czechoslovak exiles would risk no policy that might incite Soviet displeasure, and before the end of the conflict the foundations were already laid for the asymmetric relationship that was to deepen in the post-war era, notably following the Communist takeover of Czechoslovakia in 1948. Within the wartime

---

617 Masaryk, *Volá Londýn* (1990), 174.
618 Such phrases were commonly used in the First Republic, for both domestic and international audiences. František Krejčí claimed that "In our relations to the west and to the east we feel such equality as no other European nation [...] we gladly name our country the heart of Europe"; Krejčí, *Češství a Evropanství: Úvahy o naší kulturní orientaci* (Prague: Orbis, 1931), 106. Karel Čapek, writing in English, explained that the long, thin shape of the republic was not due to mountains or coastline, as with Chile or Norway, but because "Narrow and long are the bridges that connect two riverbanks. Czechoslovakia is long by virtue of her position and by her mission she links up West and East"; see Čapek et al., *At the Cross-Roads of Europe: A Historical Outline of the Democratic Idea in Czechoslovakia* (London: Hutchinson, 1938), 9.

British propaganda structure, criticism of the allied Soviet Union was also not permitted to be broadcast and the Czechoslovaks found this easier to comply with than many other governments (notably the Polish exiles). No listener to the government broadcasts – which praised the "heroic Red Army," the "mighty" Soviet Union, and that "great friend of Czechoslovakia, Marshall Stalin" – was left in any doubt that a close relationship with the Soviet Union was to be a definitive characteristic of post-war Czechoslovakia.[619] While many figures from President Beneš downwards predicted a "close and intimate" co-operation with the USSR in Czechoslovakia's future, Soviet respect for Czechoslovak sovereignty was also much trumpeted. In light of post-war events, comments such as those by Jan Masaryk, quoted above, seem naïve, but what is of principal interest to this project is how the exile government's changing relations with the Soviet Union affected its propaganda throughout the war period.

This chapter will argue that, although the two grew steadily closer throughout the war, relations between Czechoslovakia and the Soviet Union moved through three distinct phases, each of which had a notable effect on the exile government's propaganda. In the first phase, from the outbreak of the war until the German attack on the USSR in June 1941, the Soviet Union was presented as neither an ally nor an enemy of Czechoslovakia, although Beneš proclaimed confidence in the USSR's eventual entry into the conflict on the side of the Allies.[620] In this period, the Czechoslovak government programme focused only infrequently on Soviet matters, but when they did appear broadcasters were frank in their assessment and encouraged listeners to judge the Soviet system on both its achievements and its failings. Following the German invasion, the Soviet Union joined the Allies and an immediate change was evident in all Allied propaganda, including that of the Czechoslovak exiles; the Soviet Union was now mentioned frequently and listeners were urged not to dwell on criticism of the country's political structure but were instead reminded of the ethnic and cultural ties between the two states. In this second phase, lasting from June 1941 until approximately early 1943, the USSR was a close ally of the exiled Czechoslovaks but had

---

619 BBC Czechoslovak Programme, 23 February 1942, LN Z 1942 – 12; 14 December 1943, LN Z 1943 – 28; 10 May 1945, LN Z 1945 – 46, CRA.
620 Beneš told listeners on 19 June 1940 that the USSR was aware of German plans against it and reminded them of his foresight on 24 June 1941 following the German attack; Beneš, Šest let exilu, 51, 73–74.

not yet begun to exert dominance over their policy. As such, the Soviet Union was presented increasingly favourably but the exile government also continued to promote its own policies and future plans within its broadcasts.

The third and final phase followed the USSR's first significant military victories over German forces. From early 1943 until the end of the war the Soviet Union gained influence among all the Allies, and the Czechoslovaks, having accepted the inevitability of their future reliance on the USSR, found all their policy decisions subject to the whims of Soviet goodwill. This subjugation to Soviet policy meant that topics and future plans which had previously been much promoted, such as close cooperation with the Polish government-in-exile in London, became taboo and largely disappeared from the broadcasts. Subcarpathian Ruthenia – a region incorporated into Czechoslovakia in 1919, partially annexed by Hungary in 1938 and fully occupied from 1939, before being transferred to the Soviet Union in 1945 – was also greatly affected by the changing Czechoslovak–Soviet relationship, both in terms of propaganda and policy. Listeners were told that "Subcarpathian Ruthenia is Czechoslovak" and "Subcarpathian Ruthenia never stopped seeing itself as an inseparable part of the republic"; but, behind the scenes, diplomatic negotiations regarding the future of the territory reveal a more complex story, and propaganda on the region's imminent return to Czechoslovakia bore increasingly little resemblance to reality.[621] Study of the government's wartime broadcasts thus reveals the impossibility of trying to broadcast a concrete image of the future from London when decisions were being made in Moscow, showing the dangers of propaganda divorced from policy.

Neither Hell nor Paradise: 1940 to June 1941

In the first of the three phases outlined above, broadcasters on the Czechoslovak government programme attempted to take an objective stance on the Soviet Union, encouraging listeners to think for themselves and draw their own conclusions. While these broadcasts were never hostile and often reminded listeners that the USSR had been innocent in

---

621 Speech given by President Beneš on 25 April 1943, in Beneš, *Šest let exilu*, 129; Government declaration on Red Army reaching the border of Subcarpathian Ruthenia, BBC Czechoslovak Programme, 8 April 1944, LN Z 1944 – 32, CRA.

the Czechoslovak crisis of 1938, they were also free of baseless praise and lacked any suggestion of the fawning tone that was to become commonplace later. Prior to March 1941, the Soviet Union featured very rarely in the broadcasts and was generally only mentioned in relation to German plans, with listeners being told on more than one occasion that the Molotov–Ribbentrop pact of non-aggression between the two countries meant next to nothing in the long term.[622] Between March and June 1941, however, Minister Jaroslav Stránský devoted a series of longer broadcasts to discussion of the Soviet Union's achievements and failings, encouraging a fair but critical assessment based on evidence rather than assumptions. Stránský, a staunch democrat who would later be forced to leave Czechoslovakia following the Communist takeover in 1948, acknowledged the range of opinion regarding the Russian Revolution with his observation that "to some it appears as the most fiendish hell, to others as the wide gate to paradise on earth." In a series of talks in this period, however, Stránský encouraged listeners to employ what he called "tried and tested Czech soberness" in evaluating both sides of the argument, and to seek a conclusion that was "without prejudice" and "sensible rather than passionate."[623]

In these early talks, preceding Soviet entry into the war, Stránský did not shy away from discussing the ideological basis of the USSR, nor from criticising it. In a broadcast outlining Karl Marx's predictions for the rise and fall of capitalism, Stránský commented that "actual events did not confirm Marx's prognosis, however," citing the lack of proletarian revolutions in developed capitalist societies. Given the extremely low level of capitalist development in Tsarist Russia, Stránský concluded that, "Although the Russian revolution was carried out by Marxists, it would be a mistake to think that it was therefore the revolution predicted by Marx. It had different preconditions and a different course."[624] In fact, he argued, none of Marx's "Russian devotees" cared that the conditions in 1917 were the "exact opposite" of those the theorist had described as necessary to proletarian revolution: they simply "saw a strategic

---

[622] For example, BBC Czechoslovak Programme, 6 December 1940, LN Z 1940 – 3; 13 January 1941, LN Z 1941 – 4, CRA.
[623] BBC Czechoslovak Programme, 28 March 1941, LN Z 1941 – 5, CRA. Stránský (1884–1973) had been elected to the National Assembly several times during the First Republic: as a member of the National Democrats (Československá národní demokracie) in 1920 and then the National Socialists (Československá strana národně socialistická) in 1929 and 1935.
[624] BBC Czechoslovak Programme, 4 April 1941, LN Z 1941 – 6, CRA.

opportunity and they capitalised on it."[625] Stránský's presentation of the Russian Revolution and the conditions that led to it was entirely in keeping with the official view prevalent in the First Republic, as standardised in the work of T. G. Masaryk. Referring to Masaryk's writings on Russia, Stránský supported his conclusion that "Russia is Europe, but Europe two hundred years ago," adding that "anyone who wants to understand the Russian Revolution must know that it was just a postscript to the great catastrophe of the feudal age which Europe went through at the turn of the nineteenth century."[626] Stránský was critical but not damning, characterising Soviet Russia as a dictatorship (a system that was clearly inferior to democracy) but also arguing that democratic conditions would not have been sufficient to modernise Russia, so backward had the country been in 1917.[627]

In his determination to promote sober judgement of the Soviet Union based on facts, Stránský was dismissive of the kind of emotional appeals to historic Slav unity that were to become commonplace in government broadcasting once the country entered the war. Without denying the existence of historical and cultural connections between Czechoslovakia and the USSR, Stránský sought to convince his audience that such nineteenth-century thinking was no longer appropriate. He did not seek to dissociate Soviet Russia from the Tsarist Russia of the past but rather emphasised the continuity of national spirit that bridged the gap of the revolution, stating that "Revolutionary Russia is no less Russian than Tsarist Russia, quite the reverse." Nor did he deny the historic bonds of friendship and admiration between Czechs, Slovaks, and Russians, reminding listeners that "there was a time when we sang *Hej Slované* with the well-known concluding verse: 'Russia is with us, whoever is against us the French will destroy'" (citing an alternative to the traditional lyrics of "God is with us, whoever is against us Perun [leader of the gods in Slav mythology] will destroy"). "Such faith, such hope, and such love was placed in the promise of that song by our fathers and grandfathers, that it can only be remembered with emotion," Stránský stated, before adding, "but that was then." He advised that Czechoslovaks must not let old

---

[625] BBC Czechoslovak Programme, 18 April 1941, LN Z 1941 – 6, CRA.
[626] BBC Czechoslovak Programme, 4 April 1941, LN Z 1941 – 6, CRA. See also T. G. Masaryk, *Rusko a Evropa: studie o duchovní proudech v Rusku*, vols. 1–3 (Prague: Ústav T. G. Masaryka, 1995; 1996). For more on Masaryk's view of Russia, see Vratislav Doubek, *Česká politika a Rusko (1848–1914)* (Prague: Academia, 2004), 264–79.
[627] BBC Czechoslovak Programme, 18 April 1941, LN Z 1941 – 6, CRA.

emotional ties influence their judgement, but must rather be prepared for "the confrontation of thoughts with experiences," they must "seek the truth" and approach Russia with "determination to judge it according to the truth and not according to desires, or fashion, or trends."[628]

When the Soviet Union joined the Allies in the aftermath of the launch of the German invasion on 22 June 1941, the BBC and all its associated services had to adapt to a sudden change in policy as pro-Russian feeling "took hold with extraordinary rapidity" in Britain, following an example set by Churchill himself.[629] Stránský was forced to change tack swiftly: "Friends," he began, speaking on the evening that news of the invasion broke, "if you want to judge the current situation of Soviet Russia and its meaning for us and our affairs, you cannot let yourself be confused by ideological sympathies or ideological disagreement. Soviet ideology and practise could and can be controversial, but that is not at all what this is about." In this new battle, Russia was once again "the ancient homeland of the largest Slav nation," "a nation of great poets and thinkers who inspired our greatest figures," which faced being "torn to pieces" should Germany triumph.[630] Thus, from urging objective and balanced discussion of Soviet ideology and governance, Stránský performed a complete volte-face and encouraged traditional pro-Slav feeling towards Czechoslovakia's newest ally.

"Our Brother Slavs": June 1941 to 1943

In his study of changing Czech political views of Russia in the late nineteenth and early twentieth centuries, Vratislav Doubek concluded that the disappearance of Tsarist Russia in 1917 meant the loss of the traditional foundation for pro-Russian and Slavophile arguments, as international Marxism was incompatible with Slav nationalism.[631] However, when the Soviet Union joined the Allied powers, the Czechoslovak exile government's immediate outpouring of pro-Slav rhetoric marked the bombastic return of Russophilic feeling. The BBC had also immediately adopted a policy of promotion of the new ally, encouraging the British

---

628 BBC Czechoslovak Programme, 2 May 1941, LN Z 1941 – 6, CRA.
629 Nicholas, *Echo of War*, 165. For more on representations of the USSR in British domestic broadcasting, see ibid., 163–71.
630 BBC Czechoslovak Programme, 22 June 1941, LN Z 1941 – 7, CRA.
631 See Doubek, *Česká politika a Rusko*, 292–93.

public's already generally positive feeling towards the Soviet people, and Czechoslovak government broadcasts therefore had to comply with this policy.[632] There was a perceived need to combat the attempts of German propaganda to spread fear of the Soviet system throughout occupied Europe, with a 1943 PWE regional Czechoslovak propaganda directive warning that "the bogey of Bolshevism is being used by the Nazis and the Magyars to frighten a simple population into compliance." The various BBC language services were therefore encouraged to argue against this by presenting the Soviet Union as a reliable ally, a tone which spread also to the "free time" programmes of exile governments, such as that of Czechoslovakia.[633] Where some other exile governments caused problems in this regard – notably the BBC was concerned by Polish government figures criticising "our ally Russia" in their broadcasts – Czechoslovak compliance and history of good relations with Russia were noted, with PWE commenting that the exiles in London represented "a country which suffers less from Russophobia than almost any other."[634] Pro-Russian sentiment, under the influence of fellow feeling among Slavs, was to become a major theme in Czechoslovak government propaganda throughout the rest of the war.

In the second phase of Czechoslovak–Soviet relations, the two thus became allies once more and propagandists fell back on the traditional and established themes of Slav unity and kinship. These themes had been influential in the eighteenth- and nineteenth-century Czech and Slovak national revivals, featuring heavily in much popular nineteenth-century literature and art, and the violent anti-Slav rhetoric of Nazi Germany and appearance of the Soviet Union on the side of the Allies reinvigorated the idea. Exile figures such as Clementis also worked to promote the idea of Slav unity among the British public, publishing propaganda pamphlets on the "organic factor" that reciprocity among Slavs played in their respective national revivals, and its position as part of their "living spiritual heritage."[635] As described above, this theme was par-

---

632 The corporation would later be criticised in this regard, as other British departments such as the Ministry of Information wanted to ensure Soviet representation was positive without pushing public opinion too far to the left; Nicholas, *Echo of War*, 163.
633 PWE Regional Directive for BBC Czech Service, 14–20 January 1943, C 194/194/12, FO 371/34333, TNA. See also 18–24 February 1943; 1–7 July 1943, etc.
634 Kirkpatrick, *The Inner Circle*, 161; PWE Regional Directive for BBC Czech Service, 11–17 February 1943, C 194/194/12, FO 371/34333, TNA.
635 Vladimír Clementis, *Panslavism: Past and Present* (London: Czechoslovak Committee for Slav Reciprocity in London, 1943), 59. Clementis was a Slovak Communist who had been investigated by the KSČ before the war due to his criticism of the Molotov–Ribbentrop pact.

ticularly widely used in government broadcasts to Slovakia and it also played a role in propaganda to Subcarpathian Ruthenia, but references to brotherly feeling and historical ties among Slavs were commonplace throughout the government programme from mid-1941 onwards.

Russians were frequently referred to as "brother Slavs" and listeners were urged to attend events linked to Slav solidarity, such as Slovak celebrations honouring St. Cyril and St. Methodius, Orthodox saints and "apostles to the Slavs."[636] Pro-Slav gatherings, such as the All-Slav Congresses held in April of 1942 and 1943, both in Moscow, were given extensive coverage, and the appeal to the Czech nation by the attendees of the latter event was broadcast by Prokop Maxa. The congress praised the Czechs for having "always been loyal sons of our Slav clan" who were "proud of your Slav origin," while emphasising the need for pro-Slav action in the present: "To be a Slav today means being a brave fighter for freedom [...] act as your Slav hearts implore you."[637] Listeners were also reminded of historical and cultural ties, however, when they were advised in a further programme that "the principal idea of our national existence is, without question, the idea of purely Slav culture."[638] Contemporary politics were mingled with historical and cultural allusions in talks such as that of Minister Ripka on 14 December 1943 in response to the Czechoslovak–Soviet agreement, quoted in Chapter Three. There, he listed Czech, Slovak, Russian, and Ukrainian figures together and asserted that the recent treaty was been signed in their "spirit" and "blessed" by them, the "culmination" of a pro-Slav tradition.[639] The idea that Czechoslovaks had been waiting for generations for help to come from Russia (harking back to hopes for military aid from Tsarist Russia in earlier periods of struggle) was further emphasised in the announcement of the entry of Red Army troops onto Czechoslovak territory. Following the formal government declaration on 8 April 1944, planned programming the following day was cancelled in favour of three announcements of the arrival of the Red Army, one each in Czech, Slovak, and Ukrainian (although only the Czech and English texts survive in the archive). In the Czech version, Prokop Drtina proclaimed that, in the liberation by

---

[636] For example, BBC Czechoslovak Programme, 16 July 1941, LN Z 1941 – 7; 24 February 1942, LN Z 1942 – 12, CRA. Cyril and Methodius Day is traditionally celebrated on July 5 in the Czech lands and Slovakia, and attendance was encouraged in broadcasts in the days preceding this in 1944 (LN Z 1944 – 34).
[637] BBC Czechoslovak Programme, 10 April 1943, LN Z 1943 – 20, CRA.
[638] BBC Czechoslovak Programme, 4 July 1943, LN Z 1943 – 22, CRA.
[639] BBC Czechoslovak Programme, 14 December 1943, LN Z 1943 – 28, CRA.

the Red Army, "the eternal wishes and dreams of our fathers and mothers have found their fulfilment. The Slav brothers from the east are coming together with our native brothers and they are bringing freedom to you and happiness to your children."[640]

In addition to this appeal to historical and cultural sentiments, the Czechoslovak government broadcasts also contained many predictions regarding the future power of the Soviet Union and the importance of Czechoslovak–Soviet relations, reflecting the change in these relations over time. In early broadcasts Britain was given precedence over the Soviet Union, but this changed as the latter began to make military gains. The broadcasting of announcements regarding British and Soviet recognition of the exile government in 1941 show the preference given to the former at this early stage. In a series of broadcasts that July, it was announced that the Czechoslovak exile government had been accorded full recognition by both the British and the Soviets, and that an agreement of co-operation had been signed with the USSR. Despite the fact that Soviet recognition was awarded first and after much less negotiation, it was the announcement of British recognition that opened the programme, with Foreign Minister Masaryk proclaiming the exile government's gratitude and the significance of the recognition, concluding that "today, the path to our goal grew significantly shorter." Masaryk then read the text of the Czechoslovak–Soviet agreement and explained its significance, commenting that Czechoslovakia now had "one more powerful ally." Jiří Hronek followed by praising the significance of the agreement, but he also let the figures speak for themselves: "We are fighting alongside two hundred million citizens of that [Soviet] empire" and "five hundred million citizens of the British Empire."[641] Gradually, as news of the losses on the Eastern Front spread, sympathy grew, and broadcasters noted in October 1941 that the British could not rival the Soviets in terms of the sacrifices being made.[642]

Wartime talks by some Communist and pro-Soviet broadcasters showed the roots of what was to become mythologised as the official

---

[640] BBC Czechoslovak Programme, 9 April 1944, LN Z 1944 – 32, CRA.
[641] BBC Czechoslovak Programme, 18 July 1941, LN Z 1941 – 7, CRA. The Soviet Union had offered full recognition several months previously, in fact, and the pressure of this offer did much to hasten British action in the matter. The final agreement of Soviet recognition was signed at noon and the British note was received from Eden some four hours later. For a personal account of the day from the point of view of the British representative to the Czechoslovak government, see Lockhart, *Comes the Reckoning*, 119–21.
[642] BBC Czechoslovak Programme, 24 October 1941, LN Z 1941 – 9, CRA.

narrative of Czechoslovak–Soviet friendship from 1948 onwards. Listeners were reminded that "the Soviet Union did not recognise Munich" and that in those "sad days" of September 1938, unlike other allies, "the Soviet Union stood on the side of Czechoslovakia come what may, and did not recognise the breaking up of Czechoslovakia carried out by Hitler in March 1939."[643] After 1948, the image of the Soviet Union as the only state willing to stand by Czechoslovakia at the time of Munich would become central to the myth of friendship between the two states that was promoted by the Communist regime.[644] As Robert Pynsent has pointed out, it also provided a convenient distraction from the Soviet Union's conduct between 1939 and 1941 during the Molotov–Ribbentrop pact, emphasising instead that the country had been an ally of Czechoslovakia both before the war and at its end, glossing over the intervening period.[645] In addition to being a useful means by which to promote Czechoslovak–Soviet friendship, the example of Munich also offered opportunities to discredit the democratic signatories, Britain and France, and the democratic Czechoslovak government that had accepted the terms. It was asserted that Britain and France had never truly abandoned their "Munich policy" and the USSR was presented as the only reliable ally.[646] While the roots of the Munich argument can be identified in talks by some Communist members of the London exile community, the huge sacrifices made by the Soviet Union, another important component of the myth, were respected by broadcasters of all denominations, and equal attention was paid to successes on both the Eastern and Western Fronts. While many British and other Western histories of the war came to focus heavily on the Western Front during the Cold War period, the Czechoslovak government programme had laid the foundation for

---

643 This first talk was written by Clementis; BBC Czechoslovak Programme, 2 November 1942, LN Z 1942 – 17, CRA. The second talk was written and read by Anežka Hodinová, a member of the National Council and the KSČ; BBC Czechoslovak Programme, 7 November 1941, LN Z 1941 – 10, CRA.
644 See, for example, Jan Kuklík, Jan Němeček, and Jaroslav Šebek, *Dlouhé stíny Mnichova: Mnichovská dohoda očima signatářů a její dopady na Československo* (Prague: Auditorium, 2011), 244–50. The authors show how, especially in the 1950s, the Munich myth was exploited for a variety of purposes, including the attribution of Czechoslovakia's losses to "American imperialists."
645 Pynsent provides examples of the myth in Czechoslovak sources, and attempts to redress it, in his article "Activists, Jews," esp. 211–14.
646 In his 1948 work on Munich, Rudolf Beckmann argued Churchill's policy, including the renunciation of Munich in 1942, only constituted a continuation of Chamberlain's policy; see Beckmann, *K diplomatickému pozadí Mnichova, Kapitoly o britské mnichovské politice* (Prague: Státní nakladatelství politické literatury, 1954). Kuklík, Němeček, and Šebek identify Beckmann's thesis as one of the most important works from the early Communist period, in *Dlouhé stíny Mnichova*, 244.

an alternative history which more openly acknowledged Soviet achievements and contributions.[647]

The enthusiasm of broadcasters across much of the BBC continued to grow as the war progressed, and the Soviet Union's military victories in the first months of 1943 were the subject of much congratulatory broadcasting in the Czechoslovak government programme, including jubilant renditions of Shostakovich's "Leningrad" symphony and various Russian victory marches.[648] Returning from a visit to the Soviet Union in March 1943, Bohumil Laušman – a member of the National Council and a Social Democrat who would go on to co-operate with the Czechoslovak Communist Party in post-war governments – employed language reminiscent of pro-Soviet writers of the 1930s, such as the Communist Julius Fučík. Laušman reported on the great strength of the country, telling listeners that "we have read and heard that the Soviet people are strong, determined, and brave, and that they are resolved to continue the battle until Hitlerite Germany is brought to her knees. Reading and listening is not enough, however. You have to see it and live it." After stating that this strength was made manifest "wherever people met" in the Soviet Union, Laušman concluded that "a country with such people and such moral strength [...] is unbeatable."[649] Programmes such as this thus gave establishment support to opinions that were once the domain of the left-wing opposition that Fučík represented.[650]

The signing of the Czechoslovak–Soviet treaty of December 1943 was also much lauded and its significance for the future of Czechoslovakia stated in the strongest terms; Minister for Economic Renewal František Němec even described it as "one of the greatest events of our history."[651] Speaking from Moscow after the signing of the agreement, President Beneš spoke clearly on the future of the relationship between the two nations: "Being in Moscow today, I want to especially emphasise that our co-operation with Moscow and the Soviet Union will be close and intimate." Expressing confidence in the national awareness and historical knowledge of his listeners, Beneš again listed popular national figures such as Dobrovský, Kollár, Palacký, Šafařík, and Hurban-Vajanský to

---

[647] See, for example, BBC Czechoslovak Programme, 18 July 1943, LN Z 1943 – 23; 8 August 1945, LN Z 1945 – 41, CRA.
[648] BBC Czechoslovak Programme, 19 January 1943; 19 February 1943, LN Z 1943 – 18, CRA.
[649] BBC Czechoslovak Programme, 27 March 1943, LN Z 1943 – 19, CRA.
[650] See Julius Fučík, *V zemi, kde zítra již znamená včera* (Prague: K. Borecký, 1932).
[651] BBC Czechoslovak Programme, 8 January 1944, LN Z 1944 – 29, CRA.

present the relationship as a continuation of historical ties: "you, dear Czechoslovak citizens, understand my journey today in the spirit of our entire national history of the last century: it is only an expression of that which our great national awakeners saw in the Russian nation."[652] When marking the first anniversary of the signing, Minister Ripka returned to this theme, arguing that relations between the two countries were a defining element of Czechoslovakia's national consciousness:

> Alliance with Russia is in fact one of the enduring Czechoslovak truths. It is an expression of national desires from time immemorial, it is clearly an expression of Czech and Slovak national tradition and the sovereign interest of Czechoslovak national thought.[653]

Such rhetoric was widely used after the war to justify increasingly close political relations with the Soviet Union. In his conclusion to a 1947 edited volume of papers from a conference on the importance of the Slavic idea in Czech history and culture, Professor Josef Macůrek used very similar language to that of the wartime broadcasters when he stated that a Slav policy must be the "indispensable foundation" of modern Czech life and that "it must be recognised that alliance with the Soviet Union can contribute to the strengthening of our national interests more than anything."[654]

As has been mentioned above, this increasingly positive representation of the Soviet Union in the Czechoslovak broadcasts from London was dictated to a certain extent by British propaganda requirements, and reflects the increasingly close wartime relations between the London exiles and Moscow which are well-documented elsewhere.[655] What the study of these broadcasts provides is an insight into how this positive representation was constructed and how much it relied on inherited nineteenth-century ideas of Slav unity and pro-Russian feeling among the Czechs and Slovaks, as well as showing the early appearance of what

---

[652] Beneš, *Šest let exilu*, 140–41.
[653] BBC Czechoslovak Programme, 12 December 1944, LN Z 1944 – 39, CRA.
[654] Josef Macůrek, ed., *Slovanství v českém národním životě* (Brno: Masarykova Univerzita, 1947), 245–46.
[655] In their extensive collection of documents relating to Czechoslovak–Soviet relations, Jan Němeček et al. show how relations with the Soviet Union came to be "decisive" for Czechoslovakia, and that, at the end of the war, Beneš went back to Czechoslovakia via Moscow because he knew that was where the really important decisions for the future of the country were to be made; see *Československo-sovětské vztahy*, 1:3, 2:11.

would go on to become established myths in the Communist era. Listeners to the government programme were prepared for a close relationship with the Soviet Union in the future and knew it to be a cornerstone of Beneš's foreign policy. In other areas, however, listeners were not to be so well prepared, as Soviet opposition to various policies and plans complicated propaganda efforts. Once relations with the Soviet Union had moved from the second phase, that of friendly alliance, into the third, of Soviet domination in policy decisions, the government broadcasts became prone to sudden silences and changes of policy in several areas.

When Propaganda Diverges from Policy: Mid-1943 Onwards

Former PWE employee and later historian of propaganda Michael Balfour asserted that "if propaganda is to be effective, it must be the handmaid of policy and action, not something which can be detached and dealt with on its own."[656] When propaganda is conducted separately and promotes policies that do not then come to pass, its authority and credibility – and therefore that of the government issuing it – are undermined. In the final phase of Czechoslovak–Soviet wartime relations, from mid-1943 until the end of the conflict, Soviet influence over Czechoslovakia's domestic and foreign policies became increasingly pronounced. This meant that policies concerning Czechoslovakia's future which had been promoted in the government programme up until this point, such as the co-operation between the Polish and Czechoslovak governments-in-exile and their plans for a future confederation, faltered and disappeared.

"If it doesn't work, it will not be our fault": The Changing Representation of Poland and the Central European Confederation

One notable area in which diplomatic problems and, in particular, Soviet relations came to frustrate Czechoslovak efforts to create consistent propaganda was in relations with the Polish government-in-exile. Though

---

656 Michael Balfour, *Propaganda in War, 1939–1945: Organisations, Policies and Publics in Britain and Germany* (London: Routledge & Kegan Paul, 1979), xi.

the relationship between the Polish and Czechoslovak governments in London was never free from tension, mainly due to the ongoing territorial dispute centred on Těšín/Cieszyn, its eventual breakdown was principally due to pressure from the Soviet Union and poor Polish–Soviet relations.[657] The references to Poland in the Czechoslovak government broadcasts chart this relationship, as the Poles appeared firstly as close allies and then almost disappeared from the broadcasts following the break in Polish–Soviet and, subsequently, Polish–Czechoslovak relations in April to May 1943. When mention of Poland was again made, the Polish government in London was presented as obstructing Allied unity and pursuing an anti-Soviet policy, before being abruptly dropped in favour of the Moscow-backed Provisional Polish Government in February 1945.

The topic of a proposed Central European Confederation, consisting of Czechoslovakia, Poland, and possibly other states, dominated Czechoslovak–Polish relations in London for the first half of the war. This episode also provides a useful case study for the difficulties of aligning exile politics and exile propaganda, since the policy was subject to complex and difficult diplomatic negotiations that could not be shared in radio broadcasts. On the one hand, the Czechoslovak exiles had to show their public at home that they were making plans for the future and to state these plans confidently, both to enhance their own authority and to prepare their people for post-war changes. On the other hand, the constantly changing political climate in wartime meant that decisions made in 1940 became unworkable by 1943, and topics that had been confidently promoted in early propaganda had to be abandoned. In the first years of the war, it was important for the Czechoslovaks to keep on the side of the British government – their host and most powerful ally – and to show their willingness to work with their European neighbours. Churchill had told President Beneš in the summer of 1940 that a Central European Confederation would be necessary for the security of Europe

---

657 Both Polish and Czechoslovak representatives had laid claim to the area known as Těšín in Czech and Cieszyn in Polish at the post-First World War Paris Peace Conference, and attempts to divide the territory in a way that was satisfactory to both parties was not achieved in the interwar period. Following the Munich crisis, Poland had renewed its claims and annexed the area. The refusal of the Polish exile government to support Czechoslovakia's claim to pre-Munich borders, and therefore renounce Polish claims on this territory, were a persistent obstacle to relations between the two governments in London. For more, see Jan Němeček, *Od spojenectví k roztržce: Vztahy československé a polské exilové reprezentace 1939–1945* (Prague: Academia, 2003).

as a whole. Beneš drew from this the need to appear friendly towards Poland (so as not to offend Churchill's apparent Polonophilia) and positive about negotiations, but to avoid the inevitable "contentious issues" and be patient with regards to Russia.[658]

One "contentious issue" was exactly how this proposed confederation would be structured, with the Polish vision of a much more closely unified state coming into conflict early on in discussions with the more separate Czechoslovak understanding.[659] Minister Ripka reported on these problems at cabinet meetings throughout November 1941 and his comments on the confederation project also revealed the importance of British opinion on the exile government's actions: "I am afraid of the English finding out that there are disagreements."[660] By 1943, however, Britain was no longer Czechoslovakia's most important ally and Soviet goodwill became the most important factor in policy decisions for the exiles, as well as influencing British policy in turn. In response to Polish warnings of Soviet intent to "communise" Europe and advice that Czechoslovakia should retreat from its pro-Soviet position, Jan Masaryk replied that his government had no intention of doing so and he would be "thrown down the front steps of the Foreign Office" if he suggested any such thing.[661] Conflict between Poland and the Soviet Union and the eventual severance of relations between the two forced both Czechoslovakia and Britain to take sides. Both favoured the Soviet Union, which had come out against the idea of confederation by autumn 1942, and they refused to risk offending this powerful ally by continuing negotiations on the matter with Poland.[662]

By this point, however, the proposed confederation had received a great deal of coverage in Czechoslovak propaganda, especially in the early years of the war. The two exile governments signed their first document on co-operation in November 1940, and that month Juraj Slávik told listeners that "Czechoslovakia and Poland are bringing to an end, once and for all, the period of their former disagreements and taking

---

658 Němeček et al., *Zápisy ze schůzí*, 1:117–18.
659 For example, the Poles were proposing a shared parliament while the Czechoslovaks wanted separate parliaments with a foreign policy that was *společný* (common, mutual) rather than *jednotný* (unified, single); see Němeček et al., *Zápisy ze schůzí*, 1:746–47. For more on the confederation negotiations in this period, see ibid., 730–96; for an overview of the principal ideas of the confederation, see ibid., 764–68 (Appendix C).
660 Němeček et al., *Zápisy ze schůzí*, 1:776.
661 Němeček et al., *Zápisy ze schůzí*, 3.1:348.
662 For the influence of Soviet–Polish relations on the confederation discussions, see Němeček et al., *Zápisy ze schůzí*, 2:681–84.

into consideration the unity of their fundamental interests." Despite a strained relationship between the two states during the interwar period due to disputes over the territory of Těšín/Cieszyn, further tarnished by what the Czechoslovak side viewed as the opportunistic and treacherous annexation of territory following the Munich Agreement, Slávik presented the planned confederation as heralding a future of "close political and economic association."[663] Early in 1941, listeners were updated on the progress of these negotiations, including details of the planning committees and councils that had been formed, and the members appointed to these bodies.[664] Speaking at a cabinet meeting on 11 July 1941, Ripka stressed that the exiles must "impress upon our people the need to work harder for an agreement with Poland," but by 24 November, as the negotiations encountered difficulties, Ripka warned the cabinet that they should alter their propaganda if they did *not* want a close union with Poland, in order to avoid raising expectations that would not be met.[665] Propaganda continued, however, with a fairly detailed agreement on the political and economic structure of the confederation being broadcast in January 1942 and the military implications being explained to listeners soon after, with the preparations for the confederation presented as both broad and thorough.[666] Greater attention was paid to Polish issues and historical events in the broadcasts (such as the anniversary of the Constitution of 1791 in May 1942) and more Polish speakers, from soldiers and airmen to Prime Minister General Sikorski himself, were heard on the Czechoslovak government programme.[667] When speaking to the British media, Czechoslovak politicians were also keen to promote the co-operation; in his book on the exile governments in London, published in 1942, Hans Madol quoted both Masaryk and Ripka's support for collaboration between the two states, and when he asked Beneš directly if there would have to be a Polish–Czechoslovak confederation after the war, the president replied, "It is absolutely essential."[668]

---

663 BBC Czechoslovak Programme, 19 November 1940, LN Z 1940 – 3, CRA.
664 BBC Czechoslovak Programme, 22 March 1941, LN Z 1941 – 5, CRA.
665 Němeček et al., *Zápisy ze schůzí*, 1:539, 760.
666 BBC Czechoslovak Programme, 23 January 1942, LN Z 1941/2 – 11; 4 February 1942, LN Z 1942 – 12, CRA.
667 BBC Czechoslovak Programme, 3 May 1942, LN Z 1942 – 13, CRA. Polish servicemen spoke in programmes including 2 May 1942, LN Z 1942 – 14; 17 July 1942, LN Z 1942 – 15; 1 September 1942, LN Z 1942 – 16. Sikorski spoke on 20 June 1942, LN Z 1942 – 14.
668 Hans Roger Madol, *The League of London: A Book of Interviews with Allied Sovereigns and Statesmen* (London: Hutchinson, 1942), 11–12, 8.

By November 1942, however, political relations were again under strain and doubts were beginning to surface in the broadcasts. That month, in a programme which included extracts from speeches at a meeting of the National Council, Beneš addressed the matter of post-war confederations and was heard to say, "I stress that, without the clear voice of the nation and its state institutions in the homeland, it will not be possible for any exile government to make any final decisions. It will also be necessary to agree on this with the Soviet Union, Great Britain, and the United States and, from the continental states, with France, Poland, and Yugoslavia."[669] Behind the scenes, tensions continued to rise over the disputed territory of Těšín/Cieszyn, and in January 1943 Jan Masaryk claimed that Polish intransigence on the matter was compromising the Czechoslovak government's credibility with its own representatives, as well as the people at home, stating that "I cannot stand in front of the National Council and our nation and say that we will make a confederation with the people who stole Těšín from us."[670] At a cabinet meeting on 2 February 1943, while assessing the government's position, Ripka advised that "We maintain that we must try to establish friendly relations with Poland for the future. We are therefore in favour of either a confederation or an alliance, with Poland remaining as part of our policy for the future, whatever the circumstances." However, his reservations regarding the feasibility of this project were also clear, as he concluded that the post-war situation would determine the outcome of the project, and "if it doesn't work, it will not be our fault."[671]

The British government, however, remained in favour of promoting Czechoslovak–Polish friendship and the confederation project for as long as possible. It was noted in a PWE propaganda directive of January 1943 that the Hungarian press was widely proclaiming conflict between the Polish and Czechoslovak exile governments in order to disrupt the idea of confederation, and broadcasters were encouraged to "use every opportunity in order to foster the Czecho-Polish co-operation and friendship."[672] In a subsequent propaganda directive, PWE acknowledged tension between the London exiles, but advised broadcasters that, "despite differences aired in this country, Polish and Czech statesmen are agreed

---

669 BBC Czechoslovak Programme, 12 November 1942, LN Z 1942 – 17, CRA.
670 Němeček et al., *Zápisy ze schůzí*, 3.1:64.
671 Němeček et al., *Zápisy ze schůzí*, 3.1:126 (Appendix A).
672 PWE Regional Directive for BBC Czech Service, 28 January – 3 February 1943, C 194/194/12, FO 371/34333, TNA.

that in view of the innumerable affinities that link the two nations a very close co-operation must inevitably be entered on after the war, and there is still considerable interest in the confederation scheme. There is also evidence that the suffering populations are drawing closer together in adversity." As German propaganda tried to convince the public that Soviet–Polish tensions would split the Czechoslovak–Polish alliance, PWE advised "positive propaganda" on topics which united the two countries, such as the scorn Nazi Germany expressed for both Slav nations and the threat both faced of incorporation into the Reich.[673] According to its own intelligence, PWE considered the confederation project to have been widely accepted by listeners at home, claiming that "reports from the Protectorate show that this co-operation is fully accepted there as an absolute necessity."[674] In March 1943, PWE acknowledged the effect that Polish–Soviet territorial disputes were having on Polish–Czechoslovak relations, in a directive which noted that, "whilst the open question of the eastern frontier of Poland has had almost visibly a withering effect on the growth of the sensitive plant of co-operation between the two allied governments in London, no such effects are discernible as far as the mass of the Czech and Polish people in the occupied territories are concerned."[675] "Free time" programming for exile governments was not compelled to observe PWE propaganda directives, however, and references to Poland in the Czechoslovak government programme became increasingly less frequent from early 1943 onwards.

That Polish and Czechoslovak listeners were not aware of the political conflict behind the scenes is illustrated in a contemporaneous letter sent to Sheila Grant Duff, editor of the BBC Czech Section, by a Czechoslovak serving in the RAF at St. Athan in the Vale of Glamorgan. Despite struggling to express himself in written English, K. Plananský had felt moved to write after hearing Churchill speak on the importance of European confederations. "I should say this is the most important thing for us," Plananský wrote, "now I think it is your duty to explain." He continued: "you should prepare people [for the] federation and for all that it means. Federation is again not a political agreement only. It means to live in it and all

---

[673] PWE Regional Directive for BBC Czech Service, 11–17 February 1943, C 194/194/12, FO 371/34333, TNA.
[674] PWE Regional Directive for BBC Czech Service, 28 January – 3 February 1943, C 194/194/12, FO 371/34333, TNA.
[675] PWE Regional Directive for BBC Czech Service, 4–10 March 1943, C 194/194/12, FO 371/34333, TNA.

that implies the living with neighbours as co-citizens." Plananský's letter also shows that listeners had noticed the increasingly less friendly tone in which the Poles were discussed in the broadcasts, as well as an increasingly pro-Soviet line: "We want to hear something positive about Poles and Poland. We will have to live with them and therefore we must like them at least a bit. I am not interested in this conflict with Russians, or at least I cannot take the purely antiPolish [sic] bias because I know I will have to live with them and not with Russians." Plananský feared that arguing with Poland over Soviet issues was unwise, warning that "we should not be on principle too disagreeable for our neighbours and future co-citizens, because otherwise we might become unacceptable for them owing to many unnecessary resentments."[676] In his hopes for more pro-Polish coverage and greater detail regarding the future confederation, this correspondent was to be disappointed as, in the face of diplomatic difficulties, the topic disappeared from the Czechoslovak broadcasts altogether.

The tense nature of Polish–Soviet relations had made the position of the Czechoslovak exiles, as proposed neighbour and ally to both, increasingly difficult, especially as Czechoslovakia grew closer to the Soviet Union while Poland was pulling away. PWE directives show an awareness of these tensions and their potentially damaging effect on the Czechoslovak audience, as they recommended in late February 1943 that propaganda to the region "avoid the subject wherever possible."[677] When news broke on 13 April 1943 of the mass graves of Polish officers discovered in the forests at Katyn, near Smolensk, and German propaganda attributed the killings to the Red Army, tensions reached their peak. PWE noted that the controversy surrounding the killings represented "a specially delicate problem for the Czechoslovak broadcasts, as of all the Allied nations, Czechoslovakia is the most directly interested in Russian–Polish friendship."[678] The Polish government-in-exile demanded an international investigation and the Soviet Union, angry at the imputation of guilt for a crime it would continue to deny for nearly fifty years, broke off relations on 25 April.[679] Over the next forty-eight hours, the BBC

---

676 K. Plananský to Miss Grant Duff, 25 March 1943, E1/645, BBC WAC. Emphasis in original.
677 PWE Regional Directive for BBC Czech Service, 25 February – 3 March 1943, C 194/194/12, FO 371/34333, TNA.
678 PWE Regional Directive for BBC Czech Service, 22–28 April 1943, C 194/194/12, FO 371/34333, TNA.
679 The Soviet Union did not admit responsibility for the killing of approximately 20,000 Polish officers until 1990. For more, see George Sanford, *Katyn and the Soviet Massacre of 1940: Truth, Justice and Memory* (London: Routledge, 2005).

broadcast an announcement of the split in all languages.[680] Despite PWE's desire for "extreme caution," the Czechoslovak government programme did occasionally refer to the Katyn massacre.[681] Responsibility for the killings was always attributed to Germany, with Clementis (as Hron) describing Goebbels's attempt to blame the USSR as "a cynical comedy with the corpses of the unfortunate Polish officers killed by the Germans," and Ivo Ducháček dismissing claims of Soviet guilt as *"báchorka,"* "a cock and bull story."[682] On 19 May, the National Council in London issued what even the Czechoslovak cabinet considered to be an overtly anti-Polish statement, accusing the Polish government-in-exile of pursuing an anti-Soviet policy in regard to Katyn.[683] The London Poles responded by breaking off relations with the Czechoslovak exile government and the confederation project formally came to an end, although it had disappeared from the government's broadcasts some time earlier.

This was not to be the last area in which the Soviet Union dictated Czechoslovak–Polish relations, however. The Soviet Union's establishment of the Polish Committee of National Liberation (Polski Komitet Wyzwolenia Narodowego, PKWN, also known as the Lublin Committee) in opposition to the Polish government-in-exile in London, and the subsequent Czechoslovak recognition of the provisional government formed by the PKWN, marked the total domination of Soviet will over Czechoslovak–Polish relations. In a speech to the cabinet on 17 June 1943, Beneš claimed that he had warned the Soviets against setting up a rival Polish government and that he had been able to pass on to President Roosevelt the assurances he had received from Ambassador Bogomolov that the USSR had no such intention.[684] Just over a year later, however, in July 1944, the PKWN announced itself as the sole bearer of authority over liberated Poland – authority which it officially received from the Red Army during the process of liberation. With the full support of the Soviet Union, the PKWN was eventually able to enter Warsaw in January 1945 and declared itself to be the provisional government in Poland. Czechoslovak ambassador to the Soviet Union Zdeněk Fierlinger was put under pressure to ensure his government's recognition

---

680 Output Report, BBC European Service, 23–29 April 1943, E2/209/2, BBC WAC.
681 PWE Regional Directive for BBC Czech Service, 3–9 June 1943, C 194/194/12, FO 371/34333, TNA.
682 BBC Czechoslovak Programme, 3 May 1943, LN Z 1943 – 21; 5 June 1943, LN Z 1943 – 22, CRA.
683 Němeček et al., *Zápisy ze schůzí*, 3.1:401.
684 See Němeček et al., *Zápisy ze schůzí*, 3.1:408.

of the new Polish government and made to understand that failure to do so would be interpreted in Moscow as evidence that Czechoslovakia was not committed to co-operation with the USSR.[685] Under direct Soviet pressure and in fear of its own position as an exile government of a country facing liberation by the Red Army, the Czechoslovak government-in-exile announced its recognition of the Polish provisional government in February 1945.

To attentive listeners of the Czechoslovak government programme, this definitive break with the London Poles may not have come as a great surprise, since broadcasts relating to Polish matters had become increasingly critical. Having almost totally disappeared from Czechoslovak government propaganda throughout 1944, the topic of Poland then returned to the broadcasts and the divisive issue of the Polish–Soviet border was finally discussed. At the end of that year, a programme by Communist and regular broadcast-writer Fridrich Biheller presented the failure of the London Poles to reach an agreement with the Soviet Union as posing a significant threat to the Allied bloc, and he asserted that the PKWN was already carrying out the majority of governmental work. Biheller also sought to impress upon listeners where British sympathies lay on the matter. He informed them of Churchill's support for the Curzon Line – the border between Poland and the Soviet Union claimed by the USSR, which brought territory that had been included within Poland between 1921 and 1939 under Soviet authority – and the British public's rejection of the pre-war borders favoured by the London Poles, and he quoted the *Daily Mail*'s comment that "the justice of the Curzon Line can hardly be denied."[686] Two days later, Josef Kodíček reminded listeners again of British support for the Curzon Line and interpreted a US statement refusing to guarantee any pre-war borders as showing "great support" for the British point of view and as an indication that the Americans "indirectly support Churchill's opinion that Polish representatives in exile should do everything possible to reach agreement both with the Soviet Union and with the Lublin Committee." It is interesting to note that the original end of this sentence – "which is supported by the Moscow government" – was removed from the text before broadcasting, suggesting a possible desire to play down Soviet involvement in the matter.[687]

---

685 Ivan Pop, *Chekhoslovakiia – Sovetskii sojuz: 1941–1948gg.* (Moscow: Nauka, 1990), 158.
686 BBC Czechoslovak Programme, 17 December 1944, LN Z 1944 – 39, CRA.
687 BBC Czechoslovak Programme, 19 December 1944, LN Z 1944 – 39, CRA.

In his closing broadcast of 1944, on New Year's Eve, Jan Masaryk spoke to listeners of the Czechoslovak government's hopes for Poland and made clear whom the exiles prioritised as an ally: "We want a democratic, strong Poland, but only one which will co-operate with the Soviet Union. We have neither the time for, nor any interest in, any other solution to the Polish question."[688] The following February the government programme repeated the statement of recognition of the provisional government in Warsaw and followed this with a series of quotations from the London-based government magazine *Čechoslovák*, condemning the aggressive attitude of Poland in the aftermath of the Munich Agreement.[689] Further distaste for the previous Polish administration was encouraged several days later in a programme following the Yalta Conference of Allied leaders. The only voice speaking out against the agreements made at the conference was that of the Polish government in London, and the Czechoslovak programme quoted British press reactions which judged this as a lack of maturity.[690]

The contrast between their respective wartime relations with the Soviet Union was the dominant factor in Polish–Czechoslovak relations in the period, although the dispute over Těšín/Cieszyn also presented a considerable obstacle. Study of the cabinet minutes confirms Vít Smetana's conclusion that, while it is "very difficult, if not impossible, to establish the actual degree of Czechoslovak devotion to the confederation project," it is nevertheless clear that it was considerably smaller than Polish and British interest.[691] Despite this relative lack of commitment and extensive disagreement between the two exile governments from the very start, plans for the project were much promoted in Czechoslovak government propaganda and encouraged all along by the British propagandists at PWE. Having been convinced of the inevitability of the confederation, some listeners (like K. Planský) were then concerned at the anti-Polish and pro-Soviet tone of government broadcasting in early 1943, but this trend only strengthened in the next few months as controversies over the Katyn massacre isolated the London Poles from both the Soviet Union and the Czechoslovak exiles. The Czechoslovaks considered themselves to be acting as realists in their relations with the Soviet Union and some judged the Polish government for failing to do

---

688 Masaryk, *Volá Londýn* (1990), 223.
689 BBC Czechoslovak Programme, 10 February 1945, LN Z 1945 – 42, CRA.
690 BBC Czechoslovak Programme, 15 February 1945, LN Z 1945 – 42, CRA.
691 Smetana, *In the Shadow*, 309.

the same; Minister of Defence Sergej Ingr criticised the Polish exiles for being unable to negotiate rationally with the Russians, complaining that "they are emotionally prejudiced against them."[692] If any one party was to blame for the breakdown in relations there was no doubt on the Czechoslovak side that the fault lay with the intransigent Poles. That the Soviet Union came to dictate Czechoslovak foreign policy is beyond doubt, and the progression towards this end is well-documented in many diplomatic histories.[693] In the context of propaganda, however, erratic and unpredictable changes in policy create awkward situations in which topics which have previously been proclaimed with confidence become taboo. The same lack of control over policy was to result in similarly inconsistent propaganda on another topic: that of the future of Subcarpathian Ruthenia.

"Subcarpathian Ruthenia is Czechoslovak": Broadcasting to a Lost Territory

As a territory which formed part of pre-war Czechoslovakia and was officially ceded to the Soviet Union just a few weeks after the end of the conflict, Subcarpathian Ruthenia could be expected to feature significantly in any discussion of wartime Czechoslovak–Soviet relations – but this is rarely the case. The region has received relatively little attention from scholars in general and even less work has been done on the war period, despite its significance in understanding Czechoslovak views of the territory and its people. As the wartime government programme featured regular programming specifically targeting Subcarpathian Ruthenia, this project offers an opportunity to investigate changing Czechoslovak understandings of the region in this pivotal period. From a diplomatic perspective, the discussions on the future of the region and the eventual transfer of territory to the Soviet Union also provide an interesting case study of Soviet tactics. The Czechoslovak exiles showed their willingness to cede Subcarpathian Ruthenia very early on, but the Soviets continued to deny interest until they had occupied the territory, at which point they sidelined the Czechoslovak government delegation and fostered

---
692 Jan Masaryk described friendly policy towards the USSR as "realistic" at a cabinet meeting on 11 July 1941; Němeček et al., *Zápisy ze schůzí*, 1:536. Ingr was speaking at a cabinet meeting on 7 May 1943; Němeček et al., *Zápisy ze schůzí*, 3.1:272.
693 See, for example, Němeček et al., *Československo-sovětské vztahy*, 1:3.

a pro-Soviet movement among locals who consequently demanded incorporation into the USSR.[694]

From a propaganda perspective, this study also highlights the difficulties of producing propaganda without simultaneously having control over policy decisions. The Czechoslovak government-in-exile used its broadcasts to promote its views, and, as succinctly summarised by Beneš in his speech of 25 April 1943, its stated policy was that "Subcarpathian Ruthenia is Czechoslovak" and would therefore return to the republic after the war.[695] As a result, no mention was ever made in the government broadcasts of the possible transfer of the territory, although there was (as in all of the exile government's broadcasting) an increasingly positive representation of the Soviet Union and an appeal for Slav unity. While the territory was not officially ceded until after the conflict had ended, the Czechoslovak government delegation never exerted authority in the region and it was therefore under de facto Soviet control from the time of its liberation, despite broadcasters' claims to the contrary.[696] The government programme continued to claim Czechoslovak officials had taken control of the region, and broadcasting from London to Subcarpathian Ruthenia ceased abruptly in March 1945, without any mention of it having effectively changed states. For Czech and Slovak listeners, the subsequent transfer of the territory must have seemed somewhat abrupt, but listeners with knowledge of the reality on the ground in Subcarpathian Ruthenia would have heard several months of programming that did not represent the truth. This willingness to repeatedly broadcast information it knew to be inaccurate raises some questions about the exile government's motivations. Was this propaganda line pursued in good faith by politicians still hoping to retain the territory? Was it considered low risk given the small proportion of local inhabitants with access to a radio who could identify its inaccuracy? Had the exiles already accepted that the territory was as good as lost, maintaining the propaganda line simply for the sake of appearances? It is my contention that the broadcasting from London to and about Subcarpathian Ruthenia in this period reflected

---

694 The most detailed recent study of these negotiations and the eventual transfer is Mar'ina, *Zakarpatskaia Ukraina*. Head of the Czechoslovak government delegation František Němec also published his own account of the transfer, in František Němec and Vladimír Moudrý, *The Soviet Seizure of Subcarpathian Ruthenia* (Toronto: William B. Anderson, 1955).
695 Beneš, *Šest let exilu*, 129.
696 The agreement on Subcarpathian Ukraine was signed in Moscow on 29 June 1945; for more, see Mar'ina, *Zakarpatskaia Ukraina*, 154–60. For the delegation's unsuccessful attempts to gain authority, see in particular Němec and Moudrý, *Soviet Seizure*.

the First Republic understanding of the region, and that unresolved issues from the interwar period complicated the issue of broadcasting. The war period, featuring as it did Hungarian occupation, Soviet liberation, and a change of state, was pivotal in the history of this under-studied region and, as it marks the end of their communal life, an important time in which to examine Czechoslovak attitudes towards Subcarpathian Ruthenia. The 2022 Russian invasion of Ukraine and associated debates around Russian and Ukrainian national identity in a post-Soviet world also cast new light on the recurring challenges the Czechoslovak government programme faced in regard to both language and identity in the region. This contemporary confrontation, then, offers a new case study by which to examine the intersection of language and nationhood in a diverse region, and to reveal how complex regional issues can be hijacked by larger states to their own ends.[697]

As terminology is so easily politicised on this topic, those terms favoured in this study should be explained. The term *Subcarpathian Ruthenia* has been chosen as a clear and unambiguous English term that, as far as possible, avoids outright political implications. This territory has been part of several different states and known by many different names throughout history, and even now the terminology varies. Some historians of the region prefer the term *Subcarpathian Rus* and others, largely historians of Ukraine, prefer *Transcarpathia* or *Transcarpathian Ukraine*, an Anglicisation of the region's current name as an administrative oblast of Ukraine.[698] Given the Czechoslovak focus of this work, the adjective *Subcarpathian* is used as the direct translation of the Czech/Slovak *Podkarpatská* (from the contemporary name for the region, *Podkarpatská Rus*), in which the prefix *pod-* denotes a position "beneath" or at the foot of the Carpathian Mountains. The alternative English adjective

---

[697] Russia invaded Ukraine on 24 February 2022. Russian President Vladimir Putin has been explicit in his rejection of a Ukrainian national identity that is distinct and separate from Russia, and of the validity of an independent Ukrainian state. He published an extensive essay on his views in July 2021 and reiterated his views in a speech given on 21 February 2022; see Vladimir Putin, "On the Historical Unity of Russians and Ukrainians," 12 July 2021, Presidential Executive Office, The Kremlin, Moscow, accessed 6 June 2022, http://www.en.kremlin.ru/misc/66182; Vladimir Putin, "Address by the President of the Russian Federation," 21 February 2022, Presidential Executive Office, The Kremlin, Moscow, accessed 6 June 2022, http://www.en.kremlin.ru/events/president/transcripts/67828.

[698] For example, historian Paul Robert Magocsi, whose work acknowledges a distinct regional identity, favours *Subcarpathian Rus* in his works such as *Shaping of National Identity*. Historians of Ukraine such as Andrew Wilson and Orest Subtelny favour *Transcarpathia* and *Transcarpathian Ukraine*; see Wilson, *The Ukrainians: Unexpected Nation* (New Haven: Yale University Press, 2009); Subtelny, *Ukraine: A History* (Toronto: University of Toronto Press, 1988).

of *Transcarpathian*, from the Ukrainian *zakarpatska*, denotes a position "beyond" the Carpathians that implies a different geographical viewpoint, looking westwards from Kyiv rather than eastwards from Prague. The term *Subcarpathian*, as opposed to simply *Carpathian*, is used not only because it is closer to the Czech/Slovak terminology, but also because it clearly differentiates the territory in question from other areas that have been termed *Ruthenia*, such as Galicia and Bukovina.[699] The term *Ruthenia* comes from Latin and has been chosen as a fairly widely used English term that avoids the pro-Russian or pro-Ukrainian implications of the terms *Rus* and *Ukraine*. Terms such as *Carpathian Russia* and variations on it, although widely used in English-language sources at the time, have been rejected for the same reason.[700] When quoting from other texts, I have preserved the original term and/or included a direct translation into English to reflect most accurately the original writer's usage. While the adjective *Ruthenian* is thus used when referring to the territory or citizens, the term *Rusyn* is mainly used when discussing both an identity and language distinct from both Russian and Ukrainian, reflecting usage in contemporary sources.

In order to understand wartime developments relating to Subcarpathian Ruthenia it is necessary to examine them in the context of the region's history. The region known in this work as Subcarpathian Ruthenia had, prior to the First World War, formed part of the Kingdom of Hungary. Following the end of the conflict, the territory was occupied by Hungarian troops and the Hungarian government proclaimed it an autonomous region of the country in December 1918.[701] Local opinion was divided as to which state Subcarpathian Ruthenia should join, and different national councils in different towns favoured different solutions (usually in favour of the state with the closest border to that particular town).[702] There was a movement to join with the recently declared Ukrainian National Republic but, when its independence was not recognised by the Paris Peace Conference, this option was abandoned.[703] This decision

---

[699] Magocsi, *Shaping of National Identity*, 277.
[700] The terms *Carpathian Russia* and *Carpatho-Russia* can be seen in FO documents such as C 2878/96/12 and C 3366/96/12, FO 371/34329, TNA. Terminology relating to the region varies hugely in contemporary English-language sources, betraying in some instances a particular political standpoint and, in others, simply ignorance of the region or significance of associated terms. It is not uncommon to find multiple terms used within a single document, without comment or explanation.
[701] Mar'ina, *Zakarpatskaia Ukraina*, 3.
[702] Magocsi, *Shaping of National Identity*, 86.
[703] Mar'ina, *Zakarpatskaia Ukraina*, 3–4.

was later interpreted in Soviet historiography as the manifestation of the people's will to join with the Soviet Union, overlooking the fact that it was the threat of being overwhelmed by Bolshevist Russia which put many people off the connection at the time.[704] Czechoslovak troops first entered the region at the request of local groups in January 1919 and, working with Romanian troops moving in from the east, chased out the remaining Hungarian forces by April of that year.[705] Delegates from three separate national councils gathered in Uzhorod on 8 May 1919 and voted in favour of joining Czechoslovakia, with minorities supporting unions with Ukraine, Russia, and Hungary.[706] The Paris Peace Conference subsequently awarded the territory to Czechoslovakia – whose claim (championed by Beneš, then foreign minister) also had the support of émigré communities from the region in the United States – in the Treaty of Saint Germain-en-Laye, signed on 10 September 1919.[707] At the time of its official incorporation into Czechoslovakia, the territory bordered Slovakia to the west, Poland to the north and east, Romania to the south-east, and Hungary to the south-west. The union therefore gave Czechoslovakia a precious land border with Romania, its ally in the Little Entente, as well as bringing Czechoslovakia closer to Russia.[708]

The incorporation of Subcarpathian Ruthenia into Czechoslovakia was agreed, on the condition that the region would receive its own regional government and a significant degree of autonomy in domestic issues such as education. However, despite these guarantees being recorded in the Czechoslovak Constitution of 1920, this autonomy was not realised during the twenty years of the First Republic. It was not until October 1938, in the wake of the Munich Agreement, that both Slovakia and Subcarpathian Ruthenia were awarded autonomy, and the long delay was the cause of much contention between Prague and Uzhorod. During the 1920s and 1930s this unmet promise was the subject of several complaints – some of which were made by Hungary and others by émigré groups in the USA – which were lodged with the League of Nations,

---

704 Mar'ina, *Zakarpatskaia Ukraina*, 4; on fears of Russian domination of a potential Ukrainian state, see Vincent Shandor, *Carpatho-Ukraine in the Twentieth Century: A Political and Legal History* (Cambridge, MA: Harvard University Press, 1997), 10–11.
705 Magocsi, *Shaping of National Identity*, 92, 94–95.
706 Mar'ina, *Zakarpatskaia Ukraina*, 4.
707 On US support for the union with Czechoslovakia, see Magocsi, *Shaping of National Identity*, 77–85.
708 Jaroslav Zatloukal described these advantages in his edited volume, *Podkarpatská Rus: Sborník hospodářského, kulturního a politického poznání Podkarpatské Rusi* (Bratislava: Klub Přátel Podkarpatské Rusi, 1936), 9.

but that organisation always supported the government in Prague.[709] Czechoslovak leaders maintained throughout the First Republic that Subcarpathian Ruthenia was not yet ready for autonomy – in particular they cited the extremely low levels of education and literacy – warning that it would give disproportionate power to the Hungarian and Jewish minorities and would not actually benefit the majority of the public. President Beneš maintained that Prague was committed to the promises made in 1919, but that "autonomy, if it is to be brought about successfully – and none among us, the Subcarpathoruthene [*podkarpatoruský*] people included, would wish for an autonomy that is condemned to failure from the start – must come about in suitable conditions."[710]

Subcarpathian Ruthenia was formally granted autonomy on 11 October 1938, and its first group of leaders was soon replaced with a Ukrainian nationalist government under Avgustyn Voloshyn. In the five months of its existence, autonomous Carpatho-Ukraine (*Karpatska Ukraina*), as it was then called, pursued a strongly Ukrainophile policy and formed close relations with Nazi Germany which, for a while, encouraged grand ideas of a "Greater Ukraine." In March 1939, following Slovakia's split from the Czech lands and the beginning of the Nazi occupation of Prague, Carpatho-Ukraine declared its independence – but the republic lasted only one day.[711] Hungary, which had already been awarded a large swathe of former Subcarpathian Ruthenia in the First Vienna Arbitration of November 1938, had been restrained only by German prevarication. Thus, when Berlin decided the Ukrainian national movement was no longer useful and turned its back on Voloshyn's government, Carpatho-Ukraine had no way to defend itself against the incoming Hungarian troops which took control of the territory between 15 and 18 March 1939.[712] The territory remained under Hungarian control until the arrival of the Red Army in April 1944.

The Czechoslovak government in London prioritised neither the political representation of Subcarpathian Ruthenia nor propaganda to the region. Although a representative of the region (Russian-speaking Pavel Tsibere) had been appointed to the National Council at its

---

709 Beneš cited the League of Nations' support in defence of Prague's policy in his essay "Podkarpatská Rus z hlediska zahraničně-politického," in Zatloukal, *Podkarpatská Rus*, 18–19.
710 Beneš, "Podkarpatská Rus," 18.
711 For an observer's account of autonomous Carpatho-Ukraine and the short-lived republic, including its nationalist policy, see Michael Winch, *Republic for a Day: An Eye-witness Account of the Carpatho-Ukraine Incident* (London: Robert Hale, 1939).
712 Mar'ina, *Zakarpatskaia Ukraina*, 8–10.

formation in July 1940, no related government department was established until the following May. The Office for Subcarpathian Ruthenia (Kancelář pro Podkarpatskou Rus) was then formed and Tsibere appointed its head, charged principally with propaganda work relating to the region: writing questions and articles for the Czech and British press in London; maintaining contact with Subcarpathian Ruthenians in the armed forces in Britain, the USA, Canada, and elsewhere; and editing Subcarpathian Ruthenian and English-language propaganda on the region.[713] As its work was centred on propaganda, the Office for Subcarpathian Ruthenia was located in the MZV, the home of the government's Information Department, but, for political reasons, it officially fell under the Ministry of the Interior. Minister of the Interior Juraj Slávik complained frequently about the incompatibility of the office with his ministry, but he was met with a blunt refusal that reveals the perceived importance of administrative unity: Ripka told Slávik in no uncertain terms that officially moving the department to the MZV was impossible, because "it could then be inferred that Subcarpathian Ruthenia is a territory which is not an integral part of the republic."[714]

The Czechoslovak government in London was also delayed in its efforts to broadcast to Subcarpathian Ruthenia by British opposition. At a cabinet meeting on 21 March 1941, Minister Bečko complained that, "at the BBC, currently we aren't allowed to even speak about Subcarpathian Ruthenia." This was attributed to Britain's conciliatory approach towards Hungary, while the two countries were not yet at war, and Bečko predicted that a future break in diplomatic relations between Britain and Hungary would "free the way for us."[715] Rather than raising their complaints with the BBC, the Czechoslovaks approached their British representative, Robert Bruce Lockhart, regarding pro-Hungarian broadcasts and references to a shared border between Hungary and Poland (only made possible by Hungarian occupation of former Czechoslovak territory).[716] Their indignation was compounded by censorship of Czechoslovak broadcasts referring to the territory and, on 4 April, Ripka told his cabinet colleagues that he would be taking the matter to the Foreign Office after British censors removed an "innocent mention" of Subcarpathian Ruthenia from

---

[713] "Důvodová zpráva ministerstva vnitra k rozpočtu kanceláře pro Podkarpatské Rus na rok 1941," Appendix G to meeting on 8 August 1941, in Němeček et al., *Zápisy ze schůzí*, 1:589.
[714] Němeček et al., *Zápisy ze schůzí*, 2:674.
[715] Němeček et al., *Zápisy ze schůzí*, 1:378.
[716] Němeček et al., *Zápisy ze schůzí*, 1:380.

the Wednesday evening military programme.[717] At a cabinet meeting on 5 December, Ripka was able to report that they had successfully "forced through" programming to the region, and stated clearly what he wanted from the broadcasts: "It's important that they allow [us] to speak to them as to our own territory."[718] Prime Minister Jan Šrámek then commented that "they are allowing it because war is going to be declared on Hungary," which Britain did that same day.[719]

Given the immediate British declaration of war and the fact that the first Czechoslovak government broadcast to Subcarpathian Ruthenia was transmitted just over a week later, on 13 December 1941, Šrámek's assertion that the two are linked is not unjustified.[720] However, Russian historian Valentina Mar'ina has suggested an alternative British motivation behind allowing broadcasting to the region, which brings the Soviet Union into play. She suggests that, while the British had indeed wished to avoid guaranteeing the territory to any particular state after the war, the fear that the Soviet Union might seize it (in addition to the large areas of Eastern Europe which the Soviets had already occupied by this point) was too great. Mar'ina suggests that Beneš used this fear to his advantage, leveraging British opposition to the cession of the territory to extract British support regarding Czechoslovakia's pre-Munich borders, and some sources support this claim.[721] In his notes from a conversation with Beneš on 18 July 1941, the president's assistant Jaromír Smutný quoted Beneš as having alluded to a British fear of Russia on the western side of the Carpathians that lingered from the end of the First World War: "When it comes to Subcarpathian Ruthenia, all punctiliousness aside, they [the British] would give it to us tomorrow just so the Russians wouldn't get it. Just like at the peace conference. Lockhart told me there are no longer any objections against broadcasting to Subcarpathian Ruthenia."[722]

Other archival sources reveal alternative motivations, however. Discussions among Foreign Office officials, following Beneš's complaints at the ban on broadcasting in November 1941, show complete awareness that "Dr. Beneš's main object was not so much to broadcast to the

---

717 Němeček et al., *Zápisy ze schůzí*, 1:400.
718 Němeček et al., *Zápisy ze schůzí*, 1:805.
719 Němeček et al., *Zápisy ze schůzí*, 1:805.
720 BBC Czechoslovak Programme, 13 December 1941, LN Z 1941 – 10, CRA.
721 Mar'ina, *Zakarpatskaia Ukraina*, 25.
722 Němeček et al., *Československo-sovětské vztahy*, 1:87.

Ruthenians as to get us to agree to a first step down the slippery slope of accepting the Czech contention that Czechoslovakia should be restored within her old frontiers." Apart from resenting Beneš's "peremptory tone," those present at the Foreign Office's Central Department meeting on the subject agreed that "the question was not of very great importance in itself one way or the other," and permission was granted.[723] Lockhart's main argument for allowing the broadcasts was principally one of avoiding embarrassment: "if the news of this ban [on broadcasting to Subcarpathian Ruthenia] were made public there would be very violent criticism both of PWE and the BBC." When he wrote to Beneš to confirm broadcasts could begin, Lockhart quoted in his note the paragraph from Foreign Secretary Anthony Eden's letter conferring recognition on the exile government, which explicitly stated British refusal to acknowledge borders.[724] No mention has been found in British sources to support Mar'ina's argument of fear regarding Soviet influence, merely evidence of further British disinterest in Czechoslovak affairs.

Despite having apparently waited impatiently to begin broadcasting to Subcarpathian Ruthenia, the Czechoslovaks did not immediately do so on a great scale and it was never a high propaganda priority. This was likely influenced, at least in part, by the knowledge that radio ownership was not widespread in this largely rural region; data from 1933 shows that, outside the cities of Uzhorod and Mukachevo, there were at least 100 people per radio receiver in all regions of Subcarpathian Ruthenia (rising to more than 400 in some places), confirming that radios were considerably more scarce than in the Czech lands and much of Slovakia.[725] After broadcasting twice in December 1941, programming remained sporadic for the first year, with several months sometimes passing between broadcasts. Although Tsibere had been promised a weekly programme to the region from the very start, Tsibere himself had long ceased broadcasting by the time weekly transmissions began in April 1943.[726] In July 1944, Ripka was informed by the Ministry of National Defence (Ministerstvo národní obrany, MNO) that "the representative for Subcarpathian Ruthenia complains that they have been totally forgotten about" and

---

723 Central Department, minutes of meeting, 26 November 1941, FO 371/24618, TNA.
724 Lockhart to Strang, 23 November 1941; Lockhart to Beneš, 2 December 1941, C 13338/10893/12, FO 371/24618, TNA.
725 This region-level data is presented in a map in Patzaková, *Prvních deset let*, obr. 2 (between pp. 672 and 673).
726 Tsibere's frustrated hopes for a weekly programme were expressed in his letter to Ripka from 21 April 1942, LA (D) 42, MZV.

that "they are requesting at least one radio programme per week at 20.45 in their language."[727] Access to this peak listening slot was denied and broadcasting to the region was not increased until December 1944, when an additional Sunday afternoon slot was added to the existing Monday morning. Broadcasting to the region was the subject of much discussion within the exile government, and a close study of the broadcasts and the debate surrounding them reveals a great deal about Czech and Slovak perceptions of the region. More than anything else, they show how little knowledge and understanding of the region had increased since 1919, and how the complex problem of the population's national identity remained unresolved after nearly twenty years as part of the Czechoslovak Republic.

Broadcasting to Subcarpathian Ruthenia involved strongly patriotic and nationalist themes, but the national identity of the region and its population, as understood and represented by broadcasters, underwent a fundamental change. Exactly where the population of Subcarpathian Ruthenia "belonged" in terms of national identity had been a topic of much debate during the First Republic, and this continued in the early years of the war. Such was the sensitivity surrounding the subject that the London exiles stated their intention of allowing all appointed speakers to address listeners in whichever language they chose. Receiving demands from rival language groups, the Czechoslovak government broadcasts for Subcarpathian Ruthenia began as a purely Russian-language programme, before being taken over by a Ukrainian-speaking team of broadcasters who gradually altered the tone of the programmes to one of overtly Ukrainian nationalist (and pro-Soviet) sympathies.

A study of this change in representation, from Russian-leaning to decidedly Ukrainian, provides historians with the final chapter on the questions of language and identity in Subcarpathian Ruthenia during the Czechoslovak period, and thereby contributes to the existing literature on the territory's identity.[728] Since the nineteenth century, three different movements had competed for political and linguistic supremacy in the region, with outlooks that are either pro-Russian, pro-Ukrainian, or supportive of the local Rusyn identity. Although the first two had come to dominate the debate from the 1930s onwards, the theory of

---

727 MNO to Ripka, 7 July 1944, AHR 181, CNA.
728 The most prolific historian in this field is undoubtedly Paul Robert Magocsi, whose regional Rusyn focus conflicts with the work of those of a pro-Ukrainian disposition, such as Vincent Shandor and Orest Subtelny.

local exceptionalism – the idea that the population of Subcarpathian Ruthenia constituted an individual nation distinct from both Russia and Ukraine – also had deep roots. The impossibility of debate during the period of enforced Magyarisation at the end of the nineteenth century meant that the topic re-emerged when the region was incorporated into Czechoslovakia in 1919.[729] During the First Republic, different movements were favoured at different times, and this led to accusations that the Prague government was exacerbating the language issue by playing rival groups off against each other.[730] The Czechoslovaks were not alone in this, however, as all the various powers that ruled the territory in the modern era preferred different national and linguistic movements within the region at different times, pursuing their own interests at the expense of the region's own identity. Even though the territory has now been part of Ukraine for over sixty years, pro-Rusyn and even pro-Hungarian movements have returned since Ukraine gained independence from the Soviet Union, and a Ukrainian national identity is by no means accepted by all to this day.[731] This confusion of national identities has been viewed by some as characteristic of the geographically isolated region, and supports the claim of Andrew Wilson that Subcarpathian Ruthenia serves as an "an excellent illustration of the dangers of assuming that a given national identity is ever fixed or final."[732] A study of the broadcasts to Subcarpathian Ruthenia also provides an interesting comparison to the broadcasts to Slovakia that were analysed in Chapter Three. While the complex themes of Czechoslovakism and the debate as to whether Czechs and Slovaks constitute one nation or two divided government representatives, the inhabitants of Subcarpathian Ruthenia were always viewed, both by their own broadcasters and in Czech- and Slovak-language programming, as being distinctly separate from their fellow Czechoslovak citizens. As will be shown below, the broadcasts themselves did not interrogate how the Subcarpathian Ruthenians related to the Russian and Ukrainian nations.

---

729 On local exceptionalism, see Wilson, *Ukrainians*, 111; on the unresolved conflict, see Magocsi, *Shaping of National Identity*, 131.
730 An example of such accusations can be seen in Michael Yuhasz, *Petition Concerning the Educational Complaints of the Autonomous Carpatho-Russian Territory South of the Carpathian Mountains* (Homestead, PA: Amerikansky Russky Viestnik, 1932), which was sent to the League of Nations and published by a Ruthenian organisation in the United States.
731 Wilson, *Ukrainians*, 114. It is as yet too early to know how this region will be affected by the Russian invasion of 2022, which has been associated with a rise in Ukrainian national feeling elsewhere.
732 Subtelny, *Ukraine*, 250; Wilson, *Ukrainians*, 111.

Exactly who the people of Subcarpathian Ruthenia were and what they wanted were complex questions for the governments of the First Republic. The region was geographically distant from Prague and the Czech lands (the westernmost town in what was then Czechoslovakia, Aš, is closer to London than it is to Yasinya, the town that then marked the easternmost point in Subcarpathian Ruthenia), but there were also great cultural and economic differences. In an attempt to increase knowledge and understanding of the region in the rest of the Czechoslovakia, state-sponsored books published in the 1920s and 1930s contained essays by prominent academics and politicians that stressed to teachers and the general public the importance of the region to the republic as a whole.[733] "What does the Czechoslovak public know about Subcarpathian Ruthenia? Still very little," complained the contributors, attributing some blame to the exoticisation of the region in fiction and the press: "this is not helped by the many books emphasising romantic elements, with bandits, bears, and wolves popping up all the time."[734] While a romanticised image of the region remained in some wartime British sources, the Czechoslovak government programme was largely free of such references.[735] In fact, although there was dedicated broadcasting to the region from December 1941, it received almost no attention whatsoever in Czech- and Slovak-language programming.

The language spoken in the broadcasts to Subcarpathian Ruthenia constituted the single most telling change in the identity of the region as it was understood in London, and therefore marked a turning point in the "language question" that had dominated the national debate previously. Under the First Republic a liberal approach had been taken to the language of the region, as the Prague government supported use of the "local language" but left the choice of Ukrainian, Russian, or Rusyn up to local bodies and individuals. The Czechoslovak census of 1930 included a question on "mother tongue" that was used to determine nationality,

---

[733] Examples such as Josef Chmelař, Stanislav Klíma, and Jaromír Nečas, eds., *Podkarpatská Rus: Obraz poměrů přírodních, hospodářských, politických, církevních, jazykových a osvětových* (Prague: Orbis, 1923); and Zatloukal, *Podkarpatská Rus*.

[734] Jaroslav Zatloukal, "Za hlubším a objektivním poznáním Podkarpatské Rusi," in Zatloukal, *Podkarpatská Rus*, 8–9. Popular First Republic writers such as Vladislav Vančura and Ivan Olbracht wrote a great deal about Subcarpathian Ruthenia, but their works often stressed the differences between this exotic region and the Czech lands; see Veronika Krabsová, "Prostor Zakarpatska v české literatuře" (PhD thesis, Charles University, Prague, 2012).

[735] An example of such an exotic representation can be seen in short books on the region's partisan warfare published in English during the war, such as Jan Čech, *Death Stalks the Forest: The Story of the Russo-Carpathian Guerrillas* (London: Lindsay Drummond, 1943).

but no distinction was made between those self-identifying as Russian, Rusyn, or Ukrainian. Similarly, the number of schools teaching in the "local" language (an important regional issue given the enforced dominance of Hungarian language-teaching before the First World War) was counted as a single unit, regardless of which of the three was spoken.[736] In the first years following incorporation into Czechoslovakia, Prague officials made several statements proclaiming Ukrainian as the language of the region.[737] As it became apparent that no attempt to formalise the various Rusyn dialects into a new written language was likely to succeed, the growing educated population and intelligentsia was split in support for Russian and Ukrainian, and the preference for the latter among the younger generation of teachers and students led many Czechs and Slovaks to view this as the more dynamic and popular movement. There was still deep-rooted support for Russian, however, mostly among older figures and the émigré population in the USA, and Ukrainian did not hold majority support.[738] Given this chequered history – American organisations had sent petitions to the League of Nations on the issue that the Prague government had considered suitably threatening as to respond to them – it is maybe not surprising that Czech and Slovak representatives in London acted with caution.[739] It is perhaps also unsurprising that their attempts at compromise continued to be unsuccessful.

As by far the most prominent representative of the region in London, Pavel Tsibere took charge of broadcasts to Subcarpathian Ruthenia when they finally began in December 1941, and his pro-Russian perspective characterised the early broadcasts. Tsibere gave all his broadcasts exclusively in Russian and his "greater-Russian" mentality was criticised for not representing the majority of the region's population. In the first meeting of the PRS after the inaugural broadcast to Subcarpathian

---

[736] See Yuhasz, *Petition*.
[737] An enquiry into the issue of language carried out by the Czechoslovak Ministry of Culture in 1919 returned with the conflicting findings that only members of a given group could make decisions regarding their own language, but simultaneously that the promised recognition of local languages meant it was "necessary to recognize as the literary language of the population, the Little Russian literary language, used by their closest neighbours and fellow countrymen, i.e. the Galician Ukrainian language"; quoted in Magocsi, *Shaping of National Identity*, 136. Five years later, the first superintendent of schools in Subcarpathian Ruthenia, Josef Pešek, announced that the language issue had been settled, claiming it had been confirmed that "the Subcarpathoruthenian [*podkarpatoruský*] language is Little Russian and consequently it is necessary to use the Ukrainian language in Subcarpathian Rus"; *Lidové noviny*, 29 July 1923, quoted in Magocsi, *Shaping of National Identity*, 137.
[738] Magocsi, *Shaping of National Identity*, 144.
[739] See Magocsi, *Shaping of National Identity*, 217.

Ruthenia, editor Spurný criticised the "pure Russian" nature of Tsibere's broadcasting and dubbed him a *Velkoruss* (Pan-Russianist). Referring to his own experience of visiting the region, Spurný argued that "they speak Ukrainian there, a Russian speech cannot engage the people." He warned that the pro-Russian movement in Subcarpathian Ruthenia was being enforced by "Hungarian-minded people" and "the people hate this [Hungarian] movement." He recommended consulting some Subcarpathian Ruthenians for advice, "so that these broadcasts bring real results." Drtina gave the simple explanation that "Russian was used on the basis that the political representative of Subcarpathian Ruthenia in London speaks Russian," but added that he himself "considered the language question to be very complicated politically."[740] At the next PRS meeting, however, Drtina confirmed that the committee had received requests for broadcasts in Ukrainian, and he seemed confident that this complicated problem could be easily overcome: "The question is simple. We are working on the basis of continuity. Therefore, all the languages that were legally accepted in Subcarpathian Ruthenia will be spoken. There will be no exclusivity. We must have the effectiveness of the propaganda foremost in our minds."[741] This had been the policy when broadcasting to the region from within Czechoslovakia itself began in 1934; provincial programming had been transmitted from Košice in the Rusyn dialect, as well as in Russian and Ukrainian.[742] When put under pressure, Minister Ripka advocated an objective stance: "I ask the ministerial council to take the position that whoever wants to speak Russian, let them speak Russian, whoever wants Ukrainian, let them speak Ukrainian, otherwise we won't get out of this argument."[743]

In addition to Ukrainian nationalist feeling, which had grown significantly in the short period of autonomy and was then suppressed by the occupying Hungarians, the exile government also received conflicting information that the pro-Rusyn movement was believed to be gaining ground. The Hungarian leadership in Subcarpathian Ruthenia had reverted to the same policy that the country had pursued during its last occupation, immediately after the First World War. This strategy promoted the

---

740 PRS, 17 December 1941, MV–L 271: 2-82-4, CNA.
741 PRS, 22 January 1942, MV–L 271: 2-82-4, CNA.
742 Magocsi, *Shaping of National Identity*, 223n72. For more on early radio broadcasting to the region, see also Fedir Ivanchov, ed., *Hovorit Priashiv: 30 rokiv Ukrainskoho radiomovlennii v Chekhoslovachchini* (Prešov: TsK Kulturnoho Soiuzu Ukrainskikh Trudiashchyk v USSR, 1968), 13–23.
743 Němeček et al., *Zápisy ze schůzí*, 2:191–93.

Rusyn or "Uhro-Rusyn" movement, which encouraged residents to think of themselves as a separate nation that shared a long history with Hungary, and not as Ukrainians or Russians with ethnic or linguistic ties to any other Slav nations.[744] At a cabinet meeting on 6 March 1942, Jaromír Nečas told colleagues he had heard the "Ruthenian radio" (*rusínský rozhlas*) broadcasting from Budapest two weeks before, making propaganda capital out of the fact that the London broadcasts to the region were all in Russian. He reported comments such as "Do you hear how they speak to you? They not only took your land, but your language too," and he encouraged Ripka, as head of the MZV Information Department, to look into the matter, as Tsibere had appointed only Russian-speakers to help with the broadcasts. Šrámek responded that Ripka (who was absent from the meeting) had received requests from Subcarpathian Ruthenia insisting that only Tsibere should be put in charge of radio to the region, showing the continuing divisions among the home population.[745] As the Hungarian authorities proceeded to suppress Ukrainian-nationalist views in the occupied territory and more and more Ukrainian-speakers gathered in London, it was perhaps natural for them to become involved in broadcasting to their homeland and expressing their pro-Ukrainian stance. Until August 1942, when Ivan Petrushchak made his first speech in Ukrainian, Tsibere was the only person to address Subcarpathian Ruthenia via the government programme.[746] From that point onwards, however, his influence and involvement declined swiftly, and this was principally due to his position on the ever-present "language question."

The exile government's attempt to compromise by including multiple languages in regional broadcasts was not to prove possible in wartime London, as Tsibere was highly resistant to co-operating in the production of broadcasts in languages other than Russian; indeed, his reaction to the request showed the symbolic significance of language in Subcarpathian Ruthenia. In a letter to Ripka from 21 April 1942, Tsibere explained that he had received the request for broadcasting to begin in other languages but was unable to comply. His description of broadcasting in "Russian, Ukrainian, and, as I understood from a brief conversation with you, also in some sort of compromise 'Rusyn' language" suggests a scepticism or

---

744 Magocsi, *Shaping of National Identity*, 142.
745 Němeček et al., *Zápisy ze schůzí*, 2:152–53. Ripka did receive such a request and circulated it to several departments, saying that the MZV would not comply with it; Ripka, message, 25 February 1942, LA (D) 42, MZV.
746 PRS, 3 September 1942, MV–L 271: 2-82-4, CNA.

disregard for using a local dialect which is compounded by the fact that he did not refer to it again. Focusing instead on the threat to Russian posed by the Ukrainian language, Tsibere explained his support for using Russian by quoting from his own memorandum on the language question that he had already sent to President Beneš. According to Tsibere, his people had fought to protect their "native language," which he described as "the single cultural element which unites the entire nation and ensures its further spiritual development."

However, Tsibere then took a more controversial position, by claiming that, "For us, the term 'Russian' [*rusky*] is the same as the term 'national,'" and he denied accusations of pan-Russianism by asserting that, when used with adjectives such as *Carpatho-*, this term could not be interpreted as implying any kind of "international orientation." Although the Czech adjective *rusky* is indeed used to denote association with both Ruthenia (*Rus*) and Russia (*Rusko*), it is inaccurate to suggest that the similarity between the two terms was not understood to imply a political and linguistic connection, as this was precisely the reason that the pro-Ukrainian movement in the nineteenth century had moved away from the term.[747] Tsibere concluded his letter with the comment that "the Russian language always and exclusively served our nation as a means to express cultural-national consciousness," and he informed Ripka that, as a representative of Subcarpathian Ruthenia, he was bound to these beliefs and could not forsake them. Tsibere then expressed his hope that Ripka would "take the appropriate steps" to enable him to continue broadcasting in Russian, and he ended by referring to the support he received from listeners and the "many emphatic requests" he had received for his reinstatement.[748] Contrary to Tsibere's hopes, he made his last broadcast on 25 July 1942 and the Office for Subcarpathian Ruthenia was disbanded at the end of the year.[749] Tsibere's fall from grace marked the end of Russian-language broadcasting, and as the Czechoslovak government never actively pursued broadcasting in local Rusyn dialects, Ukrainian was left as the only alternative.

---

747 Subtelny, *Ukraine*, 307.
748 "I consider it my duty to inform you that, from the moment at which the broadcasts to Subcarpathian Rus were cancelled, many emphatic requests have reached me from different circles within our audience for the renewal of the broadcasts as soon as possible, and their incorporation into constant and regular propaganda"; Tsibere to Ripka, 21 April 1942, LA (D) 42, MZV.
749 The last broadcast by Tsibere that survives in the archive is BBC Czechoslovak Programme, 25 July 1942, LN Z 1942 – 15, CRA. The decision to disband the office was agreed at a cabinet meeting on 27 November 1942; see Němeček et al., *Zápisy ze schůzí*, 2:765.

Broadcasting to the region became a weekly event from April 1943, transmitted in the early morning programme on Mondays. This was then expanded by adding a Sunday afternoon slot in December 1944. Following Tsibere's departure, all broadcasting to the region was carried out in Ukrainian, with the exception of one or two broadcasts given in Russian by non-native speakers.[750] As Ukrainian-speakers came to dominate broadcasting, so too did the understanding of the region as inherently Ukrainian come to dominate the exile government. A gradual shift towards a pro-Ukrainian stance in the broadcasts can be traced not only in the ascendancy of Ukrainian over Russian but also in the changing terminology used by speakers of all languages when referring to the region. In a spoken medium such as radio, every nuance of language is accentuated, and the political motivations behind the transition from Russian-dominated broadcasting to Ukrainian-dominated broadcasting, despite the exile government's desire to avoid the issue, were then displayed in every spoken word and every allusion to the territory in question. Even broadcasters speaking Czech and Slovak were not free from problems caused by the politicisation of terminology regarding what a territory and its population should be called.

From the start of broadcasting to Subcarpathian Ruthenia in December 1941 until mid-1943, a variety of different terms were used to refer to the region and its inhabitants. In Czech and Slovak, the territory was mostly referred to as Subcarpathian Ruthenia (*Podkarpatská Rus*), the name that had been used in official Czechoslovak documents such as the Constitution of 1920.[751] Occasionally, however, the shorter name Subcarpathia (*Podkarpatsko*) was also used. The population of the region was referred to as the Subcarpathian people (*Podkarpatský lid*), the Carpathian people (*karpatský lid*), the Carpathorusyn nation (*karpatoruský národ*), or Carpathorusyns (*Karpatorusové*). In the introductions to the broadcasts, listeners were informed, in Czech or Slovak, that they were addressed to "Czechoslovak citizens in Subcarpathian Ruthenia." In the earliest broadcasts, Russian-speaking broadcaster Pavel Tsibere used the Russian equivalent of Subcarpathian Ruthenia (*Podkarpatskaia Rus'*) and also referred to the population as Carpathorusyns (*Karpatorossy*). In this early period,

---

750 For example, a talk by member of the National Council Prokop Maxa, BBC Czechoslovak Programme, 14 February 1944, LN Z 1944 – 29, CRA.
751 "Zákon ze dne 29. února 1920, kterým se uvozuje Ústavní listina Československé republiky," 29 February 1920, Parlament České republiky: Poslanecká sněmovna, accessed 8 July 2014, http://www.psp.cz/docs/texts/constitution_1920.html.

Ukrainian-speaking broadcasters Ivan Petrushchak and Mikhail Bilitskii also referred to Subcarpathian Ruthenia (*Pidkarpatska Rus*), the Subcarpathian people (*Pidkarpatskii narod*), and the people of Subcarpathia (*narod Pidkarpattia*), as well as "our country under the Carpathians." In these early Ukrainian-language broadcasts a broad variety of terms were used; in a single broadcast, Mikhail Bilitskii spoke of "Carpathian Ukrainians [*Karpatski Ukraintsi*] or Carpathorusyns [*Karpatorosi*]," as well as referring to "Subcarpathian Rus," "Carpathian Ukrainian," "Subcarpathian people," and "the Rusyn language," showing the diversity of terms in use in this early period.[752]

This heterogeneity can be traced back to the lack of official policy regarding the appropriate terminology to describe the region and its population. In January 1943, the Ministry of National Defence passed on a request from the head of the Czechoslovak military mission in the Soviet Union asking for confirmation of the "official terminology," providing examples of the three most commonly used denominations among soldiers serving in the USSR: Subcarpathian Russians (*Podkarpatští Rusové*), Subcarpathian Ukrainians (*Podkarpatští Ukrajinci*), and Subcarpathian Rusyns (*Podkarpatští Rusíni*).[753] The Ministry of the Interior's response revealed the lack of official policy; explaining that the matter had never been legally resolved in Czechoslovakia and that, therefore, "there is no official title for the population of Subcarpathian Ruthenia as an ethnographic unit," it suggested that whichever term was most popular among soldiers should be used.[754] The MZV also responded to this query, concluding that, given there had been no legal resolution in the pre-war republic, it had therefore decided "not to interfere in the tangle of nationality and language questions" in the region, instead allowing all various national movements "as much freedom as possible." The letter also warned that the time was not right for such discussions: "As these are still very delicate and complex questions, the Ministry of Foreign Affairs is of the opinion that, since this problem was not resolved in the pre-war period, it is an even less convenient time now and it is hardly likely to contribute to the united spirit of the [Czechoslovak] army if this question is stirred up now."[755] However, this question could not be avoided in broadcasting, and, allowed the freedom to choose their preferred

---

752 BBC Czechoslovak Programme, 21 June 1943, LN Z 1943 – 21, CRA.
753 MNO to MV, 12 January 1943, MV-L 114: RPR 2-10-9, CNA.
754 MV to MNO, 18 January 1943, MV-L 114: RPR 2-10-9, CNA.
755 MZV to MNO, 28 January 1943, MV-L 114: RPR 2-10-9, CNA.

terminology, Ukrainian-speaking broadcasters moved in an increasingly pro-Ukrainian direction.

Even so, it was not until the end of 1943 that Czech-speaking broadcasters openly identified any of the inhabitants of Subcarpathian Ruthenia as Ukrainians. In a talk "to our citizens in Subcarpathian Ruthenia," Chairman of the National Council Prokop Maxa spoke. Although it is not immediately clear in which language Maxa gave this talk (he did give later talks in Russian but, in this instance, only the Czech text and English translation of this talk survive), it shows a Czech-speaker referring to "Subcarpathian Ukrainians," "representatives of Subcarpathian Ruthenia," and "Subcarpathorusyns" (*Podkarpatorusové*), all in one short talk.[756] Throughout 1944, Ukrainian-language broadcasts increasingly referred to the population as Ukrainian, whether they were "Carpathian Ukrainians," "Subcarpathian Ukrainians," or "Carpatho-Ukrainians," and Czech/Slovak terminology began to mirror this trend.[757] March 1944 saw the transmission of a Slovak-language broadcast and an excerpt of a speech by Czechoslovak Communist Party leader Klement Gottwald which referred to "Carpatho-Ukrainians," as well as a talk by Minister Ripka using the unusual term "Subcarpatho-Rusyns" (*Podkarpato-Rusové*).[758] In the D-Day programme of 6 June 1944, Ripka called for renewed resistance efforts from "the citizens of the historic lands! Citizens of Slovakia, citizens of Subcarpathian Ukraine! Czechoslovak people!"[759] Here, Ripka identified the territory in question as sharing ethnic links with Ukraine, but also emphasised the continuing Czechoslovak identity of the people. Towards the end of the year, however, a marked change took place in the terminology used to introduce the broadcasts to Subcarpathian Ruthenia. Though there was still some variety between "Carpatho-Ukrainians," "citizens in Carpathian Ukraine," and "citizens in Subcarpathian Ukraine," there was no longer any doubt that they were all considered Ukrainians.[760]

The identity of listeners in the region was also reflected in the content of the broadcasts, specifically in their relation to other Slavs. Calls

---

[756] BBC Czechoslovak Programme, 13 December 1943, LN Z 1943 – 27, CRA.
[757] For example, BBC Czechoslovak Programme, 13 March 1944, LN Z 1944 – 30; 3 September 1944, LN Z 1944 – 36; 4 September 1944, LN Z 1944 – 35, CRA.
[758] BBC Czechoslovak Programme, 16 March 1944; 15 March 1944, LN Z 1944 – 30; 5 March 1944, LN Z 1944 – 31, CRA.
[759] BBC Czechoslovak Programme, 6 June 1944, LN Z 1944 – 33, CRA.
[760] For example, BBC Czechoslovak Programme, 9 October 1944, LN Z 1944 – 36; 2 November 1944; 20 November 1944, LN Z 1944 – 37, CRA.

for unity among Slavs were common in the broadcasts but they did not deny the existence of differences, even among the population of Subcarpathian Ruthenia itself. In his broadcast of 5 April 1943, marking the start of weekly broadcasting to the region, Petrushchak called for unity with Czechs, Slovaks, and all other Slavic peoples.[761] One week later, in a broadcast that also branded conflict with the Soviet Union a "fratricidal war," Petrushchak ended with a call for unity: "all unite, whether Ukrainians, Russians, or Rusyns."[762] The following week, fellow Ukrainian-speaking broadcaster Mikhail Bilitskii spoke in a similar vein, urging listeners to put decades of linguistic and national conflict behind them and unite "without distinction of political adherence or religion, without distinction of the language to which you adhere."[763] As the war progressed, however, this openness to diversity and general Slav kinship was replaced with a more assertively Ukrainian identity. Some examples of this can be seen in the assumption that all listeners would identify with the term *Ukrainian* and its implied loyalties. Reporting on the composition of Czechoslovak military units, Petrushchak claimed that "Czechs, Slovaks, and Ukrainians have joined together as equals among equals and will maintain their strong internal unity regardless of social differences, religion, or political convictions."[764] No longer, then, were listeners to be given the option of identifying as Carpathorusyn (*Karpatorus*). A similar assumption can be heard in a broadcast by Fedir Rozniichuk, a member of the Czechoslovak army in Great Britain. After repeating Beneš's promise for a "democratic national state of Czechs, Slovaks, and Carpathorusyn people," Rozniichuk went on to comment that "only Czechs, Slovaks, and Carpathian Ukrainians can be the bearers of the state idea."[765]

In relation to Czechoslovak–Soviet relations, it should be noted that the Subcarpathian Ruthenian Communist Party had formally acknowledged its countrymen as members of the Ukrainian nation at a congress of 1926 and this view was shared by the Comintern.[766] According to the Czechoslovak minister in the Soviet Union, Zdeněk Fierlinger, there the

---

[761] BBC Czechoslovak Programme, 5 April 1943, LN Z 1943 – 19, CRA.
[762] BBC Czechoslovak Programme, 12 April 1943, LN Z 1943 – 19, CRA.
[763] BBC Czechoslovak Programme, 19 April 1943, LN Z 1943 – 19, CRA.
[764] BBC Czechoslovak Programme, 11 October 1943, LN Z 1943 – 25, CRA.
[765] BBC Czechoslovak Programme, 13 March 1944, LN Z 1944 – 30, CRA.
[766] Magocsi, *Shaping of National Identity*, 229; Mar'ina, *Zakarpatskaia Ukraina*, 6. The Communist International (Comintern) was an international association of Communist parties which was backed by the USSR and advocated for Communist revolutions around the world.

inhabitants of Subcarpathian Ruthenia were also officially classified as Ukrainians.[767] Although this project has revealed no evidence of direct Soviet pressure regarding the classification of the region's population as Ukrainians, the appointment of some staff members was calculated to win Soviet approval. When Ivan Petrushchak, the most frequent broadcaster after Tsibere's departure in 1942, was appointed to the National Council in 1943, it was as a Ukrainian Communist, and the exiles were keen to show the Soviets the attention they were paying to the region. Stressing agreement with the Soviet view of the population as Ukrainians, head of the National Council Prokop Maxa told Soviet diplomat Val'kov in April 1943 that, "on that basis, we recently brought Petrushchak into the National Council: a Ukrainian, a Communist, a worker, a very wise, intelligent person."[768]

National identity was not the only topic discussed in the broadcasts, however; in the early programmes, favourable references to a joint Czechoslovak and Subcarpathian Ruthenian state were also prominent. While nostalgia for the First Republic was considerably less prevalent than in Czech-language programming, the discussions of the period that were broadcast stressed the benefits that membership of Czechoslovakia had brought the region. There was a strongly Czechoslovak tone to Tsibere's early broadcasts, as he referred to "our Czechoslovak government" and "our Czechoslovak airmen," assuring listeners that "neither the Germans nor the Hungarians will be able to destroy the brotherly union of *Karpatorossy* with Czechs and Slovaks."[769] In his next broadcast on the eve of Orthodox Christmas, 6 January 1942, Tsibere referred to the future liberation of "our shared motherland" and life with "our brother Czechs and Slovaks."[770] On 8 May 1942, he looked back to the same date in 1919, when the National Council had declared its desire for Subcarpathian Ruthenia to be part of Czechoslovakia. Tsibere insisted that no details on how their future autonomy would be arranged had been necessary, as the Subcarpathian Ruthenians had held such trust in Czechoslovakia and the values they shared, and continued to share, with T. G. Masaryk.[771]

Petrushchak also referred to the First Republic several times in his broadcasts, often using religious terminology. Twice in early 1943

---

767 Němeček et al., *Československo-sovětské vztahy*, 1:391.
768 Quoted in Mar'ina, *Zakarpatskaia Ukraina*, 30.
769 BBC Czechoslovak Programme, 6 January 1942, LN Z 1941 – 10, CRA.
770 BBC Czechoslovak Programme, 6 January 1942, LN Z 1941 – 11, CRA.
771 BBC Czechoslovak Programme, 8 May 1942, LN Z 1942 – 14, CRA.

Petrushchak referred to the First Republic as a period of national "resurrection" for the people of Subcarpathian Ruthenia, reminding listeners in both broadcasts of how many schools teaching in Russian, Ukrainian, and Rusyn were opened during those years.[772] That October, Petrushchak argued that "twenty years of common life with the Czechs and Slovaks meant salvation to our people," but his primary example of just how the people had been saved was that "their national consciousness and their feeling of Slav kinship developed."[773] Slav unity was a common theme in Petrushchak's broadcasts as he referred to "our Slav land," "our Slav brothers, the Russians, Ukrainians, and Belarusians," and ended an April broadcast with the promise that "our nation was and will remain a true son of the great Slav family."[774] This pro-Slav tone was common to Czech- and Slovak-language broadcasting too but, once again, the Russian–Ukrainian conflict within the broadcasts to Subcarpathian Ruthenia is reflected in discussion of Slav kinship. For Tsibere, unsurprisingly, the Russian nation formed the centre of the Slav world, but later broadcasters moved away from his strongly pro-Russian stance to one of more general fellow feeling among all Slavs.

As in many of the broadcasts to Slovakia, Russians were presented in the broadcasts to Subcarpathian Ruthenia as "our Russian brothers," but Tsibere went even further.[775] In an appeal to listeners to resist the attempts being made by Hungary to enlist them to fight Soviet troops, he urged, "Do not commit this terrible crime." If forced to enlist, they should desert to the Russian side as quickly as possible, Tsibere advised, reminding his audience that, "in Russia, you are not foreign, there you are among your own."[776] This statement goes beyond an appeal for unity among Slav peoples, as Tsibere states that the two nations are not merely as close as brothers, they are one and the same. Other broadcasters stopped short of this while acknowledging a close relationship with Russia. In one of three short talks broadcast on 8 November 1943 to mark the twenty-sixth anniversary of the founding of the Soviet Union, one broadcaster claimed the people of Subcarpathian Ruthenia were closer than others to these particular brothers: "The whole of Czechoslovakia

---

[772] BBC Czechoslovak Programme, 15 January 1943, LN Z 1943 – 18; 12 April 1943, LN Z 1943 – 19, CRA.
[773] BBC Czechoslovak Programme, 25 October 1943, LN Z 1943 – 25, CRA.
[774] BBC Czechoslovak Programme, 15 January 1943, LN Z 1943 – 18; 12 April 1943, LN Z 1943 – 19, CRA.
[775] BBC Czechoslovak Programme, 21 June 1942, LN Z 1942 – 14, CRA.
[776] BBC Czechoslovak Programme, 25 July 1942, LN Z 1942 – 15, CRA.

and first and foremost the Subcarpathian people have particularly warm brotherly links with their great Slav brothers in the east, and all the nations of the USSR."[777] Petrushchak also predicted the certain failure of the Hungarian attempt to win the support of the Orthodox population by opening an Orthodox theological faculty in Budapest, on the basis that "the Orthodox people of Subcarpathia consider the Russian Orthodox Church to be their mother."[778]

Hungarian efforts to promote a Rusyn national identity that emphasised a shared history with Hungary rather than ethnic ties to other Slav nations were roundly rebutted in the broadcasts. Having previously described Hungary as "our nation's age-old enemy," Petrushchak struck out against the apparent attempts of Hungarian propaganda to undermine unity between Slavs.[779] "It is a blatant lie to say that we sons of the Slav family are in any way bound to the Hungarians," Petrushchak complained. "They brought us shackles once and they bind us in shackles again now, but the time is approaching when the Slav people of Subcarpathia will throw off their shackles and will gain their freedom by shedding enemy blood."[780] The following week, Bilitskii spoke on the same topic and again implied that, while there might be pro-Russian or pro-Ukrainian groups within the population, they were united against the Hungarians in their Slavness: "they even want to prove that we Carpathian Ukrainians or *Karpatorosi* aren't Slavs at all. That we are some sort of Rusyn-speaking Magyars. [...] They are striving with all their strength to tear Slav feelings and sympathies from the hearts of the Subcarpathian people." According to Bilitskii, Hungarian attempts to complete the work of "Magyarising" the population of the region, which had begun in the nineteenth century, was doomed to fail as their Slav feelings were preserved.[781]

Despite the broadcasts positively representing the Soviet Union and embracing a Ukrainian national identity for the citizens of Subcarpathian Ruthenia, Czechoslovak government propaganda remained insistent that the region would return to Czechoslovakia after the war. The policy of the exile government that everything following the Munich Agreement should be considered invalid meant the rescindment of the autonomy that Subcarpathian Ruthenia had waited nearly twenty years to receive,

---

[777] BBC Czechoslovak Programme, 8 November 1943, LN Z 1943 – 26, CRA.
[778] BBC Czechoslovak Programme, 26 July 1943, LN Z 1943 – 22, CRA.
[779] BBC Czechoslovak Programme, 12 April 1943, LN Z 1943 – 19, CRA.
[780] BBC Czechoslovak Programme, 14 June 1943, LN Z 1943 – 21, CRA.
[781] BBC Czechoslovak Programme, 21 June 1943, LN Z 1943 – 21, CRA.

but listeners were assured there would not be a return to centralised government. Broadcasters predicted a future in which "our nation, and no one else, will be lord," and where Subcarpathian Ruthenia would no longer be subject to any "foreign rule" but would be free to decide its own future "together with the Czechs and Slovaks."[782] All three nations would "live as equals" in the future republic, working together for the common good as "equal partners."[783] In early 1944 a broadcast quoted from Beneš's speech in Moscow, declaring the future republic to be "the national state of Czechs, Slovaks, and the Carpatho-Ruthenian people." These comments were cited again two months later in a Ukrainian-language programme, as broadcaster and soldier Fedir Rozniichuk claimed that "it can be no other way." Rozniichuk expressed his confidence that this was also the will of the people of Subcarpathian Ruthenia, maintaining that "this is not only the word of the president but also the plan of our government-in-exile and the wish of us all."[784] Though it did not occur often, Czech and Slovak listeners were also occasionally encouraged to value the return of the formerly little-known territory to the shared state. In a speech to young listeners several months after Red Army troops had first arrived in Subcarpathian Ruthenia, a Czech history professor told listeners that "it is our fundamental belief that only an independent state uniting the Slav peoples of the Czech lands, Slovakia, and Subcarpathian Ruthenia will guarantee us political, spiritual, and economic development."[785]

Listeners in all languages were repeatedly assured that the USSR respected Czechoslovakia's pre-Munich borders and her sovereignty. In spring 1944, listeners were told in a Czech broadcast that "the Soviet Union recognises the republic in its pre-Munich borders – including Subcarpathian Ruthenia – and has an agreement of friendship, mutual aid, and post-war co-operation with us in which it confirms again that it will not interfere in our internal questions."[786] Slovak- and Ukrainian-language broadcasts then repeated this message over the following weeks.[787] Towards the end of the year, Ripka announced the handing over of power from the Red Army to the Czechoslovak government delegation, headed

---

[782] BBC Czechoslovak Programme, 16 August 1943, LN Z 1943 – 23; 6 September 1943, LN Z 1943 – 24; 20 December 1943, LN Z 1943 – 27, CRA.
[783] BBC Czechoslovak Programme, 2 October 1944; 23 October 1944, LN Z 1944 – 36, CRA.
[784] BBC Czechoslovak Programme, 17 January 1944, LN Z 1944 – 28; 13 March 1944, LN Z 1944 – 30, CRA.
[785] BBC Czechoslovak Programme, 19 July 1944, LN Z 1944 – 33, CRA.
[786] BBC Czechoslovak Programme, 3 April 1944, LN Z 1944 – 32, CRA.
[787] For example, BBC Czechoslovak Programme, 8 May 1944, LN Z 1944 – 32, CRA.

by František Němec, and claimed the transfer showed "how effectively the Soviet–Czechoslovak alliance is functioning."[788] This was followed by a series of broadcasts on the transfer of power, stressing that at all stages the Soviet Union was honouring its commitments as laid down in the Soviet–Czechoslovak agreement of 8 May 1944. That November, a Slovak-language broadcast told listeners that provisional Czechoslovak stamps and banknotes were in circulation in Subcarpathian Ruthenia: "The readiness with which shopkeepers and farmers accept this currency for their goods shows their deep faith in our burgeoning state."[789] Programmes celebrating the successful handing over of power and foretelling a happy future for the region within the Czechoslovak Republic continued over the month that followed, and in his Christmas speech President Beneš described a future republic with "Czech rule in the Czech lands, Slovak rule in Slovakia, and Ukrainian-Ruthenian rule in Subcarpathian Ruthenia."[790] In reality, however, the region was already lost.

The diplomatic discussions regarding the future of Subcarpathian Ruthenia that took place between the Czechoslovak government-in-exile and the Soviet Union between 1939 and 1945 – and the ill-fated mission of the Czechoslovak government delegation – have already been presented in other studies as fully as is possible with existing archival sources.[791] For the purposes of this study, however, it is interesting to note at which points the Czechoslovak policy as presented in the broadcasts differed significantly from what was being discussed behind the scenes. At the very first meetings between Beneš and then Soviet ambassador Maisky in September 1939, Beneš claimed to have suggested that Subcarpathian Ruthenia could only be part of either Czechoslovakia or the Soviet Union, while Maisky's notes record the Czechoslovak president's conviction that the region should "certainly" join the USSR.[792] Between June 1941 and June 1942, Beneš then received repeated assurances that the USSR had no desire to take on Subcarpathian Ruthenia, and that

---

[788] BBC Czechoslovak Programme, 1 November 1944, LN Z 1944 – 38, CRA.
[789] BBC Czechoslovak Programme, 25 November 1944, LN Z 1944 – 37, CRA.
[790] Beneš, *Šest let exilu*, 157. Programmes include BBC Czechoslovak Programme, 3 December 1944; 12 December 1944, LN Z 1944 – 39, CRA;
[791] See in particular Mar'ina, *Zakarpatskaia Ukraina*; Němec and Moudrý, *Soviet Seizure*. Mar'ina notes the difficulty of studying the topic when so much about the activities of agencies like the NKVD remains unknown.
[792] Němeček et al., *Československo-sovětské vztahy*, 1:87; Mar'ina, *Zakarpatskaia Ukraina*, 20. Persistent differences in the Czech and Russian records of meetings such as these compound confusion over the negotiations.

the Soviet Union respected Czechoslovakia's pre-Munich borders.[793] Mar'ina suggests that, after Beneš's visit to Moscow in December 1943, both sides understood that the Czechoslovak government was willing to cede the territory but did not want to do so until the war was over: "Both sides understood perfectly that this would happen but preferred not to dot the 'i' at that moment."[794] Whether Beneš had privately accepted this or not, upon his return he told his government that the region would definitely stay within Czechoslovakia, and this was the view expressed in the broadcasts from this period.

While it is not to be expected that every fluctuation in diplomatic negotiations would be represented by a corresponding change in propaganda, the start of the "liberation" of Subcarpathian Ruthenia by the Red Army in October 1944 heralded an increasing divergence between reality and events as presented in the government's broadcasts. On 12 November, national committees across Subcarpathian Ruthenia held meetings and voted in favour of union with the USSR, and agitation for this move gained ground across the region. On 26 November, over six hundred delegates of various national committees gathered in Mukachevo, elected a committee as the sole authority in "Transcarpathian Ukraine," and voted unanimously in favour of joining the Soviet Union.[795] That these meetings were organised and controlled by Communists answering to Moscow, despite the USSR's repeated claims that it was a spontaneous local movement, was suspected by the Czechoslovak government's delegate Němec at the time and is accepted by both Czech and Russian historians now.[796] Němec's frantic telegrams about these events were held up in Moscow and did not make it to London for several weeks, by which time the government programme had already broadcast many updates on his successful assumption of authority and happy co-operation with the Soviets.[797] The new National Committee for Transcarpathian Ukraine broke off relations with the Czechoslovak government delegation on 5 December and, after much failed negotiation and a trip to Moscow,

---

[793] Mar'ina, *Zakarpatskaia Ukraina*, 25–28, 34–35.
[794] Mar'ina, *Zakarpatskaia Ukraina*, 37–38.
[795] See Mar'ina, *Zakarpatskaia Ukraina*, 82–85.
[796] See Němec and Moudrý, *Soviet Seizure*, 93; Mar'ina, *Zakarpatskaia Ukraina*, 82.
[797] Němec's communication with London was only possible via Moscow; see Němec and Moudrý, *Soviet Seizure*, 99. For more on the delays, see also Mar'ina, *Zakarpatskaia Ukraina*, 80, 106–7; Němeček et al., *Československo-sovětské vztahy*, 2:371–75.

Němec wrote to Beneš on 29 December, recommending that he accept the resolution of the Mukachevo meeting.[798] Broadcasting to Subcarpathian Ruthenia from London continued for another three months (the last broadcast went out 4 March 1945) without any reference being made to the turbulent political situation. References to Czechoslovakia also disappeared from programmes transmitted to Subcarpathian Ruthenia, while no further broadcasts mentioned the idea of that region forming part of the Czechoslovak state. A quote from a speech by prominent Slovak Communist Gustav Husák that was broadcast to Czechoslovakia on 9 March 1945 was censored to remove his statement that "the Slovak nation respects the will of Carpathian Ukrainians to join the Soviet Union."[799] On 26 March, Beneš finally wrote to Soviet Foreign Minister Molotov expressing his acknowledgement that Subcarpathian Ruthenia should join the Soviet Union, and the agreement marking the transfer was signed on 29 June.[800] The text of the agreement claimed that the transfer marked the reunion of "Transcarpathian Ukraine" with her "ancient homeland" of Ukraine, within the Ukrainian Soviet Socialist Republic.[801]

As Mar'ina notes, much is still unknown regarding the movement for Subcarpathian Ruthenia to join the Soviet Union and the role that various Soviet agencies played in it.[802] What is not in doubt, however, is that the decision was taken out of the hands of the Czechoslovak government-in-exile and its attempts at regional propaganda were thereby rendered futile; it could neither make promises for the future, nor admit its own impotence. The exiles also suffered from a lack of information as the Soviet Union obstructed communication between the government in London and its delegation in Khust. Deprived of power over policy, the Czechoslovaks in London also lost power over their propaganda, and were left with nothing to say to the people they had happily claimed as co-citizens as late as November 1944.[803] After four years of optimistic predictions for the future and proud proclamations of Slav unity, the Czechoslovak government was forced to accept the annexation of

---

798 See Mar'ina, *Zakarpatskaia Ukraina*, 118–19.
799 BBC Czechoslovak Programme, 9 March 1945, LN Z 1945 – 41, CRA.
800 Beneš's letter can be seen in Němeček et al., *Československo-sovětské vztahy*, 2:526.
801 Quoted in Mar'ina, *Zakarpatskaia Ukraina*, 3.
802 See Mar'ina, *Zakarpatskaia Ukraina*, 167.
803 In the introduction to the programme on 6 November, listeners were greeted as "Czechoslovak citizens in Subcarpathian Ruthenia"; BBC Czechoslovak Programme, 6 November 1944, LN Z 1944 – 37, CRA.

a large part of its former territory by its closest ally. Relations between the Czechoslovak exiles and the Soviet Union therefore determined not only the manner in which the territory was ceded but also the way the Czechoslovaks communicated with their former citizens, some of whom complained about being misled. One such grievance can be found in the Foreign Office archives, in a report from the British consul in Bratislava who met with a former resident of Subcarpathian Ruthenia in 1946. The man complained that he had heard Beneš say repeatedly from London that Subcarpathian Ruthenia would be part of Czechoslovakia, and he implored Britain to support this claim and do something about the Soviet takeover. However, his appeal fell on deaf ears, as the consul made it clear that Britain was not prepared to intervene in any way.[804]

* * *

The increasing diplomatic closeness between the Czechoslovak government-in-exile and the Soviet Union greatly influenced the propaganda efforts of the exiles in London. Although broadcasters had shared reasoned criticism of the USSR in the first phase of the war, before the country joined the Allies, this was swiftly abandoned in a wave of admiration and Slav kinship following the launch of Operation Barbarossa. In this second phase of relations, broadcasters fell back on familiar and established arguments regarding the position of Russia as the leading Slav nation. In addition to promoting the Soviet Union and reminding listeners of the historic bonds between their nations, however, government broadcasters still felt free to promote their own policies and keep listeners at home informed of the work they were doing on behalf of the people. Plans for a Central European Confederation or, at the very least, a friendly alliance with Poland, came to naught after the Soviet Union broke off relations with the Poles in London and the Czechoslovak exiles were eventually forced to turn their backs on the Polish government with whom they had spent four years negotiating. In propaganda terms, this resulted in proud proclamations of future co-operation, followed by a sudden disappearance of Polish themes from the broadcasts when the British discouraged communications that highlighted the tension. Propagandists were then left with nothing with which to replace the confederation project. When Poland was once again mentioned in the

---

[804] Ruthenia, Efforts to restore to Czechoslovakia, FO 817/26, TNA.

Czechoslovak government programme, it was in reference to criticism of the Polish government-in-exile, endorsement of the Soviet argument, and eventual statements of support for the Warsaw provisional government that the London Poles had rejected. In the case of Subcarpathian Ruthenia, Czechoslovak broadcasters had again actively followed the government's policy of predicting a happy future for all three nations within the reformed Czechoslovak Republic and, despite information emerging to the contrary, could not admit their failure or weakness in their propaganda. Broadcasting to Subcarpathian Ruthenia therefore petered out and ended without any acknowledgement that it had marked the last attempts of a Czechoslovak government to communicate with citizens there. The complaints of residents who had listened to the government programme and heard repeated assurances of their Czechoslovak future were left unanswered.

Those looking at the exile government's wartime broadcasts to trace the ascendency of Communism and the Communist Party will find the most compelling evidence for future political developments in Czechoslovakia in the representation of the Soviet Union; the rhetoric of Communist broadcasters in London was limited to fawning praise for this great ally, and for the efforts of "the people" for liberation. Evidence of growing unease among non-Communist Czechoslovak exiles will not be found in the broadcasts themselves – which sought above all to encourage a positive view of the USSR while fighting continued – but the roots of some concerns can be traced off air. At a cabinet meeting on 2 February 1943, Minister Ripka denied that Soviet displeasure was enough to cause the government-in-exile to change its policy, attributing changes instead to rather vague "tactical reasons." He also expressed the opinion, however, that admiration of Russia had been a rather different matter before the war: "We were Russophiles [then] because Russia was far away," he admitted, betraying perhaps the first acknowledgement that having the Soviet Union as a neighbour might mean a rather different relationship in the future.[805]

---

805 Němeček et al., *Zápisy ze schůzí*, 3:116.

Conclusions

This book has approached the government broadcasts as a performance, carefully put on by the London exiles on the only stage available to them during the war: the radio. In some ways, this performance had more than one audience; as part of a community of exiles gathered in London, a Europe in miniature, the Czechoslovaks were keen to ensure that they were accepted and treated by the British as the equal of the other governments-in-exile, and participation in the BBC's broadcasting formed part of their efforts. However, there were other opportunities to act as a government in front of the Allies on a diplomatic level, and the key audience that exile broadcasters had in mind was the home population that they could only reach over the radio. Their regular programming slot at the BBC gave them an opportunity to present themselves as a legitimate government-in-exile, claiming legal and ideological leadership of all Czechoslovaks. The image of Czechoslovakia that they presented in the broadcasts was of an ancient nation, naturally allied with the democratic western powers and the powerful "Slav empire" of the Soviet Union against their "eternal enemies," the Germans. While historical figures such as Hus and Palacký featured prominently in the broadcasts, the dominant figure of T. G. Masaryk was a mainstay of the exile government's rhetoric, and his name was used to symbolise its entire philosophy. The London exiles were initially committed to a recreation of the interwar First Republic but, as the conflict wore on, enthusiasm for the pre-war status quo began to wane and unresolved issues in Czech–Slovak relations from the First Republic resurfaced in London. The image of the nation presented in the broadcasts was distinctly Czech-centric and the propaganda broadcasts to Slovakia revealed a narrow and negative approach that does not seem calculated to win affection so much as to demand acceptance.

The exile government was not entirely free to broadcast as it chose. Its propaganda was, to some extent, constrained by British policy, especially earlier in the conflict when the British were more reluctant to engage with questions of the post-war settlement. However, both Britain and the Czechoslovak exiles were to be increasingly influenced by the whims of Soviet policy, and as Beneš's government moved diplomatically closer to Moscow its broadcasting followed suit. The foundation was thus laid for the asymmetric relationship of the post-war period, in which Soviet decisions trumped all previous promises. The exile government's propaganda on the future composition of Czechoslovakia – within its pre-1938 borders and closely allied with neighbouring Poland – was forestalled by abrupt changes in Soviet policy, and this led to increasingly erratic and inaccurate broadcasting as Subcarpathian Ruthenia left Czechoslovakia for good and the Polish government in London was abandoned in favour of a Moscow-backed alternative.

The way in which the Czechoslovaks in London used the radio also demonstrates how well-suited the medium was to wartime exile. Being able to use the human voice rather than the written word to communicate with their audience enabled broadcasters to alter the tone of their programmes and communicate something of their personality, making a more intimate connection with listeners. Jan Masaryk, without question the most celebrated Czechoslovak wartime broadcaster, was able to convey an affection, humour, and inspiration which touched listeners and forms a key part of the loving memory in which he is still held today. For speakers like Beneš, it was important to demonstrate their authority over the radio and to reassure listeners that they could be trusted to defend the Czechoslovak cause. After listening to Beneš's broadcast on the fall of France in June 1940, writer Čestmír Jeřábek described his feelings in his diary, claiming that Beneš's "calm, reliable and slightly lilting voice" gave listeners hope. Demonstrating how some listeners at least were reassured by Beneš's radio speeches, Jeřábek perceived the president's talks as the product of careful consideration and much experience, which gave his words an air of "self-assurance and certainty." Jeřábek also likened Beneš to a doctor, with listeners as recovering patients in his capable hands.[806]

---

[806] "After hearing him speak, one feels like a patient who has just been told that he has come through the worst of it and will soon be well again"; entry for 19 June 1940, in Jeřábek, *V zajetí antikristově*, 80–81.

Other speakers, such as Šrámek and Stránský, would be remembered for their more thought-provoking approach, using their broadcasts to engage listeners and encourage them to ask themselves some serious questions. The motivation behind Šrámek's broadcasts was described in the published collection of his talks: "Their intention was not for the listener to burst into applause when the speaker's voice fell at the end of a paragraph, but rather to make him think."[807] Stránský was also praised for having successfully elevated the war "above the level of a mere battle for survival" by imbuing the conflict with a national quality, a "Czech idea," which strengthened the conviction of listeners that they were fighting for "eternal values" and that this battle would "forever be held by the judgement of history and of humanity as having been worth fighting."[808] In the introduction to Stránský's collection, however, Ferdinand Peroutka noted the difference between hearing the original broadcasts and reading them later. "We read with our eyes," Peroutka commented, "but the effect of the impassioned voice is missing; it lacks the dramatic tension of the time which carried away both speaker and listener, that desperate need to say something and that desperate need to hear, and believe, and elevate oneself."[809] Due to the small number of surviving recordings from the war period, this study has likewise been largely forced to rely on a written record, and there is inevitably some element of tone, inflection, and emotion that may therefore have been overlooked.

Prokop Drtina also wrote of the wartime significance of radio in his memoirs, claiming that British microphones provided "that strange emotional magic which a connection with the forbidden and inaccessible homeland can give to an exile." As for the listeners, Drtina was satisfied that the London exiles had successfully won their allegiance, but his comments also reveal who among them was really being targeted: "those who had not lived through the war don't know and cannot imagine what the London radio meant during the war and how it was listened to with great care and, in the overwhelming majority of cases, also with love by the entire nation, at least in Bohemia and Moravia." Drtina seems aware of the possible failings of the exile government's propaganda beyond the borders of the Protectorate, but not greatly troubled by it. He also opined that the London broadcasts deserved proper research and a study

---

807 J. S. [possibly Jaroslav Stránský], "Předmluva," in Šrámek, *Politické projevy v zahraničí*, 8.
808 Ferdinand Peroutka, "Předmluva," in Stránský, *Hovory k domovu*, 6.
809 Peroutka, "Předmluva," 5.

of their own, predicting that such a work would be a "useful contribution to the study of our psychology for the future."[810]

A full and comprehensive analysis of all aspects of the exile government's broadcasting is beyond the scope of this project and the research done so far has raised several suggestions for further study. The single greatest question that this project prompts is whether the performance worked: were listeners at home convinced by what they heard from London and did the broadcasts succeed in winning support from those not already predisposed to favour the exiles? In terms of sources, research into the contemporary reception of the broadcasts could be problematic, as the ban on listening meant they could not be discussed in a public forum. Diaries, such as those of Čestmír Jeřábek, can offer brief insights, but a concrete body of sources would be difficult to collect. At the time, the Czechoslovaks in London inferred a great deal from the Protectorate press and concluded, for example, that the more virulent the attacks made upon a broadcaster in the papers, the more popular he was suspected to be by the Protectorate authorities. A study of the contemporary press could therefore shed some light on the reception of the exiles, as could any surviving records of Protectorate radio monitoring, and any records held by resistance organisations. Even if sources could be identified, however, the very nature of propaganda means it is difficult to accurately assess its reception. Propaganda is most effective when it is accepted subliminally; asking someone's opinion immediately causes them to reflect on the material as propaganda and this can alter their interpretation.[811]

The texts of the government programme also offer further possibilities for case studies in the style of Jan Láníček's paper on "The BBC Czechoslovak Service and the Jews in World War II."[812] The representation of women in the broadcasts is an area of study that has already attracted some interest and further research into the programming produced by and for women could contribute a great deal to the understanding of the role of women in the Czechoslovak exile movement in Britain more generally. Although relatively few women wrote for the radio, there were prominent female announcers in the London broadcasts and regular programmes that specifically targeted a female audience. Although these tended to cover predictably domestic topics, such as rationing and family

---

810 Drtina, *Československo: Můj osud*, 535–36.
811 Cruickshank, *Fourth Arm*, 159.
812 Láníček, "Czechoslovak Service."

life, the contribution made by women to the war effort was also widely promoted and praised. The quality of the Český rozhlas Archive means that these texts are accessible to researchers on a wide range of topics, and they are sufficiently dense as to support even quite niche topics. Some other questions raised by this project would extend beyond the war period, however. The sensitive issue of the transfer of the Czechoslovak German population is touched on in this project, but a comparative analysis of what key figures such as Beneš said publicly on the issue during the war and how they approached it once they returned to liberated Czechoslovakia would likely yield interesting results. This book provides a foundation for further research by presenting an analysis of the war period that can then be placed in a wider context by later scholars.

Reading through six years of the exile government's radio scripts offers a unique opportunity to look over its work as a whole, in the exiles' own words. When read alongside the minutes from meetings, memos, and correspondence of the time, a picture emerges of a fractured exile group working for uncertain goals in a difficult and unstable situation. The generally confident tone demanded by the microphone belies the reality of the off-air discussions and disagreements, as well as the persistent uncertainty of political exile. The exiles shared the fear of their British hosts, that exile governments inevitably become increasingly less connected to their people the longer they are away from home, and a study of all the Czechoslovak government's broadcasts suggests that this did indeed come to pass. Although the London exiles did return home to a liberated Czechoslovakia and were not ousted in exile like their former Polish colleagues, a study of their broadcasting gives an impression of stagnation. After the initial novelty of having regular access to microphones, the Czechoslovak government programme seems to have really hit its stride early in 1941, with a wide variety of content and a large number of speakers. By late 1943, however, the broadcasts became increasingly repetitive and monotonous, with the same themes and programmes being recycled constantly. Despite the upturn in the Allies' military fortunes, the spirit of the broadcasts seemed to falter, and even listeners like Jeřábek, so enthusiastic and attentive early in the conflict, appear to have eventually lost interest.[813]

---

813 Jeřábek's lengthy expositions on the London broadcasts and the characters of particular speakers disappear from his diaries from March 1943 onwards; see Jeřábek, *V zajetí antikristově*.

Enthusiasm for the return of the First Republic also petered out in the broadcasts, possibly reflecting a shift in opinion at home. Josef Horal's novel *Mlčení*, completed in 1943 but not published until 1945, is one of the earliest attempts at a faithful literary treatment of the German occupation. In it, Horal describes the life of a fictional Czech family that undergoes a similar disenchantment, as the characters' initial nostalgia for the First Republic is gradually discarded in favour of a different future.[814] A BBC intelligence report from December 1942 also warned that "the Czechs resent the idea of the restoration of the pre-Munich state: they visualise a socially progressive Federation of Czechs, Slovaks and Carpatho-Russians, within the German boundaries of the old Czechoslovakia, but excluding the Sudeten Germans."[815] Without the anchor of the First Republic, on which so much of the exile government's performance depended, the London exiles were left treading water, with nothing to offer listeners beyond what they had already been saying for four years. The support of the Allies was enough to get the exiles back to liberated Czechoslovakia but, upon their return, they found the reality of the post-war state was to differ significantly from the "free republic" they had imagined in London. In his speech for the BBC's Silver Jubilee celebrations in 1977, Ripka praised the corporation's commitment to honesty and fairness, claiming that the BBC had created an environment in which "Czechoslovak broadcasting from London was able to become exactly what we wanted it to be, the true Voice of the free Republic."[816] Yet while this fits nicely into the British narrative about both the country and its public broadcaster offering a safe haven to allies during the war period, in reality the broadcasts were the voice of the exiles themselves, and the republic at the centre of their performance never existed beyond the fictional Europe of the wartime broadcasts.

---

[814] Josef Horal, *Mlčení* (Prague: Družstevní Práce, 1945).
[815] SEA, EOCOTF (Central-Southern Europe), 24 December 1942, 51/42, EIP series 1c (b), E2/192/6, BBC WAC.
[816] Hubert Ripka, "The BBC's Silver Jubilee," 12 November 1947, E1/641/2, BBC WAC.

Bibliography of Sources[817]

Archival Collections

Český rozhlas Archive (CRA), Prague
BBC Wartime Broadcasts Collection [Working title]
BBC Londýn – Zpravodajství [LN Z] 1–52 Texts of Czechoslovak Government Programme, BBC, Aug 1940 – April 1945

BBC Written Archives Centre (WAC), Caversham
E1/638	Czechoslovakia, Czechoslovak Service, Meetings, 1940–42
E1/641/1	Czechoslovakia, Miscellaneous Correspondence A–M, 1936–52
E1/641/2	Czechoslovakia, Miscellaneous Correspondence N–Z, 1935–49
E1/645	Czechoslovakia, Czech Programme Organiser, Misc. Papers, 1943–45
E1/1323	Czechoslovakia, Czech Editor's Papers, 1943–45
E2/10	Allied Government Broadcasts: General, 1940–44
E2/15	Allied Governments, 1940–45
E2/184	European Intelligence Papers, European Audience Estimates, 1943–44
E2/185	European Intelligence Papers, Intelligence Reports, 1941–43
E2/192/1–6	European Intelligence Papers, Surveys of European Audiences, Enemy Occupied Countries Other than France
E2/209/1–4	European Service, Output Reports
R13/163/1–5	London Transcription Service (General)

The National Archives (TNA), Kew
FO 371	/24610	Central, Czechoslovakia, 1941: Czechoslovak-Soviet Relations
	/24618	Central, Czechoslovakia, 1941: Broadcasts to Czechoslovakia
	/26380	Central, Czechoslovakia, 1941: Intelligence Reports
	/30835	Central, Czechoslovakia, Anglo-Czechoslovak Relations, 1942

---

817 This bibliography is composed according the English alphabet, irrespective of Czech diacritic marks (e.g., č) or alphabetic conventions (e.g., ch will be listed under c and not as a separate letter).

	/30852	Central, Czechoslovakia, 1942, Proposed publication of a book by Dr. Benes in Czech
	/34329	Central, Czechoslovakia, 1943, Czechoslovak Government in London, activities of
	/34333	Central, Czechoslovakia, 1943, Czechoslovak broadcasts
	/34355	Central, Czechoslovakia, 1943, Future of Czechoslovakia
FO 800	/879	Czechoslovakia: Secret Reports, 1943, Robert Bruce Lockhart
FO 817	/26	Ruthenia, Efforts to restore to Czechoslovakia
FO 898	/220	PWE, Czechoslovakia, General Correspondence, 1941–45
	/429	Leaflet Sub-Committee, PWE/Air Ministry, 1942–44
	/506	Magyar Leaflets, Hungarian, Czech & Polish, 1942–45
FO 1093	/129	PWE Draft paper on Propaganda

Czech National Archive [CNA], Chodov, Prague

MV-L	Ministerstvo vnitra Londýn	271	MV-L (Rozhlas, zpravodajství)
		114	Referát pro Podkarpatskou Rus
LA	Londýnský archiv	2	Sbírka dokumentů (Ripka)
		25	Sbírka dokumentů
AHR	Archiv Huberta Ripky	181	Slovensko
		194	Zprávy z Podkarpatské Rusi

Czech Ministry of Foreign Affairs Archive (MZV), Černinský palác, Prague
Londýnský archiv (obyčejný)

LA (O) 254	Osvěta: Fotografie, gramofonové desky	1939–45
LA (O) 353	Osvěta, Rozhlas	1939–45
LA (O) 541	Zaměstnanci: Masaryk, Jan	1939–45

Londýnský archiv (důvěrný)
LA (D) 42	Osvěta – Rozhlas	

Londýnský archiv – Doplňky
Doplňky LA 9	Osvěta – Studijní ústav Londýn	1942–44

Published Primary Sources

Beneš, Edvard. *Šest let exilu a druhé světové války: Řeči, projevy a dokumenty z r. 1938–1945.* London: Čechoslovák, 1945.
Clementis, Vladimír. *Odkazy z Londýna.* Bratislava: Obroda, 1947.
Drtina, Prokop. *A nyní promluví Pavel Svatý...: Londýnské rozhlasové epištoly z let 1940–1945.* Prague: Vladimír Žikeš, 1945.
Masaryk, Jan. *Volá Londýn.* Prague: Lincolns-Prager, 1948.
Masaryk, Jan. *Volá Londýn.* Prague: Panorama, 1990.

Nejedlý, Zdeněk. *Hovoří Moskva: Rozhlasové projevy z let 1939–1945*. Prague: Odeon, 1977.
Němeček, Jan, Helena Nováčková, Ivan Šťovíček, and Miroslav Tejchman, eds. *Československo-sovětské vztahy v diplomatických jednáních, 1939–1945: Dokumenty*. Vols. 1–2. Prague: Státní ústřední archive, 1998; 1999.
Němeček, Jan, Ivan Šťovíček, Helena Nováčková, and Jan Kuklík, eds. *Zápisy ze schůzí československé vlády v Londýně*. Vol. 1, *1940–1941*. Prague: Historický ústav Akademie věd ČR, Masarykův ústav a Archiv Akademie věd ČR, 2008.
Němeček, Jan, Ivan Šťovíček, Helena Nováčková, Jan Kuklík, and Jan Bílek, eds. *Zápisy ze schůzí československé vlády v Londýně*. Vol 2, *1942*. Prague: Historický ústav Akademie věd ČR, Masarykův ústav a Archiv Akademie věd ČR, 2011.
———, eds. *Zápisy ze schůzí československé vlády v Londýně*. Vol. 3.1, *leden–červen 1943*. Prague: Pravnická fakulta Univerzity Karlovy, Historický ústav Akademie věd ČR, Masarykův ústav a Archiv Akademie věd ČR, 2012.
———, eds. *Zápisy ze schůzí československé vlády v Londýně*. Vol. 3.2, *červenec–prosinec 1943*. Prague: Pravnická fakulta Univerzity Karlovy, Historický ústav Akademie věd ČR, Masarykův ústav a Archiv Akademie věd ČR, 2013.
———, eds. *Zápisy ze schůzí československé vlády v Londýně*. Vol. 4.1, *leden–červen 1944*. Prague: Pravnická fakulta Univerzity Karlovy, Historický ústav Akademie věd ČR, Masarykův ústav a Archiv Akademie věd ČR, 2014.
———, eds. *Zápisy ze schůzí československé vlády v Londýně*. Vol. 4.2, *červenec–prosinec 1944*. Prague: Pravnická fakulta Univerzity Karlovy, Historický ústav Akademie věd ČR, Masarykův ústav a Archiv Akademie věd ČR, 2015.
———, eds. *Zápisy ze schůzí československé vlády v Londýně*. Vol. 5, *1945*. Prague: Historický ústav Akademie věd ČR, Pravnická fakulta Univerzity Karlovy, Masarykův ústav a Archiv Akademie věd ČR, 2016.
Otáhalová, Libuše, and Milada Červinková, eds., *Dokumenty z historie československé politiky 1939–1943*. Vols. 1–2. Prague: Academia, 1966.
Prečan, Vilém, ed. *Slovenské národné povstanie: dokumenty*. Bratislava: Vydavateľstvo politickej literatúry, 1965.
Šrámek, Jan. *Politické projevy v zahraničí*. Prague: Výkonný výbor československé strany lidové, 1945.
Stránský, Jaroslav. *Hovory k domovu*. Prague: Fr. Borový, 1945.

Secondary Literature

Unpublished Theses
Krabsová, Veronika. "Prostor Zakarpatska v české literature." PhD thesis, Charles University, Prague, 2012.
Ullrich, Simon. "*Odsun/Vyhnání*: The Eviction of the German-Speaking Minority from the Republic of Czechoslovakia 1945/46 and Its Reception in Austrian Newspapers." PhD thesis, University of Graz, 2021.

Web Sources
"Nariadenie zo dňa 9. septembra 1941 o právnom postavení Židov," 9 September 1941. Ústav pamäti národa (Nation's Memory Institute), Slovakia. Accessed 8 December 2014. https://www.upn.gov.sk/data/pdf/vlada_198-1941.pdf.

Putin, Vladimir. "On the Historical Unity of Russians and Ukrainians," 12 July 2021. Presidential Executive Office, The Kremlin, Moscow. Accessed 6 June 2022. http://www.en.kremlin.ru/misc/66182.
Putin, Vladimir. "Address by the President of the Russian Federation," 21 February 2022. Presidential Executive Office, The Kremlin, Moscow. Accessed 6 June 2022. http://en.kremlin.ru/events/president/news/67828.
"Ústavný zákon zo dňa 21. júlia 1939 o ústave Slovenskej republiky," 21 July 1939. Ústav pamäti národa (Nation's Memory Institute), Slovakia. Accessed 8 December 2014. https://www.upn.gov.sk/data/pdf/ustava1939.pdf.
"Zákon ze dne 29. února 1920, kterým se uvozuje Ústavní listina Československé republiky," 29 February 1920. Parlament České republiky: Poslanecká sněmovna. Accessed 8 July 2014. http://www.psp.cz/docs/texts/constitution_1920.html.

Articles and Book Chapters

Bakke, Elisabeth. "The Making of Czechoslovakism in the First Czechoslovak Republic." In *Loyalitäten in der Tschechoslowakischen Republik 1918–1938: Politische, nationale und kulturelle Zugehörigkeiten*, by Martin Schulze Wessel, 23–44. Munich: R. Oldenbourg, 2004.

Čábelová, Lenka. "Československý rozhlas a stát 1923–1945." In *Konsolidace vládnutí a podnikání v České republice a v Evropské unii*. Vol. 2, *Sociologie, prognostika a správa, Média*, edited by Jakub Končelík, Barbara Köpplová, and Irena Prázová, 291–306. Prague: Matfyzpress, 2002.

Casteel, James. "Historicizing the Nation: Transnational Approaches to the Recent European Past." In *Transnational Europe: Promise, Paradox, Limits*, edited by Joan DeBardeleben and Achim Hurrelmann, 153–69. Basingstoke: Macmillan, 2011.

Corner, John. "Mediated Persona and Political Culture: Dimensions of Structure and Progress." *European Journal of Cultural Studies* 3, no. 3 (2000): 386–402.

Cornwall, Mark. "Stirring Resistance from Moscow: The German Communists of Czechoslovakia and Wireless Propaganda in the Sudetenland, 1941–1945." *German History* 24, no. 2 (2006): 212–4.

Hronek, Jiří. "Československý rozhlas v Londýně za války." In *Kapitoly z dějin čs. rozhlasu*. Vol. 2, 32–62. Prague: Studijní oddělení československého rozhlasu, 1964.

Koutek, Ondřej. "Zahraniční odboj na vlnách BBC: Československé vysílání z Londýna 1939–1945." *Paměť a Dějiny* 8, no.1 (2014): 30–44.

Láníček, Jan. "The Czechoslovak Service of the BBC and the Jews during World War II." *Yad Vashem Studies* 38, no. 2 (2010): 123–53.

Masaryk, Tomáš. "Palackého idea národa českého." *Naše doba* 5 (1898): 769–95.

Němeček, Jan. "Československá exilová vláda a počátky Slovenského národního povstání." In *Slovenské národné povstanie – Slovensko a Európa v roku 1944*, by Marek Syrný et al., 239–46. Banská Bystrica: Múzeum Slovenského národného povstania, 2014.

Pečírková, Jaroslava. "Staročeská synonyma jazyk a národ." *Listy filologické* 92 (1969): 126–30.

Pynsent, Robert. "Activists, Jews, The Little Czech Man and Germans." *Central Europe* 5, no. 2 (2007): 211–333.

Pynsent, Robert B. "Die Dalimil-Chronik als polymythischer Text (Dalimil – Fichte – Havel)." In *Geschichtliche Mythen in den Literaturen und Kulturen Ostmittel- und Südosteuropas*, edited by Eva Behrig, Ludwig Richter, and Wolfgang Schwarz, 199–231. Stuttgart: Franz Steiner Verlag, 1999.

Rocucci, Adriano, and Élise Gaigenbet. "Le tournant de la politique religieuse de Stalin: Pouvoir Soviétique et Église Orthodoxe de 1943 à 1945." *Cahiers Du Monde Russe* 50, no. 4 (2009): 671–98.

Ryfe, David Michael. "From Media Audience to Media Public: A Study of Letters Written in Reaction to FDR's Fireside Chats." *Media, Culture & Society* 23 (2001): 767–81.

Smyčka, Václav. "Dějiny zachycené v síti." *Dějiny-Teorie-Kritika* (January 2014): 93–107.
Treat, Laura J., and Shawn VanCour. "Introduction: The State of Radio Preservation." *Journal of Archival Organization* 17, nos. 1–2 (2020): 1–12.

Books

Agnew, Hugh LeCaine. *Origins of the Czech National Renascence*. Pittsburgh: University of Pittsburgh Press, 1993.

Anderson, Benedict. *Imagined Communities: Reflections on the Origin and Spread of Nationalism*. London: Verso, 2006.

Antikomplex et al. *Zmizelé Sudety / Das verschwundene Sudetenland*. Domažlice: Český les, 2004.

Baár, Monika. *Historians and Nationalism: East Central Europe in the Nineteenth Century*. Oxford: Oxford University Press, 2010.

Baer, Josette. *A Life Dedicated to the Republic: Vavro Šrobár's Slovak Czechoslovakism*. Stuttgart: Ibidem Press, 2014.

Baines, Paul R., and Nicholas J. O'Shaughnessy, eds. *Propaganda*. Vol. 1, *Historical Origins, Definitions and the Changing Nature of Propaganda*. London: Sage, 2013.

Balfour, Michael. *Propaganda in War, 1939–1945: Organisations, Policies and Publics in Britain and Germany*. London: Routledge & Kegan Paul, 1979.

Baynes, Norman, ed. *The Speeches of Adolf Hitler: April 1922 – August 1939*. Vol. 2. London: Oxford University Press, 1942.

BBC Handbook 1941. London: British Broadcasting Corporation, 1941.

BBC Yearbook 1944. London: British Broadcasting Corporation, 1944.

BBC Yearbook 1945. London: British Broadcasting Corporation, 1945.

Beckmann, Rudolf. *K diplomatickému pozadí Mnichova, Kapitoly o britské mnichovské politice*. Prague: Státní nakladatelství politické literatury, 1954.

Bednařík, Petr, Jan Jirák, and Barbara Köpplová. *Dějiny českých médií: Od počátku do současnosti*. Prague: Grada, 2011.

Beneš, Eduard. *Memoirs of Dr. Eduard Beneš: From Munich to New War and New Victory*. Translated by Godfrey Lias. London: George Allen & Unwin, 1954.

Beneš, Eduard. *My War Memoirs*. Translated by Paul Selver. London: George Allen & Unwin, 1928.

Bennett, Jeremy. *British Broadcasting and the Danish Resistance Movement 1940–1945: A Study of the Wartime Broadcasts of the BBC Danish Service*. Cambridge: Cambridge University Press, 1966.

Billig, Michael. *Banal Nationalism*. London: Sage, 2010.

Borovička, Josef. *Ten Years of Czechoslovak Politics*. Prague: Orbis, 1929.

Brandes, Detlef. *Češi pod německým protektorátem: Okupační politika, kolaborace a odboj, 1939–1945*. Prague: Prostor, 2000.

Brandes, Detlef. *Exil v Londýně (1939–1943): Velká Británie a její spojenci Československo, Polsko a Jugoslávie mezi Mnichovem a Teheránem*. Prague: Karolinum, 2003.

Briggs, Asa. *The History of Broadcasting in the United Kingdom*. Vol. 3, *The War of Words*. Oxford: Oxford University Press, 1970.

Brinson, Charmian, and Richard Dove, eds. *"Stimme der Wahrheit": German-Language Broadcasting by the BBC*. Amsterdam: Rodopi, 2003.

Brown, Martin. *Dealing with Democrats: The British Foreign Office and the Czechoslovak Émigrés in Great Britain, 1939 to 1945*. Frankfurt am Main: Peter Lang, 2006.

Bryant, Chad. *Prague in Black: Nazi Rule and Czech Nationalism*. Cambridge, MA: Harvard University Press, 2007.

Buhite, Russell D., and David W. Levy, eds. *FDR's Fireside Chats*. Norman: University of Oklahoma Press, 1992.
Cantril, Hadley, and Gordon Allport. *The Psychology of Radio*. New York: Harper & Brothers, 1935.
Čapek, Karel. *Čtení o T. G. Masarykovi*. Prague: Melantrich, 1969.
———. *Hovory s T. G. Masarykem*. Prague: Fr. Borový a Čin, 1946.
Čapek, Karel, Václav Chaloupecký, J. L. Hromádka, František Hrubý, Albert Pražák, and Ferdinand Peroutka. *At the Cross-Roads of Europe: A Historical Outline of the Democratic Idea in Czechoslovakia*. London: Hutchinson, 1938.
Čech, Jan. *Death Stalks the Forest: The Story of the Carpatho-Russian Guerrillas*. London: Lindsay Drummond, 1943.
Chignell, Hugh. *Key Concepts in Radio Studies*. London: Sage, 2009.
Chmelař, Josef, Stanislav Klíma, and Jaromír Nečas, eds. *Podkarpatská Rus: Obraz poměrů přírodních, hospodářských, politických, církevních, jazykových a osvětových*. Prague: Orbis, 1923.
Clementis, Vladimír. *Panslavism: Past and Present*. London: Czechoslovak Committee for Slav Reciprocity in London, 1943.
Colley, Linda. *Britons: Forging the Nation, 1707–1837*. New Haven: Yale University Press, 1992.
Conway, Martin, and José Gotovitch, eds. *Europe in Exile: European Exile Communities in Britain 1940–1945*. New York: Berghahn Books, 2001.
Conway, Martin, and Peter Romijn, eds. *The War on Legitimacy in Politics and Culture 1936–1946*. Oxford: Berg, 2008.
Cornwall, Mark. *The Devil's Wall: The Nationalist Youth Mission of Heinz Rutha*. Cambridge, MA: Harvard University Press, 2012.
Cornwall, Mark, and R. J. W. Evans, eds. *Czechoslovakia in a Nationalist and Fascist Europe, 1918–1948*. Oxford: Oxford University Press, 2007.
Crisell, Andrew. *Understanding Radio*. London: Methuen, 1986.
———, ed. *Radio: Critical Concepts in Media and Cultural Studies*. Vol. 1, *Radio Theory and Genres*. London: Routledge, 2009.
Cruickshank, Charles. *The Fourth Arm: Psychological Warfare 1938–1945*. Oxford: Oxford University Press, 1981.
Daňhelka, Jiří, Karel Hádek, Bohuslav Havránek, and Naděžda Kvítková. *Staročeská kronika tak řečeného Dalimila*. Vol. 2. Prague: Academia, 1988.
Deutsch, Karl W. *Nationalism and Social Communication: An Investigation into the Foundations of Nationality*. Cambridge, MA: MIT Press, 1966.
Doubek, Vratislav. *Česká politika a Rusko (1848–1914)*. Prague: Academia, 2004.
Drtina, Prokop. *Československo: Můj osud*. Toronto: Sixty-Eight Publishers, 1982.
Dussel, Konrad. *Deutsche Rundfunkgeschichte*. Cologne: Halem, 2020.
El Mallakh, Dorothea. *The Slovak Autonomy Movement, 1935–1939: A Study in Unrelenting Nationalism*. Boulder, CO: East European Quarterly, 1979.
Elgenius, Gabriella. *Symbols of Nations and Nationalism: Celebrating Nationhood*. Basingstoke: Palgrave Macmillan, 2011.
Eliot, Simon, and Marc Wiggam, eds. *Allied Communication to the Public during the Second World War: National and Transnational Networks*. London: Bloomsbury Academic, 2019.
Fisher, Herbert. *A History of Europe from the Beginning of the 18th Century to 1937*. London: Eyre & Spottiswoode, 1952.
Footitt, Hilary, and Simona Tobia. *War Talk: Foreign Languages and the British War Effort, 1940–47*. Basingstoke: Palgrave Macmillan, 2013.
Frommer, Benjamin. *National Cleansing: Retribution against Nazi Collaborators in Postwar Czechoslovakia*. Cambridge: Cambridge University Press, 2005.
Fučík, Julius. *V zemi, kde zítra již znamená včera*. Prague: K. Borecký, 1932.

Furtado, Peter, ed. *Histories of Nations: How Their Identities Were Forged*. London: Thames & Hudson, 2017.
Garnett, David. *The Secret History of PWE: The Political Warfare Executive, 1939–1945*. London: St. Ermin's Press, 2002.
Gellner, Ernest. *Encounters with Nationalism*. Oxford: Blackwell, 1994.
———. *Nations and Nationalism*. Malden, MA: Blackwell, 2006.
Gildea, Robert. *The Past in French History*. New Haven: Yale University Press, 1994.
Glees, Anthony. *Exile Politics during the Second World War: The German Social Democrats in Britain*. Oxford: Clarendon Press, 1982.
Goodman, David. *Radio's Civic Ambition: American Broadcasting and Democracy in the 1930s*. Oxford: Oxford University Press, 2011.
Grant Duff, Sheila. *Europe and the Czechs*. Harmondsworth: Penguin, 1938.
———. *A German Protectorate: The Czechs under Nazi Rule*. London: Macmillan, 1942.
Hargrave, John. *Propaganda, the Mightiest Weapon of Them All: Words Win Wars*. London: Wells Gardener, Darton & Co., 1940.
Heimann, Mary. *Czechoslovakia: The State that Failed*. New Haven: Yale University Press, 2011.
Heisler, J. B., and J. E. Mellon. *Czechoslovakia: Land of Dream and Enterprise*. [London]: Czechoslovak Ministry of Foreign Affairs Department of Information, 1945.
Heitlinger, Alena. *In the Shadows of the Holocaust & Communism: Czech and Slovak Jews since 1945*. New Brunswick, NJ: Transaction Publishers, 2006.
Henderson, Karen. *Slovakia: The Escape from Invisibility*. London: Routledge, 2002.
Hendy, David. *Noise: A Human History of Sound and Listening*. London: Profile, 2013.
———. *The BBC: A People's History*. London: Profile, 2022.
Hermand, Jost. *Culture in Dark Times: Nazi Fascism, Inner Emigration, and Exile*. New York: Berghahn Books, 2013.
Hilmes, Michele, and Jason Loviglio, eds. *Radio Reader: Essays in the Cultural History of Radio*. New York: Routledge, 2002.
Hobsbawm, Eric. *Nations and Nationalism Since 1780: Programme, Myth, Reality*. Cambridge: Cambridge University Press, 1991.
Hobsbawm, Eric, and Terence Ranger, eds. *The Invention of Tradition*. Cambridge: Cambridge University Press, 1992.
Horal, Josef. *Mlčení*. Prague: Družstevní Práce, 1945.
Horten, Gerd. *Radio Goes to War: The Cultural Politics of Propaganda during World War II*. Berkeley: University of California Press, 2003.
Hroch, Miroslav. *Na prahu národní existence: Touha a skutečnost*. Prague: Mladá fronta, 1999.
Hudek, Adam, Michal Kopeček, and Jan Mervart, eds. *Czechoslovakism*. London: Routledge, 2021.
Hurt, Zdeněk. *Czechs in RAF Squadrons of World War II in Focus*. Walton-on-Thames: Red Kite, 2004.
Hutchinson, John. *Modern Nationalism*. London: Fontana Press, 1994.
Ivanchov, Fedir, ed. *Hovorit Priashiv: 30 rokiv Ukrainskoho radiomovlenniia v Chekhoslovachchini*. Prešov: TsK Kulturnoho Soiuzu Ukrainskikh Trudiashchikh v USSR, 1968.
Iwańska, Alicja. *Exiled Governments: Spanish and Polish, An Essay in Political Sociology*. Cambridge, MA: Schenkman, 1981.
Jaksch, Wenzel. *Europe's Road to Potsdam*. London: Thames & Hudson, 1963.
Jelínek, Ivan. *Jablko se kouše*. Prague: Torst, 1994.
Jeřábek, Čestmír. *V zajetí antikristově*. Olomouc: R. Promberger, 1945.
Ješutová, Eva, ed. *Od mikrofonu k posluchačům: z osmi desetiletí Českého rozhlasu*. Prague: Český rozhlas, 2003.
Kamenec, Ivan. *Po stopach tragedie*. Bratislava: Archa, 1991.

———. *Slovenský stát*. Prague: Anomal, 1992.
Kamusella, Tomasz. *The Politics of Language and Nationalism in Modern Central Europe*. Basingstoke: Palgrave Macmillan, 2009.
Karník, Zdeněk. *České země v éře První republiky (1918–1938)*. Vol. 1, *Vznik, budování a zlatá léta republiky (1918–1929)*. Prague: Libri, 2000.
———. *České země v éře První republiky (1918–1938)*. Vol. 2, *Československo a České země v krizi a v ohrožení (1930–1935)*. Prague: Libri, 2002.
Kirkpatrick, Ivone. *The Inner Circle: Memoirs of Ivone Kirkpatrick*. London: Macmillan, 1959.
Kirschbaum, Stanislav J. *A History of Slovakia: The Struggle for Survival*. New York: St. Martin's Griffin, 1995.
Kocourek, Milan. *Volá Londýn: Historie českého a slovenského vysílání BBC*. Prague: Ottovo nakladatelství, 2013.
Komenský, Jan Amos. "Kšaft umírající matky jednoty bratrské kterýmž (v národu svém a obzvláštnosti své dokonávající) svěřené sobě někdy od Pána Boha poklady mezi syny a dcery a dědice své rozděluje, Léta páně 1650." Private publication for participants at the conference of Skupina moravských knihomilů, Uherské Hradiště, 5 June 1938.
Končelík, Jakub, Pavel Večeřa, and Petr Orság. *Dějiny českých médií 20. století*. Prague: Portál, 2010.
Köpplová, Barbara, Petr Bednařík, Lenka Čábelová, Václav Moravec, Jitka Kryšpínová, and Eva Šádová. *Dějiny českých médií v datech: Rozhlas, Televize, Mediální právo*. Prague: Karolinum, 2003.
Körbel, Josef. *Twentieth-Century Czechoslovakia: The Meaning of Its History*. New York, NY: Columbia University Press, 1977.
Kosatík, Pavel, and Michal Kolář. *Jan Masaryk: Pravdivý příběh*. Prague: Mladá Fronta, 1998.
Kovtun, Jiří. *Republika v nebezpečném světě: Éra prezidenta Masaryka 1918–1935*. Prague: Torst, 2005.
Krejčí, František. *Češství a Evropanství: Úvahy o naší kulturní orientaci*. Prague: Orbis, 1931.
Křen, Jan. *Bílá místa v našich dějinách?* Prague: Lidové noviny, 1990.
Krofta, Kamil. *Dějiny československé*. Prague: Sfinx, 1946.
Kuklík, Jan. *Londýnský exil a obnova československého státu 1938–1945: Právní a politické aspekty obnovy Československa z hlediska prozatímního státního zřízení ČSR v emigraci*. Prague: Karolinum, 1998.
Kuklík, Jan, and Jan Němeček. *Proti Benešovi! Česká a slovenská protibenešovská opozice v Londýně 1939–1945*. Prague: Karolinum, 2004.
Kuklík, Jan, Jan Němeček, and Jaroslav Šebek. *Dlouhé stíny Mnichova: Mnichovská dohoda očima signatářů a její dopady na Československo*. Prague: Auditorium, 2011.
Langer, František. *BBC Londýn*. Prague: Fr. Borový, 1947.
Laštovička, Bohuslav. *V Londýně za války: Zápasy o novou ČSR, 1939–1945*. Prague: Státní nakladatelství politické literatury, 1961.
Launchbury, Claire. *Music, Poetry, Propaganda: Constructing French Cultural Soundscapes at the BBC during the Second World War*. Oxford: Peter Lang, 2012.
Leff, Carol Skalnik. *National Conflict in Czechoslovakia: The Making and Remaking of a State, 1918–1987*. Princeton: Princeton University Press, 1988.
Leuchtenburg, William. *Franklin D. Roosevelt and the New Deal: 1932–1940*. New York: Harper & Row, 1963.
Lo Biundo, Ester. *London Calling Italy: BBC Broadcasts during the Second World War*. Manchester: Manchester University Press, 2022.
Lockhart, Robert Bruce. *Comes the Reckoning*. London: Putnam, 1947.
———. *My Europe*. London: Putnam, 1952.

Lommers, Suzanne. *Europe – On Air: Interwar Projects for Radio Broadcasting*. Amsterdam: Amsterdam University Press, 2012.

Luneau, Aurélie. *Radio Londres: les voix de la liberté, 1940–1945*. Paris: Perrin, 2005.

Macura, Vladimír. *Masarykovy boty a jiné semi(o)fejetony*. Prague: Pražská imaginace, 1993.

———. *Znamení zrodu: České národní obrození jako kulturní typ*. Prague: Nakladatelství H&H, 1995.

Macůrek, Josef, ed. *Slovanství v českém národním životě*. Brno: Masarykova Univerzita, 1947.

Madol, H. R. *The League of London: A Book of Interviews with Allied Sovereigns and Statesmen*. London: Hutchinson, 1942.

Magocsi, Paul. *The Shaping of a National Identity: Subcarpathian Rus' 1848–1948*. Cambridge, MA: Harvard University Press, 1978.

Mansell, Gerard. *Let Truth Be Told: 50 Years of BBC External Broadcasting*. London: Weidenfeld and Nicolson, 1982.

Mar'ina, Valentina. *Zakarpatskaia Ukraina (Podkarpatskaia Rus') v politike Benesha i Stalina: 1939–1945: dokumental'nyi ocherk*. Moscow: Novyi chronigraf, 2003.

Masaryk, Tomáš. *Cesta demokracie: soubor projevů za republiky*. Vol. 2, 1921–1923. Prague: Čin, 1934.

———. *Rusko a Evropa: studie o duchovní proudech v Rusku*. Vols. 1–3. Prague: Prague: Ústav T. G. Masaryka, 1995; 1996.

———. *Světová revoluce: za války a ve válce, 1914–1918*. Prague: Čin a Orbis, 1925.

Mastný, Vojtěch. *The Czechs Under Nazi Rule: The Failure of National Resistance, 1939–1942*. New York: Columbia University Press, 1971.

Mazower, Mark. *Dark Continent: Europe's Twentieth Century*. London: Allen Lane, 1998.

Moravec, František. *Master of Spies: The Memoirs of General František Moravec*. London: Bodley Head, 1975.

Nedelsky, Nadya. *Defining the Sovereign Community: The Czech and Slovak Republics*. Philadelphia: University of Pennsylvania Press, 2009.

Nejedlý, Zdeněk. *O smyslu českých dějin*. Prague: Svoboda, 1952.

Němec, František, and Vladimír Moudrý. *The Soviet Seizure of Subcarpathian Ruthenia*. Toronto: William B. Anderson, 1955.

Němeček, Jan. *Od spojenectví k roztržce: Vztahy československé a polské exilové reprezentace 1939–1945*. Prague: Academia, 2003.

Nicholas, Siân. *The Echo of War: Home Front Propaganda and the Wartime BBC, 1939–45*. Manchester: Manchester University Press, 1996.

Nižňanský, Eduard. *Politika antisemitizmu a holokaust na Slovensko v rokoch 1938–1945*. Banská Bystrica: Múzeum SNP, 2016.

Noakes, Lucy, and Juliette Pattinson, eds. *British Cultural Memory and the Second World War*. London: Bloomsbury Academic, 2014.

Ornest, Ota. *Hraje váš tatínek ještě na housle? Rozhovor Marie Valtrové s Otou Ornestem*. Prague: Primus, 1993.

Orzoff, Andrea. *Battle for the Castle: The Myth of Czechoslovakia in Europe, 1914–1948*. Oxford: Oxford University Press, 2011.

Patzaková, A. J., ed. *Prvních deset let Československého rozhlasu*. Prague: Radiojournal, 1935.

Pekař, Josef. *O smyslu českých dějin*. Prague: Rozmluvy, 1990.

Pinard, Peter Richard. *Broadcast Policy in the Protectorate of Bohemia and Moravia: Power Structures, Programming, Cooperation and Defiance at Czech Radio 1939–1945*. Frankfurt: Peter Lang, 2015.

Placák, Petr. *Svatováclávské milenium: Češi, Němci a Slováci v roce 1929*. Prague: Babylon, 2002.

Plock, Vike. *The BBC German Service during the Second World War: Broadcasting to the Enemy*. Basingstoke: Palgrave Macmillan, 2021.

Ponsonby, Arthur. *Falsehood in Wartime, Containing an Assortment of Lies Circulated throughout the Nations during the Great War.* Torrance, CA: Institute for Historical Review, 1980.
Pop, Ivan Ivanovich. *Chekhoslovakiia – Sovetskii soiuz, 1941–1948.* Moscow: Nauka, 1990.
Potter, Simon J. *This is the BBC: Entertaining the Nation, Speaking for Britain, 1922–2022.* Oxford: Oxford University Press, 2022.
Potůček, Jaroslav, ed. *Ročenka čs. Rozhlasu 1937: Popisuje vývoj československého rozhlasu od roku 1934 do počátku roku 1937.* Prague: Radiojournal, 1937.
Pszenicki, Krzysztof. *Tu mówi Londyn: Historia Sekcji Polskiej BBC.* Warsaw: Rosner & Wspólnicy, 2009.
Pynsent, Robert B. *Questions of Identity: Czech and Slovak Ideas of Nationality and Personality.* Budapest: Central European University Press, 1994.
———, ed. *T. G. Masaryk (1850–1937).* Vol. 2, *Thinker and Critic.* Basingstoke: Macmillan, 1989.
Pytlík, Radko. *Kniha o Švejkovi.* Prague: Československý spisovatel, 1983.
Reuth, Ralf Georg. *Goebbels.* Translated by Krishna Winston. London: Constable, 1993.
Ribeiro, Nelson. *BBC Broadcasts to Portugal in World War II: How Radio Was Used as a Weapon of War.* Lewiston, NY: Edwin Mellen Press, 2011.
Roetter, Charles. *Psychological Warfare.* London: B. T. Batsford, 1974.
Rychlík, Jan. *Češi a Slováci ve 20. století: Česko-slovenské vztahy 1914–1945.* Bratislava: Academic Electronic Press, 1997.
Sahlins, Peter. *Boundaries: The Making of France and Spain in the Pyrenees.* Berkeley: University of California Press, 1989.
Sanford, George. *Katyn and the Soviet Massacre of 1940: Truth, Justice and Memory.* London: Routledge, 2005.
Scannell, Paddy. *Broadcast Talk.* London: Sage, 1991.
———. *Radio, Television and Modern Life: A Phenomenological Approach.* Oxford: Blackwell, 1996.
Scannell, Paddy, and David Cardiff. *A Social History of British Broadcasting.* Vol. 1, *1922–1939, Serving the Nation.* Oxford: Basil Blackwell, 1991.
Seaman, Mark, ed. *Special Operations Executive: A New Weapon of War.* London: Routledge, 2006.
Seton Watson, Robert, ed. *Slovakia Then and Now: A Political Survey.* London: George Allen & Unwin, 1931.
Shandor, Vincent. *Carpatho-Ukraine in the Twentieth Century: A Political and Legal History.* Cambridge, MA: Harvard University Press, 1997.
Shingler, Martin, and Cindy Wieringa. *On Air: Methods and Meanings of Radio.* London: Arnold, 1998.
Skey, Michael. *National Belonging and Everyday Life: The Significance of Nationhood in an Uncertain World.* Basingstoke: Palgrave Macmillan, 2011.
Šmahel, František. *Idea národa v husitských Čechách.* Prague: Argo, 2000.
Smetana, Vít. *In the Shadow of Munich: British Policy towards Czechoslovakia from the Endorsement to the Renunciation of the Munich Agreement (1938–1942).* Prague: Karolinum, 2008.
Smetana, Vít, and Kathleen Geaney, eds. *Exile in London: The Experience of Czechoslovakia and the Other Occupied Nations, 1939–1945.* Prague: Karolinum, 2017.
Smith, Anthony D. *The Ethnic Origins of Nations.* Oxford: Blackwell, 1986.
Soukup, František. *T. G. Masaryk jako politický průkopník, sociální reformátor a president státu.* Prague: Ústřední dělnické knihkupectví a nakladatelství (Ant. Svěcený), 1930.
Srba, Bořivoj. *Múzy v exilu: Kulturní a umělecká aktivity čs. exulantů v Londýně v předvečer a v průběhu druhé světové války 1939–1945.* Brno: Masarykova Univerzita, 2003.
Staněk, Tomáš. *Odsun Němců z Československa 1945–1947.* Prague: Academia, 1991.

Stenton, Michael. *Radio London and Resistance in Occupied Europe: British Political Warfare 1939–1943*. Oxford: Oxford University Press, 2000.

Street, John. *Mass Media, Politics & Democracy*. Basingstoke: Palgrave Macmillan, 2011.

Subtelny, Orest. *Ukraine: A History*. Toronto: University of Toronto Press, 1988.

Talmon, Stefan. *Recognition of Governments in International Law: With Particular Reference to Governments in Exile*. Oxford: Clarendon Press, 1998.

Tampke, Jürgen. *Czech-German Relations and the Politics of Central Europe: From Bohemia to the EU*. Basingstoke: Palgrave Macmillan, 2003.

Tangye Lean, Edward. *Voices in the Darkness*. London: Seeker and Warburg, 1943.

Teich, Mikuláš. *Bohemia in History*. Cambridge: Cambridge University Press, 1998.

Teich, Mikuláš, Dušan Kováč, and Martin Brown, eds. *Slovakia in History*. Cambridge: Cambridge University Press, 2011.

Tigrid, Pavel. *Kapesní průvodce inteligentí ženy po vlasntím osudu*. Toronto: Sixty-Eight Publishers, 1988.

Tomek, Prokop, ed. *Pavel Tigrid: Volá Londýn. Ze zákulisí čs. vysílání z Londýna*. Prague: Ústav pro studium totalitních režimů, 2017.

Vaughan, David. *Battle for the Airwaves: Radio and the 1938 Munich Crisis*. Prague: Radioservis, 2008.

Vodička, Felix. *Boj o obrození národa: Výbor z díla Josefa Jungmanna*. Prague: F. Kosek, 1948.

Vondrová, Jitka. *Češi a sudetoněmecká otázka, 1939–1945: Dokumenty*. Prague: Ústav mezinárodních vztahů, 1994.

Weber, Max. *Economy and Society: An Outline of Interpretive Sociology*. Berkeley: University of California Press, 1978.

———. *Political Writings*. Cambridge: Cambridge University Press, 1994.

Webster, Wendy. *Mixing It: Diversity in World War Two Britain*. Oxford: Oxford University Press, 2018.

Weight, Richard. *Patriots: National Identity in Britain, 1940–2000*. Basingstoke: Macmillan, 2002.

Weingart, Miloš. *Slovanská vzájemnost: Úvahy o jejích základech a osudech*. Bratislava: Academie, 1926.

Wellek, René, ed. *The Meaning of Czech History by Tomáš G. Masaryk*. Chapel Hill: University of North Carolina Press, 1974.

Wilson, Andrew. *The Ukrainians: Unexpected Nation*. New Haven: Yale University Press, 2009.

Winch, Michael. *Republic for a Day: An Eye-witness Account of the Carpatho-Ukraine Incident*. London: R. Hale, 1939.

Young, Kenneth, ed. *The Diaries of Sir Robert Bruce Lockhart*. Vol. 2, *1939–1965*. London: Macmillan, 1980.

Yuhasz, Michael. *Petition Concerning the Educational Complaints of the Autonomous Carpatho-Russian Territory South of the Carpathian Mountains*. Homestead, PA: Amerikansky Russky Viestnik, 1932.

Zatloukal, Jaroslav, ed. *Podkarpatská Rus: Sborník hospodářského, kulturního a politického poznání Podkarpatské Rusi*. Bratislava: Klub přátel Podkarpatské Rusi, 1936.

Index

annexation of Bohemia and Moravia, *see* Protectorate of Bohemia and Moravia
Austrian Service (BBC), 149
  PWE, 32
Austro-Hungarian Empire, 14, 19, 122, 138–39, 187, 191–92
authority of charisma, *see* personality of political leaders
authority of legality, *see* legality and authority of exiled governments
authority of tradition, *see* mythmaking and the authority of tradition

Balkans
  PWE, 32
BBC (British Broadcasting Corporation)
  autonomy and perception of, 32–34, 252
  broadcasting by Allied governments-in-exile, 30–31
  broadcasting in foreign languages, 31–32, 38–39
    Slovak language, 154–55, 166–69
    see also language
  centenary celebrations, 12
  Czech(oslovak) Service, 12–13, 35–36, 52–53, 247–48, 250
  Czechoslovak exiles, relationship with, 11, 12–20, 30–41
  exile interference in programme making, 34–35
  "free time" for Allied governments, 12–13, 34–41
  Hlas svobodné republiky (Voice of the Free Republic), 12, 41–42
  Hovory s domovem (Conversations with Home), 12, 37–39
  international importance, 15–16, 247–48
  London Transcription Service, 54–56
  London—occupied Europe connection, 14–15
  PWE, relationship with, 31–32
  reputation, 12, 30–31, 33–34, 252
  Slovak broadcasters and representatives, 154–55, 158–60
  BBC wartime services, 16, 31–35, 38, 40, 42, 52–54
  see also individual services
BBC Handbook
  broadcasting by Allied governments-in-exile, 30–31
  foreign language broadcasting, 39
Belgium
  PWE, 32
Bečko, Ján, 158–60, 183–84, 186, 194–95
Beneš, Edvard
  Beneš decrees, 102–3
  broadcasts from London, 10–11, 45–46
  claims to legal legitimacy, 64–65, 248–49
  Czechoslovak National Committee, 47–48
  exile in London, 10, 14–15
    recognition from British government, 65–70, 248–49
  "German question", 251

Beneš decrees, 102–3
  population transfers, 101–2
  propaganda, use of, 19–20, 20–21
  recognition from British government
    Beneš' claims to legal legitimacy, 64–65, 248–49
    full recognition, 67–70
    provisional recognition, 65–67
  Soviet Union, relationship with, 248
Beneš decrees, 102–3
Bilitskii, Mikhail, 234–35, 237, 240
Bohemia, *see* Protectorate of Bohemia and Moravia
Bolshevism, demonisation of, 184, 191–93, 202
Bormann, Martin, 182–83, 184
British culture and self-perception, 11–12
British Broadcasts and Allied Governments (BBC Paper), 33–34
broadcasting by Allied governments-in-exile, 30–46
  see also radio broadcasting
broadcasting in foreign languages, 23–24
  BBC broadcasting in foreign languages, 31–32, 38–39
    Slovak language, 154–55, 166–69
  national languages and nationhood, 138–43
  Soviet broadcasters, 155–56

Čapek, Karel, 78, 129–30, 134
Čaplovič, Ján, 155, 158–60, 170, 176–77, 183–84, 194–95
Catholicism
  persecution by Catholics, 82–83, 123
  persecution of Catholics, 182–83
  see also religious broadcasting
censorship
  BBC wartime censorship, 16, 29, 33, 34–35
    broadcasting to Subcarpathian Ruthenia, 224–25, 244
    Czechoslovak broadcasters, 37–38, 56, 66, 224–25
    Polish broadcasters, 36
    Protectorate of Bohemia and Moravia, 132–34
  Radiojournal (broadcaster), 23
Central European Confederation, 209–14, 245

Český rozhlas (Czech radio station)
  archives, 12–13, 16, 54–56, 251
Chamberlain, Neville, 12
Churchill, Winston
  Central European Confederation, 209–14
  Curzon Line, support for, 216
  Polish exiles, relationship with, 209–10, 216
  Political Warfare Executive, 29–30
  propaganda, use of, 12, 29–30
  pro-Russian rhetoric, 201
Clementis, Vladimír, 174, 177–79, 181–82, 192, 202–3, 215
Communist era in Czechoslovakia (1948–89), 11, 48–49, 50–51, 207–8, 245–46
  constraints on broadcast material, 23, 34–35, 43, 248
  see also censorship
cultural material
  "free republic" notion, relationship with, 147–50
  propaganda, use as, 131–34
  literature, 134–38
  national languages, 138–43
  music, 143–44
  Protectorate propaganda, 144
  representation of Germans as the "other", 145–46
  representation of Hungarians as the "other", 146–47
custom and tradition, *see* authority of tradition
Czech imperialism, 152–54
Czech League against Bolshevism (*Česká liga proti bolševismu*), 191–92
Czech national identity, 13–14, 57–58, 72, 105–6, 122, 126, 131, 134–35, 165–66
Czech National Revival, 14, 72, 111, 122–24, 139–40, 202–3
Czech Service (BBC), 12–13, 35–36, 52–53, 56–57
  see also Czechoslovak exiles in London; Czechoslovak government programme; radio broadcasting
Czech–Slovak relations, 151–52
Czech–Slovak ideological challenges, 151–60, 166–67, 175–76
  government in exile, 153
  negative propaganda, 170

negative propaganda (political arguments), 171–76
negative propaganda (religious arguments), 179–85
negative propaganda (Slovak–Soviet relations), 186–93
negative propaganda (Slovak–US relations), 176–79
"national question", 161, 164–67
promises regarding post-war arrangements, 169–70
Czechoslovak exiles in London, 12–13, 109–10
condemnation of, 82–83
Czech–Slovak ideological challenges, 151–60, 166–67, 175–76
Czechoslovak government-in-exile, 10–11, 17
Czechoslovak–Soviet relations, 202, 245–46
official status, 65
radio broadcasts, 59, 194
Slovak Republic, 151, 160
unity and identity, 119, 160
recognition from British government
Beneš' claims to legal legitimacy, 64–65
full recognition, 67–70
provisional recognition, 65–67
Czechoslovak government programme, 45–46, 251–52
anti-German broadcasting, 119–20, 123, 145–46
cultural content
"free republic" notion, 147–50
literature, 134–38
music, 143–44
national languages, 138–43
propaganda, use as, 131–47
Protectorate propaganda, 144
representation of Germans as the "other", 145–46
representation of Hungarians as the "other", 146–47
"free republic", 108, 147–50
national identity, promotion of, 110–12, 119–20, 123, 229
Poland, relationship with, 211, 213, 214–15, 216–18, 245–46
proximity and intimacy, 89–91
Soviet Union, relationship with, 197–98, 198–99, 205–6, 220, 245–46
Czechoslovak National Committee (*Československý národní výbor*), 47–48, 64–65
Czechoslovak national identity, 13–14, 20, 44, 49–50
Czechoslovak–Polish relations, 208–9
British promotion of, 212–13
Central European Confederation, 209–14
Polish–Soviet relations, 214–15
Soviet intervention/influence, 208, 210, 213–18
strains and doubts, 212
Těšín/Cieszyn disputes, 210–11, 212
Czechoslovak–Soviet relations, 44–45, 48–49, 202, 245–46
alliance, 197–98, 201–8
ambivalence/objectivity, 197, 198–201
annexation of Subcarpathian Ruthenia, 44–45, 198, 218–19, 244–45
government-in-exile propaganda, 219–20
increasing closeness, 245–46
post-WWII Communist takeover, 196–97
subjugation, 198, 208, 245–46
Czechoslovak–Polish relations, 208–18
Subcarpathian Ruthenia issue, 218–45
Subcarpathian Ruthenia, 218–30, 237–38, 242–45
national identity, 230–34, 236–38, 240–41
Russian/Ukrainian identity, 230–34, 236–37, 240–41

Denmark
PWE, 32
Drtina, Prokop, 25–26, 65–67, 83, 84–85, 86–87, 104, 136, 140–42, 144–45, 155, 191–92, 203–4, 231, 249–50
Dyk, Viktor, 137

Eastern Front, 204
Slovak involvement, 187–88
Eliáš, Alois, 141
exile politics, 15–17, 63–64, 88–89, 109–10, 209

First Czechoslovak Republic (1918–38), 11, 19–20, 48, 222–23

Czechoslovak national identity, creation of, 20, 148–50, 196, 252
Czech–Slovak relations, 19–20, 44, 50–51, 57–58, 151–54, 158, 160, 161–64, 166–67, 169, 190, 194, 247–48
exile interpretation of, 70–75, 251–52
ideological legitimacy, 46, 62–63, 65, 70–75, 79–82, 107
political propaganda, 20–22
population transfers, 104
radio broadcasts
language, 23–24, 228
Radiojournal (broadcaster), 35–36
Subcarpathian Ruthenia, 222–23, 227–29, 238–39
see also Masaryk, Tomáš Garrigue
France, fall of, 25–26, 32–33, 47, 65–67, 78, 159, 248
"free republic" creation, 108
cultural material, relationship with, 147–50
foreign-language broadcasting, 108–9
imagined communities, 109–10
national perceptions, 110–11
reinterpretation of history, 111–13
unity and nation-building, 111–13
"free time" for Allied governments, 34, 36–37
Czechoslovak exiles, 35–41
exile interference in programme making, 34–35
Hlas svobodné republiky (Voice of the Free Republic), 12–13
Polish government, 35
freedom of the press
First Czechoslovak Republic, 21–22

"German question", 251
population transfers, 101–2
Beneš decrees, 102–3
Sudeten German population, 101–3
Germany
annexation of Bohemia and Moravia, 10, 15, 49–52
anti-German propaganda
representation of Germans as the "other", 145–46
Czechoslovakia, German invasion of, 10, 102–3, 153
France, German invasion of, 35

Munich Agreement, 11, 47–48, 51–52, 64, 153, 209–10, 217, 222–23
Subcarpathian Ruthenia, 240–43
Soviet Union, German invasion of, 183–84, 186, 189, 197–98, 201
Eastern Front, 187–88, 204
Goebbels, Josef, 137–38, 214
propaganda, 87–88
government-in-exile, 10–11, 17, 153
BBC, relationship with
broadcasting by Allied governments-in-exile, 30–31
Czechoslovak exiles, 11, 12–20, 30–41
"free time" for Allied governments, 12–13, 34–41
BBC Handbook, 30–31
Beneš, Edvard
Beneš' claims to legal legitimacy, 64–65
full recognition, 67–70
provisional recognition, 65–67
see also Beneš, Edvard
British Broadcasts and Allied Governments (BBC Paper), 33–34
broadcasting by Allied governments-in-exile, 30–31
commitment to a united Czechoslovakia, 193–94
"free time" for Allied governments, 34, 36–37
Czechoslovak exiles, 35–41
exile interference in programme making, 34–35
Hlas svobodné republiky (Voice of the Free Republic), 12–13
Polish government, 35
legality and authority of exiled governments, 63–70
legitimacy of exiled governments, 60–70
exercising authority, 98–107
formation of national committees, 100–1
Masaryk, T. G., mythology of, 99–100
population transfers, 100–5
post-war settlement, 100–4
propaganda, use of, 106–7
negative propaganda, 170
political arguments, 171–76
religious arguments, 179–85
Slovak–Soviet relations, 186–93
Slovak–US relations, 176–79

propaganda, use of, 17–18
  Beneš', 19–20, 20–21
  legitimising government, 106–7
  negative propaganda, 170–93
  radio broadcasting, importance of, 24–25, 43–44, 45–46, 51–52, 59, 247–52
    constraints on broadcast material, 247–48
    countering Nazi propaganda, 25–26, 28–30
    "free time" for Allied governments, 12–13, 34–41
    morale and general public, 26–27
    political propaganda, 24–27
    proximity and intimacy, 27–28, 89–93
  Slovakia
    negative propaganda from government in exile, 170–95
Hašek, Jaroslav, 135–36, 139, 142
Heydrich, Reinhard, 105
  appointment, 83–84, 86, 95, 103–4
  assassination, 105
  Lidice massacre, 105, 149–50
Heydrichiáda, 105, 149–50
historical narratives
  importance for nation-building, 120–31
  mythmaking and the authority of tradition, 120–31
  reinterpretation of history, 111–13
  see also mythmaking and the authority of tradition
Hitler, Adolf, 96, 172, 176–77, 193, 205
Hlas svobodné republiky (radio programme – *Voice of the Free Republic*), 12, 41–42, 43, 97, 107, 112, 134, 137, 142
Hlinka, Andrej, 174–76
Hlinka Guard, 174, 181
Hlinka Slovak People's Party (*Hlinkova slovenská ľudová strana*, HSĽS), 148–49, 174
Hovory s domovem (radio programme – *Conversations with Home*), 12, 37–39, 43, 45–46, 56, 65–66, 76–77, 174
Hron, Petr, *see* Clementis, Vladimír
Hronek, Jiří, 37–38, 166, 204
Hungary
  anti-Hungarian propaganda
    representation of Hungarians as the "other", 146–47

Austro-Hungarian Empire, 14, 19, 122, 138–39, 187, 191–92
  Subcarpathian Ruthenia
    Rusyn identity, 240
Hus, Jan, 73
  see also Hussitism
Hussitism, 73, 121–24, 126–27, 144, 179–80

imagined communities, 109–10
  national perceptions, 110–11
  reinterpretation of history, 111–13
  unity and nation-building, 111–13
Italy
  radio broadcasts to, 32, 54

Jewish population
  persecution of, 73–74, 140–41
  Slovakia, 180

Kirkpatrick, Ivone, 36–38
Körbel, Josef, 38–39, 82, 107, 112, 155–56, 166, 192

language
  BBC Handbook
    foreign language broadcasting, 39
  broadcasting in foreign languages, 23–24, 31–32
  BBC broadcasting in foreign languages, 31–32, 38–39, 154–55, 166–69
  "free republic" creation, 108–9
  Slovak language, 154–55, 166–69
  mythmaking and the authority of tradition
    language of democracy, 74–75
    language of fairness and liberalism, 73–74
  nation-building, 111–13
  propaganda and national languages, 138–43
  national languages and nationhood, 138–43
  Soviet broadcasters, 155–56
legality and authority of exiled governments, 63–64
  Beneš' claims to legal legitimacy, 64–65
  full recognition by British government, 67–70
  provisional recognition by British government, 65–67

legitimacy of exiled governments, 60–63
Beneš' claims to legal legitimacy, 64–65
full recognition by British government, 67–70
provisional recognition by British government, 65–67
exercising authority, 98–99
formation of national committees, 100–1
Masaryk, T. G., mythology of, 99–100
population transfers, 100–5
post-war settlement, 100–4
propaganda, use of, 106–7
Lichner, Ján, 156, 158–60, 175–76, 176–77, 178, 180, 186
Lidice massacre, 105, 149–50
literature
nationhood, relationship with, 134–38
Lockhart, Robert Bruce, 29–30, 47, 61–69, 129, 224–26
London
Beneš
broadcasts from London, 10–11, 45–46
exile in London, 10, 14–15
London—occupied Europe connection, 14–15
refuge for European governments, 32–33
see also BBC; Czechoslovak exiles in London
London Transcription Service (LTS), 54–56
Lublin Committee, *see* Polish Committee of National Liberation

Macháček, Pavol, 156–57, 168, 172, 174–75, 177, 180, 182–84
Masaryk, Jan
broadcasting, 11, 16, 38, 41–42, 55–56, 82–85, 195–96, 248
anti-German stance, 103–4, 146
authority of tradition and history, 127–30, 134–36
charisma, 62, 86, 107
Czechoslovak–Soviet relations, 210–12, 217
Czech–Slovak relations, 159, 167, 172, 178
idealisation of First Republic, 71, 74, 80

intimacy of radio, 92–93, 95–98, 107
language, importance of, 140, 143, 156–57
Masaryk "legend" and legacy, 62–63, 77–78, 81–82, 95–98
Masaryk, Tomáš Garrigue, 19
Czechoslovak national identity, creation of, 20
Masaryk "legend" and legacy, 62–63, 75–81, 95–98
Ministerstvo národní obrany (MNO), *see* Ministry of National Defence
Ministerstvo pošt a telegrafů, see Ministry of Post and Telegraphs
Ministerstvo sociální péče (MSP), *see* Ministry of Social Welfare
Ministerstvo zahraničních věcí (MZV), *see* Ministry of Foreign Affairs
Ministry of Foreign Affairs
archives, 54, 56–57
BBC, relationship with, 38–42
Information Department, 38–39, 80–81, 232
nationality and language questions, 235
Office for Subcarpathian Ruthenia, 224
Radio Department, 81–82, 155, 157, 166
restructuring programming, 40–41
Third Section, 20–21
see also Körbel, Josef; Ripka, Hubert
Ministry of Information (UK), 29, 32–33, 35–36, 39
Ministry of Post and Telegraphs, 23
Ministry of Social Welfare, 159
Molotov–Ribbentrop pact, 198–99, 205
Moravec, František, 34, 47
Moravia, *see* Protectorate of Bohemia and Moravia
Munich Agreement, 11, 47–48, 51–52, 64, 153, 209–10, 217, 222–23
Subcarpathian Ruthenia, 240–43
music
nationhood and, 143–44
mythmaking and the authority of tradition
collective constructions and historical myth-making, 120–31
Czech spirit and innate democracy, 123–24
evil of Germany, 124
heroism of exile, 82–85
idealisation of national traditions, 71–73

language of democracy, 74–75
language of fairness and liberalism, 73–74
Masaryk as "President Liberator", 75–81
memory of First Republic, 81–82
political tradition and shared values, 70–71
religious broadcasting, 179–85
St. Wenceslas as a national symbol, 126–28
shared ancestry and communal life, 119–25

nation-building, 111–13
  collective constructions and historical myth-making, 120–31
  propaganda, use of, 131–34
    literature, 134–38
    national languages, 138–43
    music, 143–44
    Protectorate propaganda, 144
    representation of Germans as the "other", 145–46
    representation of Hungarians as the "other", 146–47
  radio-broadcasting, role of, 113–14
    national messaging, 116–19
    unity and shared interests, 114–16
nation-state, validity of, 17
  independent and united Czechoslovak nation, 19–20, 43–44
national committees, 99–100, 106
  Czechoslovak National Committee, 47–48, 64–65
  Transcarpathian Ukraine National Committee, 243–44
national identity, 14
  collective constructions and historical myth-making, 120–22
    "Czech spirit" and innate democracy, 123–25
    united opposition to Germany, 124
  cultural homogeneity, 117
  Czech/Slovak divide, 118–19, 151–60
    "national question", 160–70
    presentation of unity, 160–70
  Czechoslovak national identity, creation of, 20, 44, 58, 112–13, 117–19
  language, importance of, 141–42
  nation-building, 115–16
  radio-broadcasting, role of, 116

Subcarpathian Ruthenia, 227–29, 238–39
  Czechoslovak–Soviet relations, 237–38
  language, 229–31, 232–33, 234–35
  pro-Soviet, 230–31, 237–38
  Russian/Ukrainian identity, 230–34, 236–37, 240–41
  Rusyn identity, 240
  Slavic identity, 236–37
  terminology, 220–21, 229–31, 232–33, 234–36
"national question", 161, 164–67
nationalism, 14, 17
Němcová, Božena, 134–35
Neruda, Jan, 136–37, 143, 191
Netherlands
  PWE, 32, 61
newspapers, 42
  Čechoslovák (Czechoslovak government newspaper in Britain), 136
  First Czechoslovak Republic, 21–22
  radio broadcasting compared, 109
  Slovák (newspaper of the HSĽS), 168
Norway
  PWE, 32, 61

Operation Barbarossa, 183–84, 186, 245–46
Ornest, Ota, 42, 136–37, 142

Paulíny-Toth, Ján, 157, 158–59, 160, 167–68, 172, 192–93
performance, concept of, 13–14, 247–48
  performance of authority, 10–11, 15–16, 43, 45, 61–62, 88–89, 250
  performance of nationhood, 108–9, 128–29, 252
    community and cohesion, 142–43
    political speech as performance, 59–60
personality of political leaders
  Beneš
    experience, 87–88
    foresight, 86–87
  charismatic authority, 85–98
  Masaryk, Jan, 93–95
    charisma, 62, 86, 107
    intimacy of radio broadcasts, 93–98
    mythology of father, 95–96
    politics and political oratory, 88–89
    proximity and intimacy of radio broadcasting, 27–28, 89–93
    Masaryk, Jan, 93–98

Petrushchak, Ivan, 232, 234–35, 236–40
Poland and Polish exiles
  BBC wartime censorship, 36
  Churchill, relationship with, 209–10, 216
  Czechoslovak–Polish relations, 208–9
    British promotion of, 212–13
    Central European Confederation, 209–14
    Polish–Soviet relations, 214–15
    Soviet intervention/influence, 208, 210, 213–18
    strains and doubts, 212
    Těšín/Cieszyn disputes, 210–11, 212
"free time" for Allied governments, 35
governments in exile
  Central European Confederation, proposals for, 209–14
  Czechoslovak–Polish relations, 208–18
  Polish–Soviet relations, 214–18
  radio broadcasting, 36–37
Polish Committee of National Liberation (*Polski Komitet Wyzwolenia Narodowego*, PKWN), 215–16
Polish–Soviet relations, 214–18
political authority
  authority of charisma, 85–98
    see also personality of political leaders
  authority of legality, 63–70
    see also legality and authority of exiled governments
  authority of tradition, 70–85
    see also authority of tradition
Political Warfare Executive (PWE), 29–30, 31
  BBC, relationship with, 31–32
popular support for exiled governments, 60–62
population transfers, 100–1
  German Czechs, 99, 101–2, 250
  Beneš decrees, 102–3
  Protectorate of Bohemia and Moravia, 103–6
propaganda, concept of, 17–18
  BBC autonomy and perception of autonomy, 32–34
    exile interference in programme making, 34–35
  Beneš' use of, 19–20, 20–21
  Bolshevism, demonisation of, 186–93, 202
  contextual positioning, 19–20
  cultural material as, 131–34
    literature, 134–38
    music, 143–44
    national languages, 138–43
    Protectorate propaganda, 144
    representation of Germans as the "other", 145–46
    representation of Hungarians as the "other", 146–47
  Czechoslovak commitment to, 20–24
  independent and united Czechoslovak nation, 19–20
  legitimising government, 106–7
  negative connotations, 18–19
  negative propaganda in Slovakia, 170
    political arguments, 171–76
    religious arguments, 179–85
    Slovak–Soviet relations, 186–93
    Slovak–US relations, 176–79
  Political Warfare Executive, 29–30
    BBC, relationship with, 31–32
  radio broadcasting
    countering Nazi propaganda, 25–26, 28–30
    morale and general public, 26–27
    political propaganda, 24–27
    proximity and intimacy, 27–28, 89–93
  Slovakia, aimed at, 151–60
    negative propaganda, 170
  Third Section, 20–21
Protectorate of Bohemia and Moravia, 10, 15, 49–52
  assassination of Heydrich, 105
  cultural material as propaganda, 144
  Heydrich, 105
    appointment, 83–84, 86, 95, 103–4
    assassination, 105
  oppression and population transfers, 103–6

radio broadcasting
  addressing Czechs and Slovaks separately, 155–56
  audiences, 153–54
  broadcasting in foreign languages, 23–24, 31–32, 38–39
    Slovak language, 154–55, 166–69
    see also language
  exiles, importance to, 24–25, 43–44, 45–46, 51–52, 59

countering Nazi propaganda, 25–26, 28–30
"free time" for Allied governments, 12–13, 34–41
morale and general public, 26–27
political propaganda, 24–27
proximity and intimacy, 27–28, 89–93
expansion of, 28
First Czechoslovak Republic, 22–24, 153
Polish exiles, 36–37
religious broadcasting, 179–85
wartime importance, 24–28
see also Czechoslovak government programme
religious broadcasting, 179–85
anti-Communism, 183–84
Ripka, Hubert, 38–39, 41, 46, 75, 81, 107, 155–58, 164, 170, 191, 207, 210–12, 224–27, 231–33, 236, 241–42, 246, 252

St. Wenceslas
national symbol, 126–28
Second Czechoslovak Republic (Oct 1938 to Mar 1939), 10
Slav unity, concept of
Slovak National Uprising, 192–93
Slovak–Soviet relations, 186–91, 202–4, 207–8
Slovakia, 186–87
Slávik, Juraj, 158–60, 168, 172, 173–74, 180–81, 193–94, 210–11
Slovak–Czech relations, *see* Czech–Slovak relations
Slovak identity and statehood, 44, 151–52
negative propaganda from government in exile, 170
political arguments, 171–76
religious arguments, 179–85
Slovak–Soviet relations, 186–93
Slovak–US relations, 176–79
Slovak National Council (*Slovenská národná rada*, SNR), 153, 164–65
Slovak National Revival, 190, 202–3
Slovak National Uprising (1944), 50–51, 164–65
Slav unity, 192–93
Slovak–Soviet relations, 186
Czechoslovak–Soviet treaty, 190–92
Slovak-language broadcasting, 189–90
unity of Slavs, 186–91, 202–4, 207–8

Slovak–US relations, 176–79
Slovakia, 49–50
declaration of independence, 10, 110–11
declaration of war on US, 172, 176–78
negative propaganda from government in exile, 170
political arguments, 171–76
religious arguments, 179–85
Slovak–Soviet relations, 186–93
Slovak–US relations, 176–79
political arguments against independent Slovakia, 171–72
radio-broadcasting
criticisms of Slovak broadcasting, 156–58
failure of government-in-exile to unite, 194–95
Slovak language, 156–57, 166–69
unity of Slavs
Slovak–Soviet relations, 186–91, 202–4, 207–8
Šrámek, Jan, 69–70, 84, 225, 232, 249
Sova, Antonín, 137
Soviet Union, 44–45
Czechoslovak–Soviet relations, 44–45, 48–49, 202, 245–46
alliance, 197–98, 201–8
ambivalence/objectivity, 197, 198–201
Czechoslovak–Polish relations, 208–18
post-WWII Communist takeover, 196–97
Subcarpathian Ruthenia issue, 218–45
subjugation, 198, 208–46
German invasion, 201
Polish–Soviet relations, 214–18
radio-broadcasting, 155–56
threat to Christianity, 183–85
see also Czechoslovak–Soviet relations
Stalin, Josef, 184–85, 186, 197
Štefánik, Milan Rastislav, 130, 173–74, 175–76, 191
Stránský, Jaroslav, 42, 74–75, 80, 141, 162–65, 167, 184–85, 199–201, 249
Subcarpathian Ruthenia, 44, 48–49
annexation by Hungary, 198
annexation by Soviet Union, 44–45, 198, 218–19, 244–45
government-in-exile propaganda, 219–20

autonomy, 223, 240–41
British attitude to, 224–25
Czechoslovak–Soviet relations, 237–38, 242–43
First Republic ideologies, 238–39
government-in-exile broadcasts to
   changing attitude to, 224–25, 227
   lack of interest, 223–24, 226–27
   motivations, 223–26
   propaganda, 219–20
joint Czechoslovak and Subcarpathian Ruthenian state, 238–41
Munich Agreement, 240–43
national identity, 227–29, 238–39
   Czechoslovak–Soviet relations, 237–38
   language, 229–31, 232–33, 234–35
   pro-Soviet, 230–31, 237–38
   Russian/Ukrainian identity, 230–34, 236–37, 240–41
   Rusyn identity, 240
   Slavic identity, 236–37
   terminology, 220–21, 229–31, 232–33, 234–36
recognition of pre-Munich borders, 240–43
regional history and background, 221–22
   autonomy, 223
   incorporation into Czechoslovakia, 222–23, 240–41
terminology and language, 220–21, 229–31, 232–33, 234–35
Sudeten German population
   "German question", 101–3
   population transfers, 101–2
   Beneš decrees, 102–3
Svatý, Pavel, *see* Drtina, Prokop

Těšín/Cieszyn disputes, 52, 208–9, 210–11, 212, 217
Third Section (Ministry of Foreign Affairs, MZV), 20–21
Tigrid, Pavel, 42, 123, 136–37
Tikhon, Patriarch of Moscow, 184–85
Tiso, Jozef, 164, 176, 178–79, 180, 182
Transcarpathian Ukraine National Committee, 243–44
Tsibere, Pavel, 223–24, 226, 230–31, 232–35, 238–39
Tuka, Vojtech, 176, 180

United States
   propaganda, references in, 176–77
   opposition to Slovak state, 178–79
   Slovakia, relationship with, 176–79
   Slovak emigration to, 176–77
   Slovakian declaration of war, 172, 176–78
Ústřední vedení odboje domáciho (Central Leadership of the Home Resistance), 79–80, 102–3

Valo, Jozef, 157, 166, 170, 179, 189
Viboch, Pavol, 157, 159
Vojenská beseda (radio programme–*Military Talk*), 42

Weber, Max, 62
   authority of charisma, 85–98
      see also personality of political leaders
   authority of legality, 63–70
      see also legality and authority of exiled governments
   authority of tradition, 70–85
      see also mythmaking and the authority of tradition